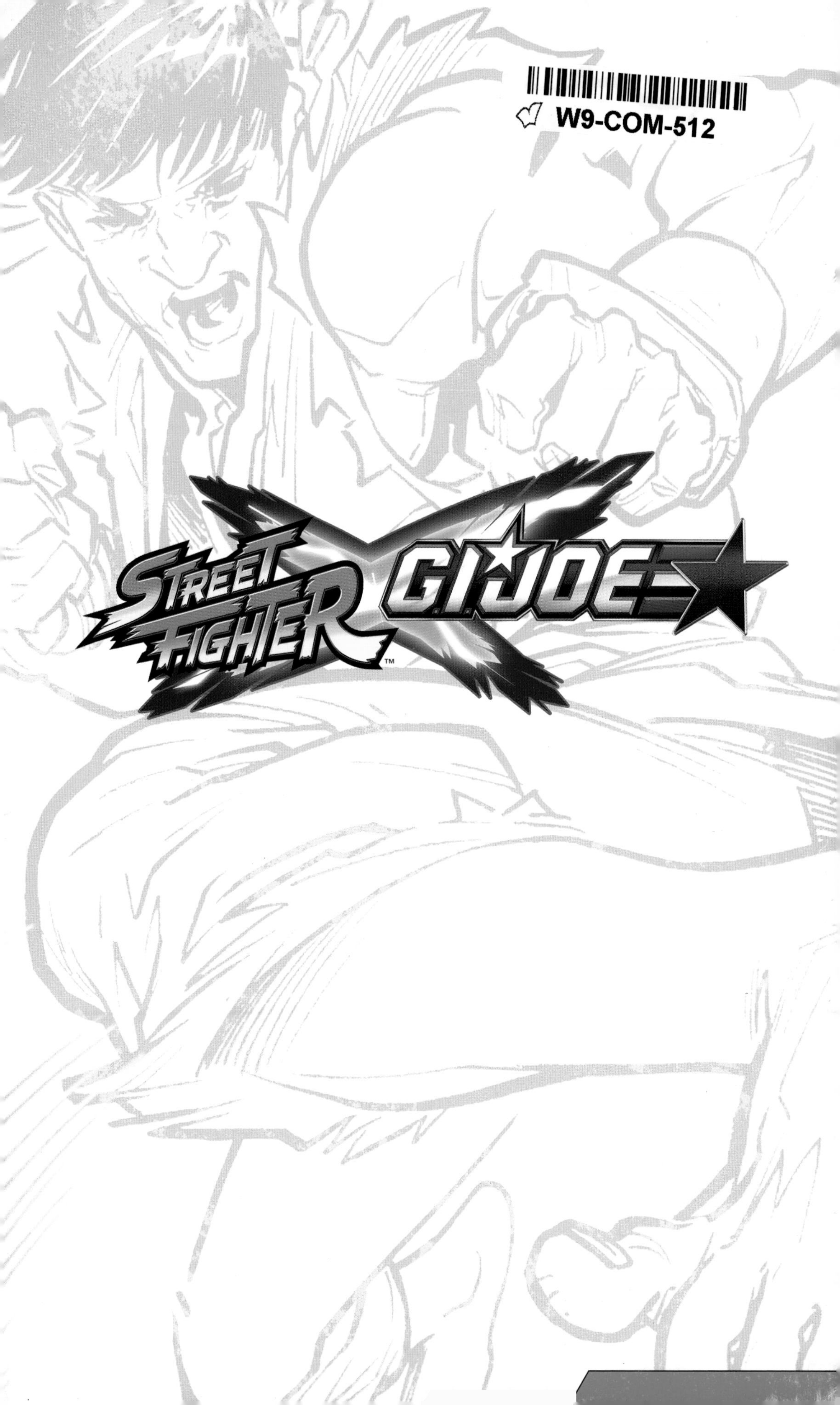
STREET FIGHTER™
G.I. JOE

COVER ART BY
MIKE CHOI

VARIANT COVER ART BY
PHIL JIMENEZ

SERIES EDITS BY
CARLOS GUZMAN

COLLECTION EDITS BY
JUSTIN EISINGER
AND ALONZO SIMON

PUBLISHER
TED ADAMS

COLLECTION DESIGN BY
GILBERTO LAZCANO

Licensed By:

Special thanks to Hasbro's Derryl
Depriest, David Erwin, Mark Weber, Ed
Lane, Beth Artale, and Michael Kelly for
their invaluable assistance.

Become our fan on Facebook **facebook.com/idwpublishing**
Follow us on Twitter **@idwpublishing**
Subscribe to us on YouTube **youtube.com/idwpublishing**
See what's new on Tumblr **tumblr.idwpublishing.com**
Check us out on Instagram **instagram.com/idwpublishing**

ISBN: 978-1-63140-744-4   19 18 17 16   1 2 3 4

Originally published as STREET FIGHTER X G.I. JOE
issues #1–6.

Ted Adams, CEO & Publisher
Greg Goldstein, President & COO
Robbie Robbins, EVP/Sr. Graphic Artist
Chris Ryall, Chief Creative Officer/Editor-in-Chief
Laurie Windrow, Senior Vice President of Sales & Marketing
Matthew Ruzicka, CPA, Chief Financial Officer
Dirk Wood, VP of Marketing
Lorelei Bunjes, VP of Digital Services
Jeff Webber, VP of Licensing, Digital and Subsidiary Rights
Jerry Bennington, VP of New Product Development

For international rights, please contact
licensing@idwpublishing.com

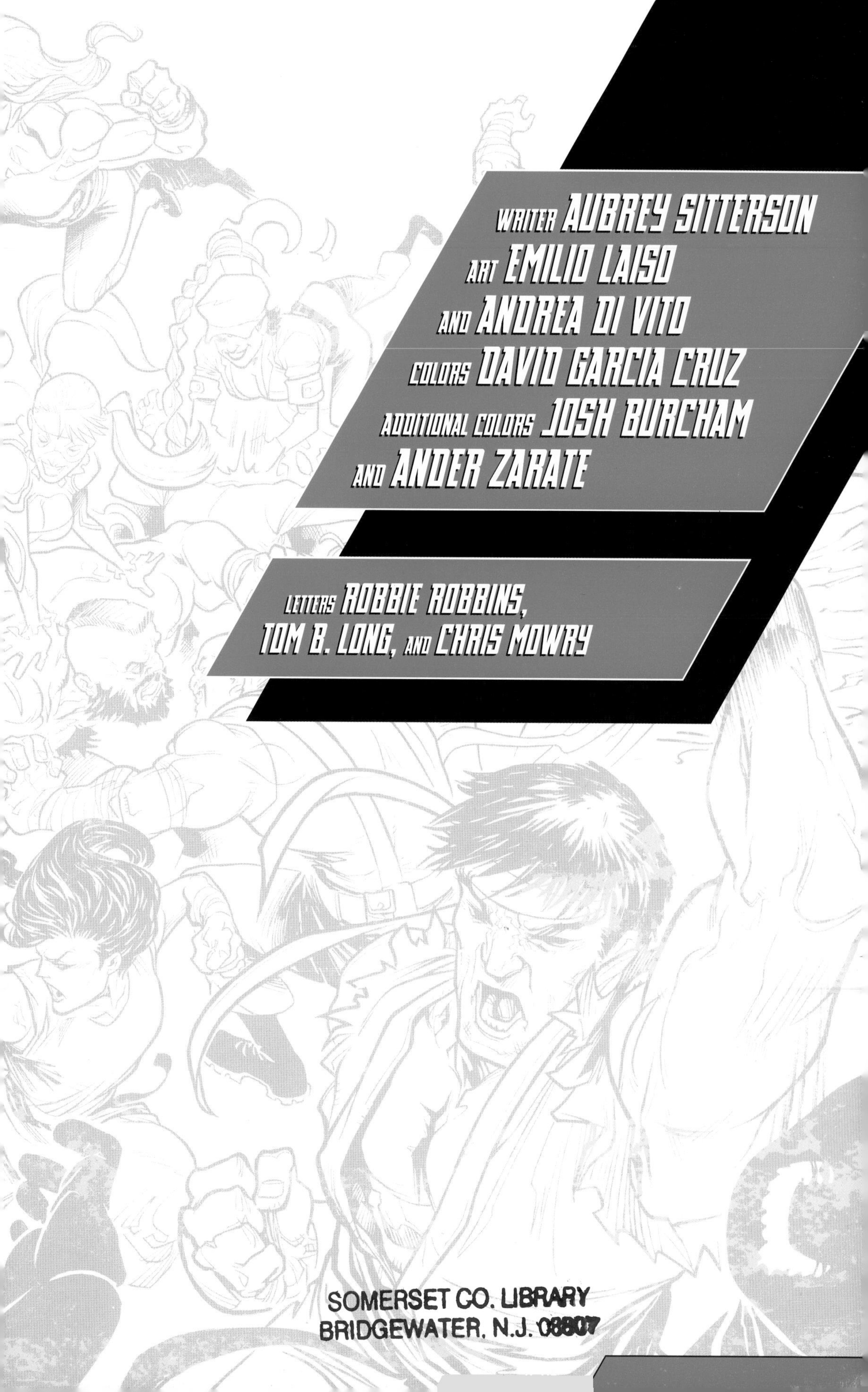

WRITER AUBREY SITTERSON
ART EMILIO LAISO
AND ANDREA DI VITO
COLORS DAVID GARCIA CRUZ
ADDITIONAL COLORS JOSH BURCHAM
AND ANDER ZARATE

LETTERS ROBBIE ROBBINS,
TOM B. LONG, AND CHRIS MOWRY

CHAPTER 1

WORLD WARRIOR
TOURNAMENT BRACKET

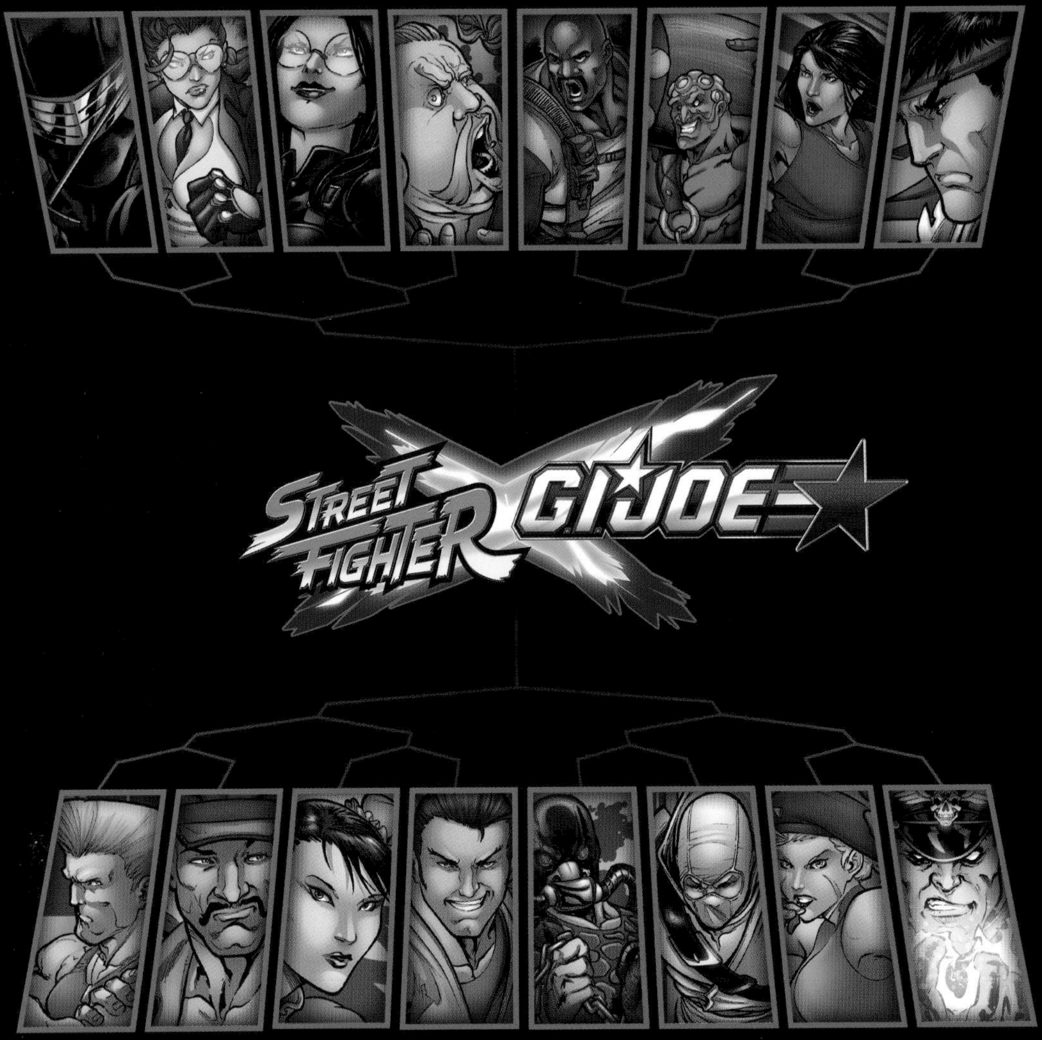
STREET FIGHTER
G.I. JOE

SNAKE EYES vs. C. VIPER

RUFUS vs. BARONESS

HAKAN vs. ROADBLOCK

RYU vs. JINX

EIGHTH-FINALS

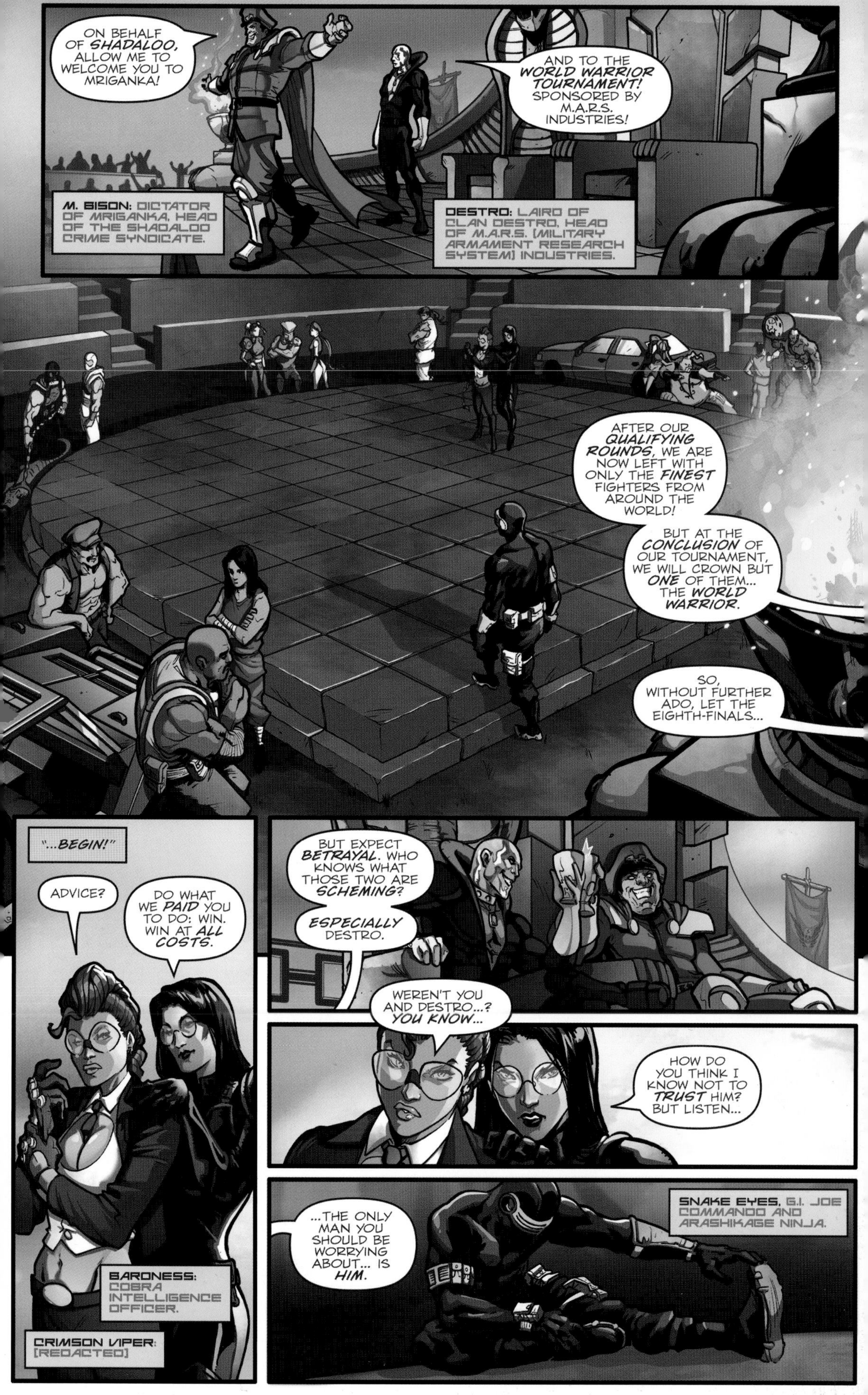

ON BEHALF OF SHADALOO, ALLOW ME TO WELCOME YOU TO MRIGANKA!
AND TO THE WORLD WARRIOR TOURNAMENT! SPONSORED BY M.A.R.S. INDUSTRIES!
M. BISON: DICTATOR OF MRIGANKA, HEAD OF THE SHADALOO CRIME SYNDICATE.
DESTRO: LAIRD OF CLAN DESTRO, HEAD OF M.A.R.S. (MILITARY ARMAMENT RESEARCH SYSTEM) INDUSTRIES.
AFTER OUR QUALIFYING ROUNDS, WE ARE NOW LEFT WITH ONLY THE FINEST FIGHTERS FROM AROUND THE WORLD!
BUT AT THE CONCLUSION OF OUR TOURNAMENT, WE WILL CROWN BUT ONE OF THEM... THE WORLD WARRIOR.
SO, WITHOUT FURTHER ADO, LET THE EIGHTH-FINALS...
"...BEGIN!"
ADVICE?
DO WHAT WE PAID YOU TO DO: WIN. WIN AT ALL COSTS.
BARONESS: COBRA INTELLIGENCE OFFICER.
CRIMSON VIPER: [REDACTED]
BUT EXPECT BETRAYAL. WHO KNOWS WHAT THOSE TWO ARE SCHEMING?
ESPECIALLY DESTRO.
WEREN'T YOU AND DESTRO...? YOU KNOW...
HOW DO YOU THINK I KNOW NOT TO TRUST HIM? BUT LISTEN...
...THE ONLY MAN YOU SHOULD BE WORRYING ABOUT... IS HIM.
SNAKE EYES, G.I. JOE COMMANDO AND ARASHIKAGE NINJA.

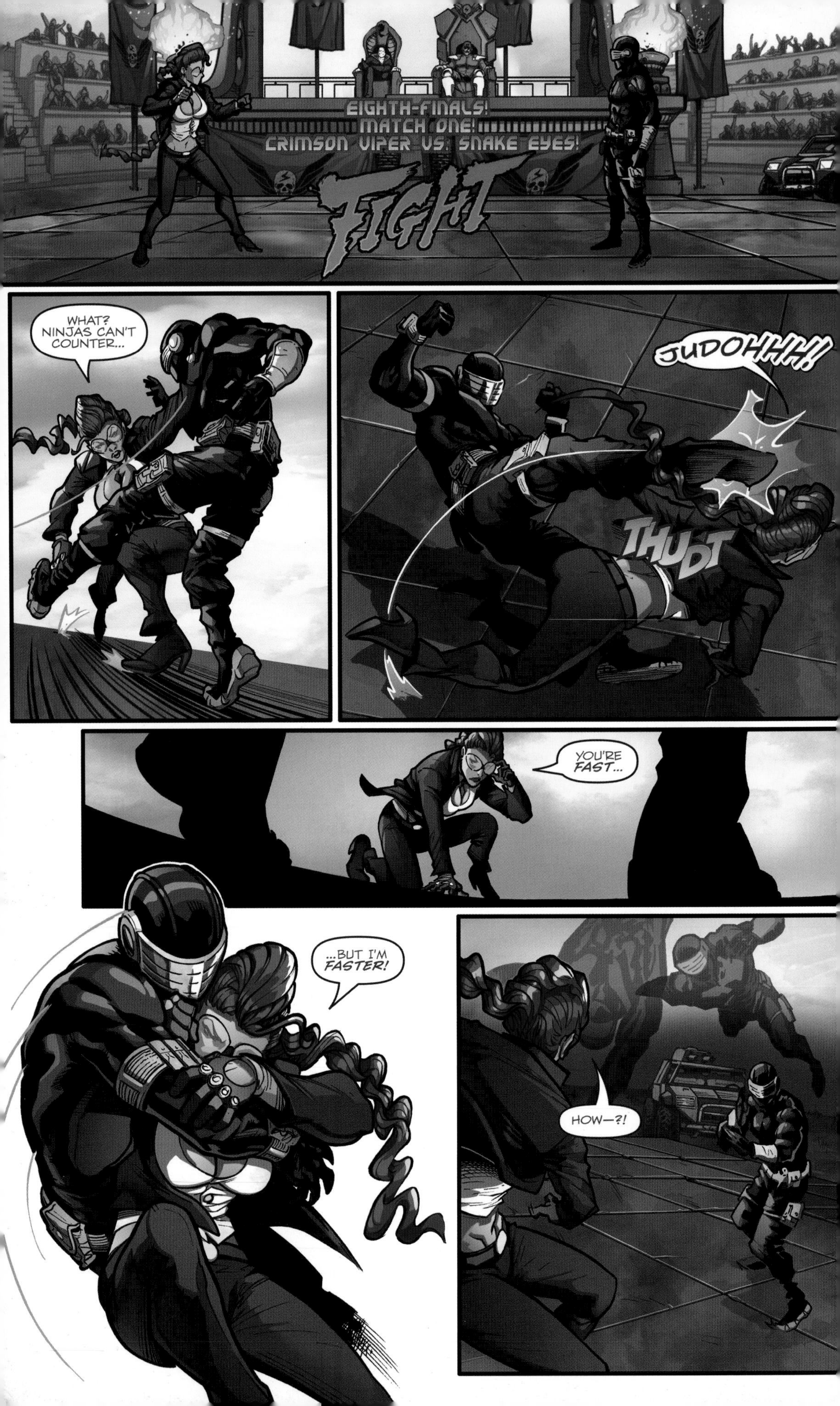
EIGHTH-FINALS!
MATCH ONE!
CRIMSON VIPER VS. SNAKE EYES!
FIGHT
WHAT? NINJAS CAN'T COUNTER...
JUDOHHH!!
THUDT
YOU'RE FAST...
...BUT I'M FASTER!
HOW—?!

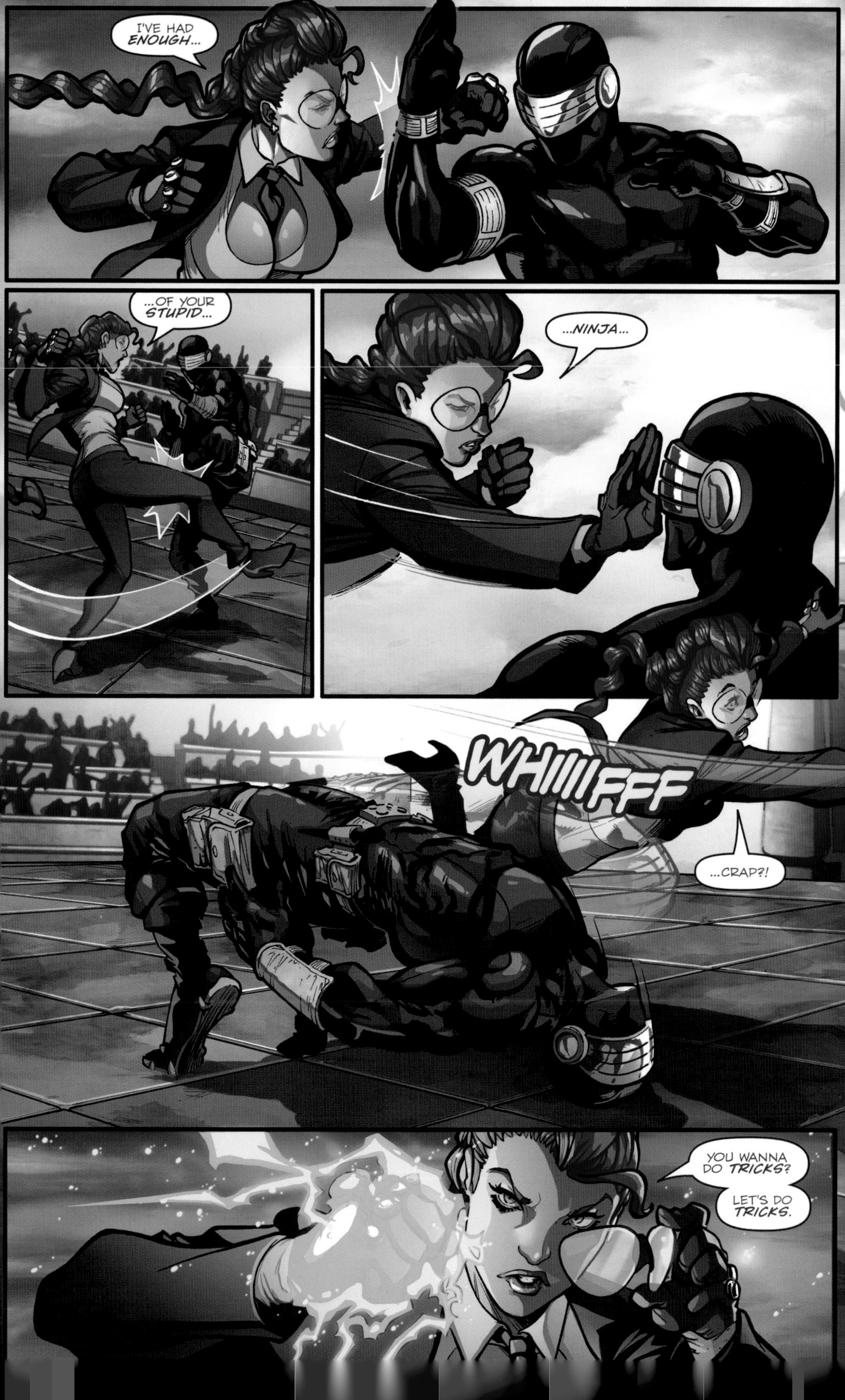
I'VE HAD ENOUGH...
...OF YOUR STUPID...
...NINJA...
WHIIIIFFF
...CRAP?!
YOU WANNA DO TRICKS?
LET'S DO TRICKS.

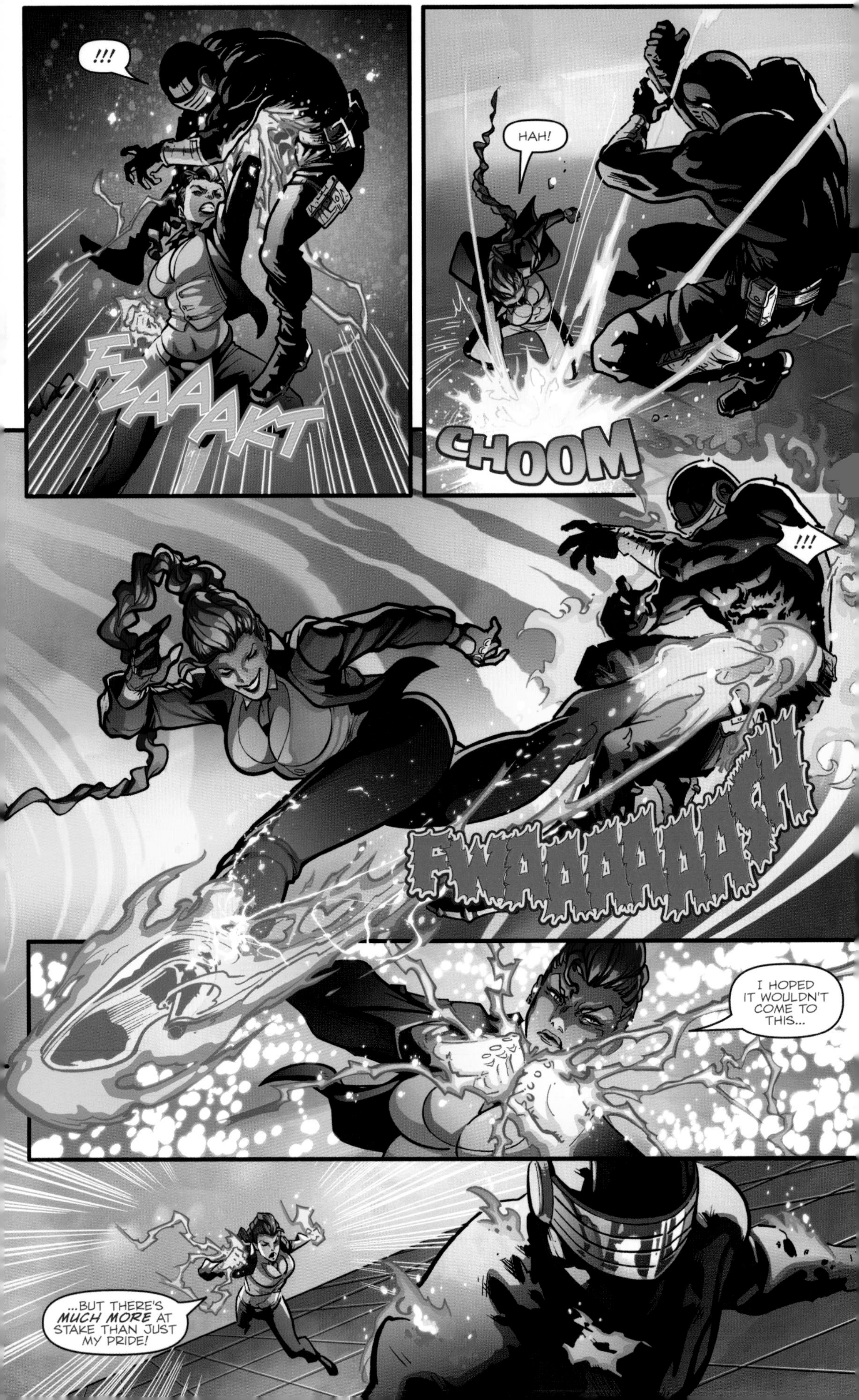
!!!
FZAAAAKT
HAH!
CHOOM
!!!
FWAAAAAASH
I HOPED IT WOULDN'T COME TO THIS...
...BUT THERE'S *MUCH MORE* AT STAKE THAN JUST MY PRIDE!

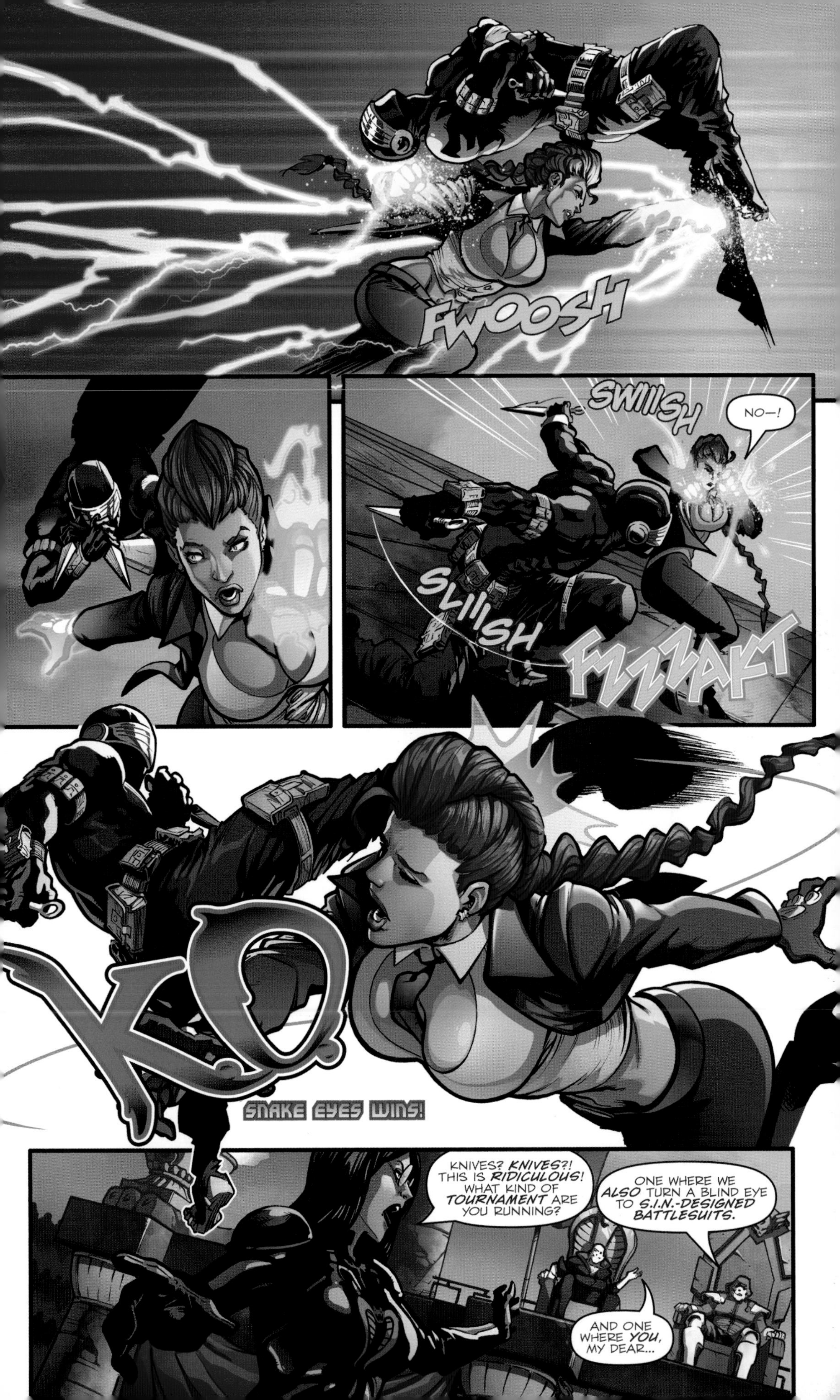
FWOOSH
SWIIISH
NO—!
SWIIISH
FZZZAKT
K.O.
SNAKE EYES WINS!
KNIVES? KNIVES?! THIS IS RIDICULOUS! WHAT KIND OF TOURNAMENT ARE YOU RUNNING?
ONE WHERE WE ALSO TURN A BLIND EYE TO S.I.N.-DESIGNED BATTLESUITS.
AND ONE WHERE YOU, MY DEAR...

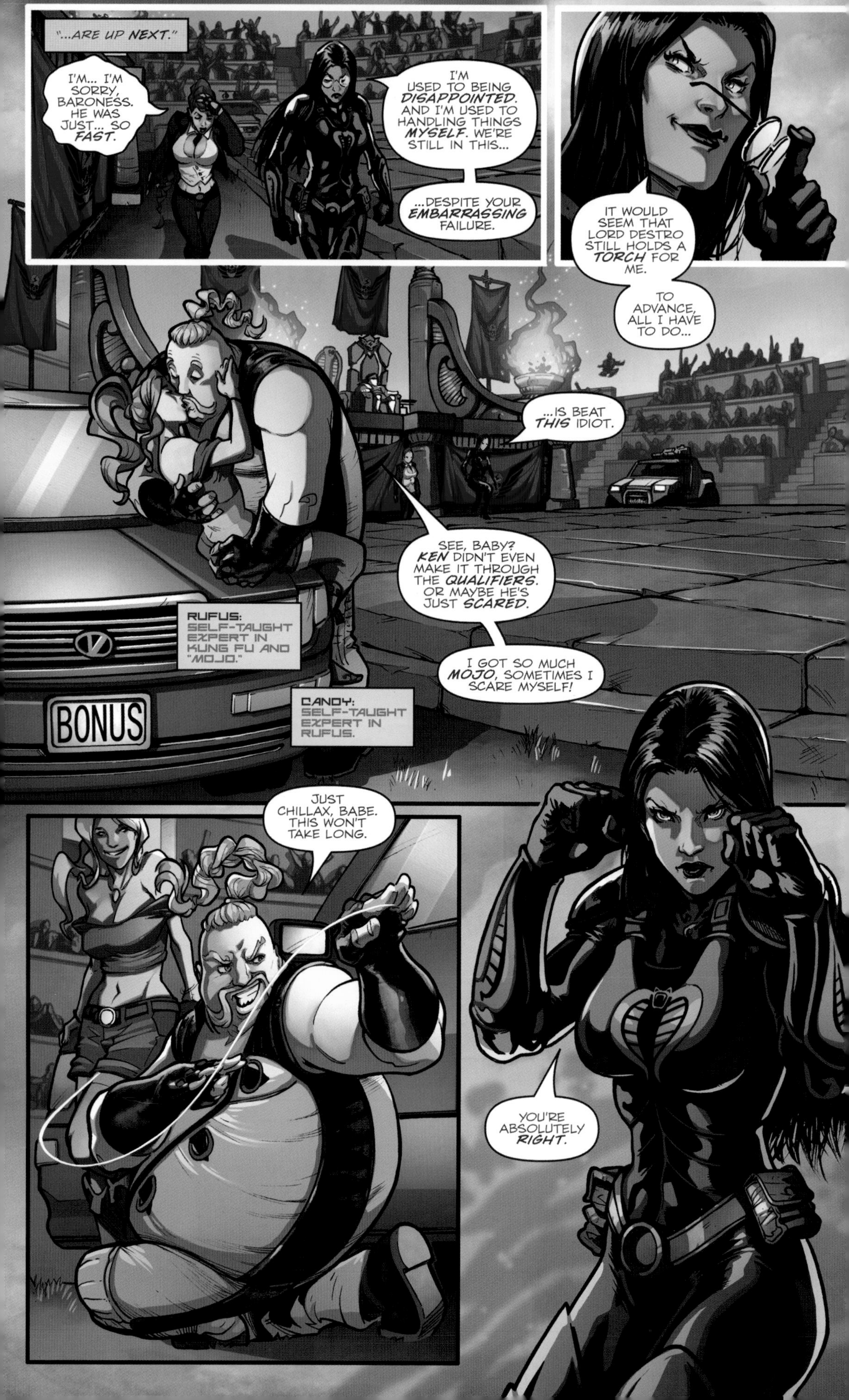
"...ARE UP NEXT."
I'M... I'M SORRY, BARONESS. HE WAS JUST... SO FAST.
I'M USED TO BEING DISAPPOINTED. AND I'M USED TO HANDLING THINGS MYSELF. WE'RE STILL IN THIS...
...DESPITE YOUR EMBARRASSING FAILURE.
IT WOULD SEEM THAT LORD DESTRO STILL HOLDS A TORCH FOR ME.
TO ADVANCE, ALL I HAVE TO DO...
...IS BEAT THIS IDIOT.
SEE, BABY? KEN DIDN'T EVEN MAKE IT THROUGH THE QUALIFIERS. OR MAYBE HE'S JUST SCARED.
I GOT SO MUCH MOJO, SOMETIMES I SCARE MYSELF!
RUFUS: SELF-TAUGHT EXPERT IN KUNG FU AND "MOJO."
BONUS
CANDY: SELF-TAUGHT EXPERT IN RUFUS.
JUST CHILLAX, BABE. THIS WON'T TAKE LONG.
YOU'RE ABSOLUTELY RIGHT.

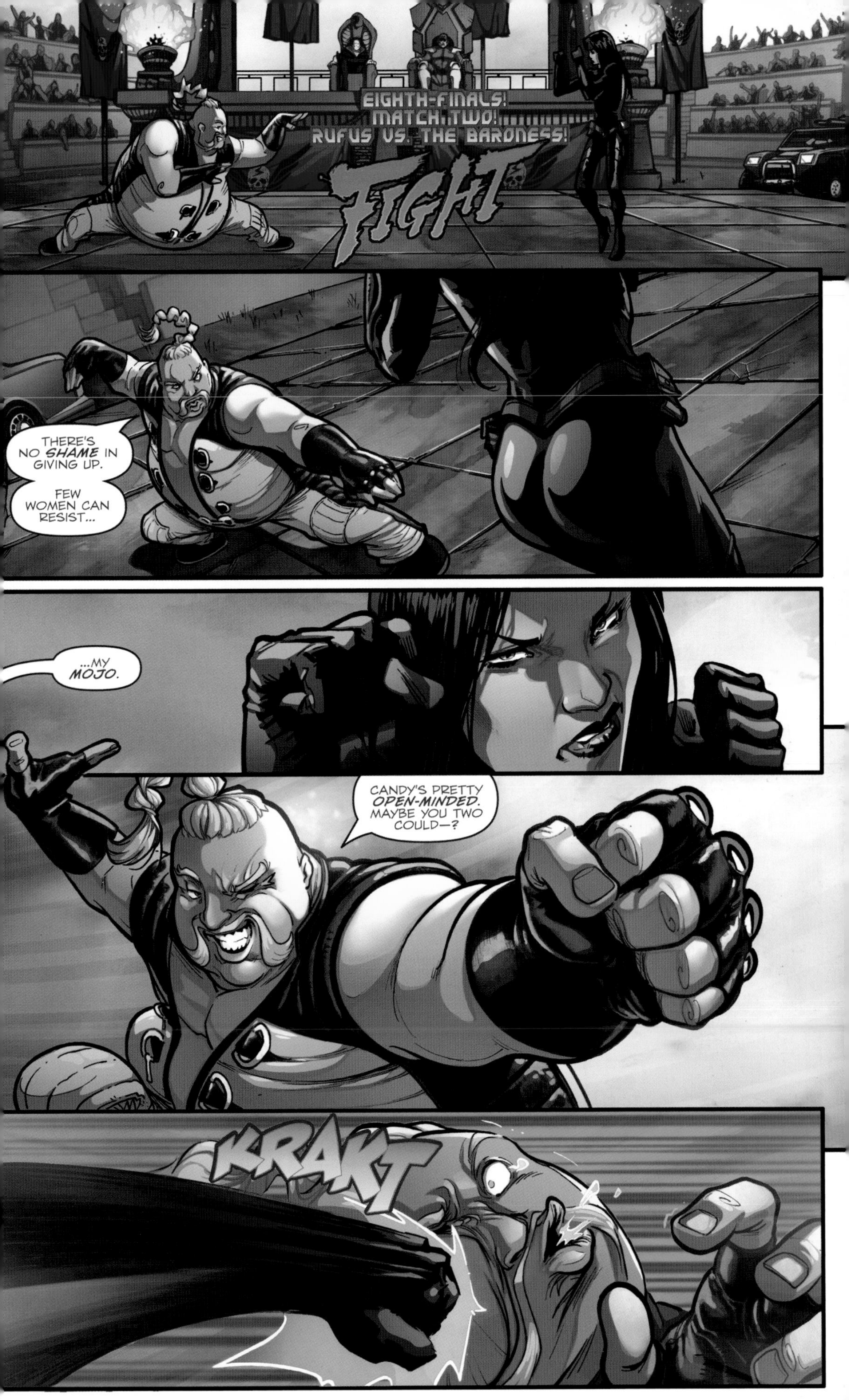
EIGHTH-FINALS!
MATCH TWO!
RUFUS VS. THE BARONESS!
FIGHT
THERE'S NO SHAME IN GIVING UP.
FEW WOMEN CAN RESIST...
...MY MOJO.
CANDY'S PRETTY OPEN-MINDED. MAYBE YOU TWO COULD—?
KRAKT

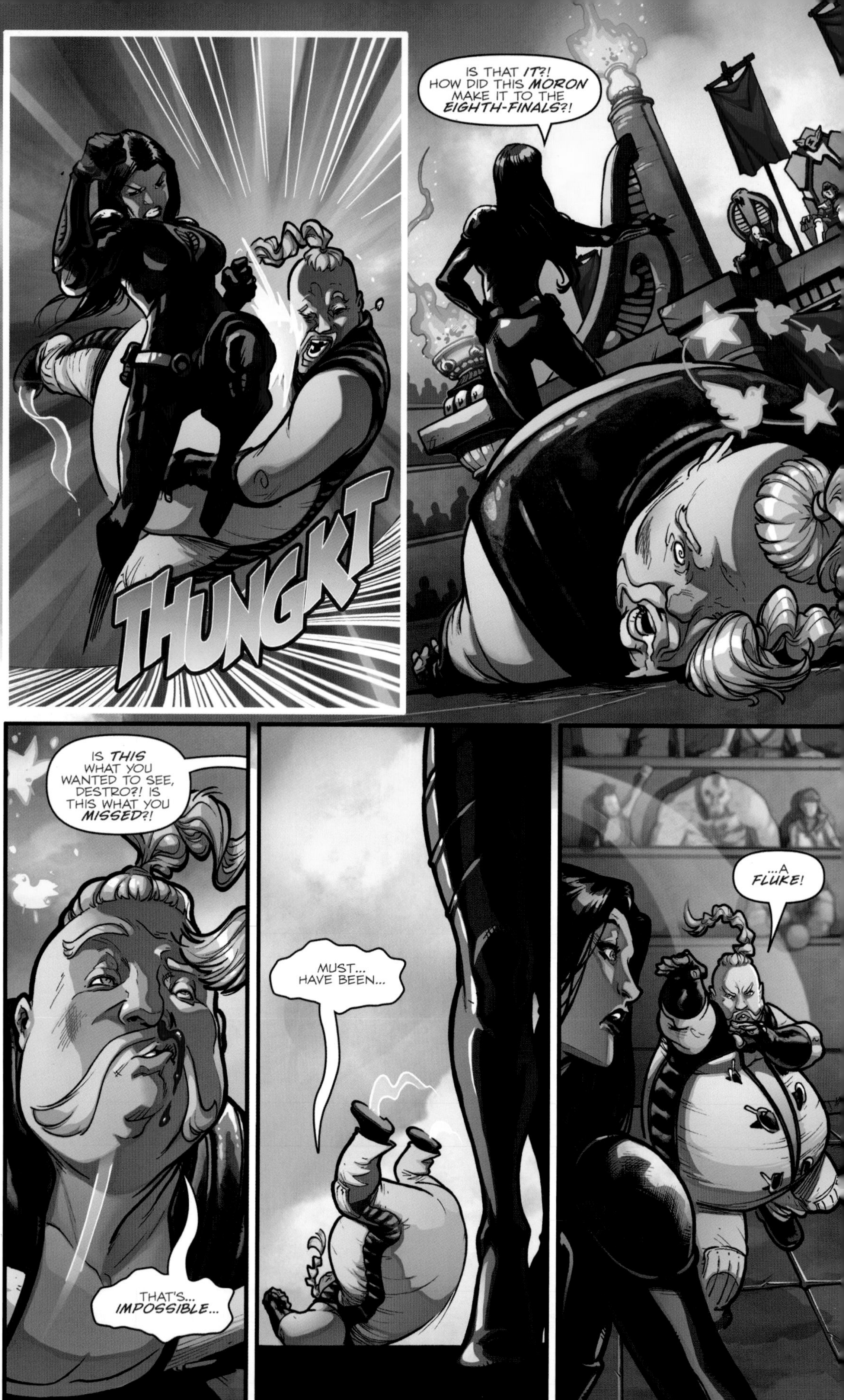
THUNGKT
IS THAT IT?! HOW DID THIS MORON MAKE IT TO THE EIGHTH-FINALS?!
IS THIS WHAT YOU WANTED TO SEE, DESTRO?! IS THIS WHAT YOU MISSED?!
THAT'S... IMPOSSIBLE...
MUST... HAVE BEEN...
...A FLUKE!

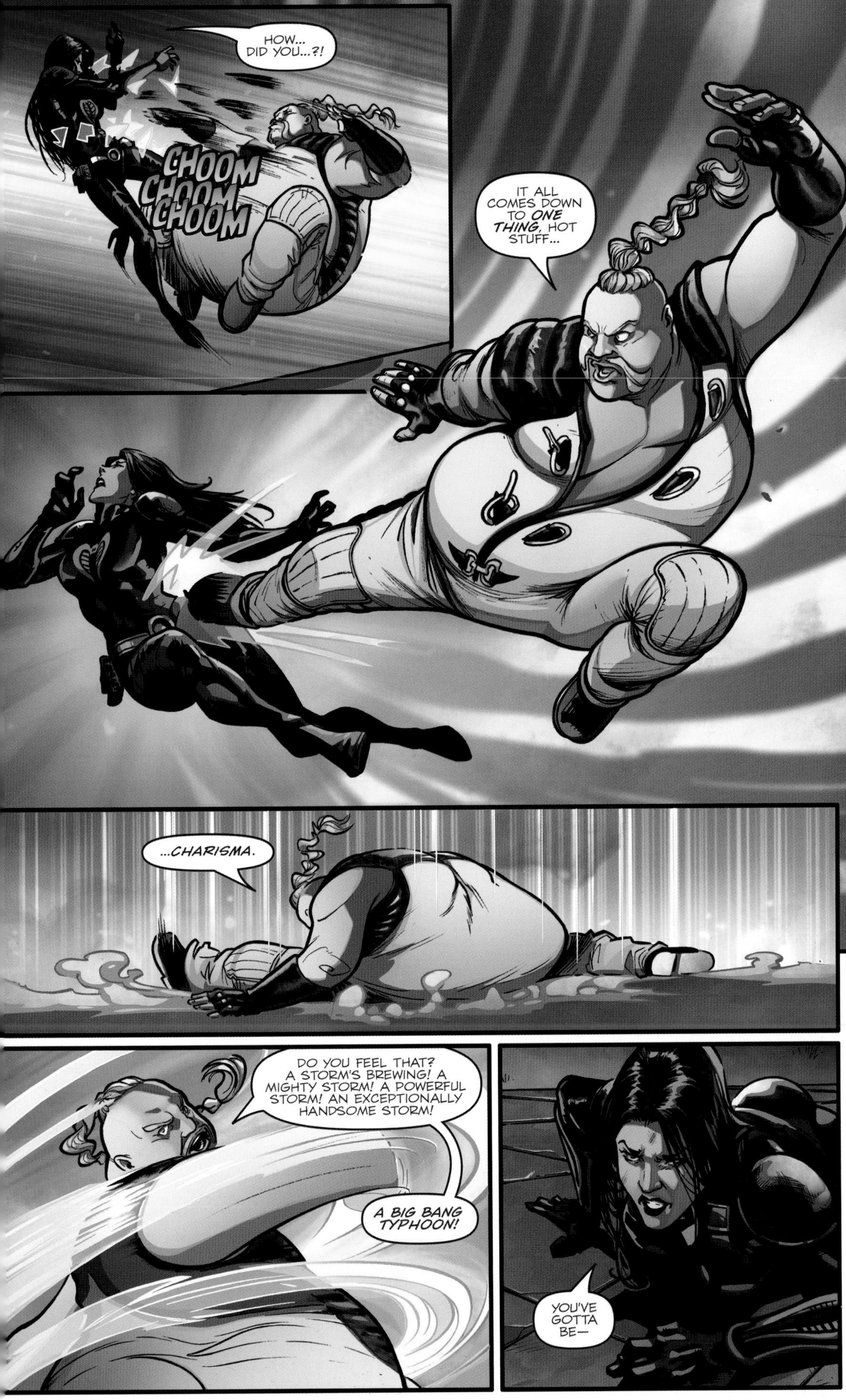
HOW... DID YOU...?!
CHOOM CHOOM CHOOM
IT ALL COMES DOWN TO ONE THING, HOT STUFF...
...CHARISMA.
DO YOU FEEL THAT? A STORM'S BREWING! A MIGHTY STORM! A POWERFUL STORM! AN EXCEPTIONALLY HANDSOME STORM!
A BIG BANG TYPHOON!
YOU'VE GOTTA BE—

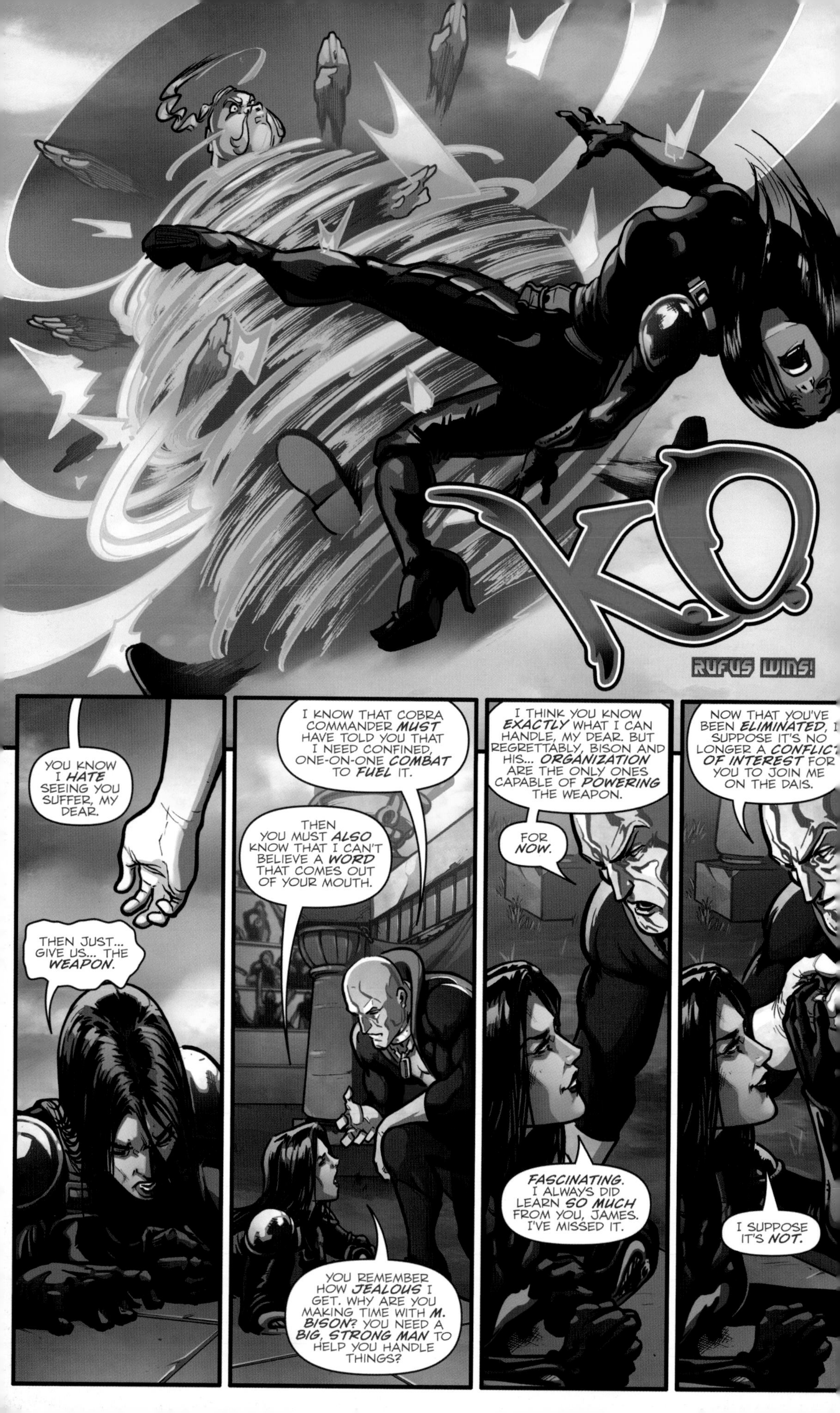
K.O.
RUFUS WINS!
YOU KNOW I HATE SEEING YOU SUFFER, MY DEAR.
THEN JUST... GIVE US... THE WEAPON.
I KNOW THAT COBRA COMMANDER MUST HAVE TOLD YOU THAT I NEED CONFINED, ONE-ON-ONE COMBAT TO FUEL IT.
THEN YOU MUST ALSO KNOW THAT I CAN'T BELIEVE A WORD THAT COMES OUT OF YOUR MOUTH.
YOU REMEMBER HOW JEALOUS I GET. WHY ARE YOU MAKING TIME WITH M. BISON? YOU NEED A BIG, STRONG MAN TO HELP YOU HANDLE THINGS?
I THINK YOU KNOW EXACTLY WHAT I CAN HANDLE, MY DEAR. BUT REGRETTABLY, BISON AND HIS... ORGANIZATION ARE THE ONLY ONES CAPABLE OF POWERING THE WEAPON.
FOR NOW.
FASCINATING. I ALWAYS DID LEARN SO MUCH FROM YOU, JAMES. I'VE MISSED IT.
NOW THAT YOU'VE BEEN ELIMINATED, I SUPPOSE IT'S NO LONGER A CONFLICT OF INTEREST FOR YOU TO JOIN ME ON THE DAIS.
I SUPPOSE IT'S NOT.

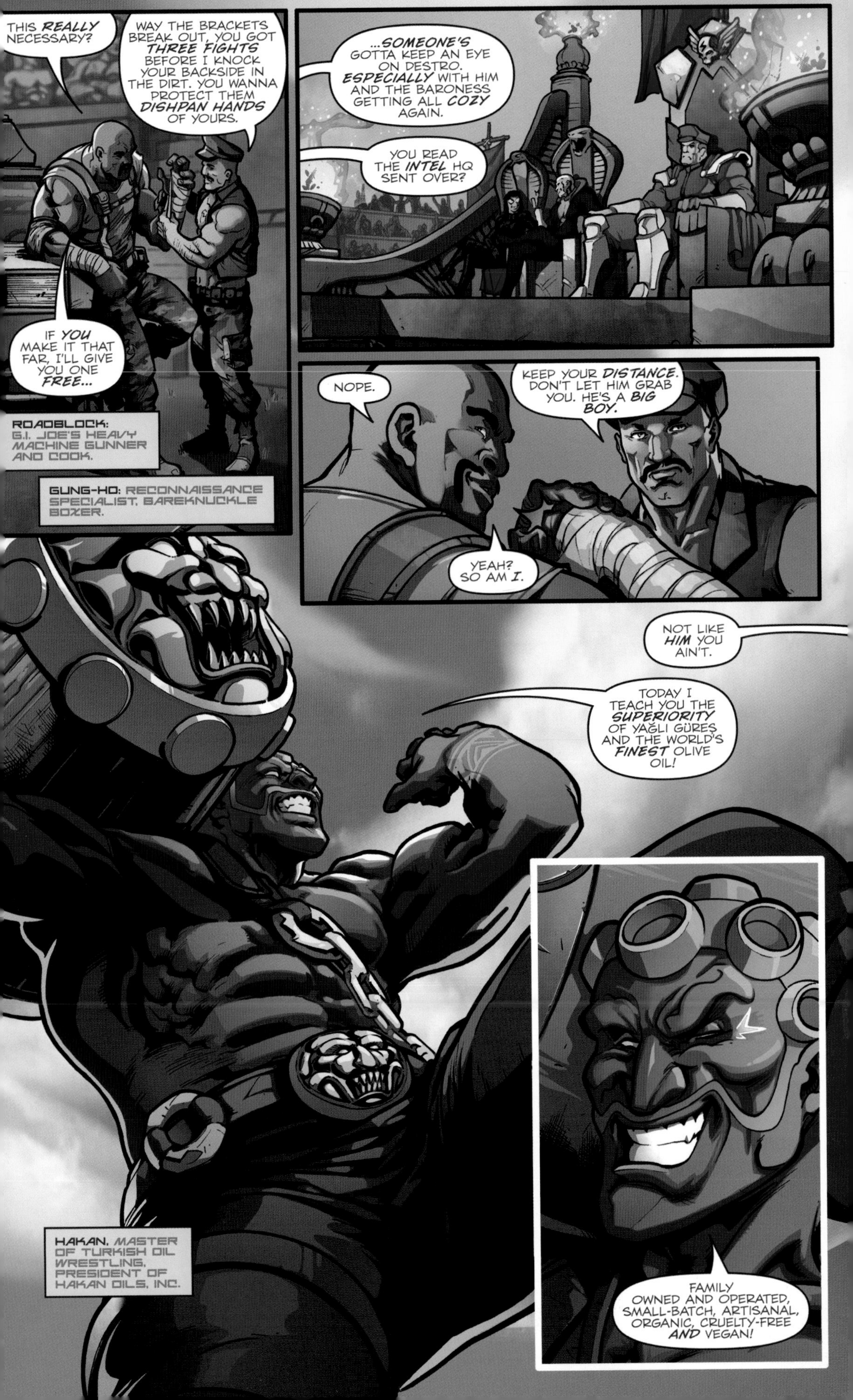
THIS REALLY NECESSARY?
WAY THE BRACKETS BREAK OUT, YOU GOT THREE FIGHTS BEFORE I KNOCK YOUR BACKSIDE IN THE DIRT. YOU WANNA PROTECT THEM DISHPAN HANDS OF YOURS.
IF YOU MAKE IT THAT FAR, I'LL GIVE YOU ONE FREE...
ROADBLOCK: G.I. JOE'S HEAVY MACHINE GUNNER AND COOK.
GUNG-HO: RECONNAISSANCE SPECIALIST, BAREKNUCKLE BOXER.
...SOMEONE'S GOTTA KEEP AN EYE ON DESTRO. ESPECIALLY WITH HIM AND THE BARONESS GETTING ALL COZY AGAIN.
YOU READ THE INTEL HQ SENT OVER?
NOPE.
KEEP YOUR DISTANCE. DON'T LET HIM GRAB YOU. HE'S A BIG BOY.
YEAH? SO AM I.
NOT LIKE HIM YOU AIN'T.
TODAY I TEACH YOU THE SUPERIORITY OF YAĞLI GÜREŞ AND THE WORLD'S FINEST OLIVE OIL!
HAKAN, MASTER OF TURKISH OIL WRESTLING, PRESIDENT OF HAKAN OILS, INC.
FAMILY OWNED AND OPERATED, SMALL-BATCH, ARTISANAL, ORGANIC, CRUELTY-FREE AND VEGAN!

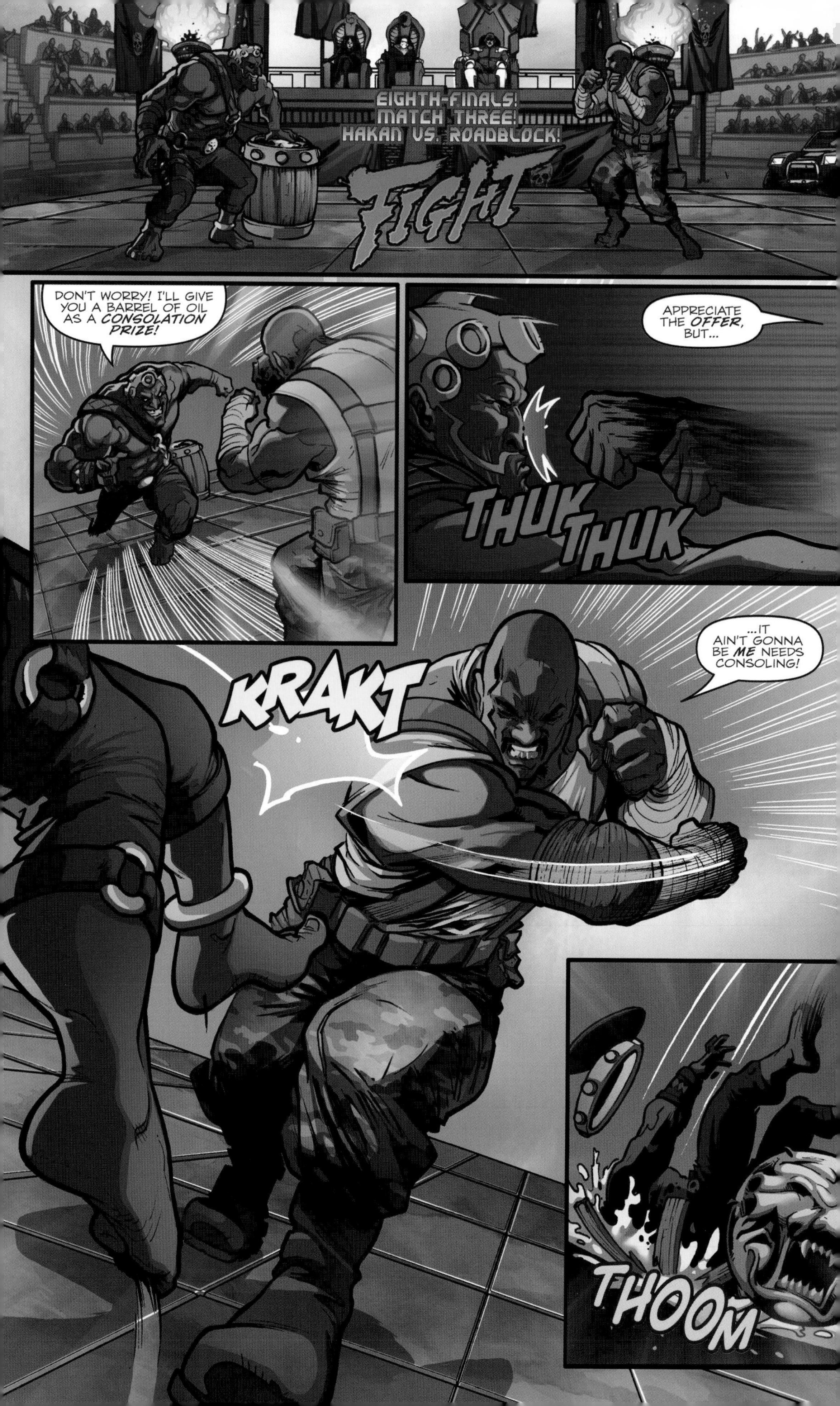

EIGHTH-FINALS! MATCH THREE! HAKAN VS. ROADBLOCK!
FIGHT
DON'T WORRY! I'LL GIVE YOU A BARREL OF OIL AS A *CONSOLATION PRIZE!*
APPRECIATE THE *OFFER*, BUT...
THUK THUK
KRAKT
...IT AIN'T GONNA BE *ME* NEEDS CONSOLING!
THOOM

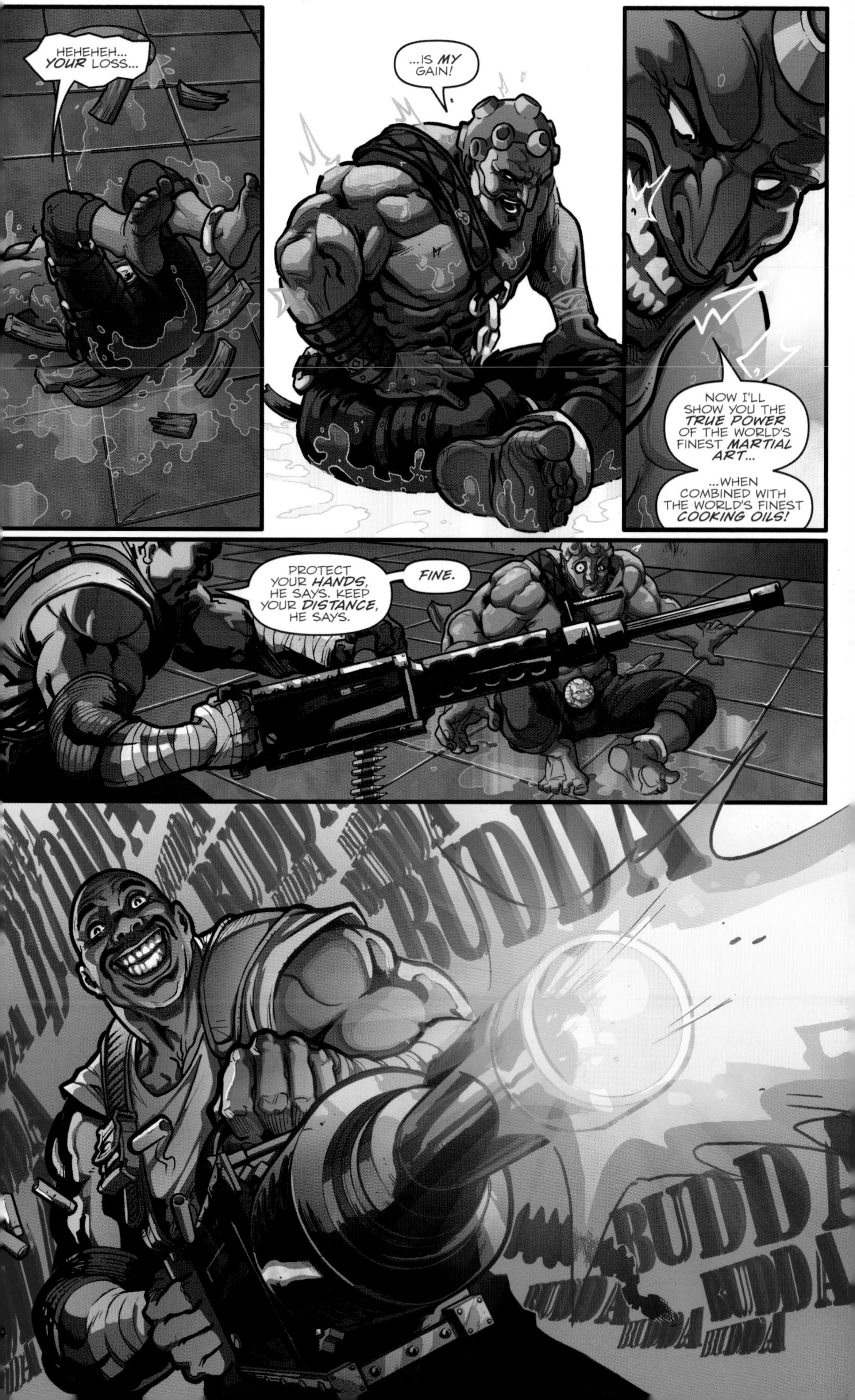
HEHEHEH... YOUR LOSS...
...IS MY GAIN!
NOW I'LL SHOW YOU THE TRUE POWER OF THE WORLD'S FINEST MARTIAL ART...
...WHEN COMBINED WITH THE WORLD'S FINEST COOKING OILS!
PROTECT YOUR HANDS, HE SAYS. KEEP YOUR DISTANCE, HE SAYS.
FINE.
BUDDA
BUDDA
BUDDA
BUDDA BUDDA

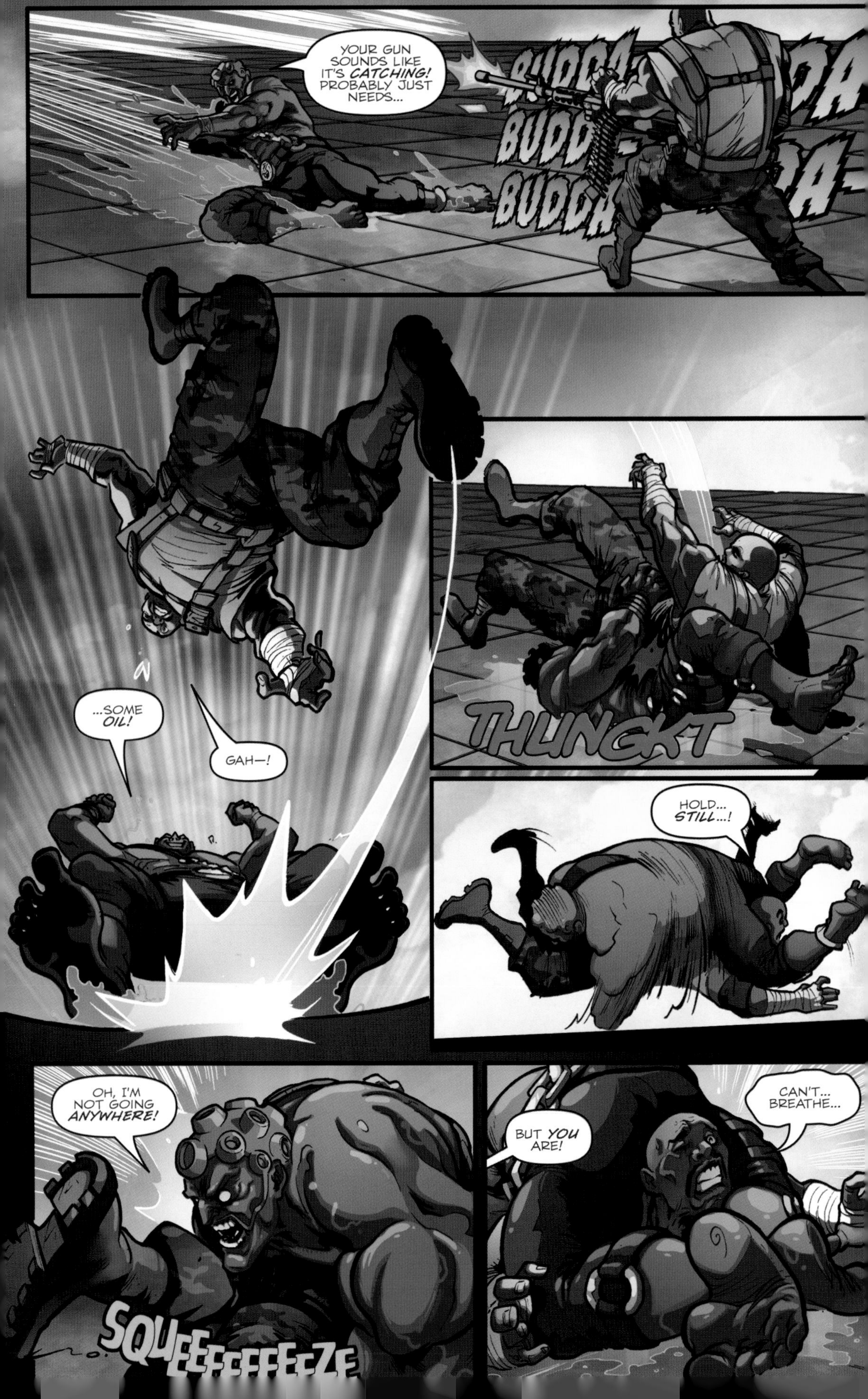

YOUR GUN SOUNDS LIKE IT'S *CATCHING!* PROBABLY JUST NEEDS...
BUDDA-BUDDA-
BUDDA-BUDDA-
BUDDA-BUDDA-
...SOME *OIL!*
GAH—!
THUNGKT
HOLD... *STILL*...!
OH, I'M NOT GOING *ANYWHERE!*
SQUEEEEEEEEEZE
BUT *YOU* ARE!
CAN'T... BREATHE...

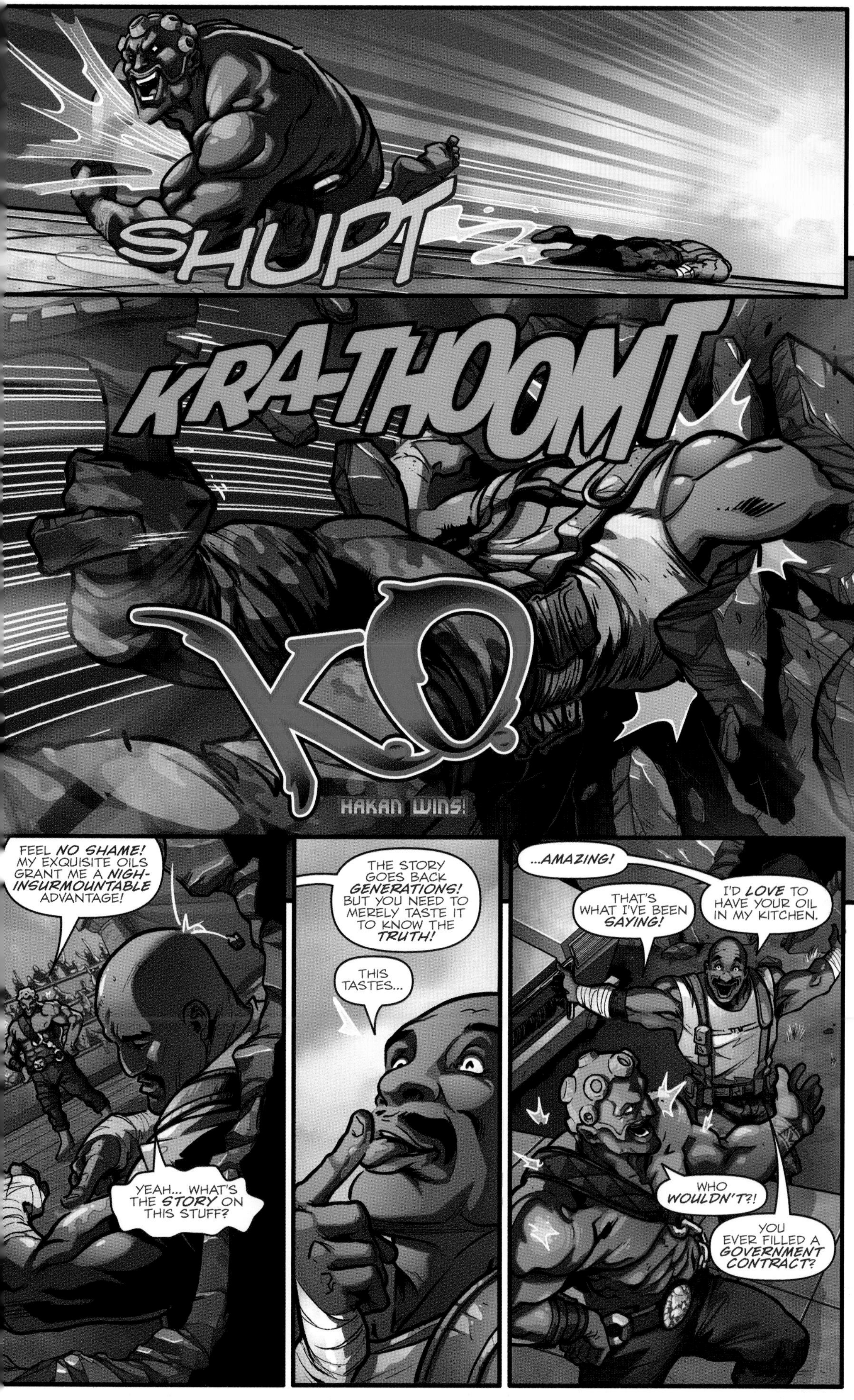
SHUPT
KRA-THOOM!
K.O.
HAKAN WINS!
FEEL NO SHAME! MY EXQUISITE OILS GRANT ME A NIGH-INSURMOUNTABLE ADVANTAGE!
YEAH... WHAT'S THE STORY ON THIS STUFF?
THE STORY GOES BACK GENERATIONS! BUT YOU NEED TO MERELY TASTE IT TO KNOW THE TRUTH!
THIS TASTES...
...AMAZING!
THAT'S WHAT I'VE BEEN SAYING!
I'D LOVE TO HAVE YOUR OIL IN MY KITCHEN.
WHO WOULDN'T?!
YOU EVER FILLED A GOVERNMENT CONTRACT?

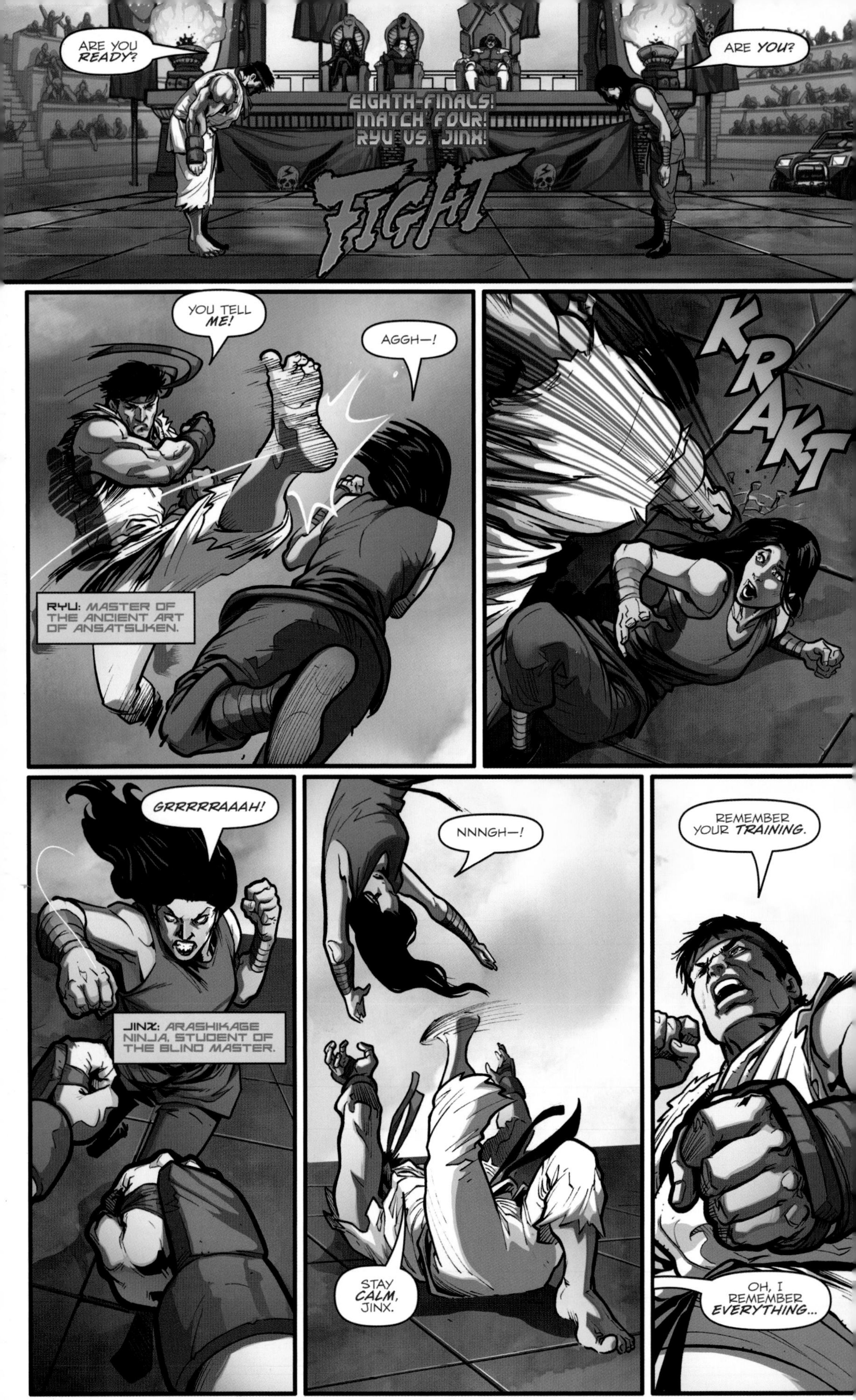
ARE YOU READY?
ARE YOU?
EIGHTH-FINALS! MATCH FOUR! RYU VS. JINX!
FIGHT
YOU TELL ME!
AGGH—!
RYU: MASTER OF THE ANCIENT ART OF ANSATSUKEN.
KRAKT
GRRRRRAAAH!
JINX: ARASHIKAGE NINJA, STUDENT OF THE BLIND MASTER.
NNNGH—!
STAY CALM, JINX.
REMEMBER YOUR TRAINING.
OH, I REMEMBER EVERYTHING...

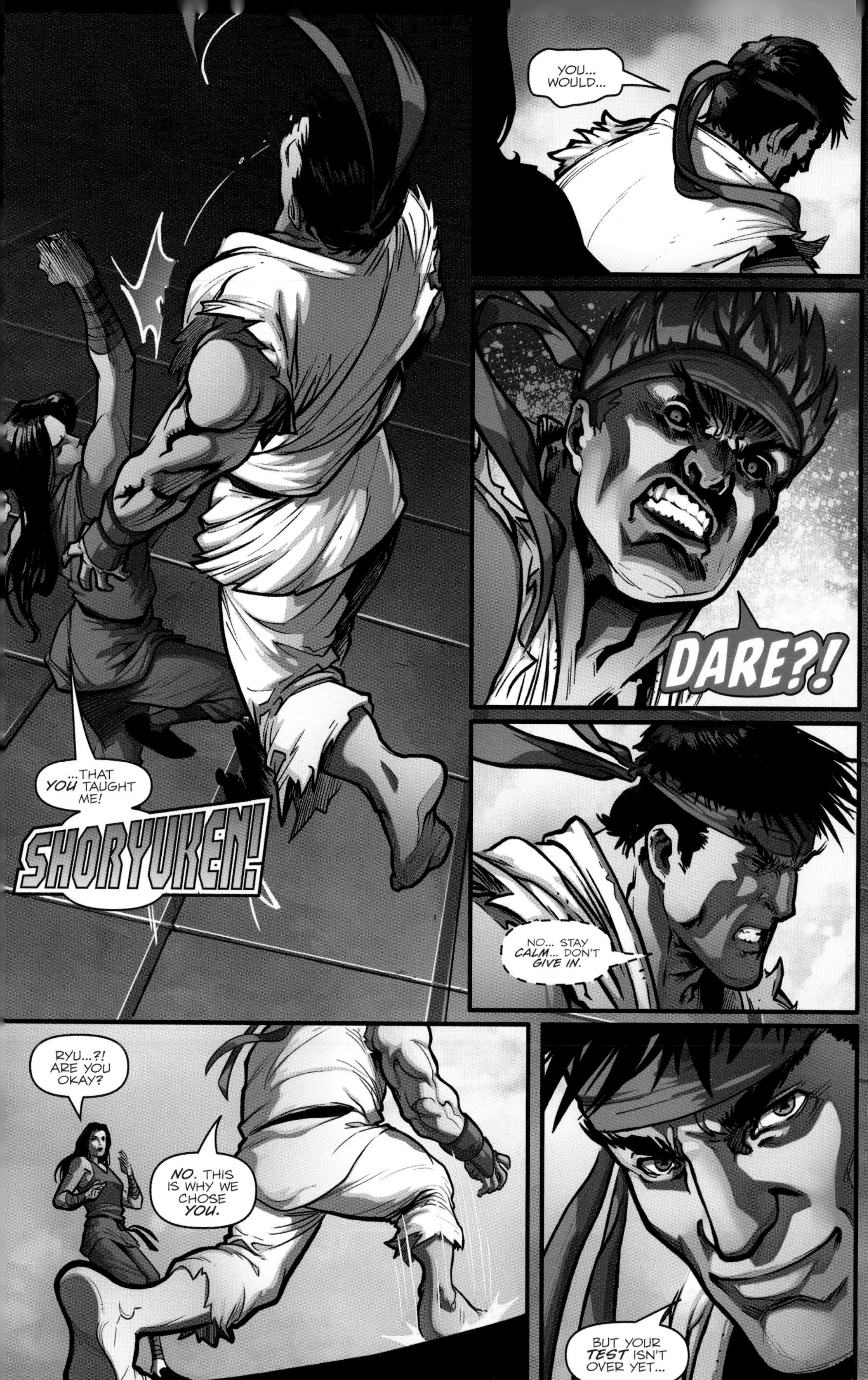
YOU... WOULD...
DARE?!
...THAT YOU TAUGHT ME!
SHORYUKEN!
NO... STAY CALM... DON'T GIVE IN.
RYU...?! ARE YOU OKAY?
NO. THIS IS WHY WE CHOSE YOU.
BUT YOUR TEST ISN'T OVER YET...

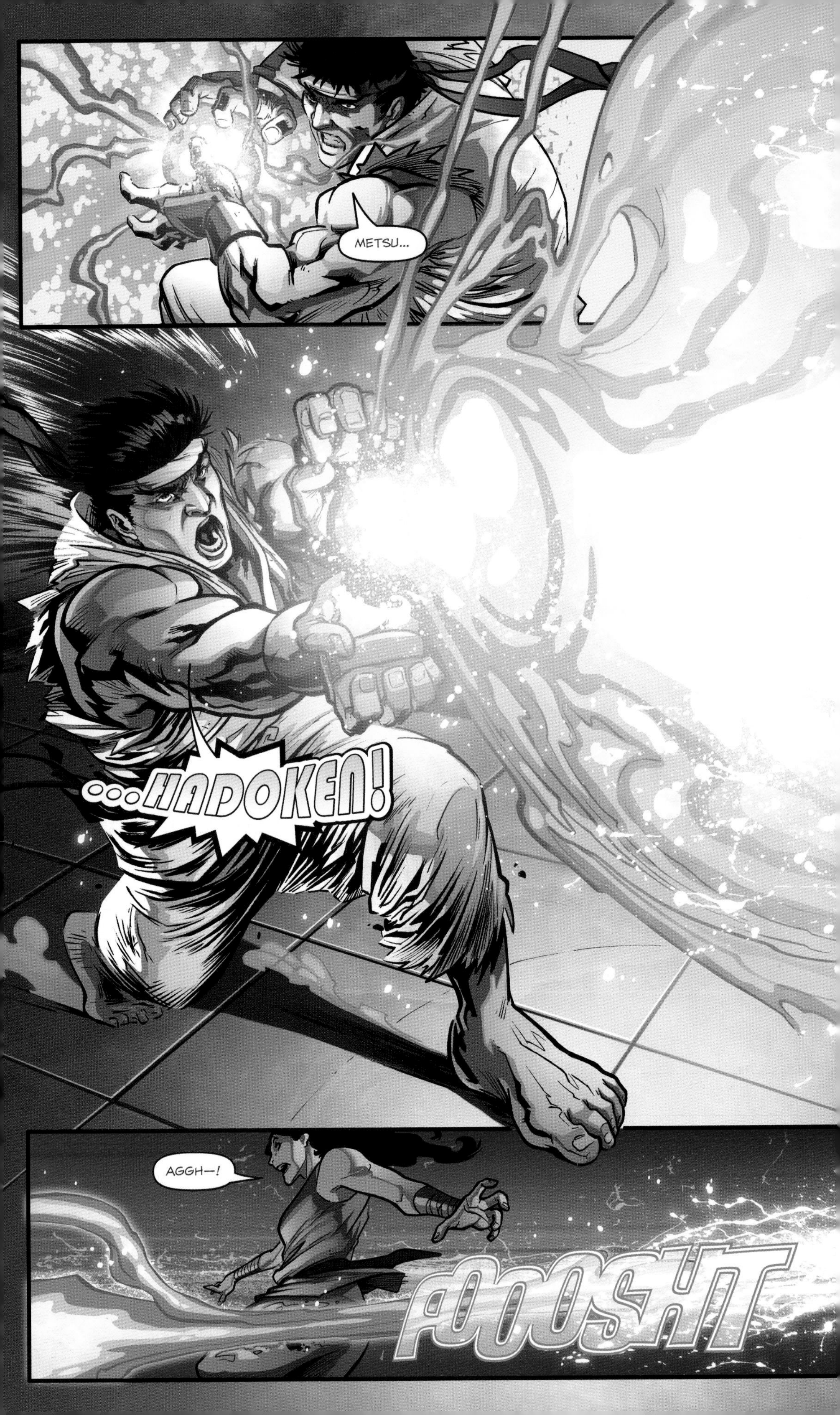
METSU...
...HADOKEN!
AGGH—!
FOOOSHT

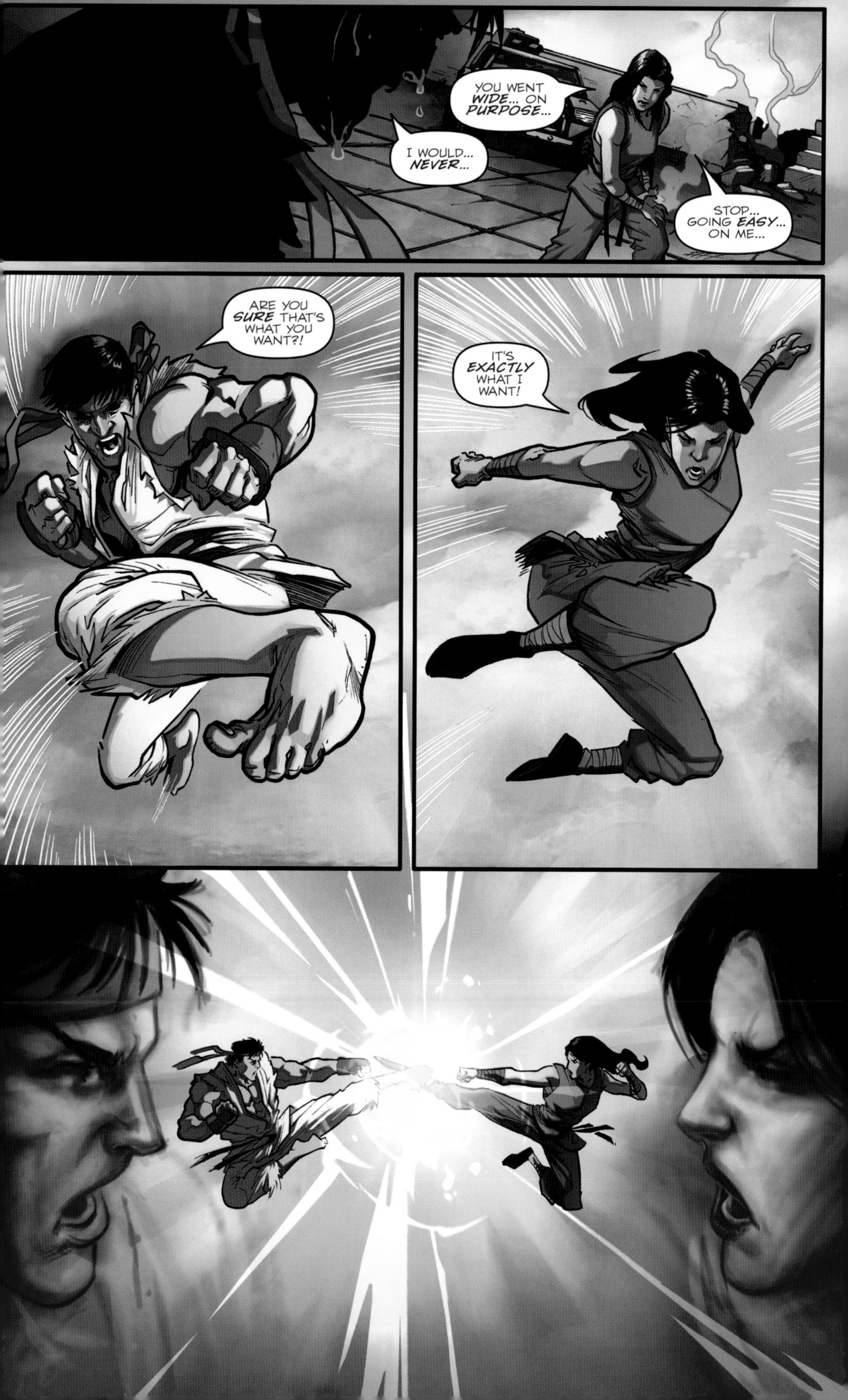
YOU WENT WIDE... ON PURPOSE...
I WOULD... NEVER...
STOP... GOING EASY... ON ME...
ARE YOU SURE THAT'S WHAT YOU WANT?!
IT'S EXACTLY WHAT I WANT!

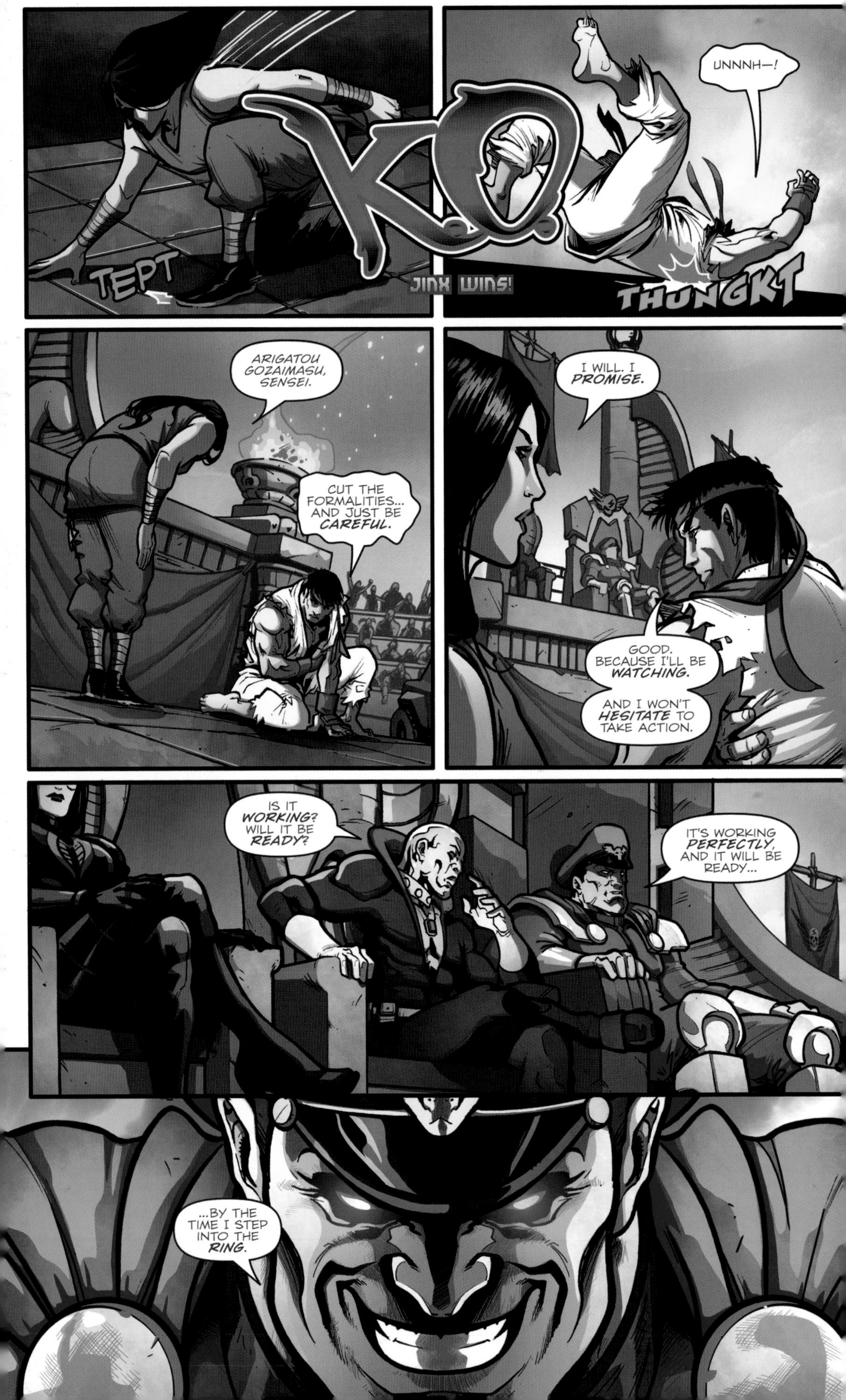
TEPT
K.O.
JINX WINS!
UNNNH—!
THUNGKT
ARIGATOU GOZAIMASU, SENSEI.
CUT THE FORMALITIES... AND JUST BE CAREFUL.
I WILL. I PROMISE.
GOOD. BECAUSE I'LL BE WATCHING.
AND I WON'T HESITATE TO TAKE ACTION.
IS IT WORKING? WILL IT BE READY?
IT'S WORKING PERFECTLY, AND IT WILL BE READY...
...BY THE TIME I STEP INTO THE RING.

ART BY PAOLO VILLANELLI
COLORS BY JOANA LAFUENTE

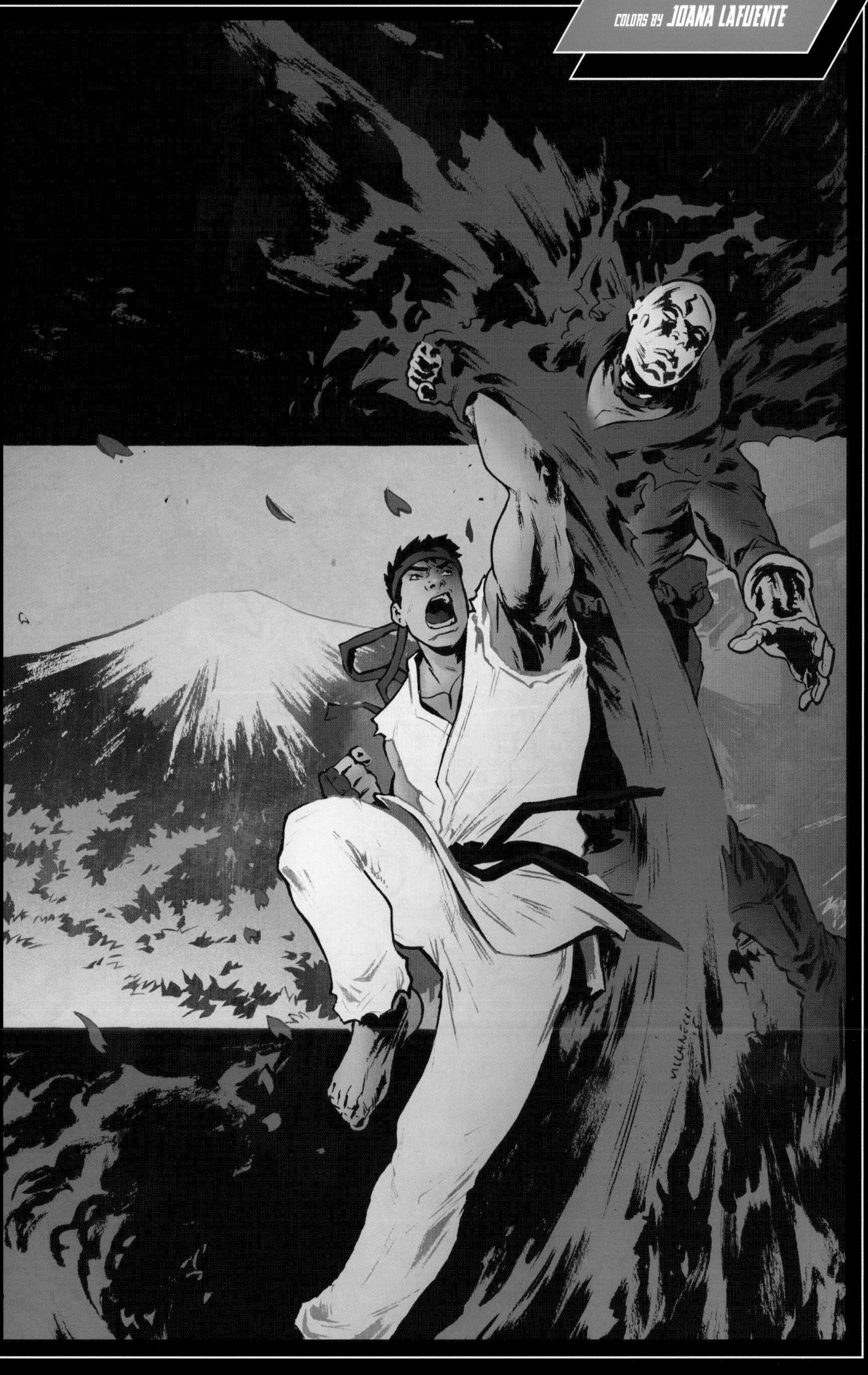

CHAPTER 2

WORLD WARRIOR
TOURNAMENT BRACKET

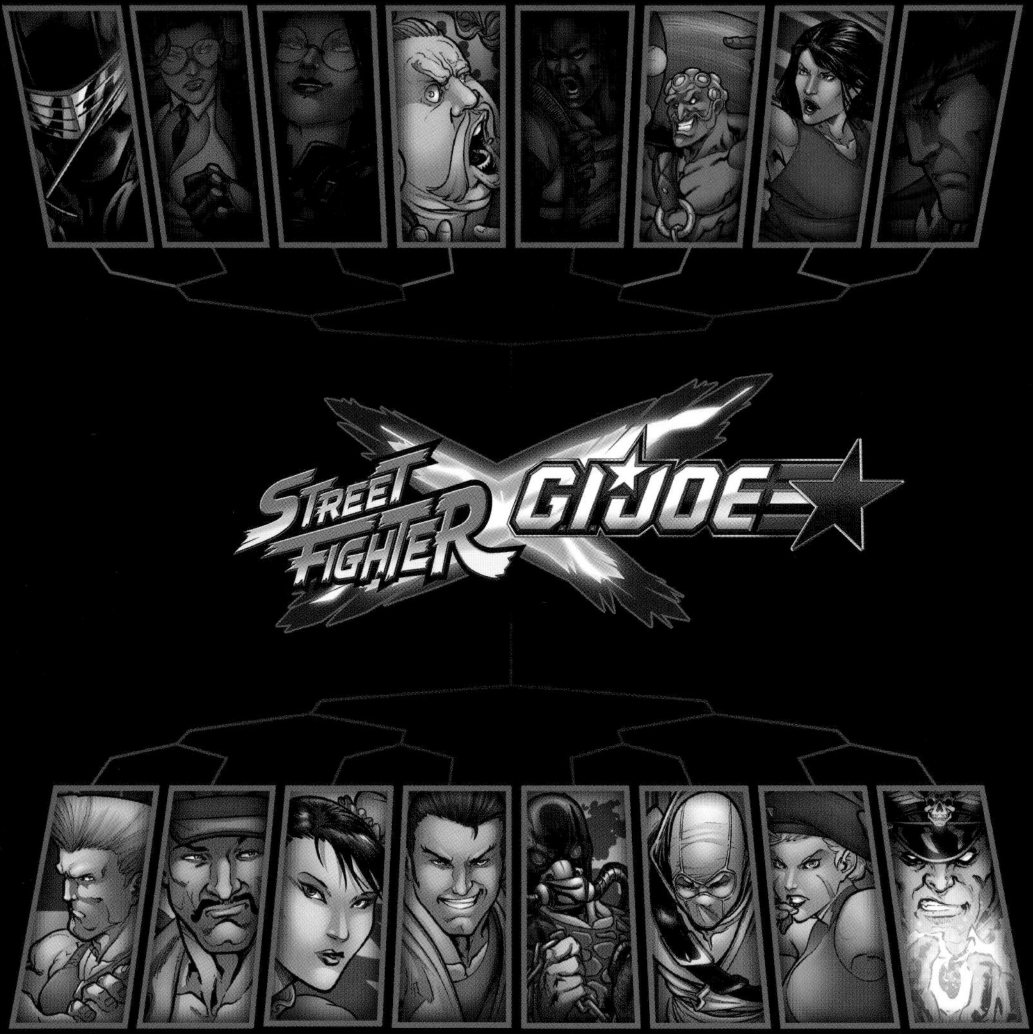
STREET FIGHTER
G.I. JOE

GUNG HO vs. GUILE
DAN vs. CHUN-LI
STORM SHADOW vs. CROC MASTER
BISON vs. CAMMY

EIGHTH-FINALS

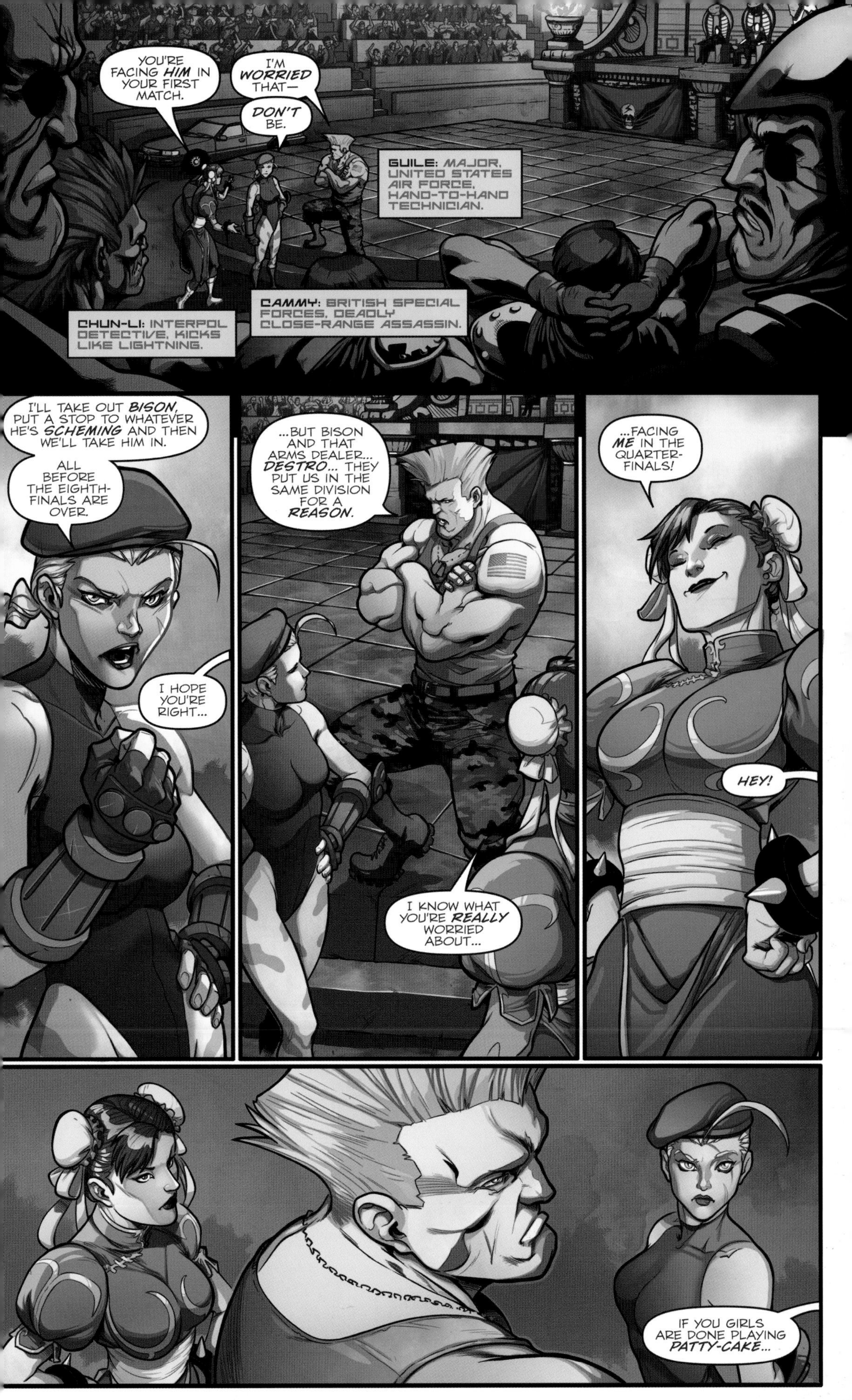
YOU'RE FACING HIM IN YOUR FIRST MATCH.
I'M WORRIED THAT—
DON'T BE.
GUILE: MAJOR, UNITED STATES AIR FORCE, HAND-TO-HAND TECHNICIAN.
CAMMY: BRITISH SPECIAL FORCES, DEADLY CLOSE-RANGE ASSASSIN.
CHUN-LI: INTERPOL DETECTIVE, KICKS LIKE LIGHTNING.
I'LL TAKE OUT BISON, PUT A STOP TO WHATEVER HE'S SCHEMING AND THEN WE'LL TAKE HIM IN.
ALL BEFORE THE EIGHTH-FINALS ARE OVER.
I HOPE YOU'RE RIGHT...
...BUT BISON AND THAT ARMS DEALER... DESTRO... THEY PUT US IN THE SAME DIVISION FOR A REASON.
I KNOW WHAT YOU'RE REALLY WORRIED ABOUT...
...FACING ME IN THE QUARTER-FINALS!
HEY!
IF YOU GIRLS ARE DONE PLAYING PATTY-CAKE...

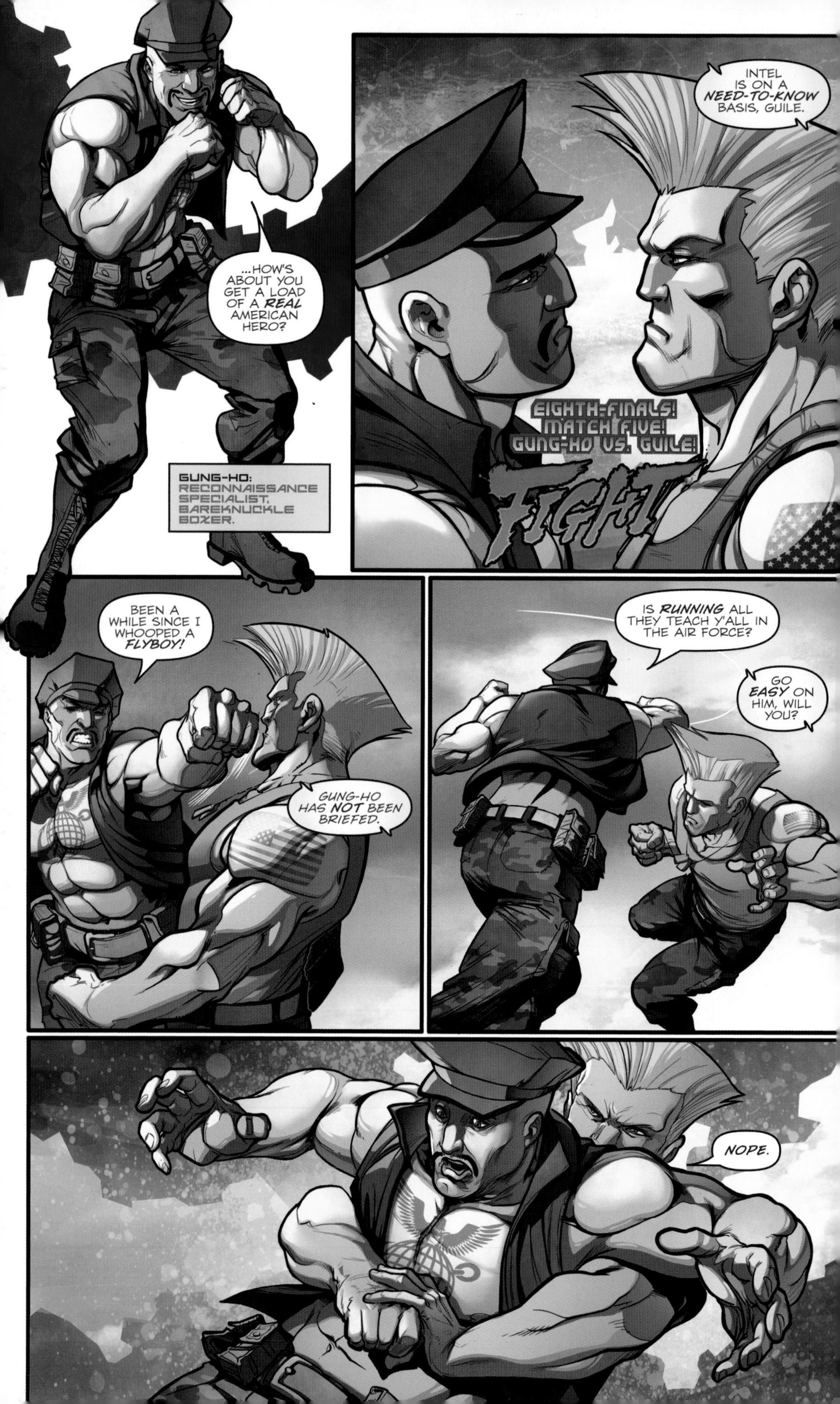
...HOW'S ABOUT YOU GET A LOAD OF A REAL AMERICAN HERO?
GUNG-HO: RECONNAISSANCE SPECIALIST, BAREKNUCKLE BOXER.
INTEL IS ON A NEED-TO-KNOW BASIS, GUILE.
EIGHTH-FINALS! MATCH FIVE! GUNG-HO VS. GUILE!
FIGHT
BEEN A WHILE SINCE I WHOOPED A FLYBOY!
GUNG-HO HAS NOT BEEN BRIEFED.
IS RUNNING ALL THEY TEACH Y'ALL IN THE AIR FORCE?
GO EASY ON HIM, WILL YOU?
NOPE.

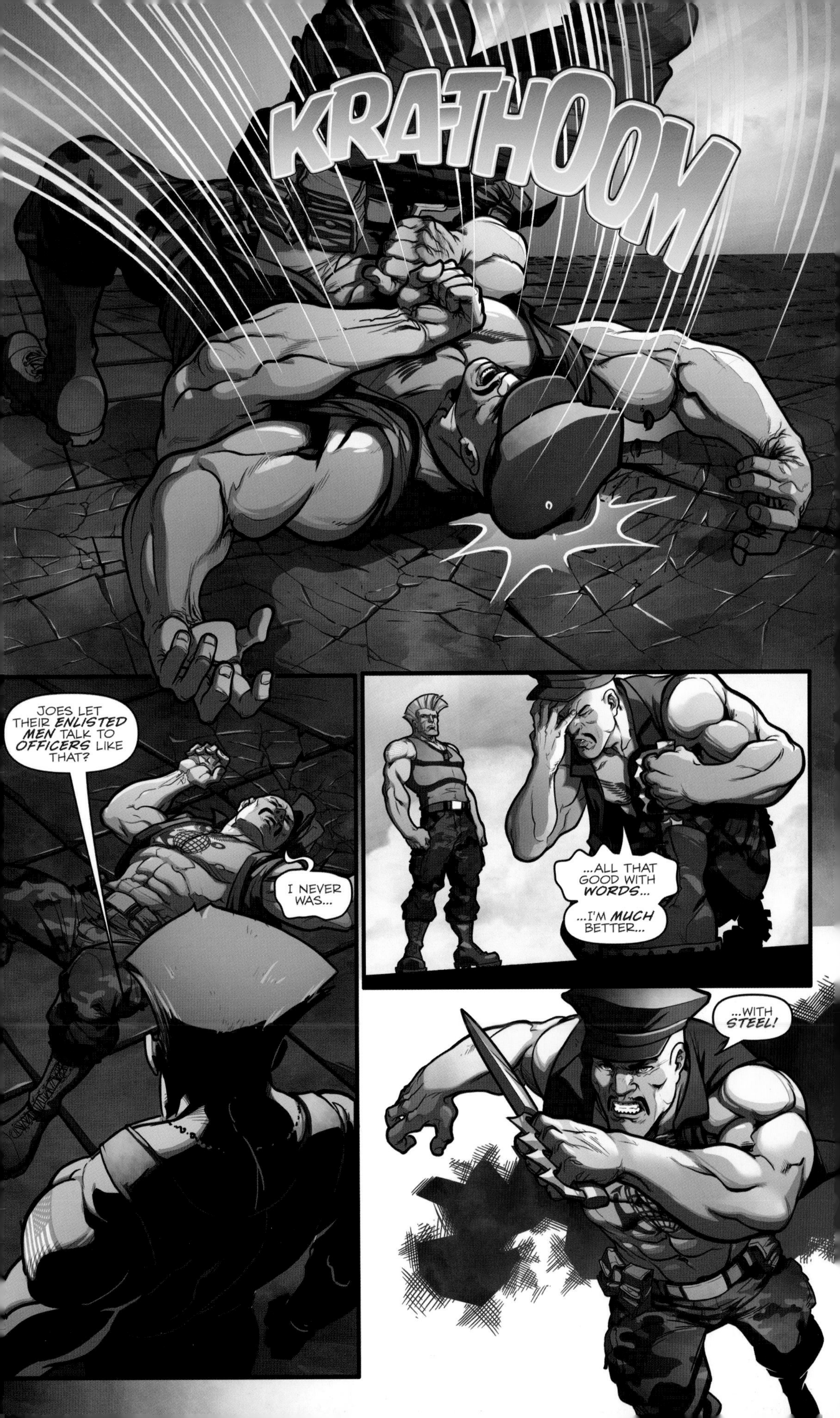
KRA-THOOM
JOES LET THEIR ENLISTED MEN TALK TO OFFICERS LIKE THAT?
I NEVER WAS...
...ALL THAT GOOD WITH WORDS...
...I'M MUCH BETTER...
...WITH STEEL!

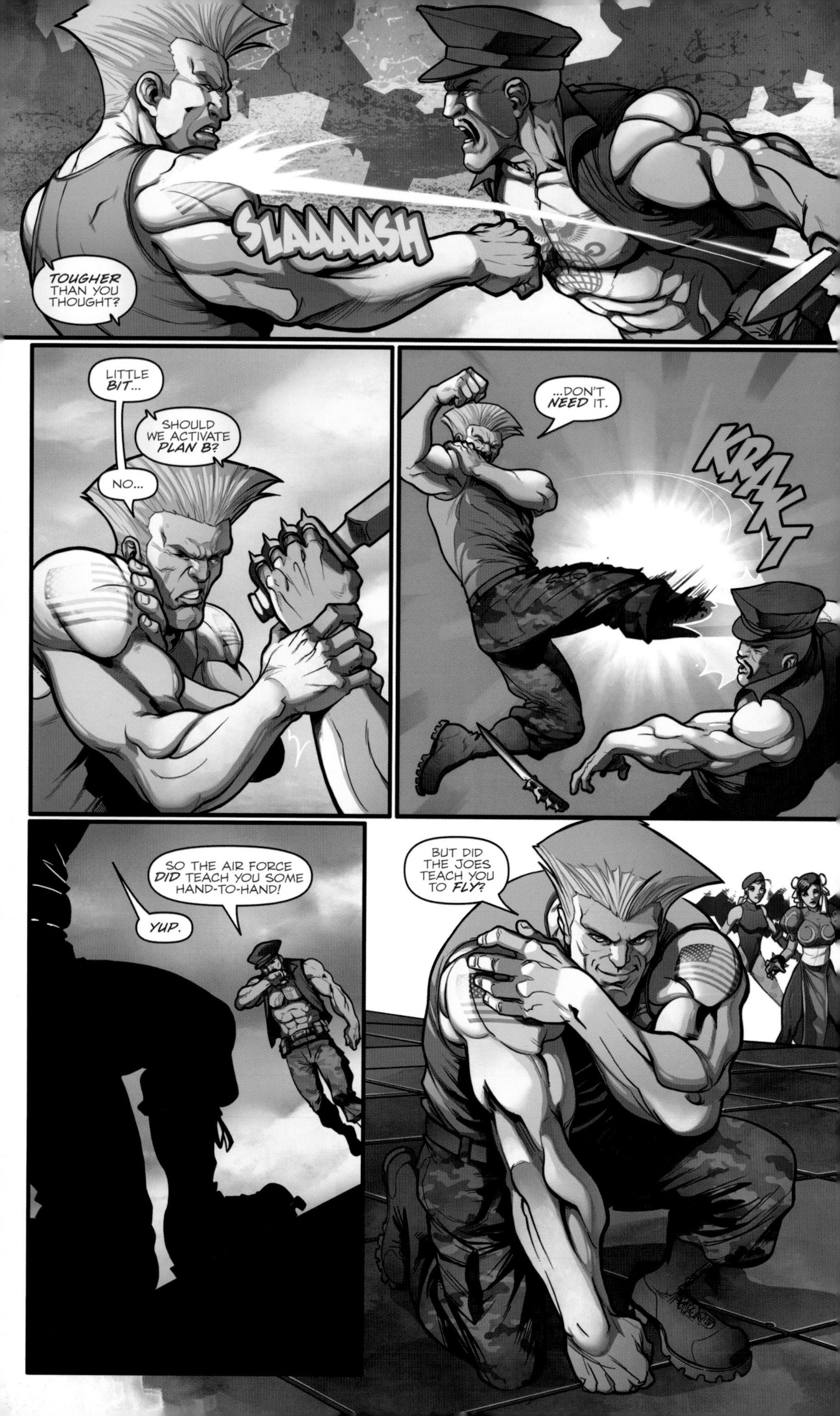

SLAAAASH
TOUGHER THAN YOU THOUGHT?
LITTLE BIT...
SHOULD WE ACTIVATE PLAN B?
NO...
...DON'T NEED IT.
KRAKT
SO THE AIR FORCE DID TEACH YOU SOME HAND-TO-HAND!
YUP.
BUT DID THE JOES TEACH YOU TO FLY?

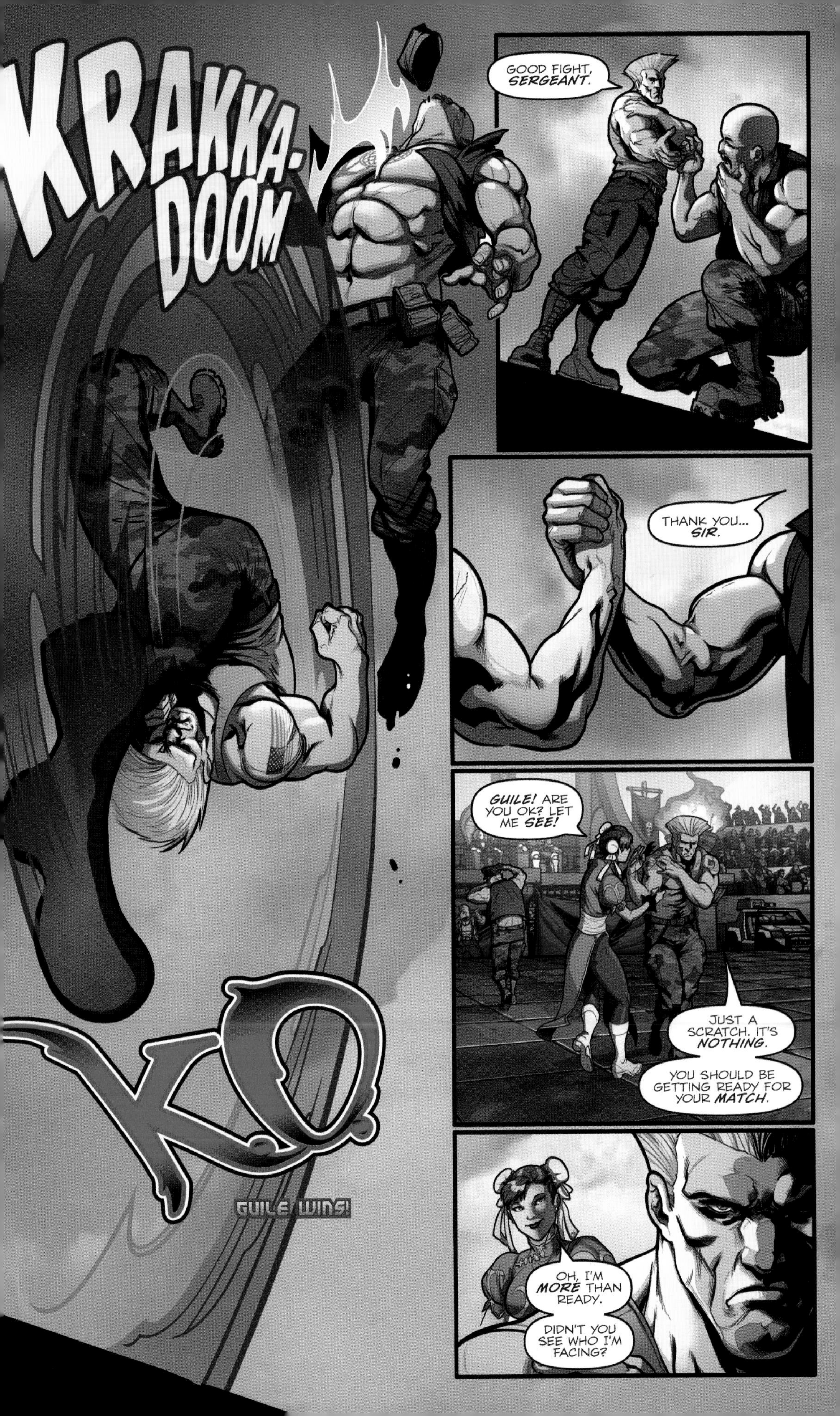
KRAKKA-DOOM
K.O.
GUILE WINS!
GOOD FIGHT, SERGEANT.
THANK YOU... SIR.
GUILE! ARE YOU OK? LET ME SEE!
JUST A SCRATCH. IT'S NOTHING.
YOU SHOULD BE GETTING READY FOR YOUR MATCH.
OH, I'M MORE THAN READY.
DIDN'T YOU SEE WHO I'M FACING?

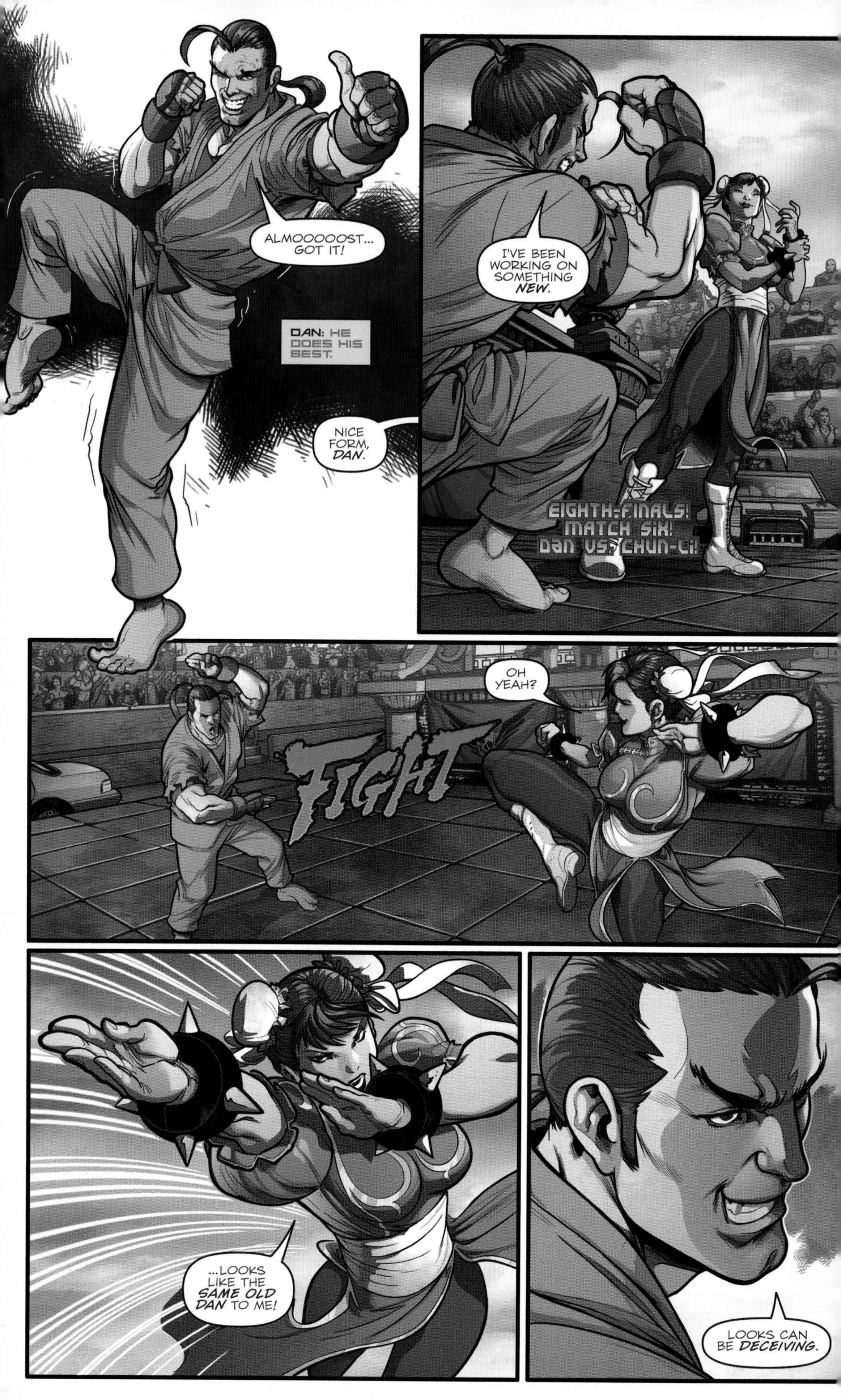
ALMOOOOOST... GOT IT!
DAN: HE DOES HIS BEST.
NICE FORM, DAN.
I'VE BEEN WORKING ON SOMETHING NEW.
EIGHTH-FINALS! MATCH SIX! DAN VS. CHUN-LI!
OH YEAH?
FIGHT
...LOOKS LIKE THE SAME OLD DAN TO ME!
LOOKS CAN BE DECEIVING.

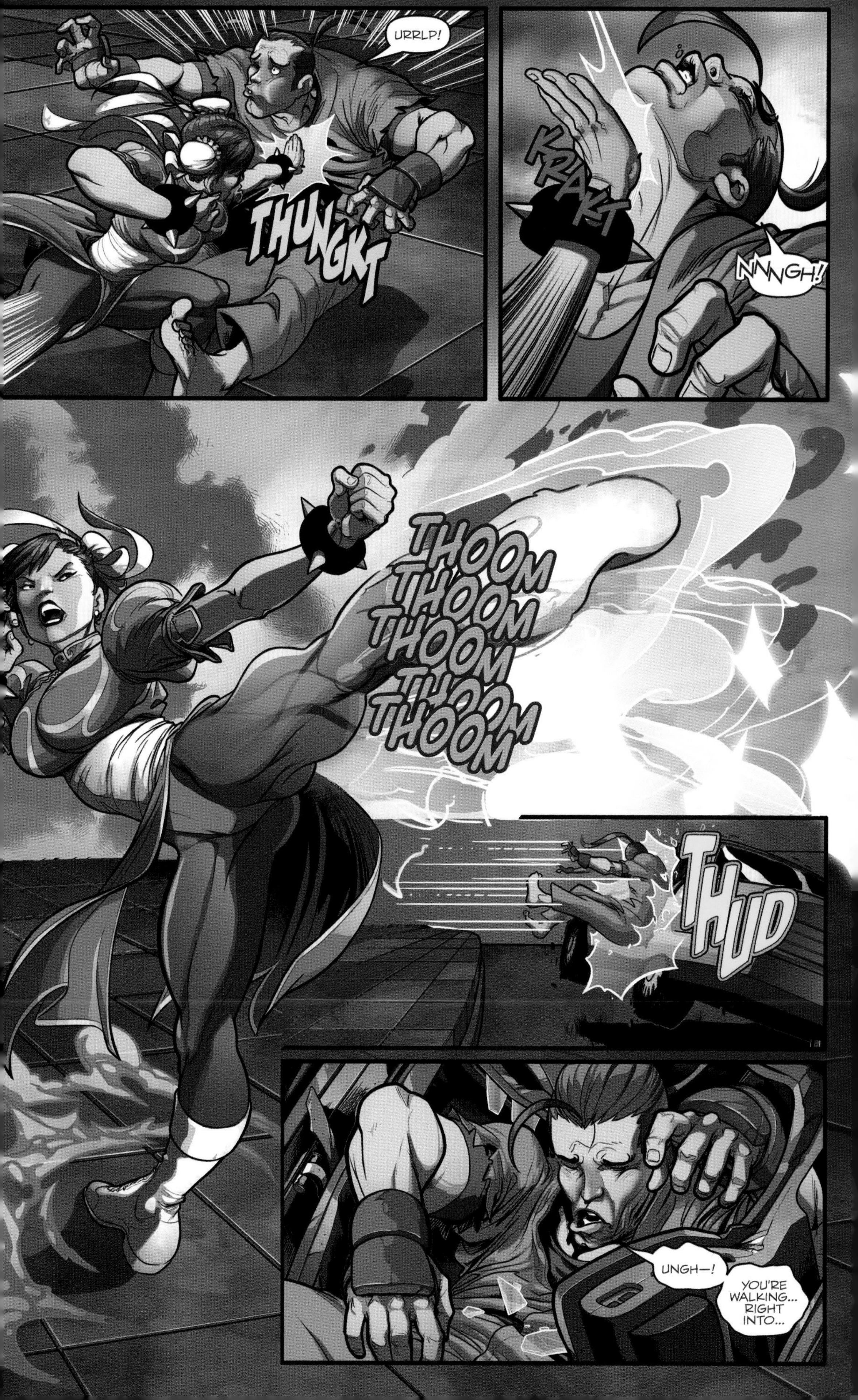
URRLP!
THUNGKT
KRAKT
NNNGH!
THOOM
THOOM
THOOM
THOOM
THOOM
THUD
UNGH—!
YOU'RE WALKING... RIGHT INTO...

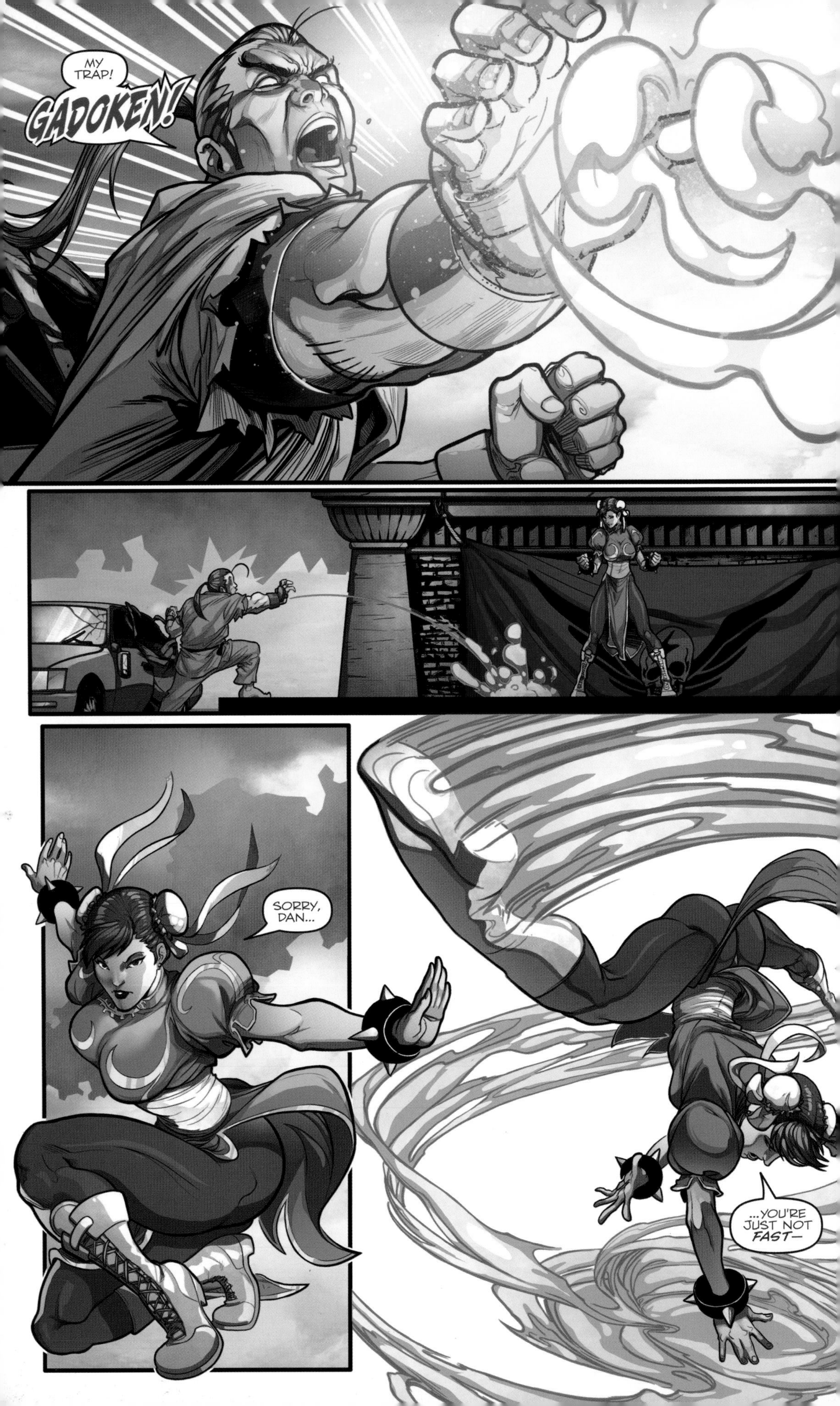
MY TRAP!
GADOKEN!
SORRY, DAN...
...YOU'RE JUST NOT *FAST*—

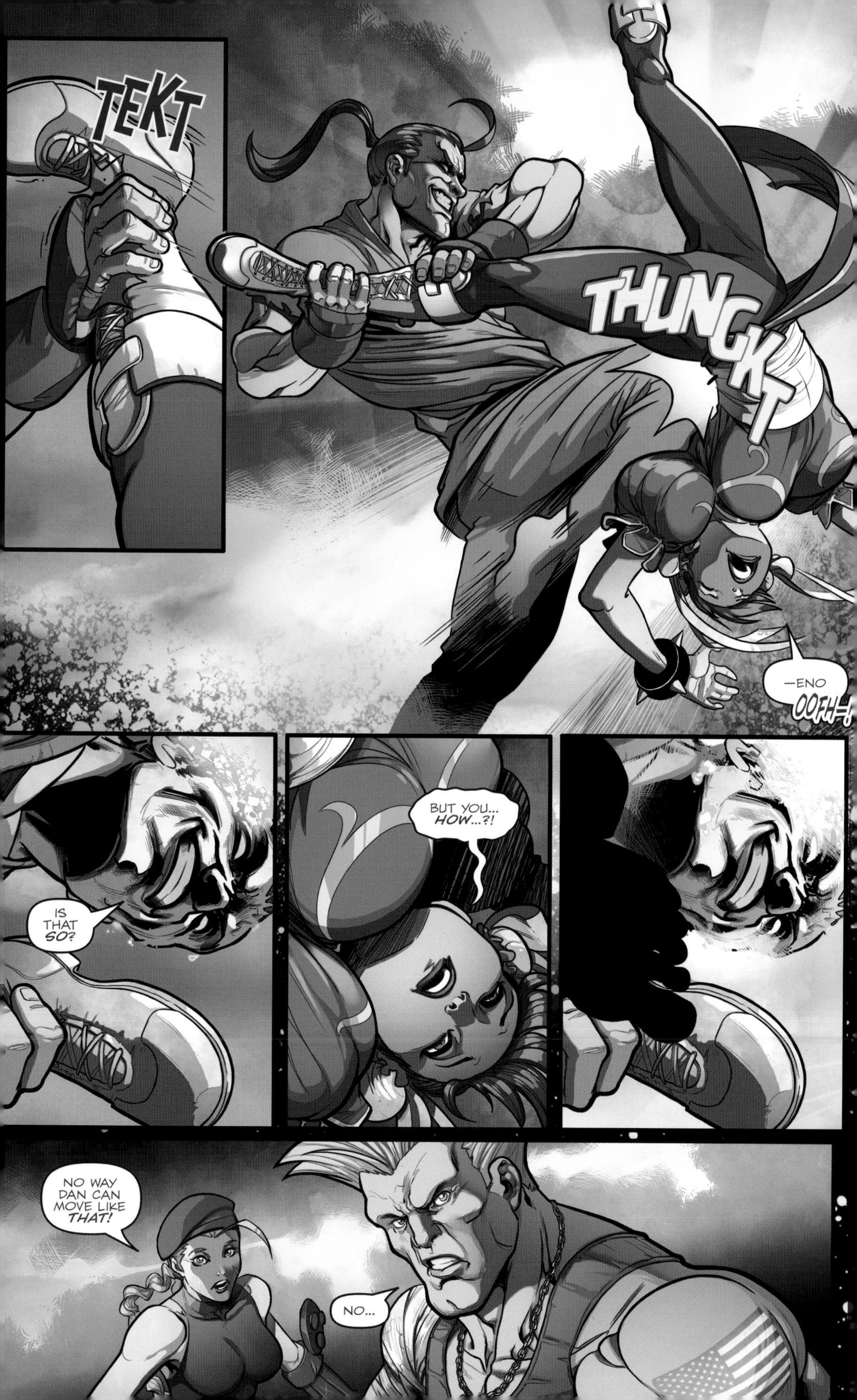

TEKT
THUNGKT
—ENO
OOFH—!
IS THAT SO?
BUT YOU... HOW...?!
NO WAY DAN CAN MOVE LIKE THAT!
NO...

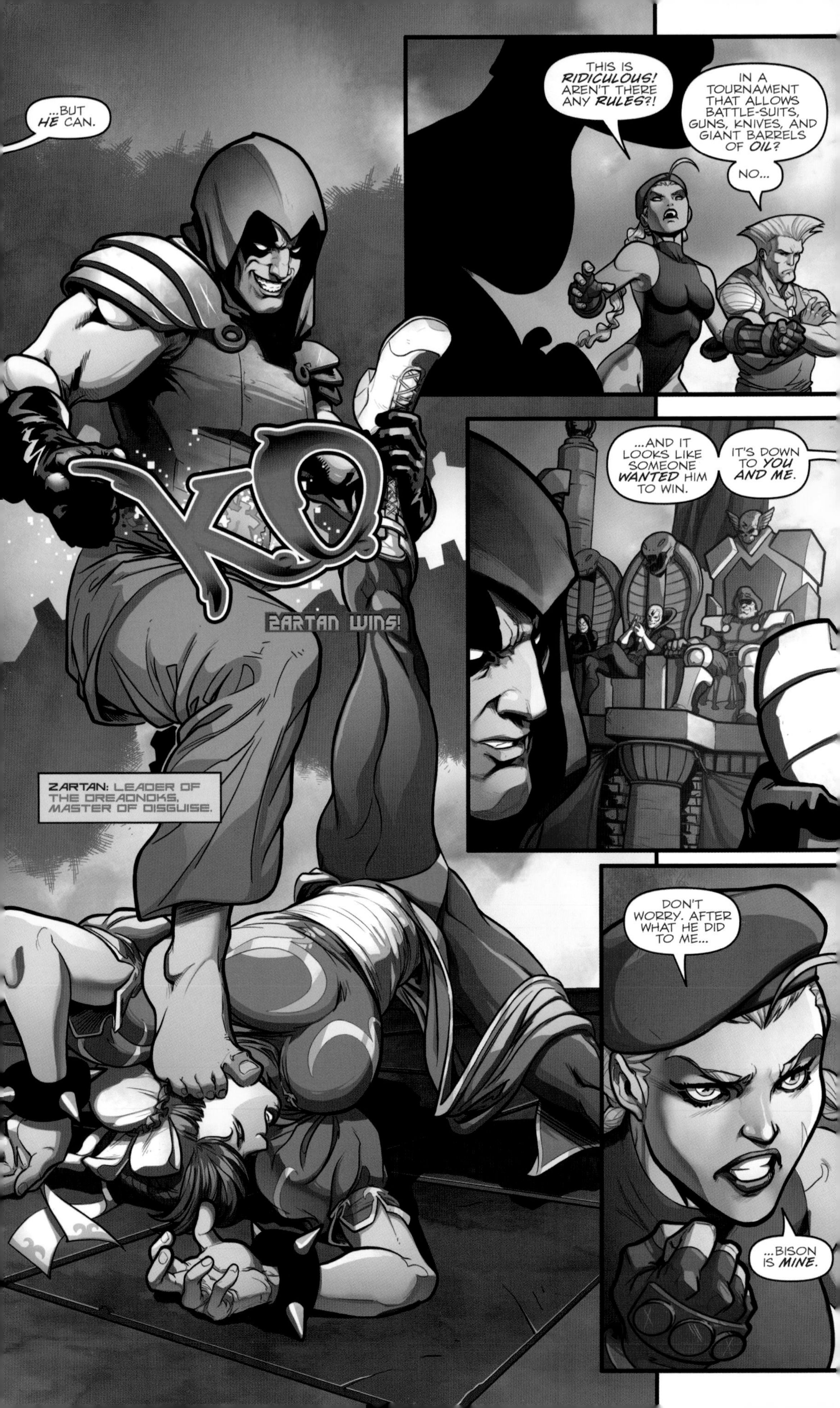
...BUT HE CAN.
KO
ZARTAN WINS!
ZARTAN: LEADER OF THE DREADNOKS, MASTER OF DISGUISE.
THIS IS RIDICULOUS! AREN'T THERE ANY RULES?!
IN A TOURNAMENT THAT ALLOWS BATTLE-SUITS, GUNS, KNIVES, AND GIANT BARRELS OF OIL?
NO...
...AND IT LOOKS LIKE SOMEONE WANTED HIM TO WIN.
IT'S DOWN TO YOU AND ME.
DON'T WORRY. AFTER WHAT HE DID TO ME...
...BISON IS MINE.

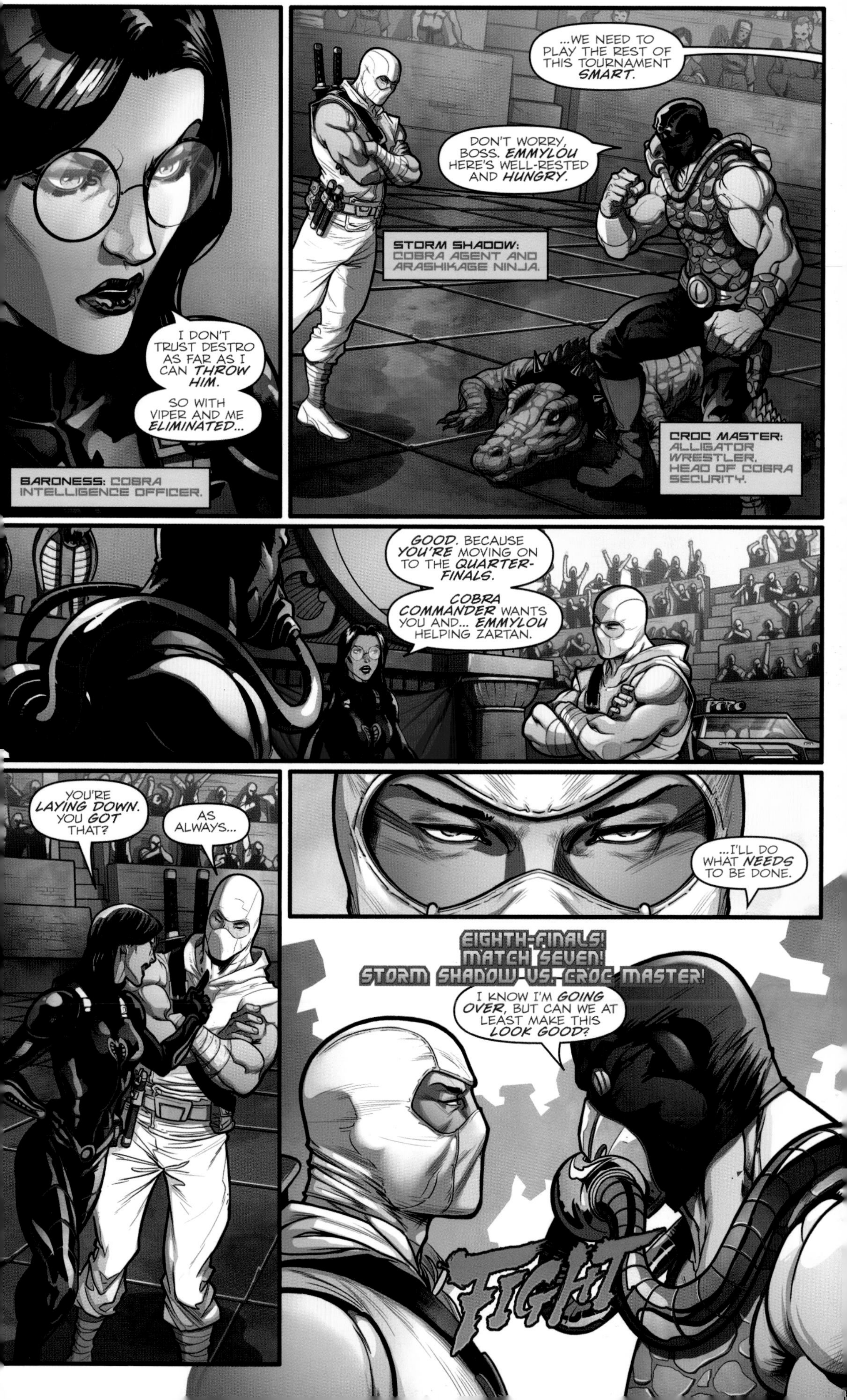
I DON'T TRUST DESTRO AS FAR AS I CAN THROW HIM.
SO WITH VIPER AND ME ELIMINATED...
BARONESS: COBRA INTELLIGENCE OFFICER.
...WE NEED TO PLAY THE REST OF THIS TOURNAMENT SMART.
DON'T WORRY, BOSS. EMMYLOU HERE'S WELL-RESTED AND HUNGRY.
STORM SHADOW: COBRA AGENT AND ARASHIKAGE NINJA.
CROC MASTER: ALLIGATOR WRESTLER, HEAD OF COBRA SECURITY.
GOOD. BECAUSE YOU'RE MOVING ON TO THE QUARTER-FINALS.
COBRA COMMANDER WANTS YOU AND... EMMYLOU HELPING ZARTAN.
YOU'RE LAYING DOWN. YOU GOT THAT?
AS ALWAYS...
...I'LL DO WHAT NEEDS TO BE DONE.
EIGHTH-FINALS! MATCH SEVEN! STORM SHADOW VS. CROC MASTER!
I KNOW I'M GOING OVER, BUT CAN WE AT LEAST MAKE THIS LOOK GOOD?
FIGHT

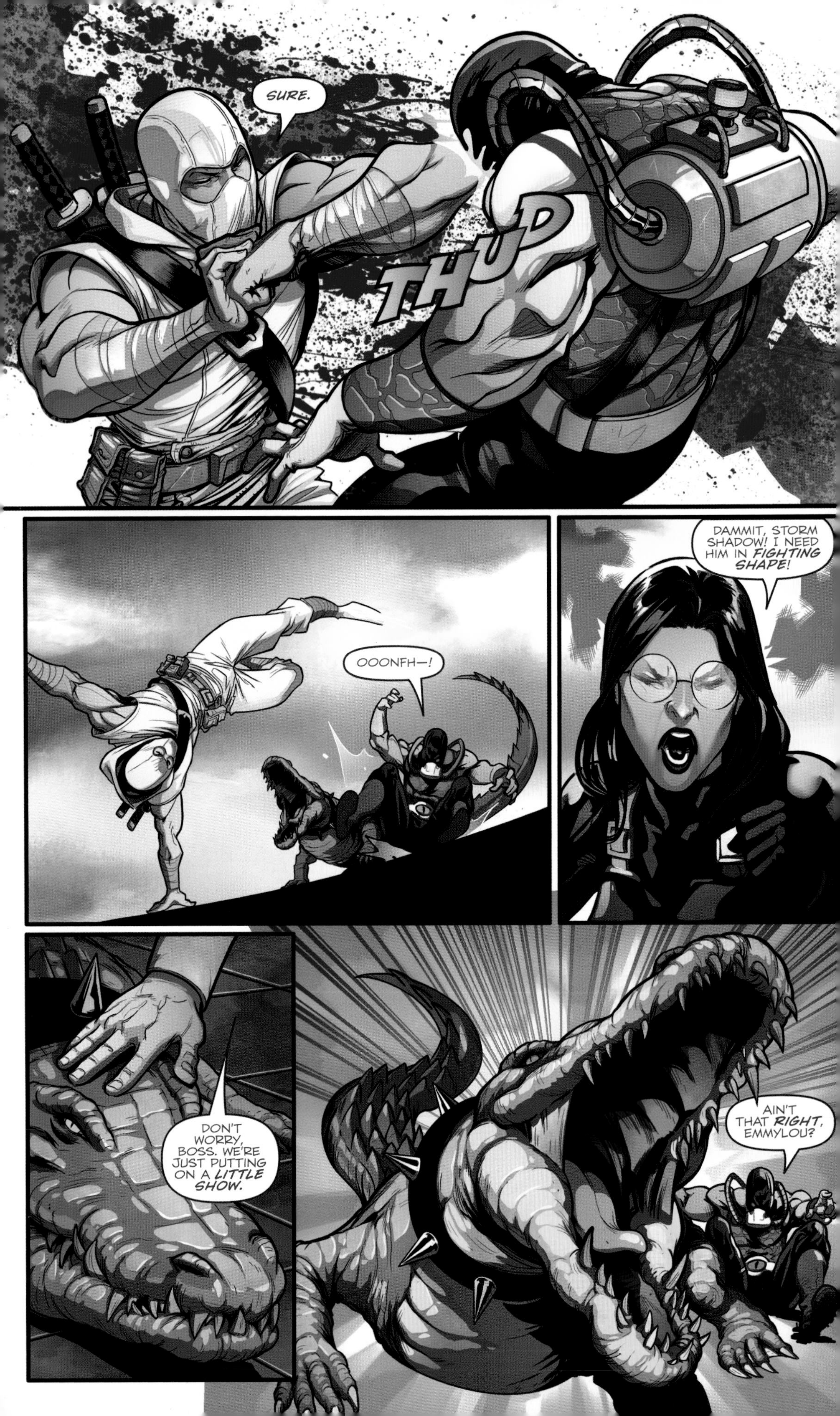
SURE.
THUD
OOONFH—!
DAMMIT, STORM SHADOW! I NEED HIM IN FIGHTING SHAPE!
DON'T WORRY, BOSS. WE'RE JUST PUTTING ON A LITTLE SHOW.
AIN'T THAT RIGHT, EMMYLOU?

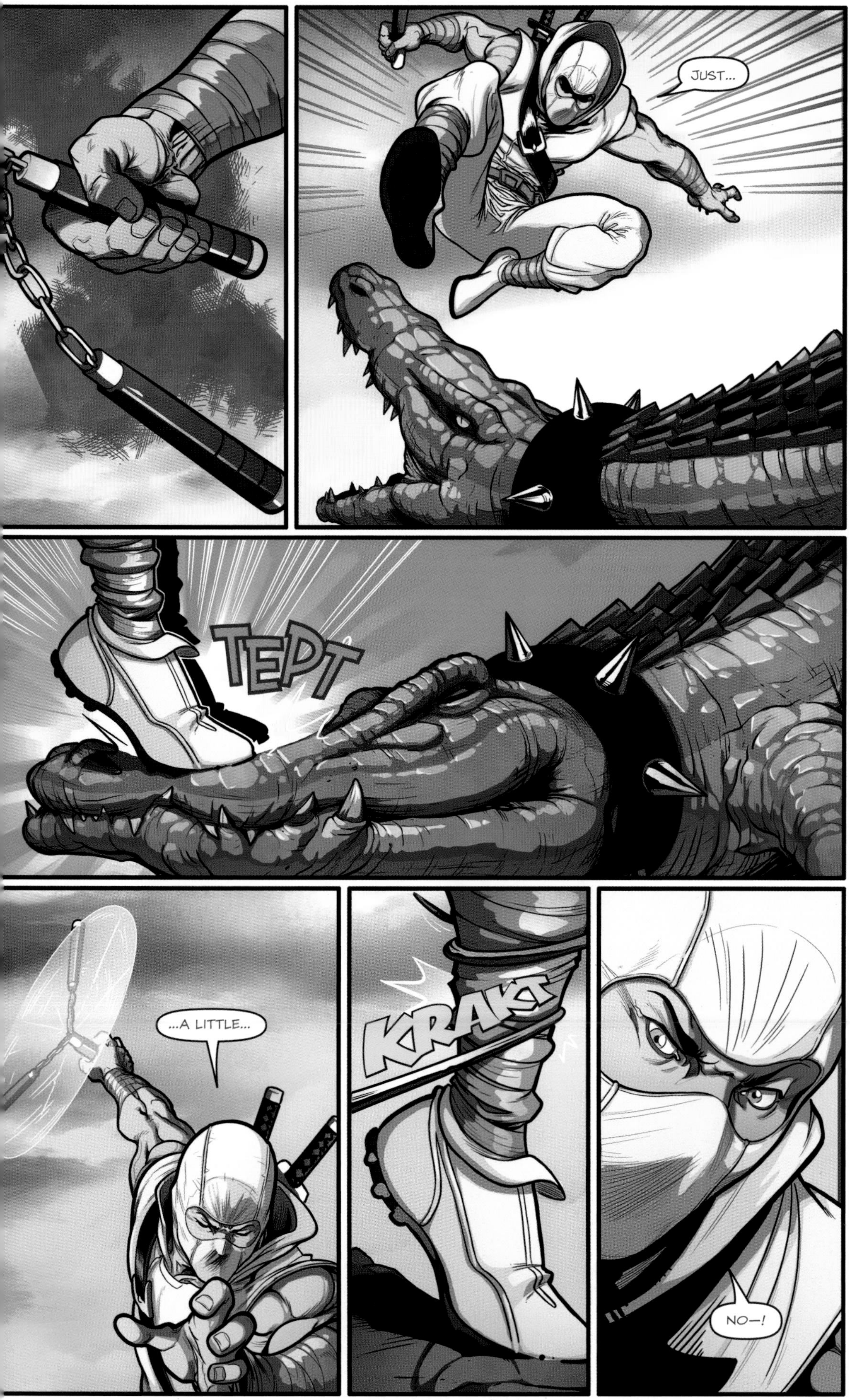

JUST...
TEPT
...A LITTLE...
KRAKT
NO—!

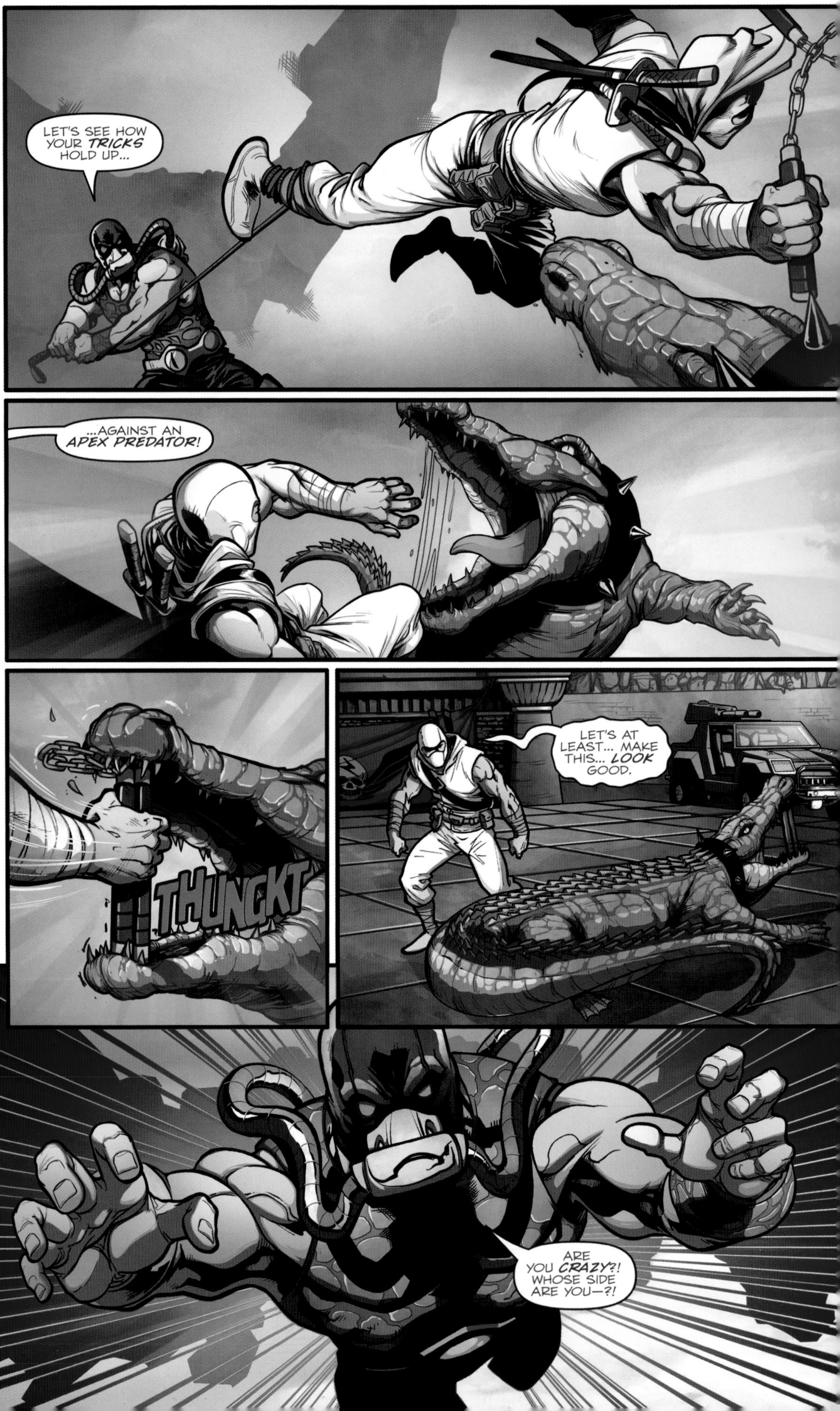
LET'S SEE HOW YOUR TRICKS HOLD UP...
...AGAINST AN APEX PREDATOR!
THUNGKT
LET'S AT LEAST... MAKE THIS... LOOK GOOD.
ARE YOU CRAZY?! WHOSE SIDE ARE YOU—?!

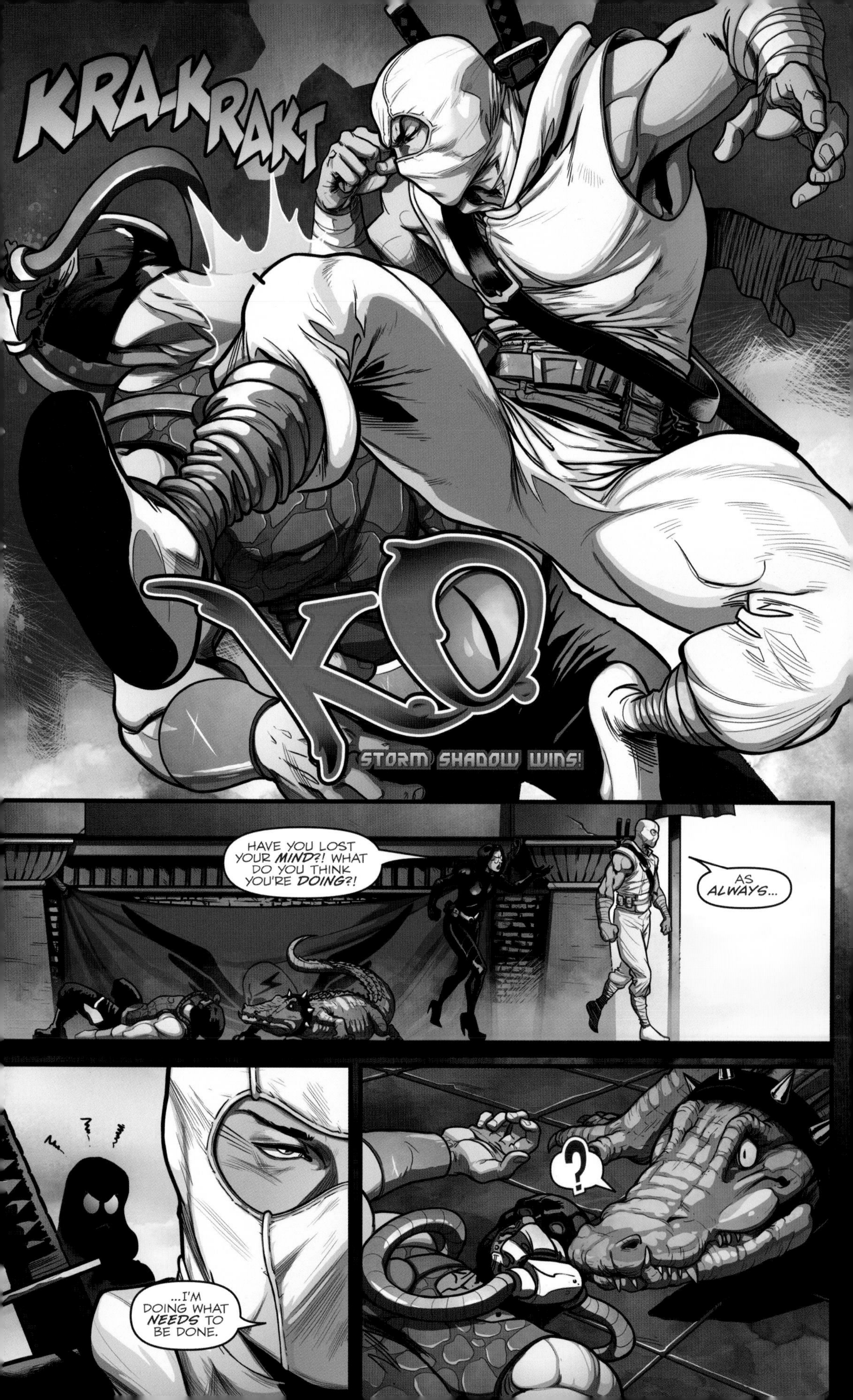
KRA-KRAKT
K.O.
STORM SHADOW WINS!
HAVE YOU LOST YOUR MIND?! WHAT DO YOU THINK YOU'RE DOING?!
AS ALWAYS...
...I'M DOING WHAT NEEDS TO BE DONE.
?

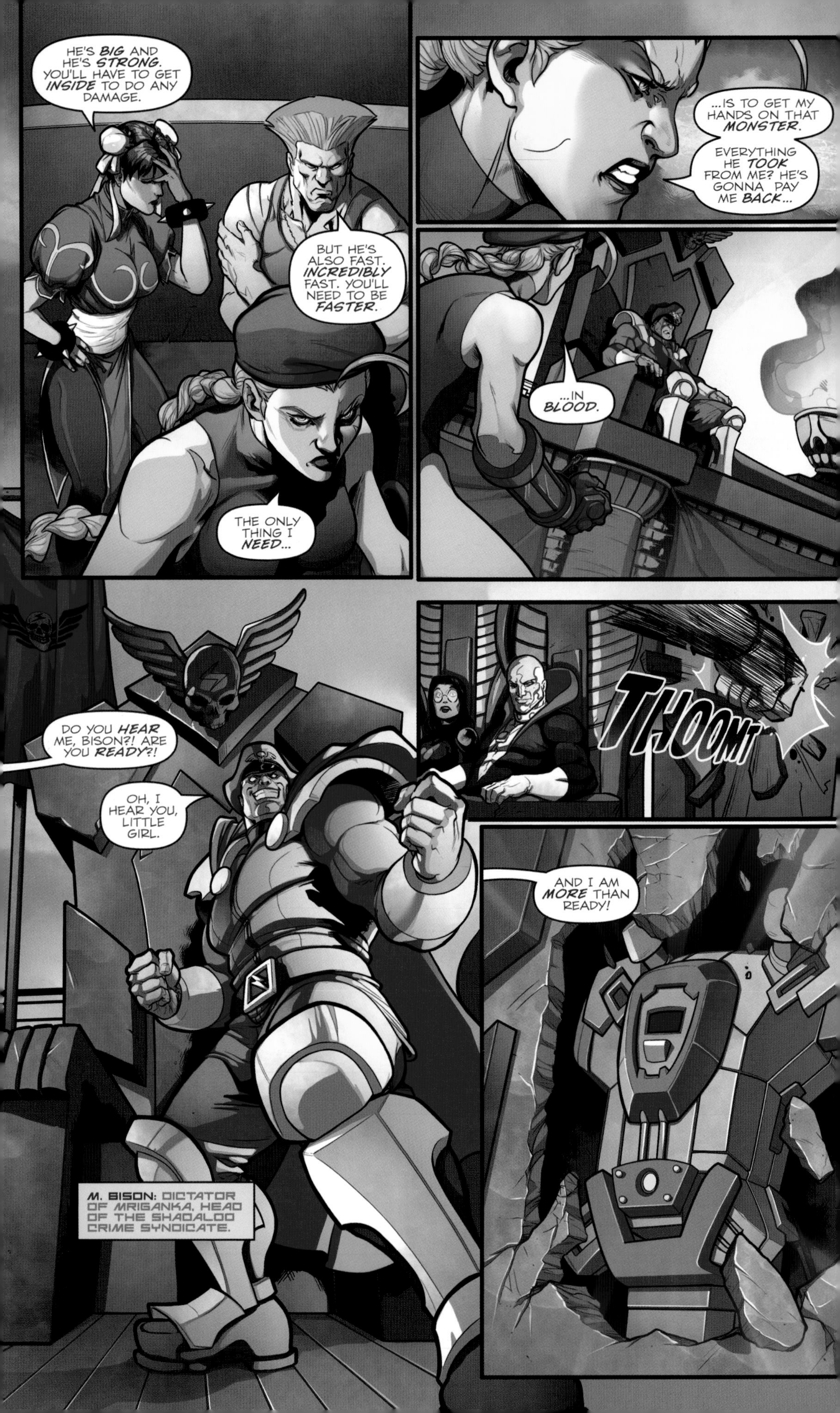

HE'S BIG AND HE'S STRONG. YOU'LL HAVE TO GET INSIDE TO DO ANY DAMAGE.
BUT HE'S ALSO FAST. INCREDIBLY FAST. YOU'LL NEED TO BE FASTER.
THE ONLY THING I NEED...
...IS TO GET MY HANDS ON THAT MONSTER.
EVERYTHING HE TOOK FROM ME? HE'S GONNA PAY ME BACK...
...IN BLOOD.
DO YOU HEAR ME, BISON?! ARE YOU READY?!
OH, I HEAR YOU, LITTLE GIRL.
M. BISON: DICTATOR OF MRIGANKA, HEAD OF THE SHADALOO CRIME SYNDICATE.
THOOM
AND I AM MORE THAN READY!

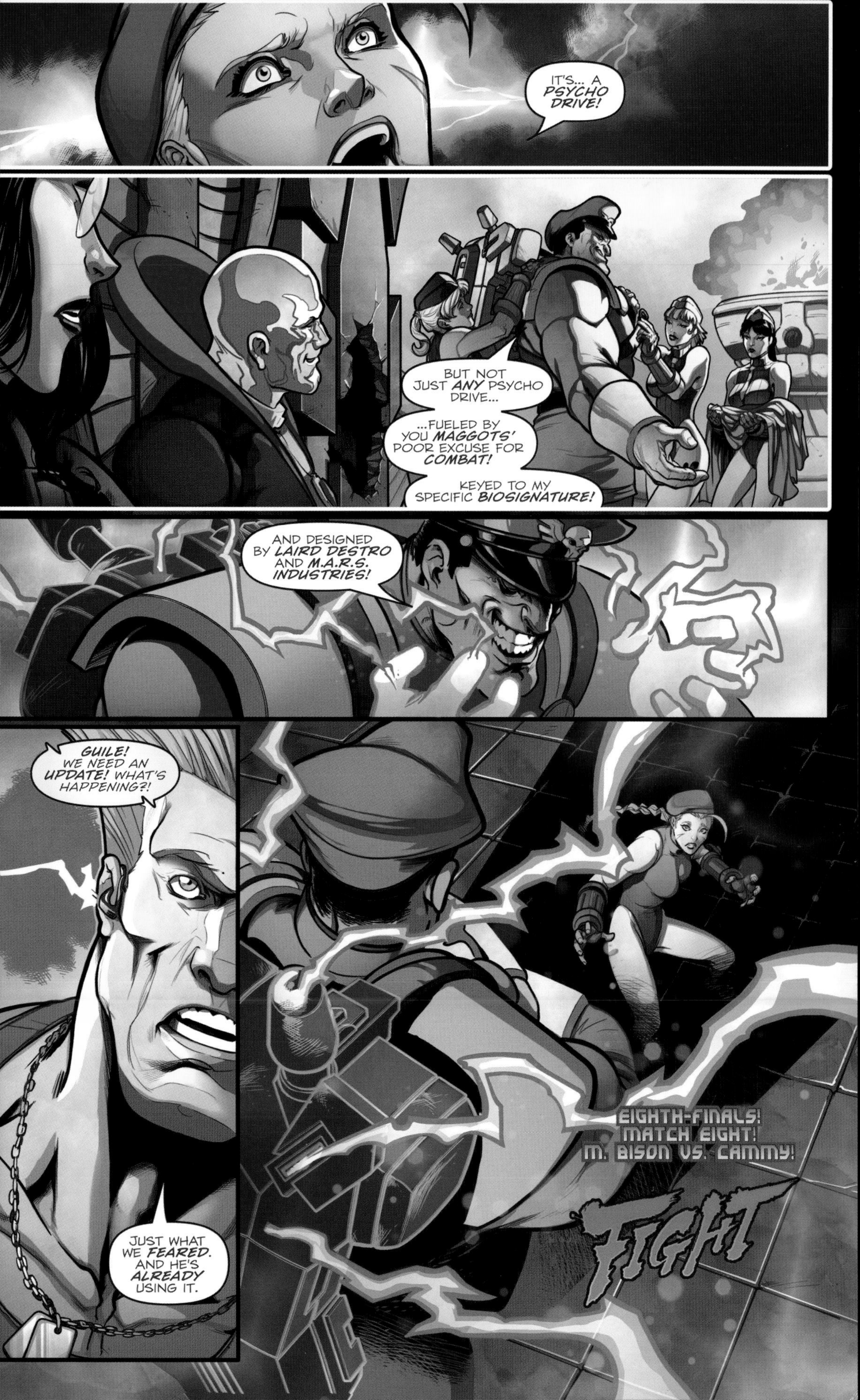
IT'S... A PSYCHO DRIVE!
BUT NOT JUST ANY PSYCHO DRIVE...
...FUELED BY YOU MAGGOTS' POOR EXCUSE FOR COMBAT!
KEYED TO MY SPECIFIC BIOSIGNATURE!
AND DESIGNED BY LAIRD DESTRO AND M.A.R.S. INDUSTRIES!
GUILE! WE NEED AN UPDATE! WHAT'S HAPPENING?!
EIGHTH-FINALS! MATCH EIGHT! M. BISON VS. CAMMY!
FIGHT
JUST WHAT WE FEARED. AND HE'S ALREADY USING IT.

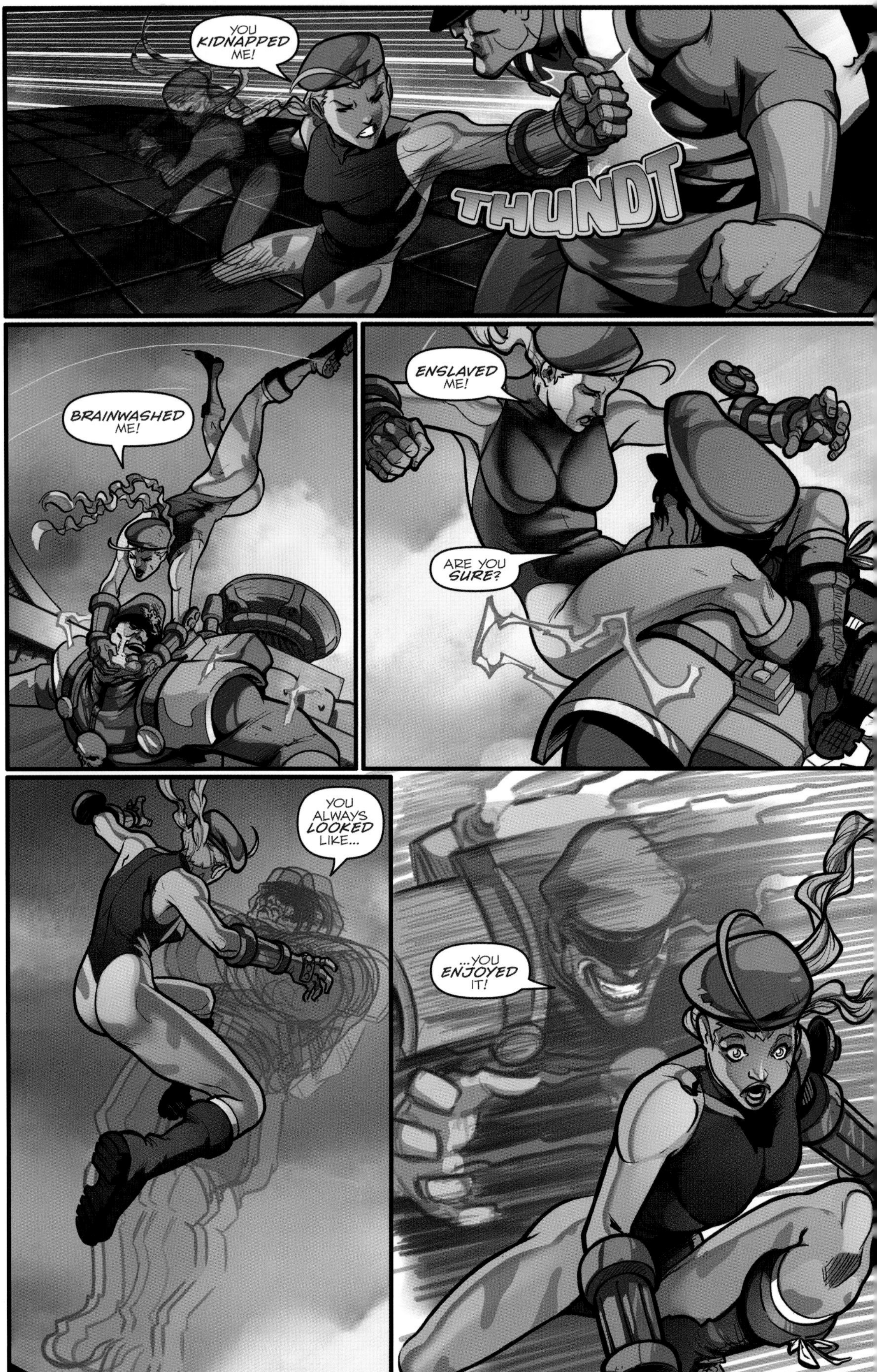
YOU KIDNAPPED ME!
THUNDT
BRAINWASHED ME!
ENSLAVED ME!
ARE YOU SURE?
YOU ALWAYS LOOKED LIKE...
...YOU ENJOYED IT!

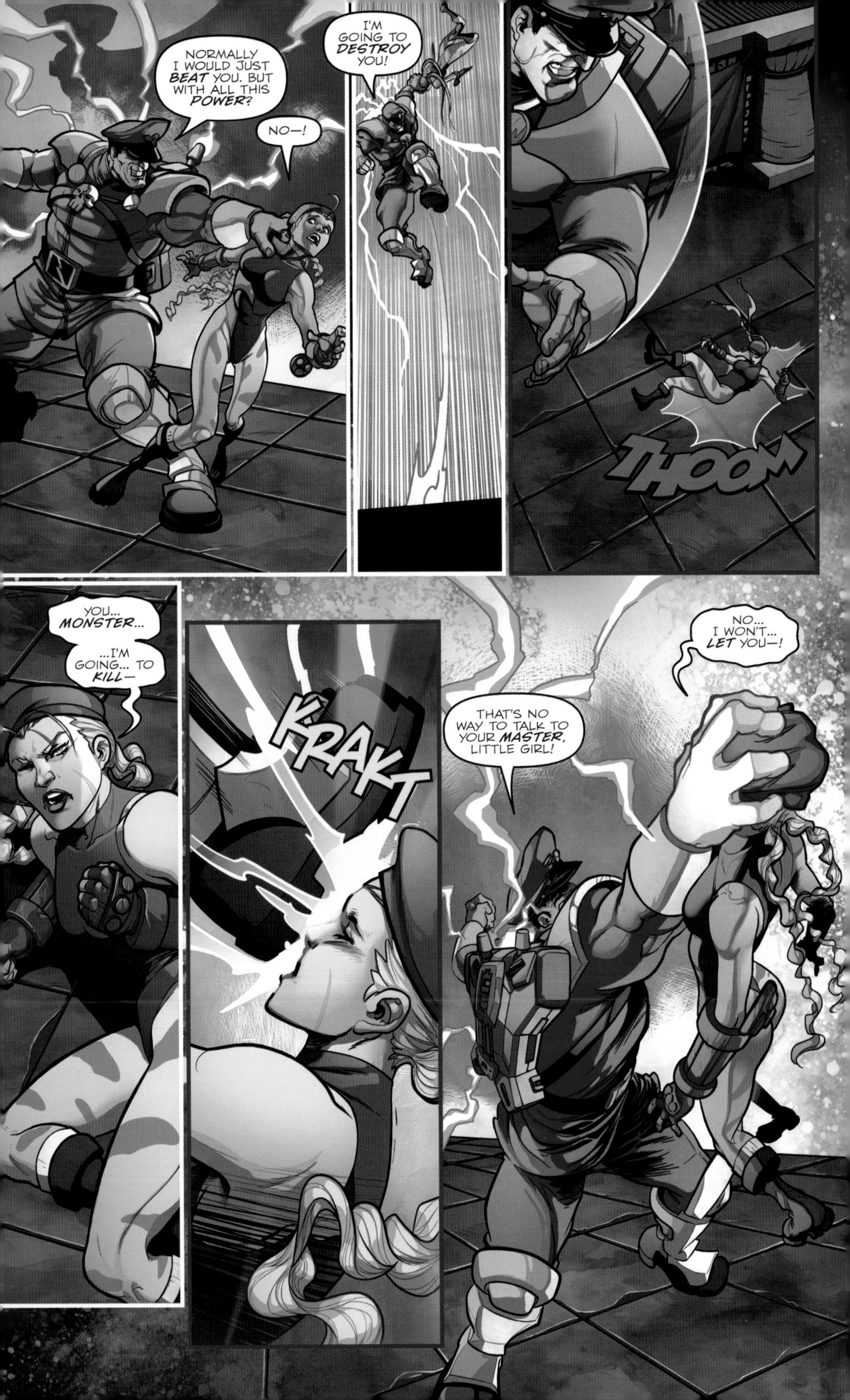
NORMALLY I WOULD JUST BEAT YOU. BUT WITH ALL THIS POWER?
NO—!
I'M GOING TO DESTROY YOU!
THOOM
YOU... MONSTER...
...I'M GOING... TO KILL—
KRAKT
NO... I WON'T... LET YOU—!
THAT'S NO WAY TO TALK TO YOUR MASTER, LITTLE GIRL!

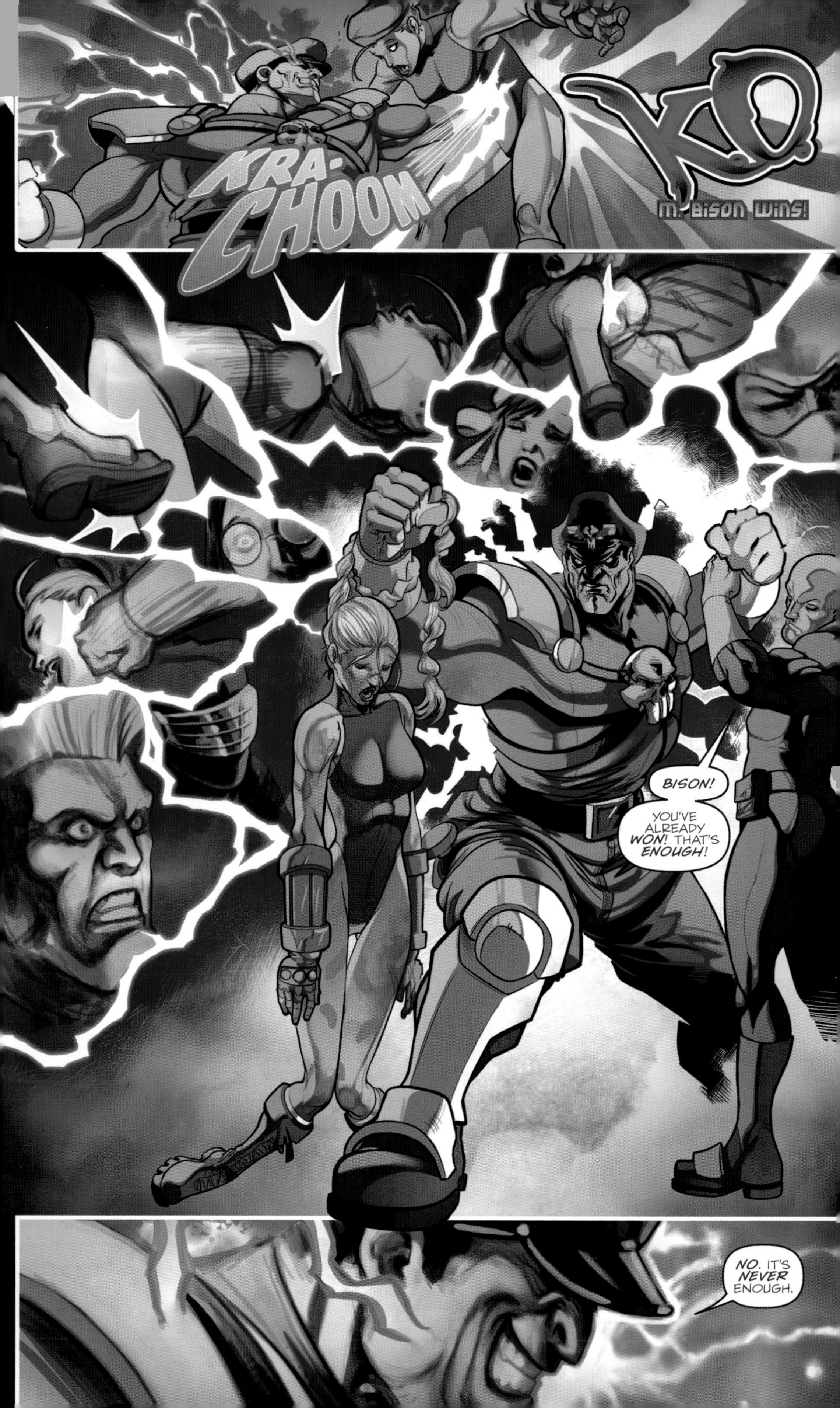
KRA-
CHOOM
K.O.
M. BISON WINS!
BISON!
YOU'VE ALREADY WON! THAT'S ENOUGH!
NO. IT'S NEVER ENOUGH.

COLORS BY MICHAEL GARLAND

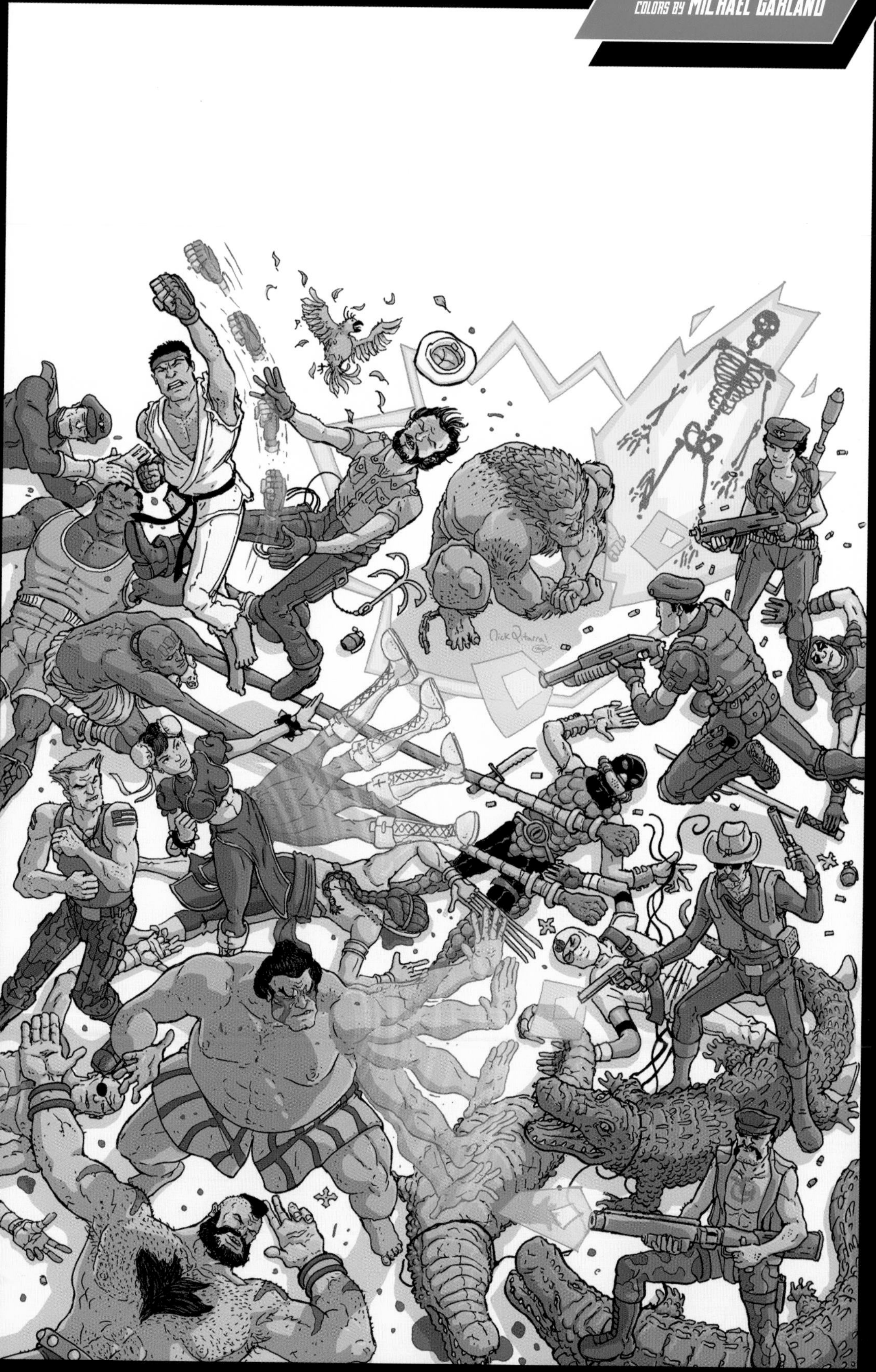

CHAPTER 3

WORLD WARRIOR
TOURNAMENT BRACKET

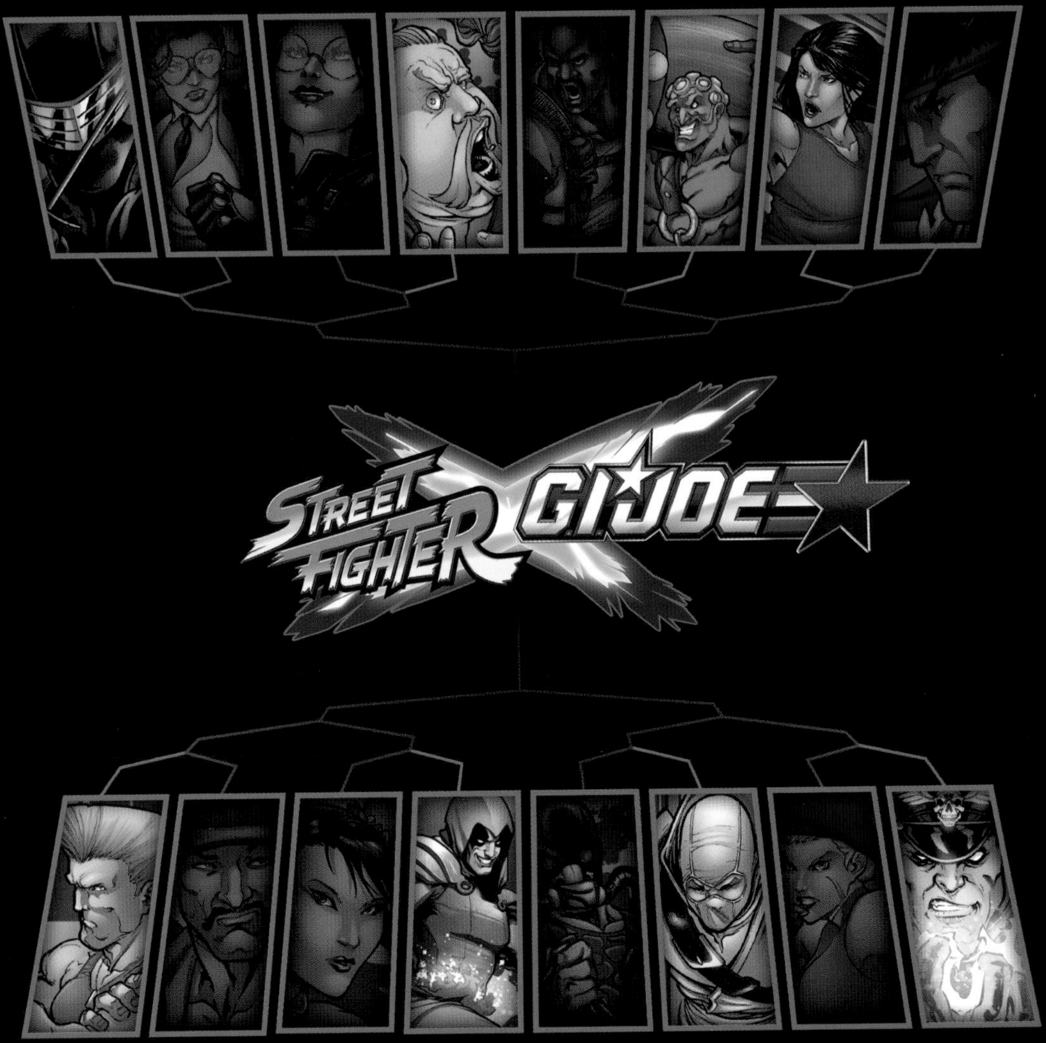
STREET FIGHTER X G.I. JOE

RUFUS vs. SNAKE EYES

JINX vs. HAKAN

ZARTAN vs. GUILE

STORM SHADOW vs. M. BISON

QUARTER-FINALS

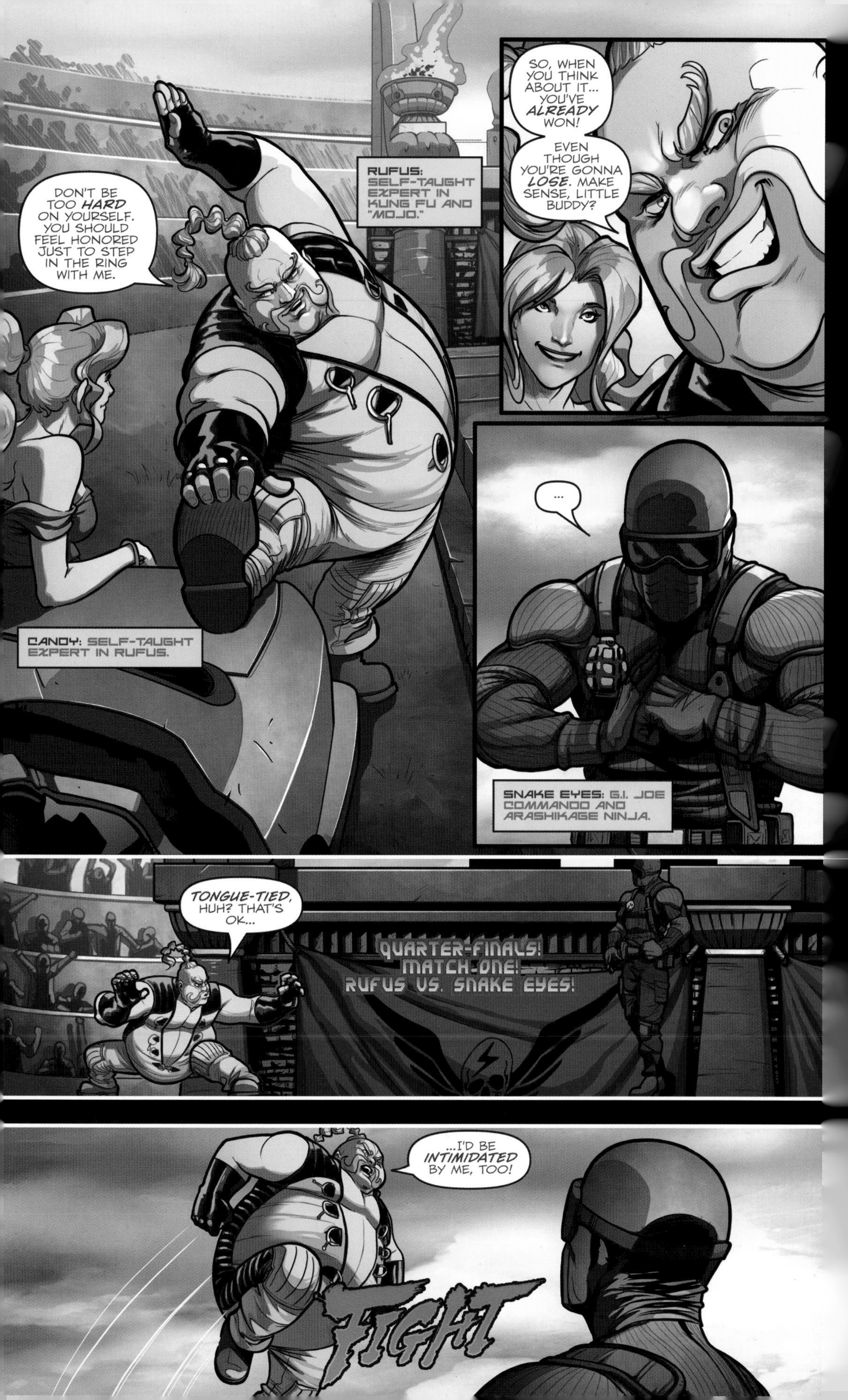
DON'T BE TOO HARD ON YOURSELF. YOU SHOULD FEEL HONORED JUST TO STEP IN THE RING WITH ME.
RUFUS: SELF-TAUGHT EXPERT IN KUNG FU AND "MOJO."
CANDY: SELF-TAUGHT EXPERT IN RUFUS.
SO, WHEN YOU THINK ABOUT IT... YOU'VE ALREADY WON!
EVEN THOUGH YOU'RE GONNA LOSE. MAKE SENSE, LITTLE BUDDY?
...
SNAKE EYES: G.I. JOE COMMANDO AND ARASHIKAGE NINJA.
TONGUE-TIED, HUH? THAT'S OK...
QUARTER-FINALS! MATCH-ONE! RUFUS VS. SNAKE EYES!
...I'D BE INTIMIDATED BY ME, TOO!
FIGHT

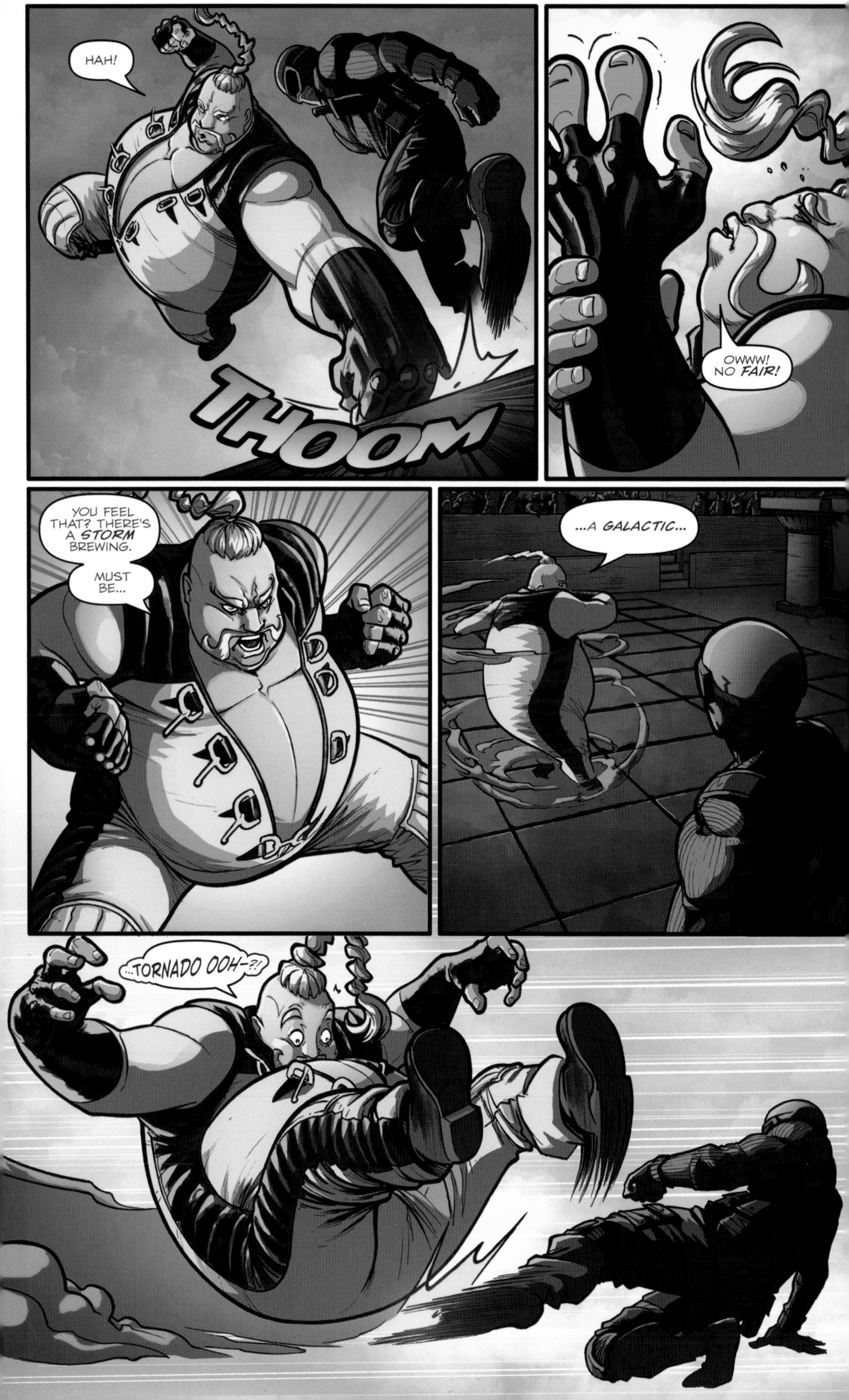
HAH!
THOOM
OWWW! NO FAIR!
YOU FEEL THAT? THERE'S A STORM BREWING.
MUST BE...
...A GALACTIC...
...TORNADO OOH-?!

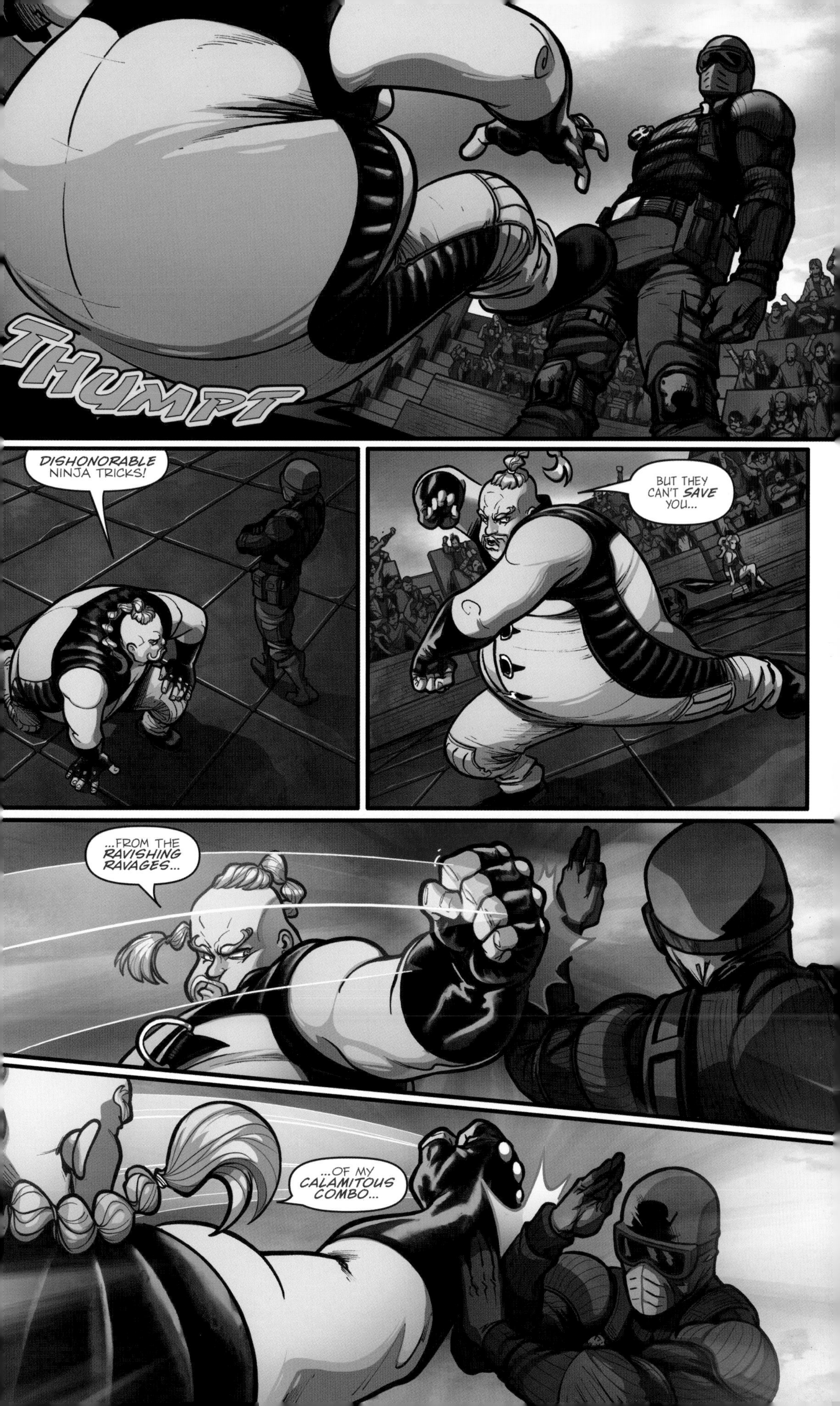
THUMPT
DISHONORABLE NINJA TRICKS!
BUT THEY CAN'T SAVE YOU...
...FROM THE RAVISHING RAVAGES...
...OF MY CALAMITOUS COMBO...

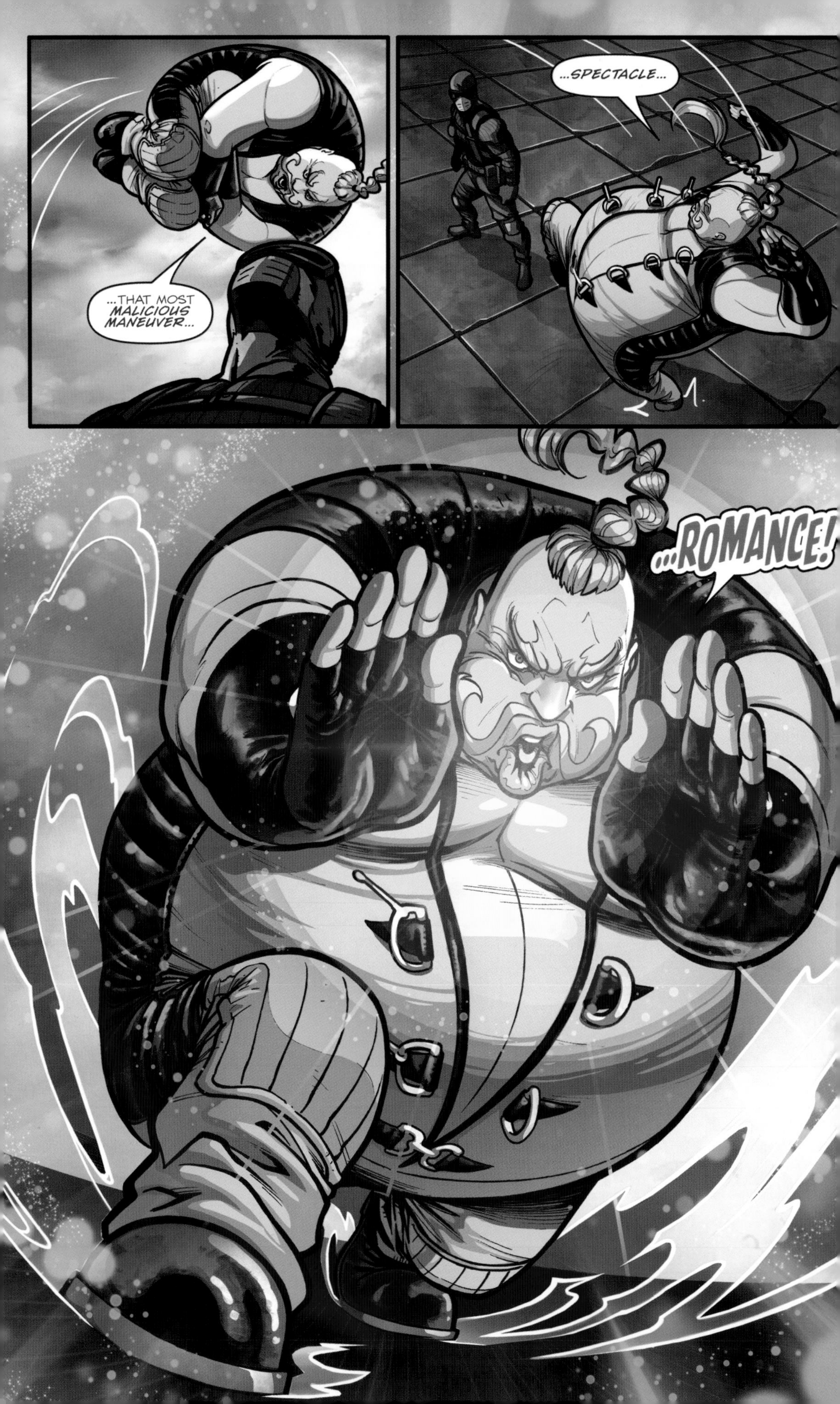

...THAT MOST MALICIOUS MANEUVER...
...SPECTACLE...
...ROMANCE!

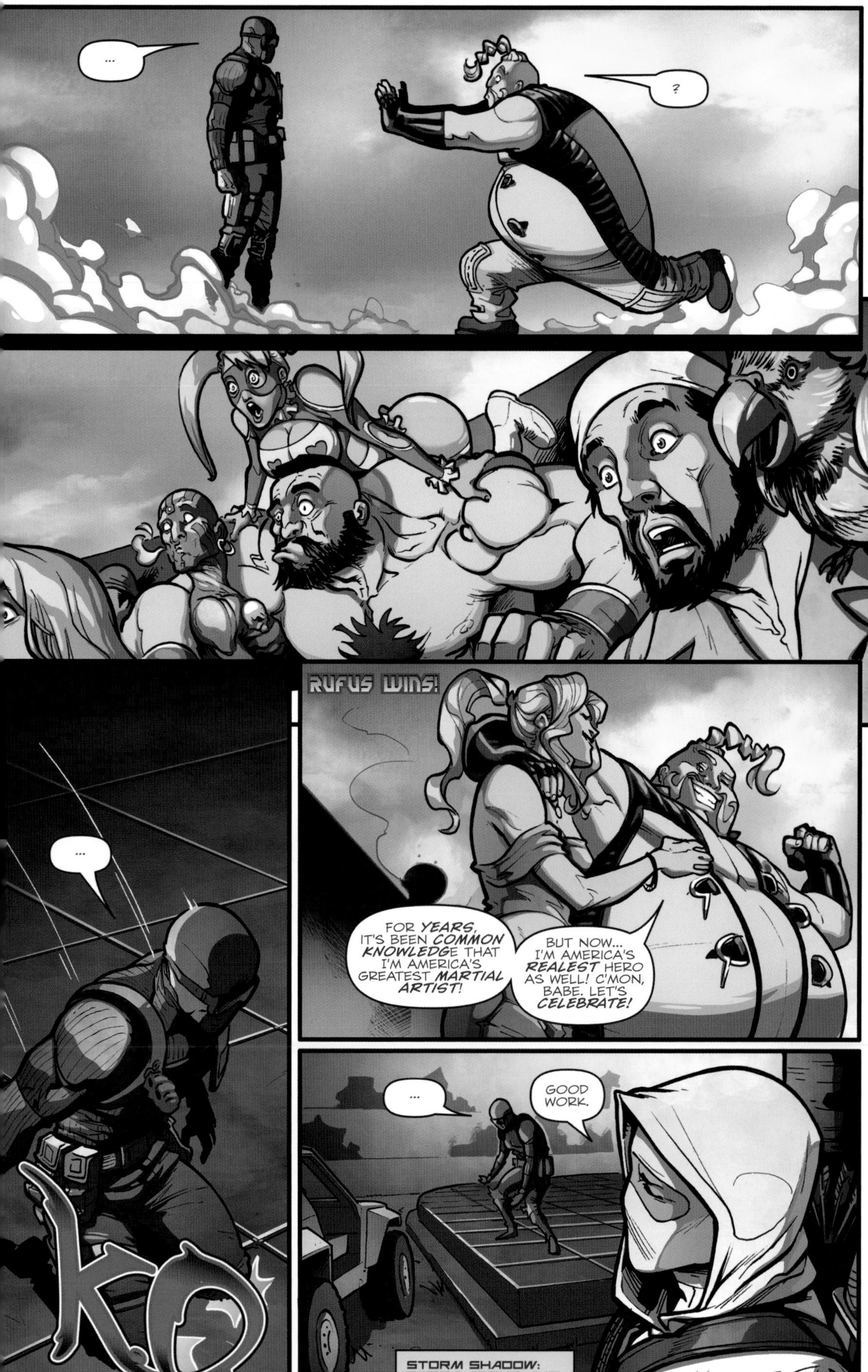
...
?
RUFUS WINS!
FOR YEARS, IT'S BEEN COMMON KNOWLEDGE THAT I'M AMERICA'S GREATEST MARTIAL ARTIST!
BUT NOW... I'M AMERICA'S REALEST HERO AS WELL! C'MON, BABE. LET'S CELEBRATE!
...
KO
...
GOOD WORK.
STORM SHADOW: [redacted] AGENT AND ARASHIKAGE NINJA.

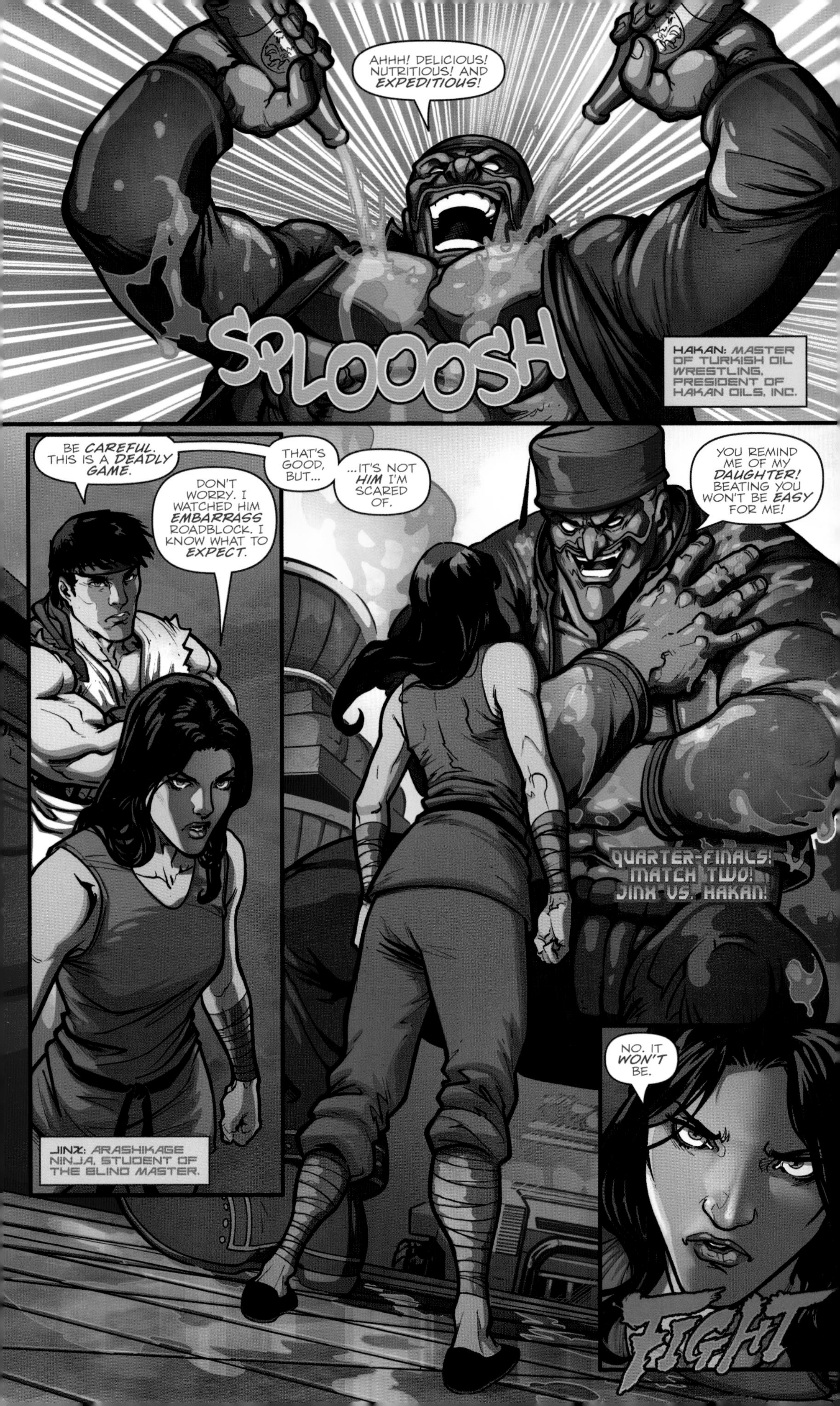
AHHH! DELICIOUS! NUTRITIOUS! AND EXPEDITIOUS!
SPLOOOSH
HAKAN: MASTER OF TURKISH OIL WRESTLING, PRESIDENT OF HAKAN OILS, INC.
BE CAREFUL. THIS IS A DEADLY GAME.
DON'T WORRY. I WATCHED HIM EMBARRASS ROADBLOCK. I KNOW WHAT TO EXPECT.
THAT'S GOOD, BUT...
...IT'S NOT HIM I'M SCARED OF.
YOU REMIND ME OF MY DAUGHTER! BEATING YOU WON'T BE EASY FOR ME!
QUARTER-FINALS! MATCH TWO! JINX VS. HAKAN!
JINX: ARASHIKAGE NINJA, STUDENT OF THE BLIND MASTER.
NO. IT WON'T BE.
FIGHT

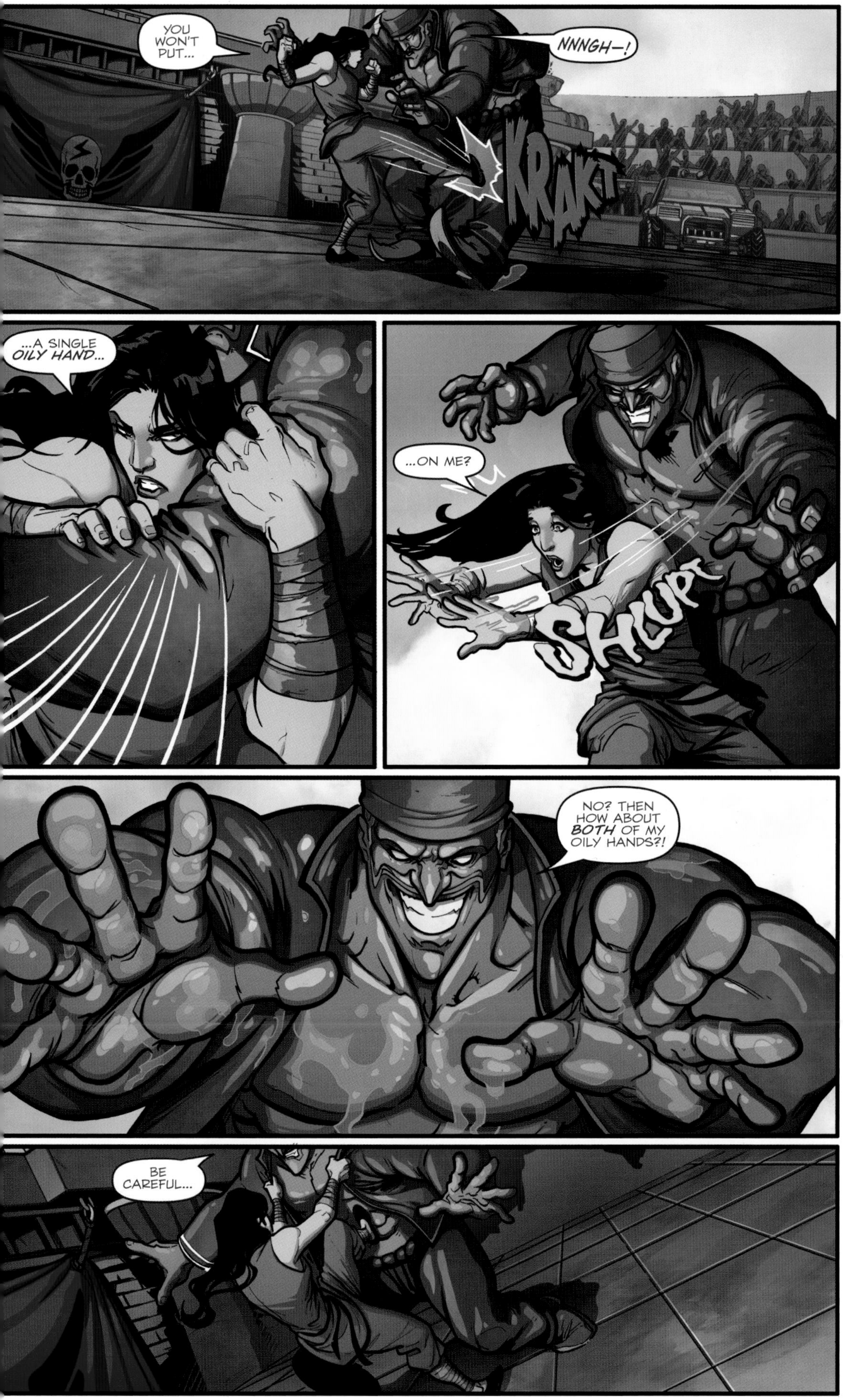
YOU WON'T PUT...
NNNGH—!
KRAKT
...A SINGLE OILY HAND...
...ON ME?
SHLUPT
NO? THEN HOW ABOUT BOTH OF MY OILY HANDS?!
BE CAREFUL...

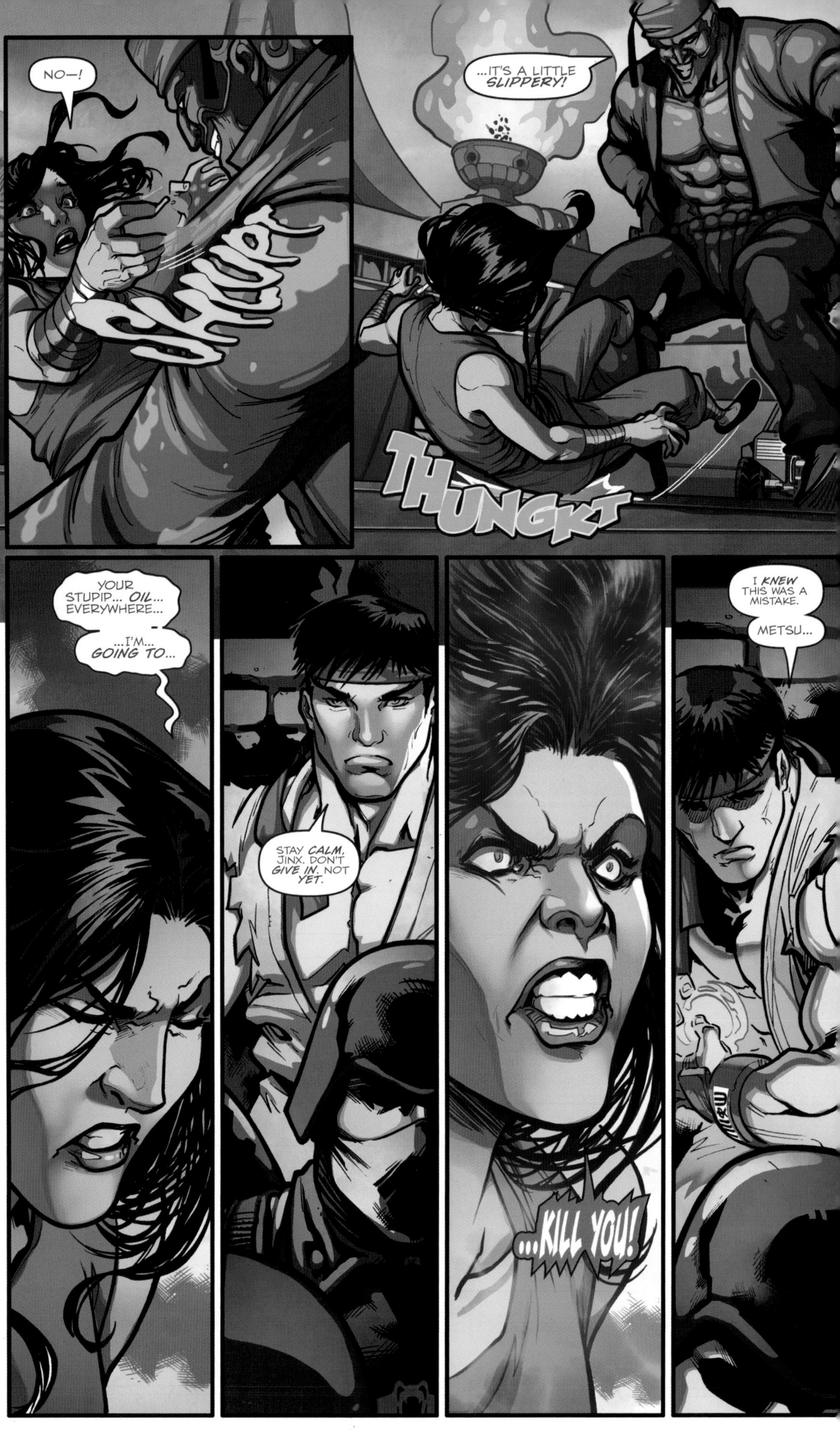
NO—!
CHHOK
...IT'S A LITTLE SLIPPERY!
THUNGKT
YOUR STUPID... OIL... EVERYWHERE...
...I'M... GOING TO...
STAY CALM, JINX. DON'T GIVE IN. NOT YET.
...KILL YOU!
I KNEW THIS WAS A MISTAKE.
METSU...

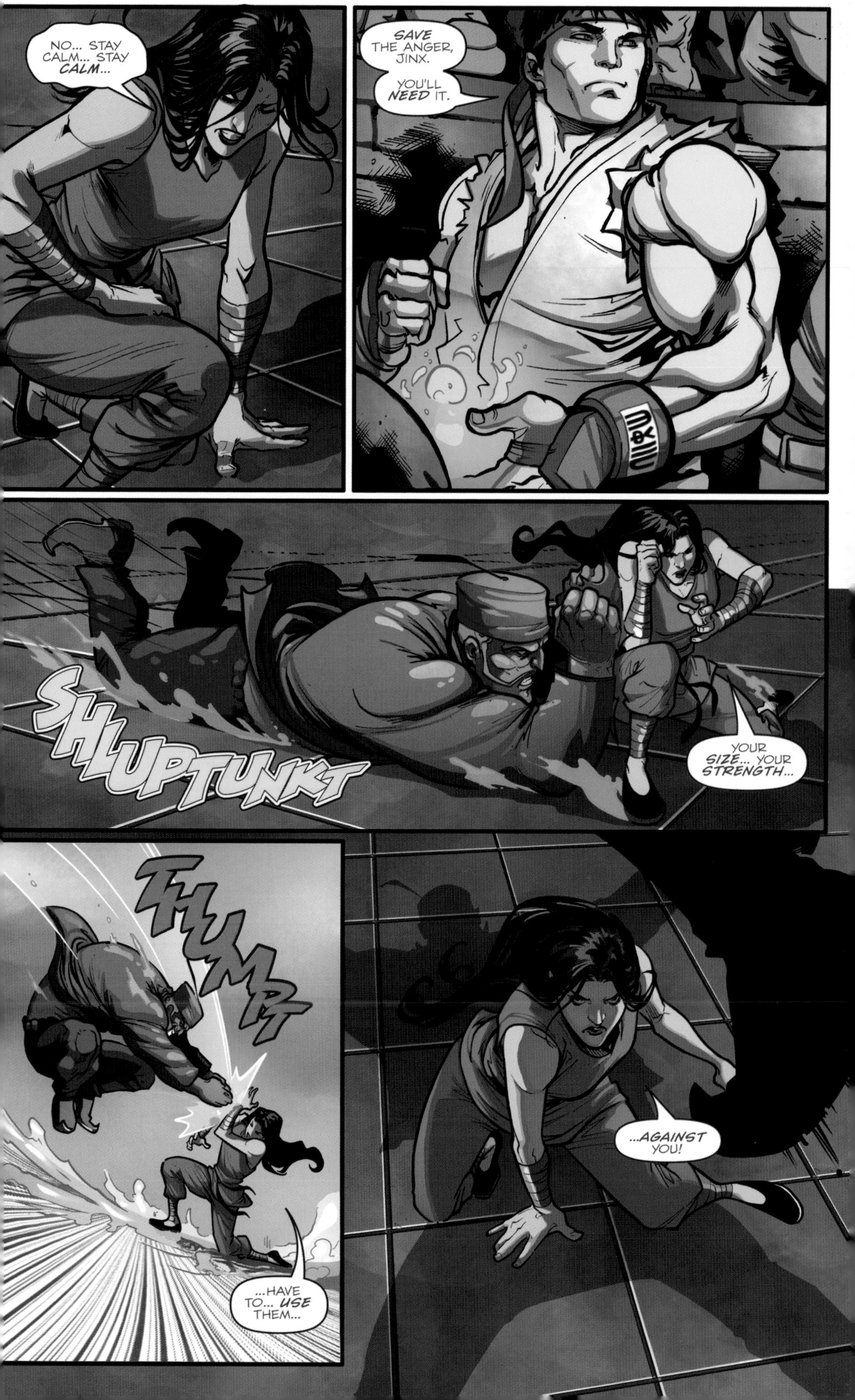
NO... STAY CALM... STAY CALM...
SAVE THE ANGER, JINX.
YOU'LL NEED IT.
SHLUPTUNKT
YOUR SIZE... YOUR STRENGTH...
THUMPT
...HAVE TO... USE THEM...
...AGAINST YOU!

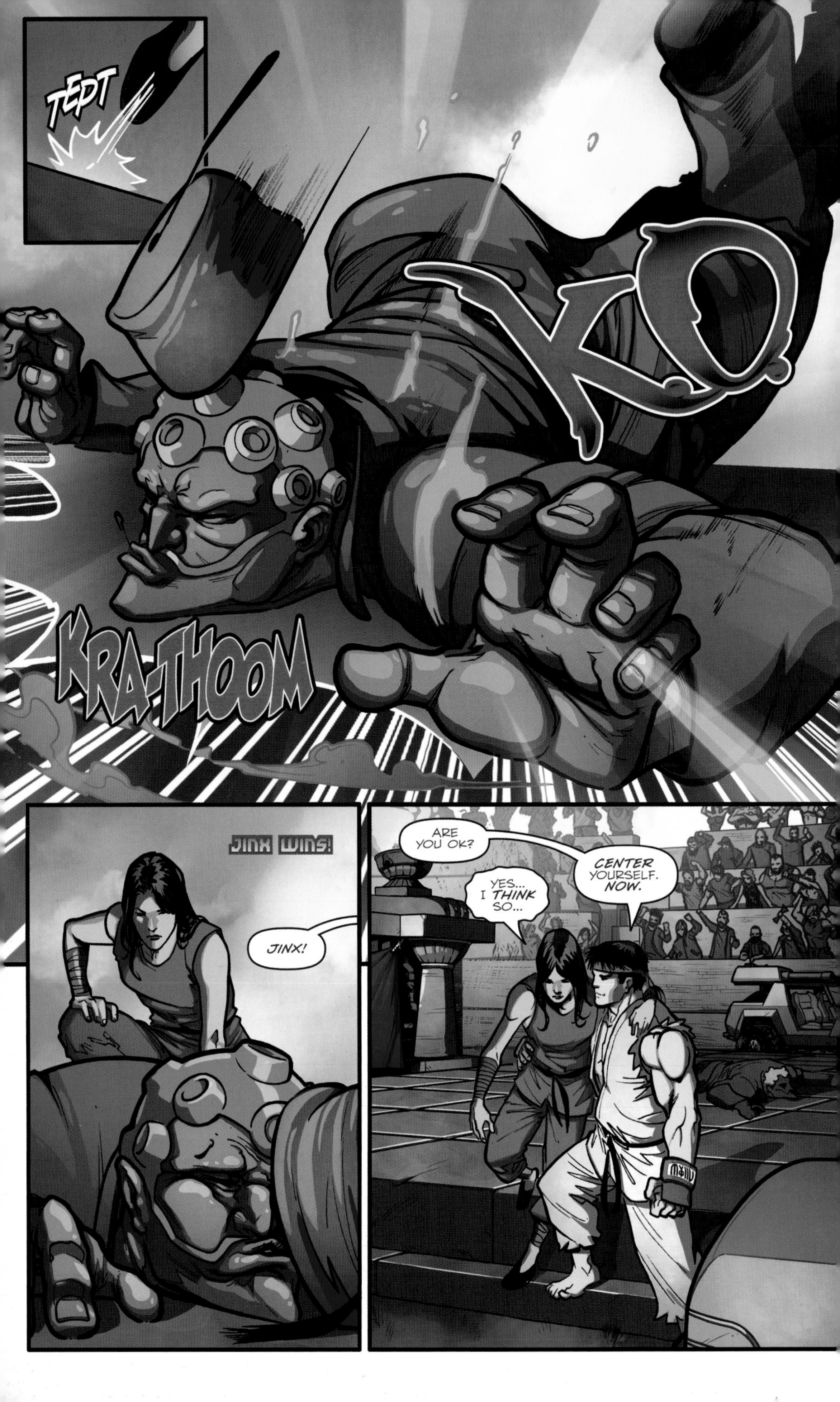

TEDT
K.O.
KRA-THOOM
JINX WINS!
JINX!
ARE YOU OK?
YES... I THINK SO...
CENTER YOURSELF. NOW.

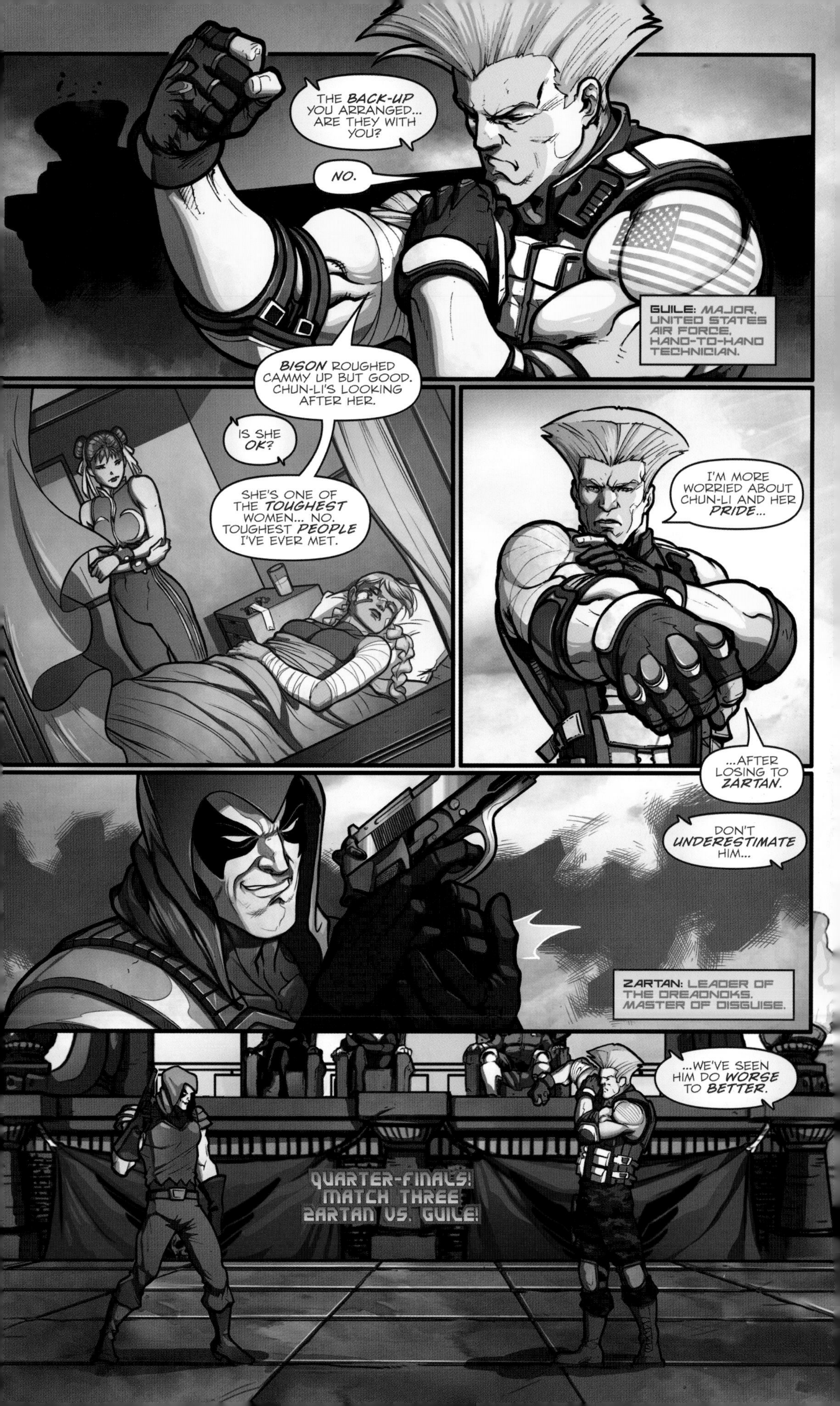
THE BACK-UP YOU ARRANGED... ARE THEY WITH YOU?
NO.
GUILE: MAJOR, UNITED STATES AIR FORCE, HAND-TO-HAND TECHNICIAN.
BISON ROUGHED CAMMY UP BUT GOOD. CHUN-LI'S LOOKING AFTER HER.
IS SHE OK?
SHE'S ONE OF THE TOUGHEST WOMEN... NO. TOUGHEST PEOPLE I'VE EVER MET.
I'M MORE WORRIED ABOUT CHUN-LI AND HER PRIDE...
...AFTER LOSING TO ZARTAN.
DON'T UNDERESTIMATE HIM...
ZARTAN: LEADER OF THE DREADNOKS. MASTER OF DISGUISE.
...WE'VE SEEN HIM DO WORSE TO BETTER.
QUARTER-FINALS! MATCH THREE ZARTAN VS. GUILE!

BLAM

FIGHT

CAREFUL, GUILE. YOU DON'T WANT TO REOPEN...

...OLD WOUNDS!

KA-KRAKT

YOU WERE SAYING?

GUILE...

...YOU JUST STOOD THERE... YOU LET HIM HURT ME...

...HOW COULD YOU...?

WHAT?! NO! I...

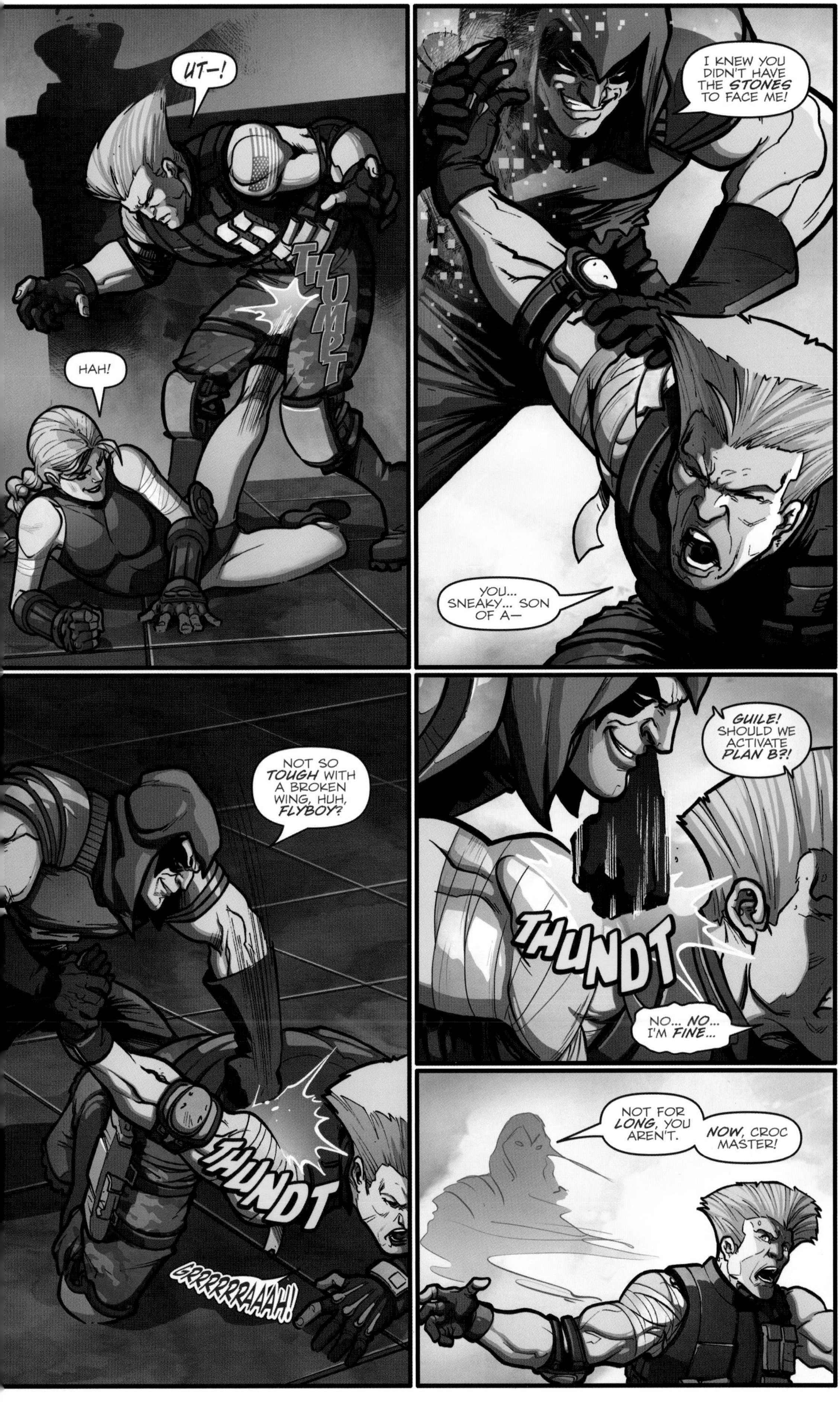
UT-!
THUMPT
HAH!
I KNEW YOU DIDN'T HAVE THE STONES TO FACE ME!
YOU... SNEAKY... SON OF A—
NOT SO TOUGH WITH A BROKEN WING, HUH, FLYBOY?
THUNDT
GRRRRRRAAAH!
GUILE! SHOULD WE ACTIVATE PLAN B?!
THUNDT
NO... NO... I'M FINE...
NOT FOR LONG, YOU AREN'T.
NOW, CROC MASTER!

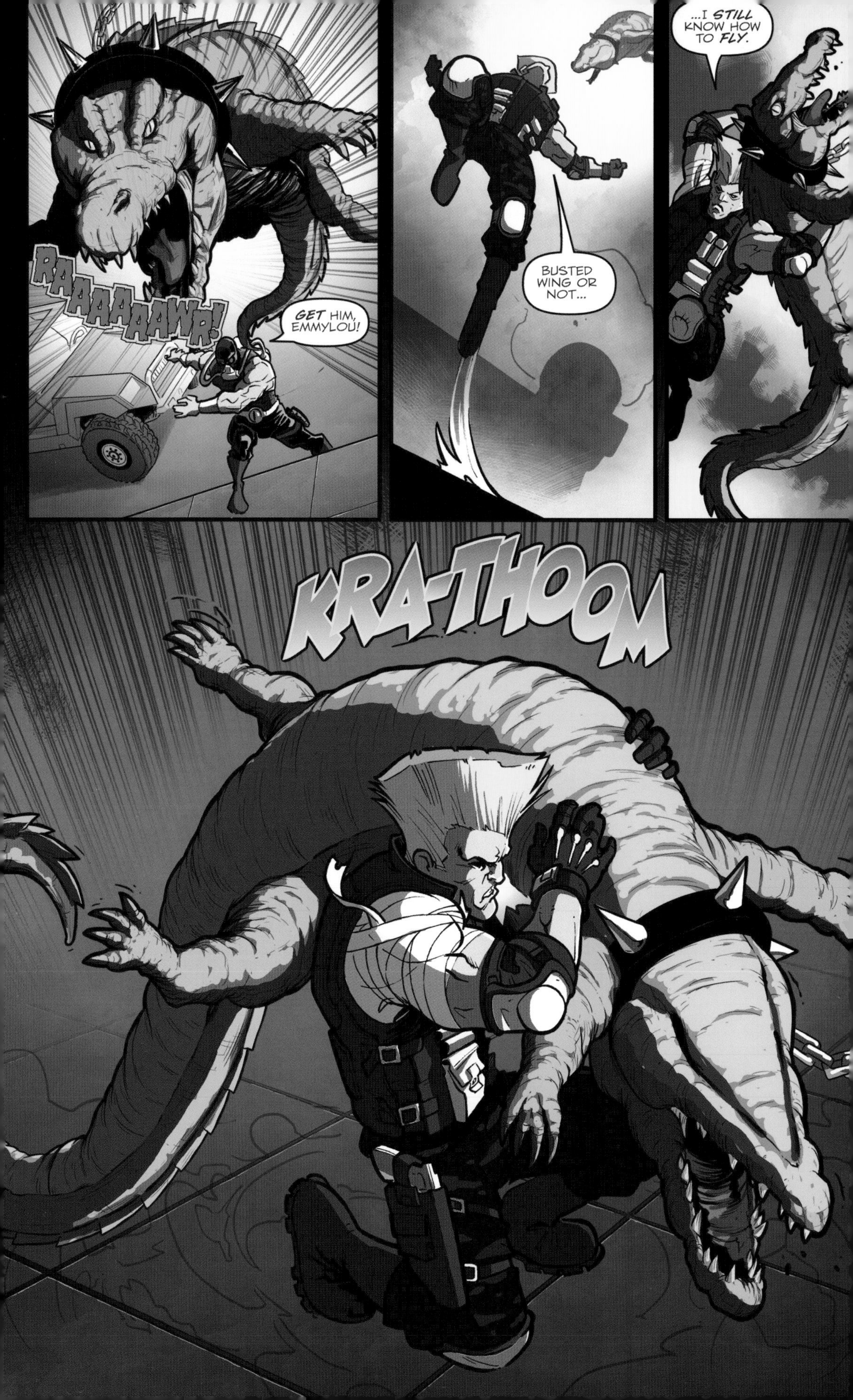
RAAAAAAAWR!
GET HIM, EMMYLOU!
BUSTED WING OR NOT...
...I STILL KNOW HOW TO FLY.
KRA-THOOM

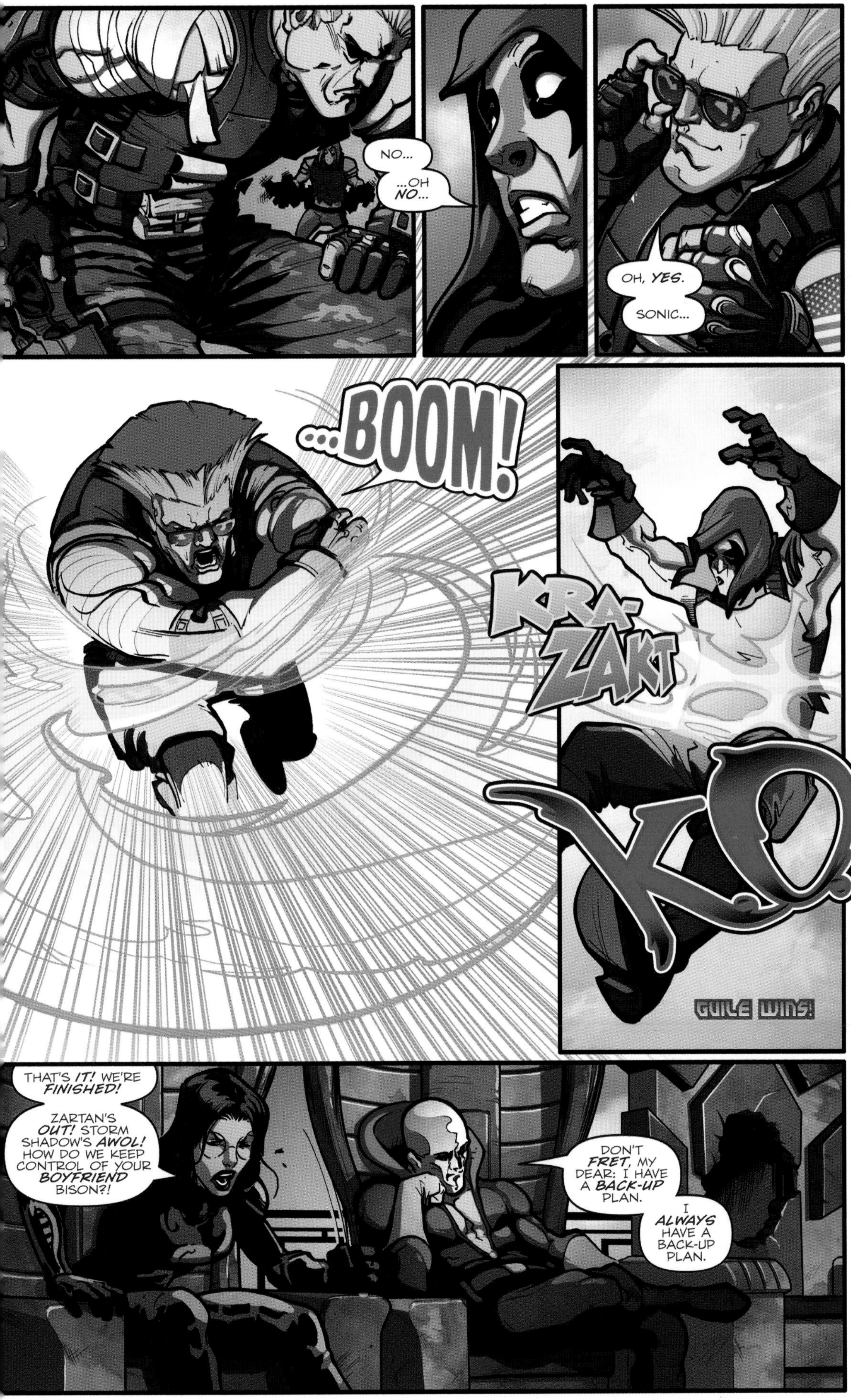
NO...
...OH NO...
OH, YES.
SONIC...
...BOOM!
KRA-ZAKT
K.O.
GUILE WINS!
THAT'S IT! WE'RE FINISHED!
ZARTAN'S OUT! STORM SHADOW'S AWOL! HOW DO WE KEEP CONTROL OF YOUR BOYFRIEND BISON?!
DON'T FRET, MY DEAR: I HAVE A BACK-UP PLAN.
I ALWAYS HAVE A BACK-UP PLAN.

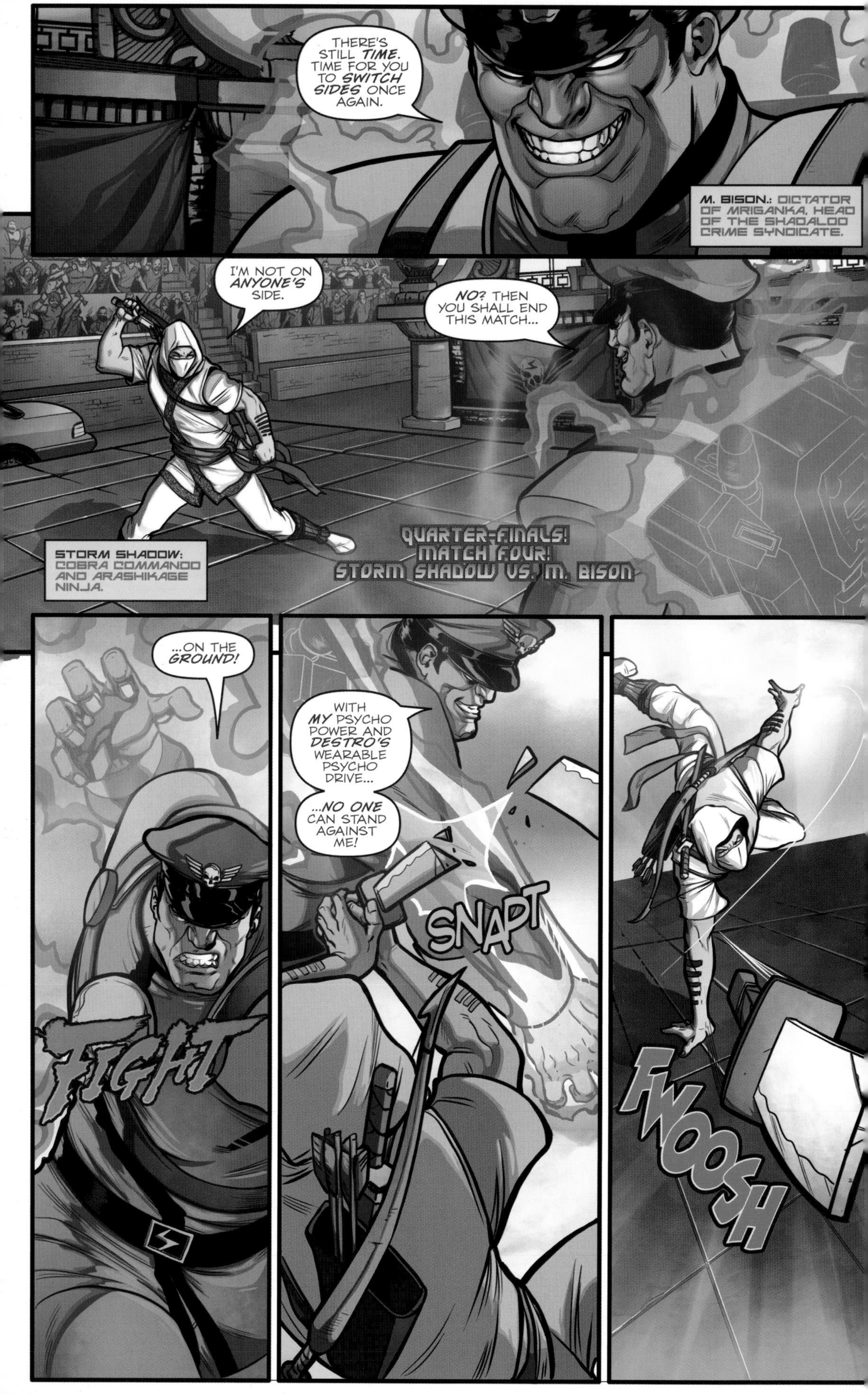
THERE'S STILL TIME. TIME FOR YOU TO SWITCH SIDES ONCE AGAIN.
M. BISON.: DICTATOR OF MRIGANKA, HEAD OF THE SHADALOO CRIME SYNDICATE.
I'M NOT ON ANYONE'S SIDE.
NO? THEN YOU SHALL END THIS MATCH...
STORM SHADOW: COBRA COMMANDO AND ARASHIKAGE NINJA.
QUARTER-FINALS! MATCH FOUR! STORM SHADOW VS. M. BISON
...ON THE GROUND!
FIGHT
WITH MY PSYCHO POWER AND DESTRO'S WEARABLE PSYCHO DRIVE...
...NO ONE CAN STAND AGAINST ME!
SNAPT
FWOOSH

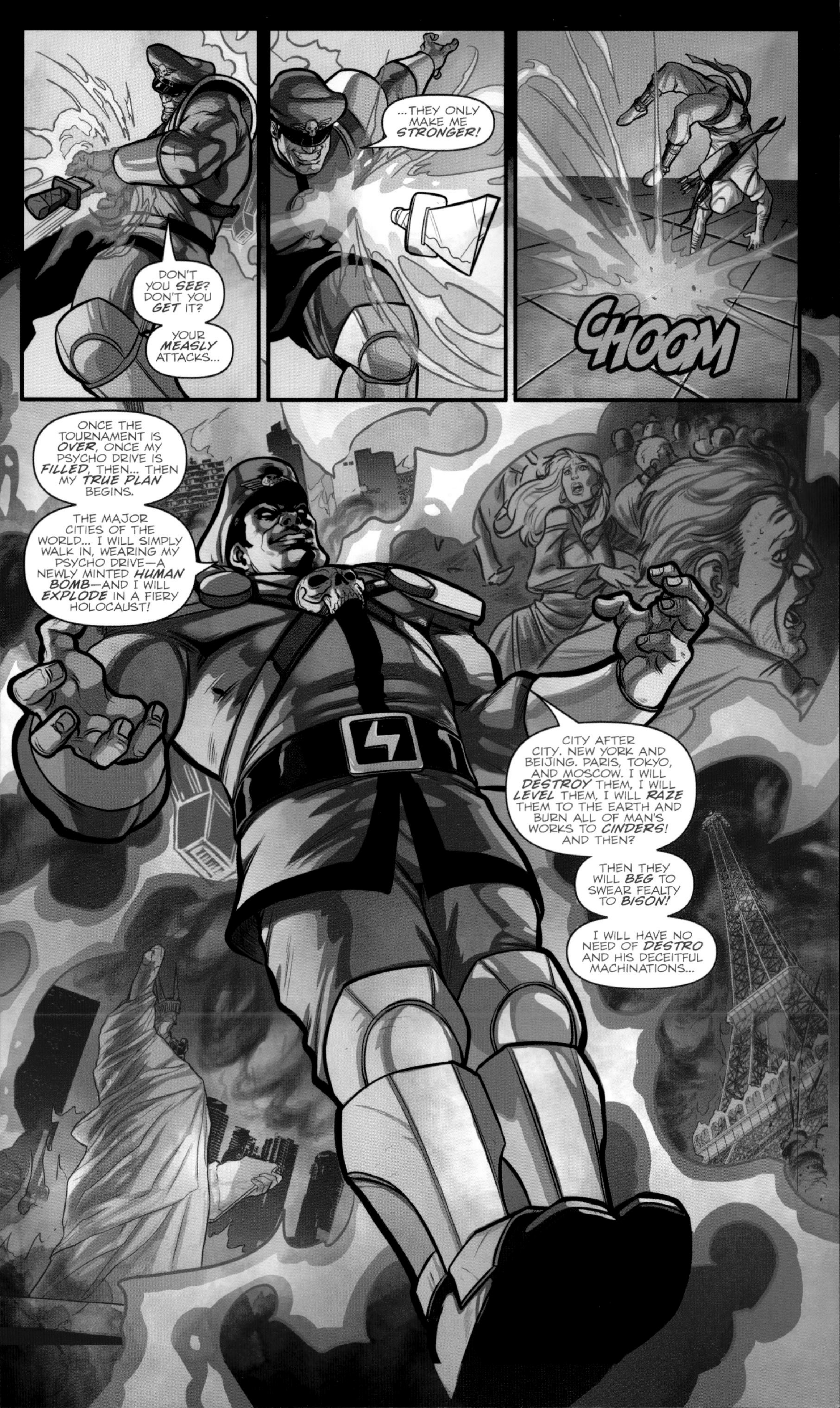

DON'T YOU SEE? DON'T YOU GET IT?
YOUR MEASLY ATTACKS...
...THEY ONLY MAKE ME STRONGER!
CHOOM
ONCE THE TOURNAMENT IS OVER, ONCE MY PSYCHO DRIVE IS FILLED, THEN... THEN MY TRUE PLAN BEGINS.
THE MAJOR CITIES OF THE WORLD... I WILL SIMPLY WALK IN, WEARING MY PSYCHO DRIVE—A NEWLY MINTED HUMAN BOMB—AND I WILL EXPLODE IN A FIERY HOLOCAUST!
CITY AFTER CITY. NEW YORK AND BEIJING. PARIS, TOKYO, AND MOSCOW. I WILL DESTROY THEM, I WILL LEVEL THEM, I WILL RAZE THEM TO THE EARTH AND BURN ALL OF MAN'S WORKS TO CINDERS! AND THEN?
THEN THEY WILL BEG TO SWEAR FEALTY TO BISON!
I WILL HAVE NO NEED OF DESTRO AND HIS DECEITFUL MACHINATIONS...

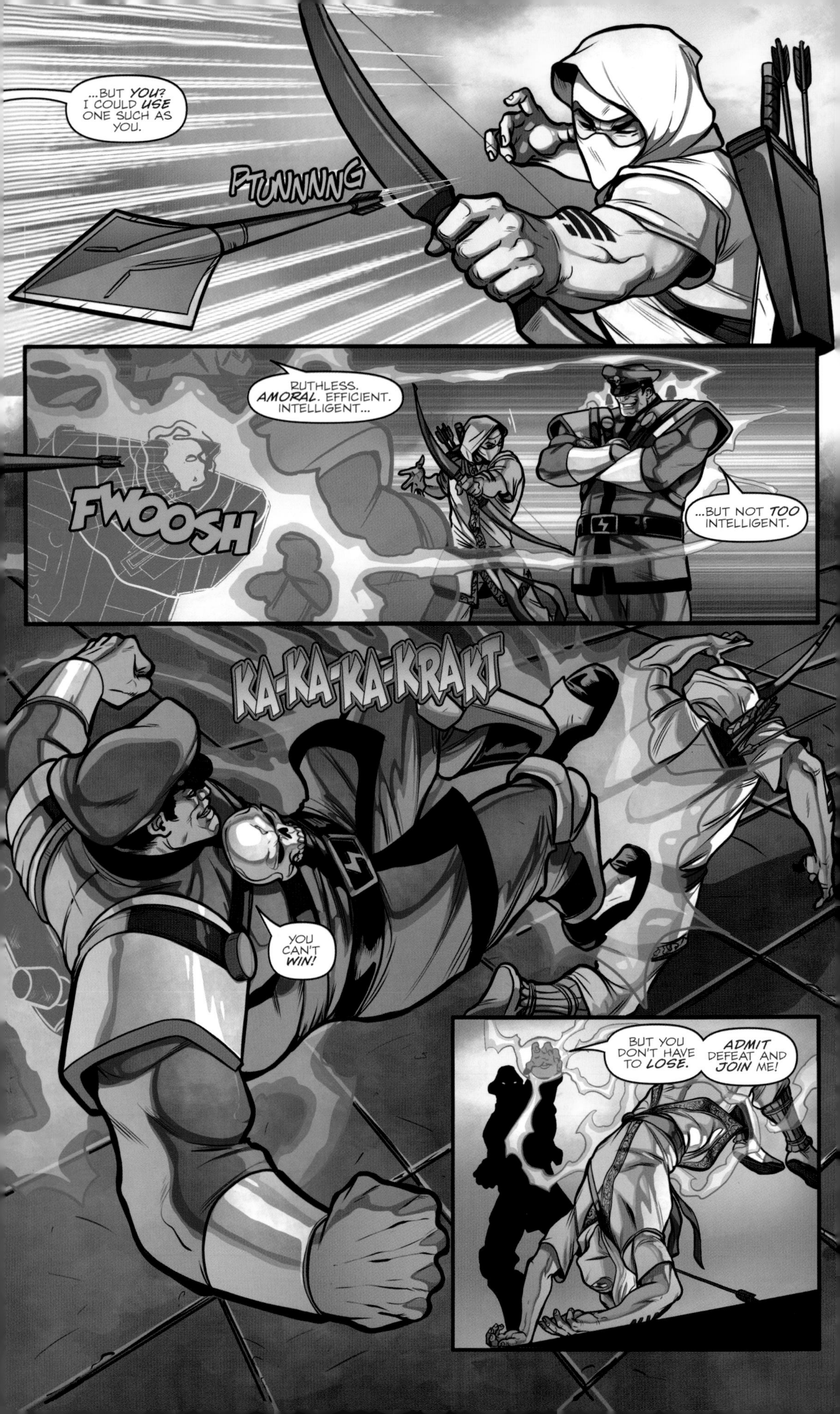
...BUT YOU? I COULD USE ONE SUCH AS YOU.
PTUNNNNG
RUTHLESS. AMORAL. EFFICIENT. INTELLIGENT...
FWOOSH
...BUT NOT TOO INTELLIGENT.
KA-KA-KA-KRAKT
YOU CAN'T WIN!
BUT YOU DON'T HAVE TO LOSE.
ADMIT DEFEAT AND JOIN ME!

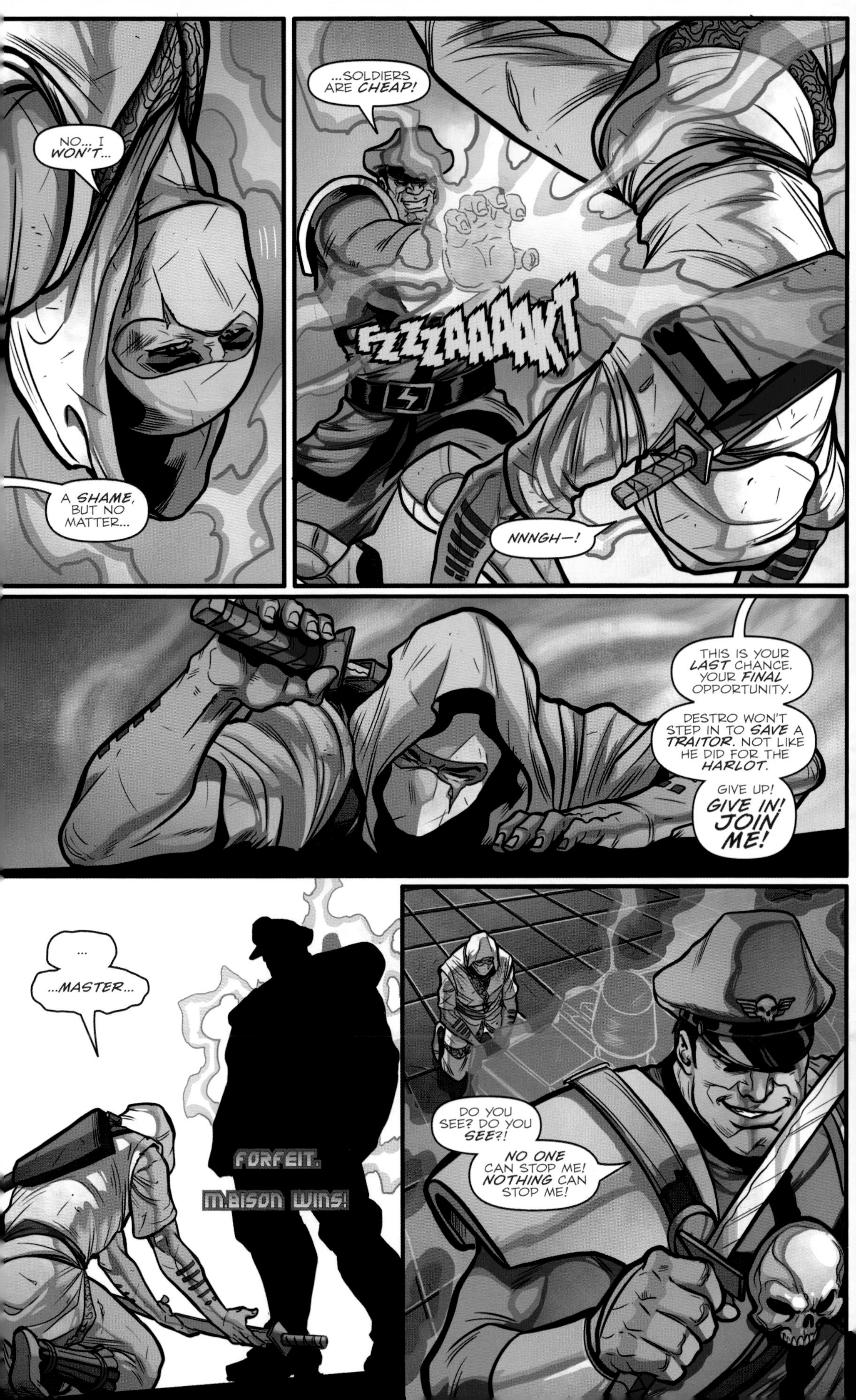
NO... I WON'T...
A SHAME, BUT NO MATTER...
...SOLDIERS ARE CHEAP!
FZZZAAAAKT
NNNGH—!
THIS IS YOUR LAST CHANCE. YOUR FINAL OPPORTUNITY.
DESTRO WON'T STEP IN TO SAVE A TRAITOR. NOT LIKE HE DID FOR THE HARLOT.
GIVE UP! GIVE IN! JOIN ME!
...
...MASTER...
FORFEIT.
M.BISON WINS!
DO YOU SEE? DO YOU SEE?!
NO ONE CAN STOP ME! NOTHING CAN STOP ME!

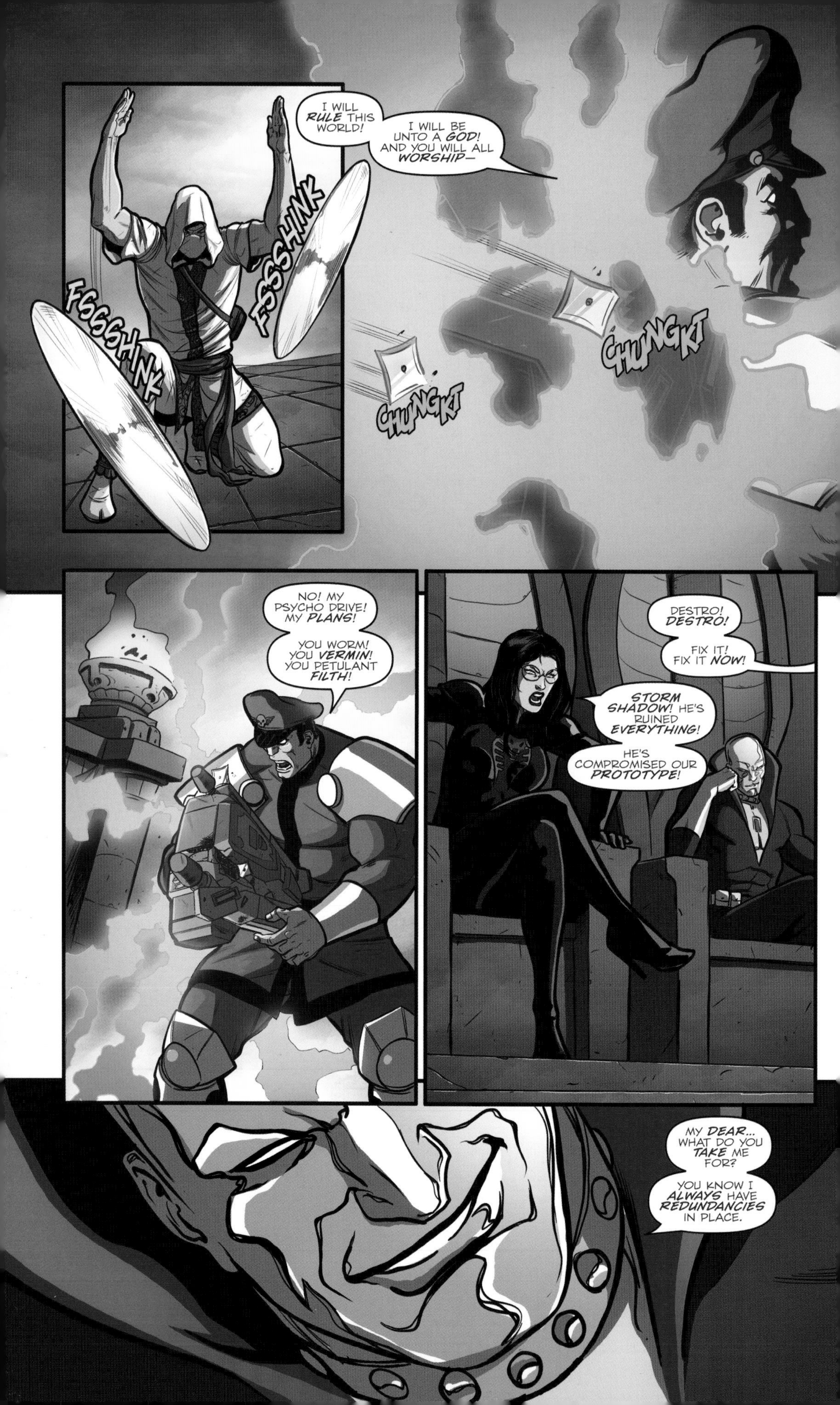
I WILL RULE THIS WORLD!
I WILL BE UNTO A GOD! AND YOU WILL ALL WORSHIP—
FSSSHNK
FSSSHNK
CHUNGKT
CHUNGKT
NO! MY PSYCHO DRIVE! MY PLANS!
YOU WORM! YOU VERMIN! YOU PETULANT FILTH!
DESTRO! DESTRO!
FIX IT! FIX IT NOW!
STORM SHADOW! HE'S RUINED EVERYTHING!
HE'S COMPROMISED OUR PROTOTYPE!
MY DEAR... WHAT DO YOU TAKE ME FOR?
YOU KNOW I ALWAYS HAVE REDUNDANCIES IN PLACE.

ART BY CHRIS EVENHUIS

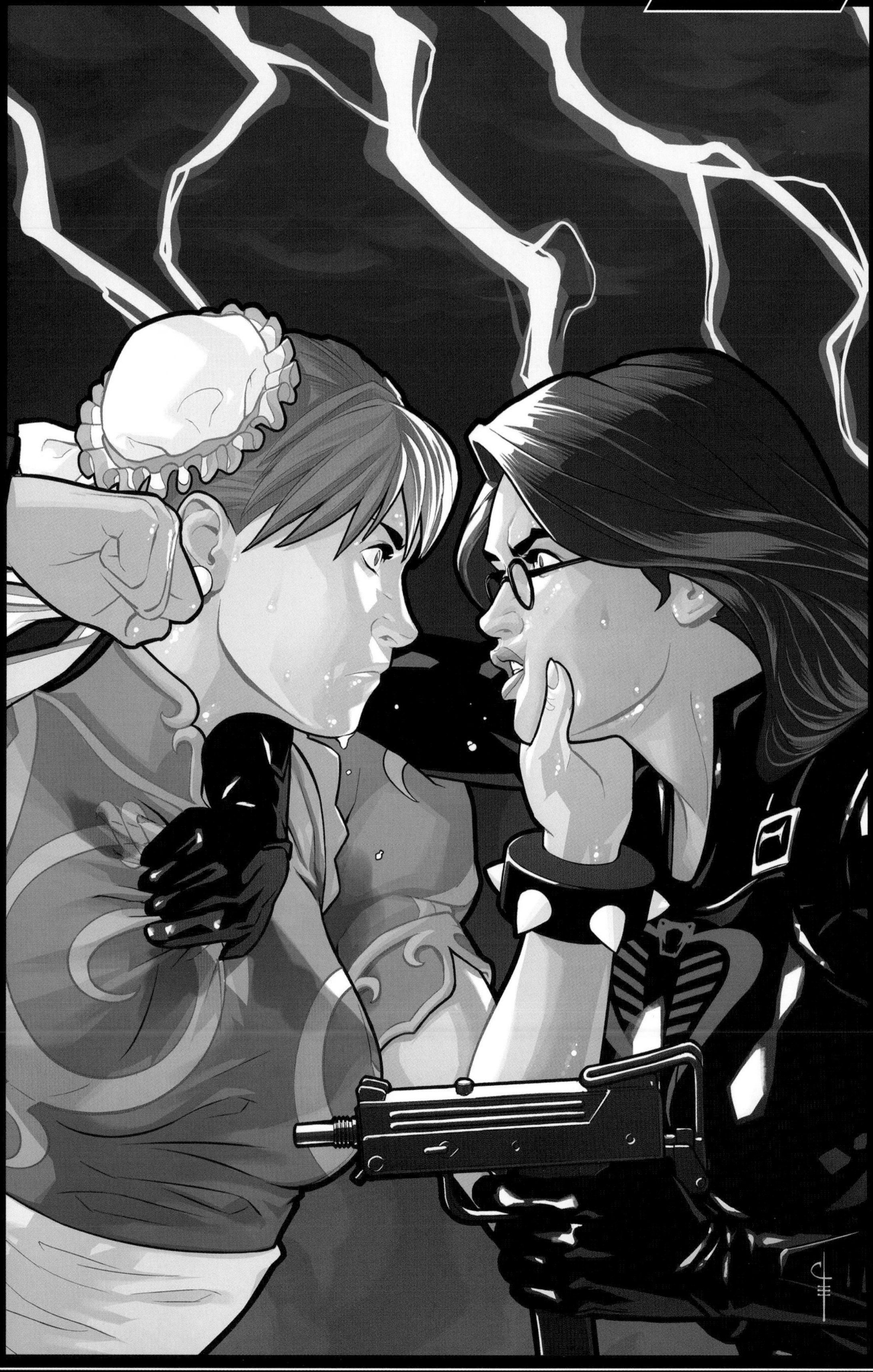

CHAPTER 4

WORLD WARRIOR TOURNAMENT BRACKET

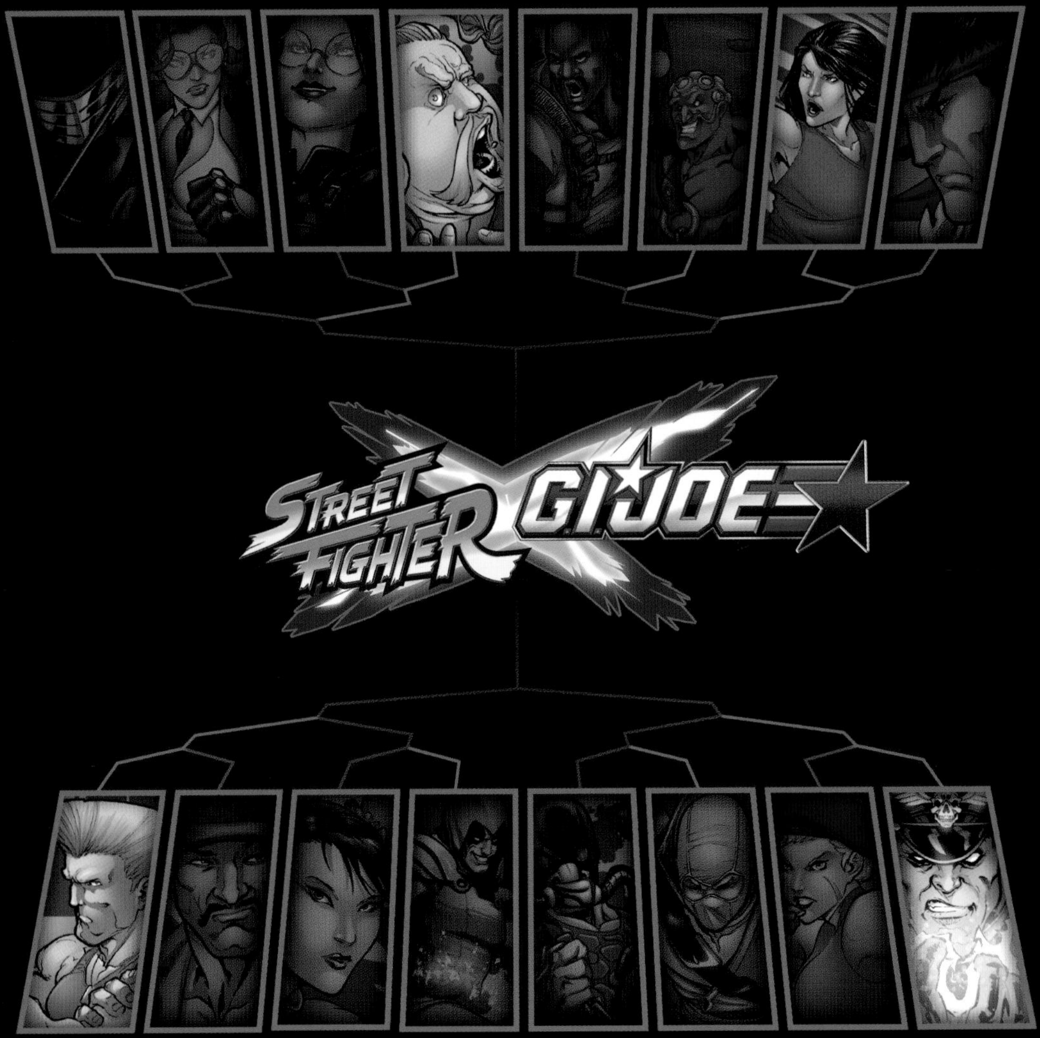
STREET FIGHTER
G.I. JOE

RUFUS vs. JINX

M. BISON vs. GUILE

SEMI-FINALS

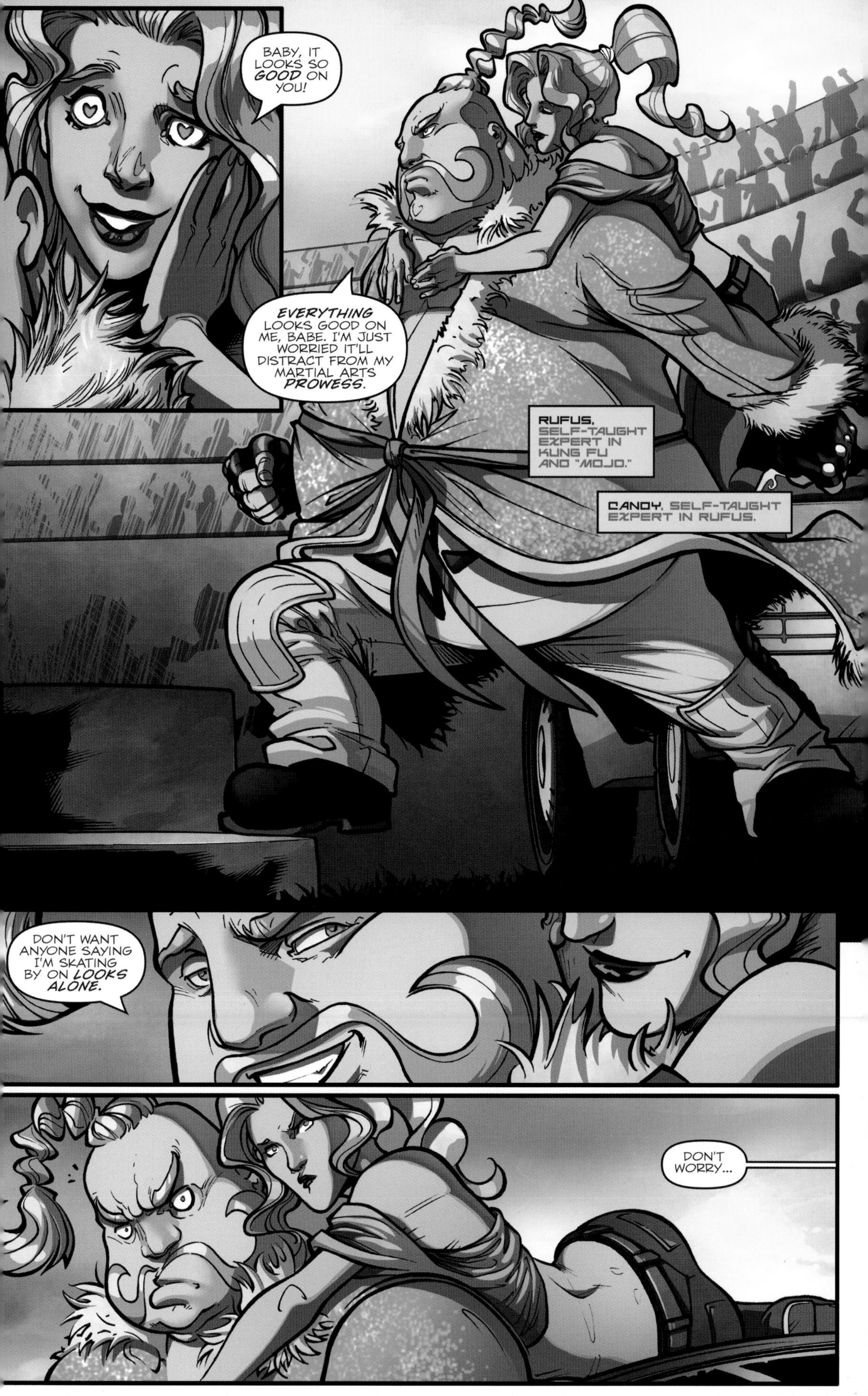
BABY, IT LOOKS SO GOOD ON YOU!
EVERYTHING LOOKS GOOD ON ME, BABE. I'M JUST WORRIED IT'LL DISTRACT FROM MY MARTIAL ARTS PROWESS.
RUFUS, SELF-TAUGHT EXPERT IN KUNG FU AND "MOJO."
CANDY, SELF-TAUGHT EXPERT IN RUFUS.
DON'T WANT ANYONE SAYING I'M SKATING BY ON LOOKS ALONE.
DON'T WORRY...

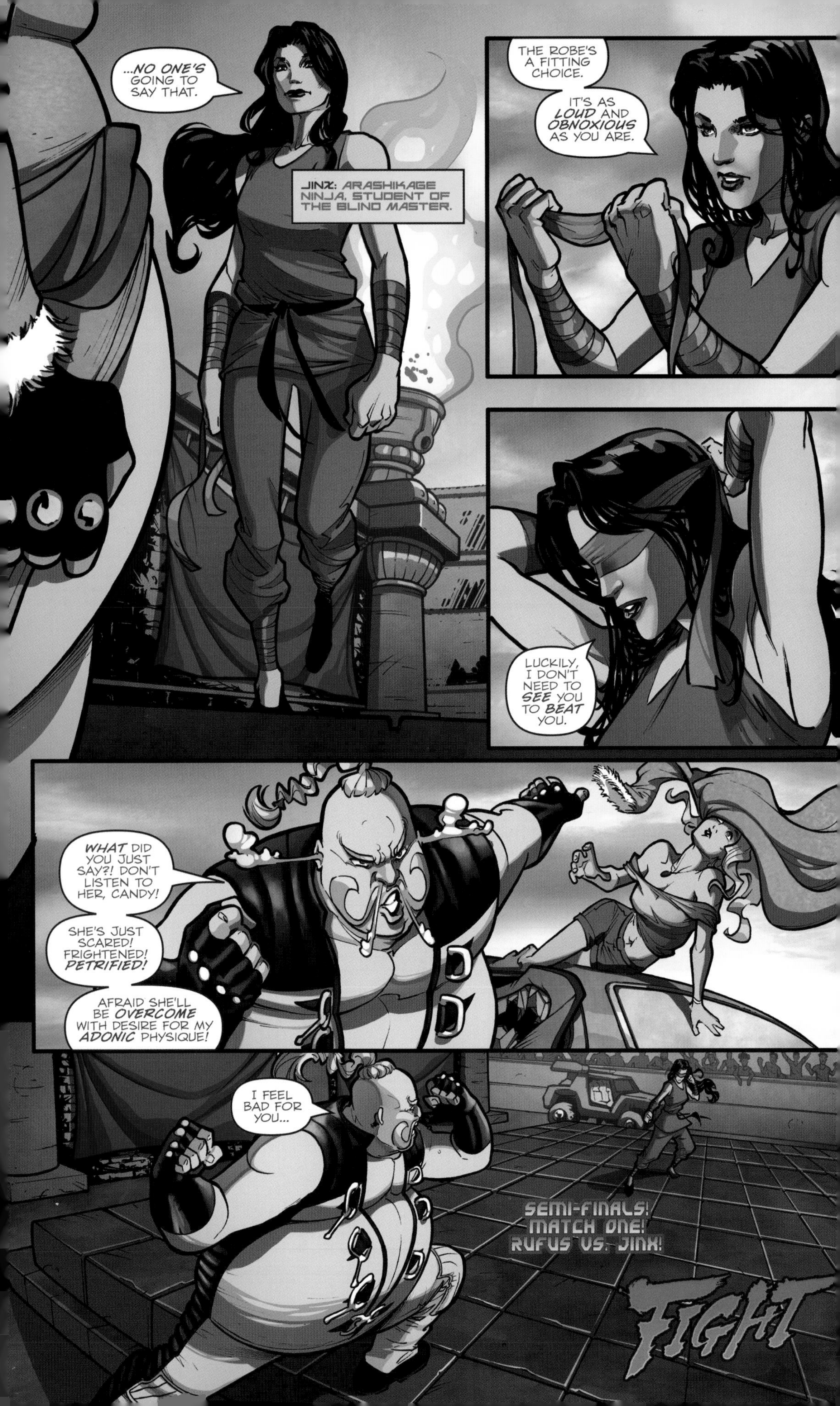
...NO ONE'S GOING TO SAY THAT.
JINX: ARASHIKAGE NINJA, STUDENT OF THE BLIND MASTER.
THE ROBE'S A FITTING CHOICE.
IT'S AS LOUD AND OBNOXIOUS AS YOU ARE.
LUCKILY, I DON'T NEED TO SEE YOU TO BEAT YOU.
WHAT DID YOU JUST SAY?! DON'T LISTEN TO HER, CANDY!
SHE'S JUST SCARED! FRIGHTENED! PETRIFIED!
AFRAID SHE'LL BE OVERCOME WITH DESIRE FOR MY ADONIC PHYSIQUE!
I FEEL BAD FOR YOU...
SEMI-FINALS! MATCH ONE! RUFUS VS. JINX!
FIGHT

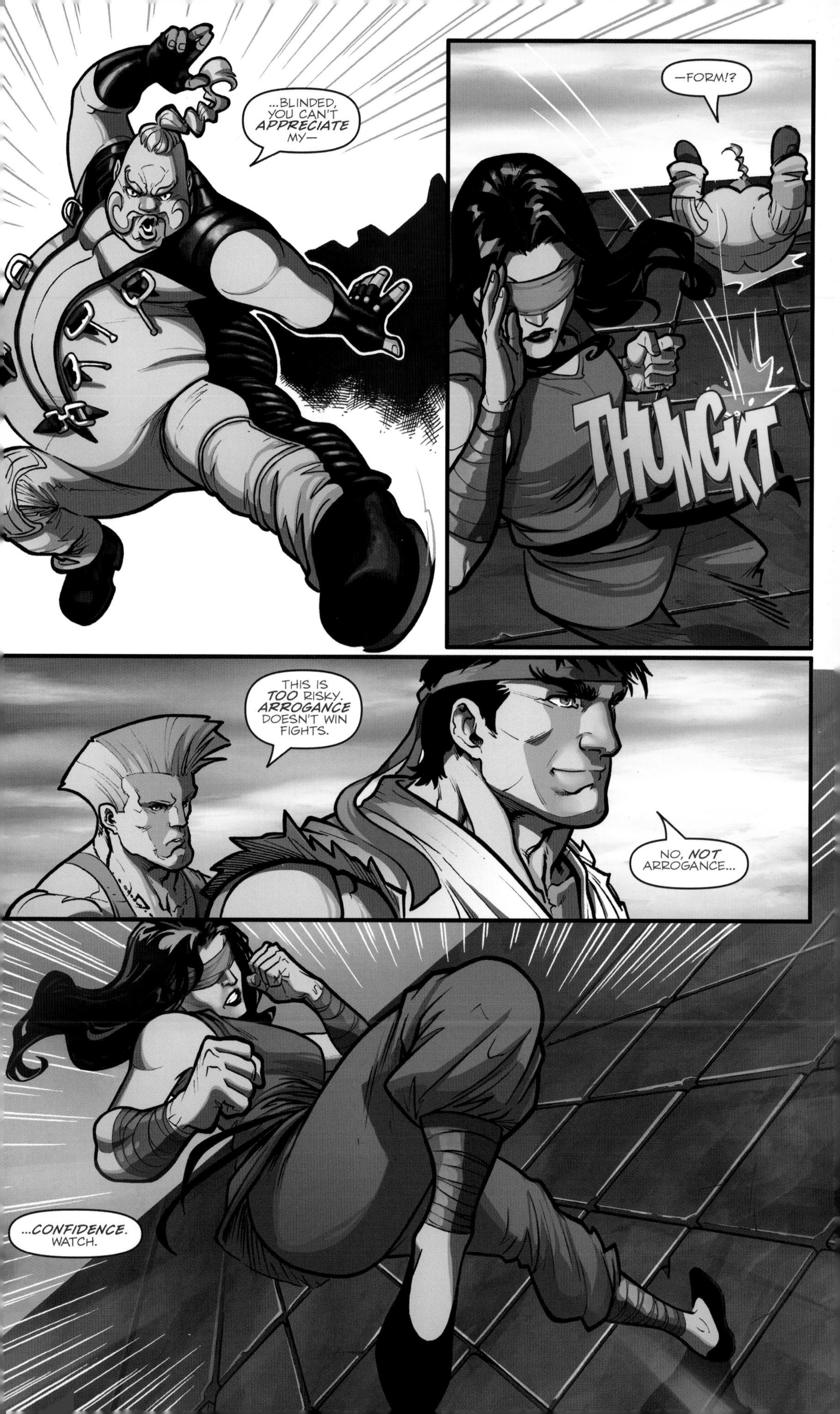
...BLINDED, YOU CAN'T APPRECIATE MY—
—FORM!?
THUNGKT
THIS IS TOO RISKY. ARROGANCE DOESN'T WIN FIGHTS.
NO, NOT ARROGANCE...
...CONFIDENCE. WATCH.

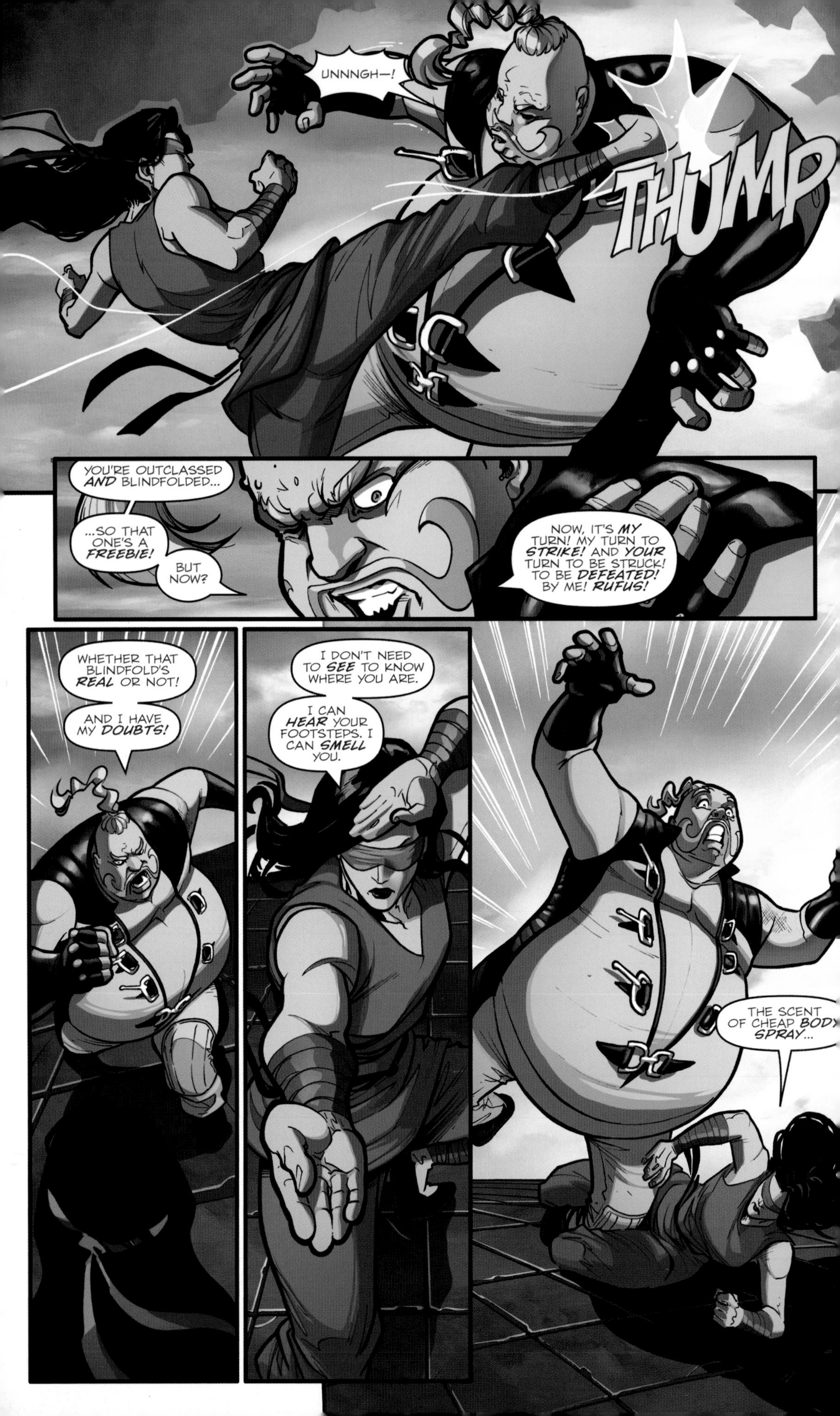
UNNNGH—!
THUMP
YOU'RE OUTCLASSED AND BLINDFOLDED...
...SO THAT ONE'S A FREEBIE!
BUT NOW?
NOW, IT'S MY TURN! MY TURN TO STRIKE! AND YOUR TURN TO BE STRUCK! TO BE DEFEATED! BY ME! RUFUS!
WHETHER THAT BLINDFOLD'S REAL OR NOT!
AND I HAVE MY DOUBTS!
I DON'T NEED TO SEE TO KNOW WHERE YOU ARE.
I CAN HEAR YOUR FOOTSTEPS. I CAN SMELL YOU.
THE SCENT OF CHEAP BODY SPRAY...

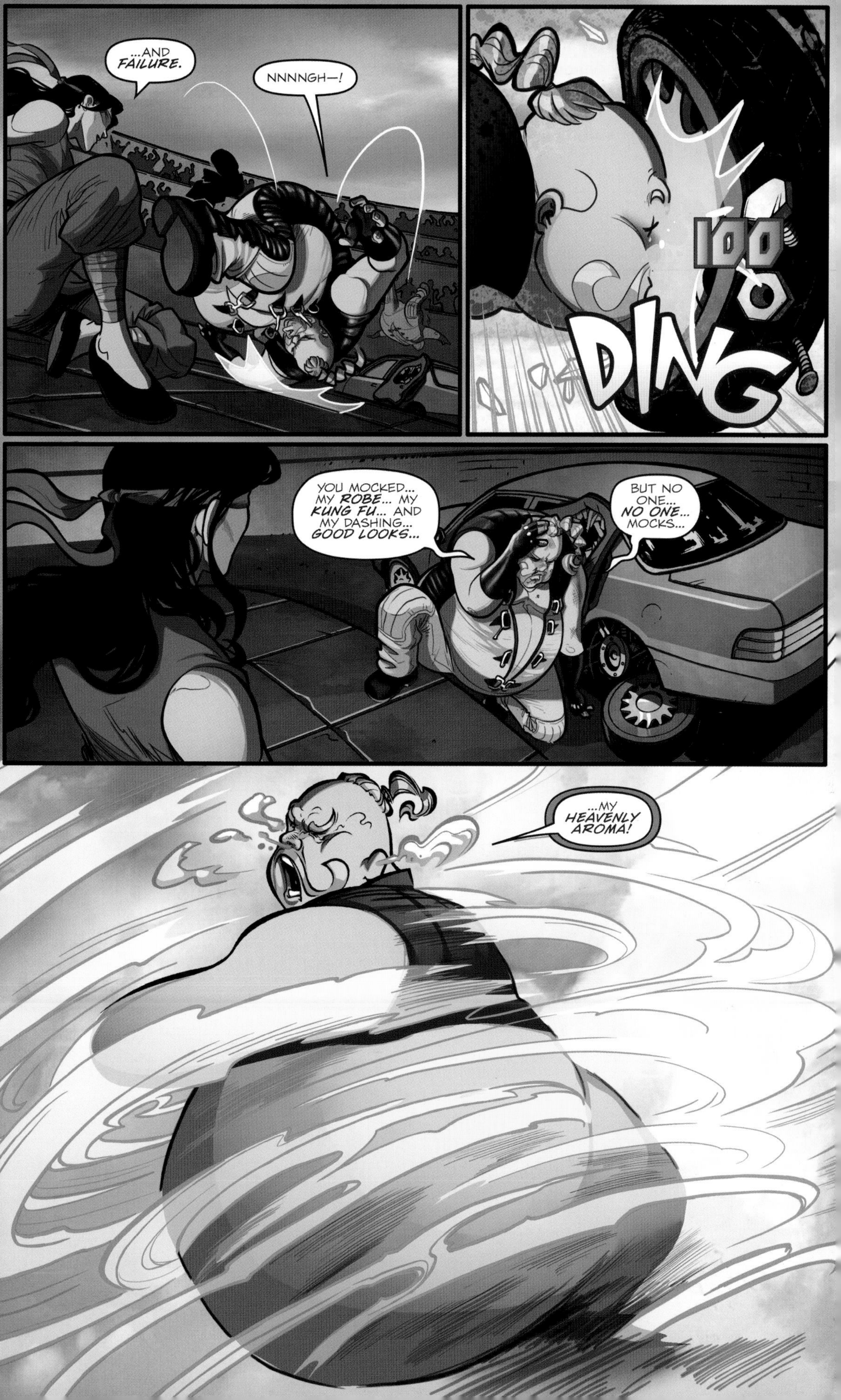
...AND FAILURE.
NNNNGH—!
100
DING
YOU MOCKED... MY ROBE... MY KUNG FU... AND MY DASHING... GOOD LOOKS...
BUT NO ONE... NO ONE... MOCKS...
...MY HEAVENLY AROMA!

PREPARE YOURSELF FOR...

...A BIG BANG...

...TYPHOOOOOOH!

POINK

WHAT... WHAT DID YOU *DO* TO ME?!

ONCE YOU GET THROUGH THE *PADDING*, PRESSURE POINTS WORK ON *EVERYONE*.

THERE'S ANOTHER ONE RIGHT...

POINK

...HERE!

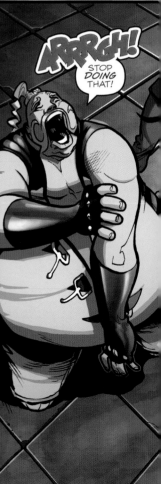

ARRRGH!

STOP *DOING* THAT!

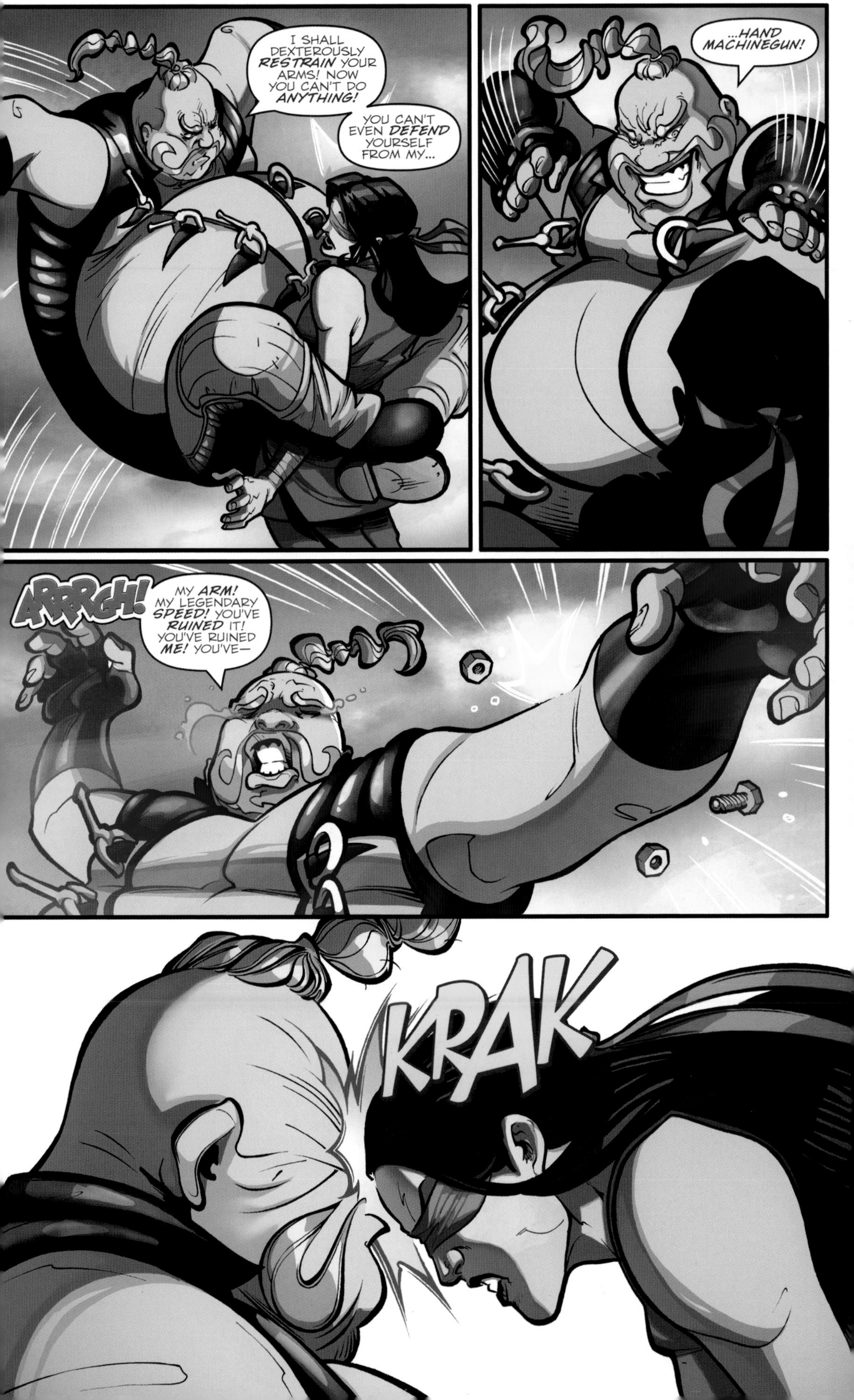
I SHALL DEXTEROUSLY RESTRAIN YOUR ARMS! NOW YOU CAN'T DO ANYTHING!
YOU CAN'T EVEN DEFEND YOURSELF FROM MY...
...HAND MACHINEGUN!
ARRRGH!
MY ARM! MY LEGENDARY SPEED! YOU'VE RUINED IT! YOU'VE RUINED ME! YOU'VE—
KRAK

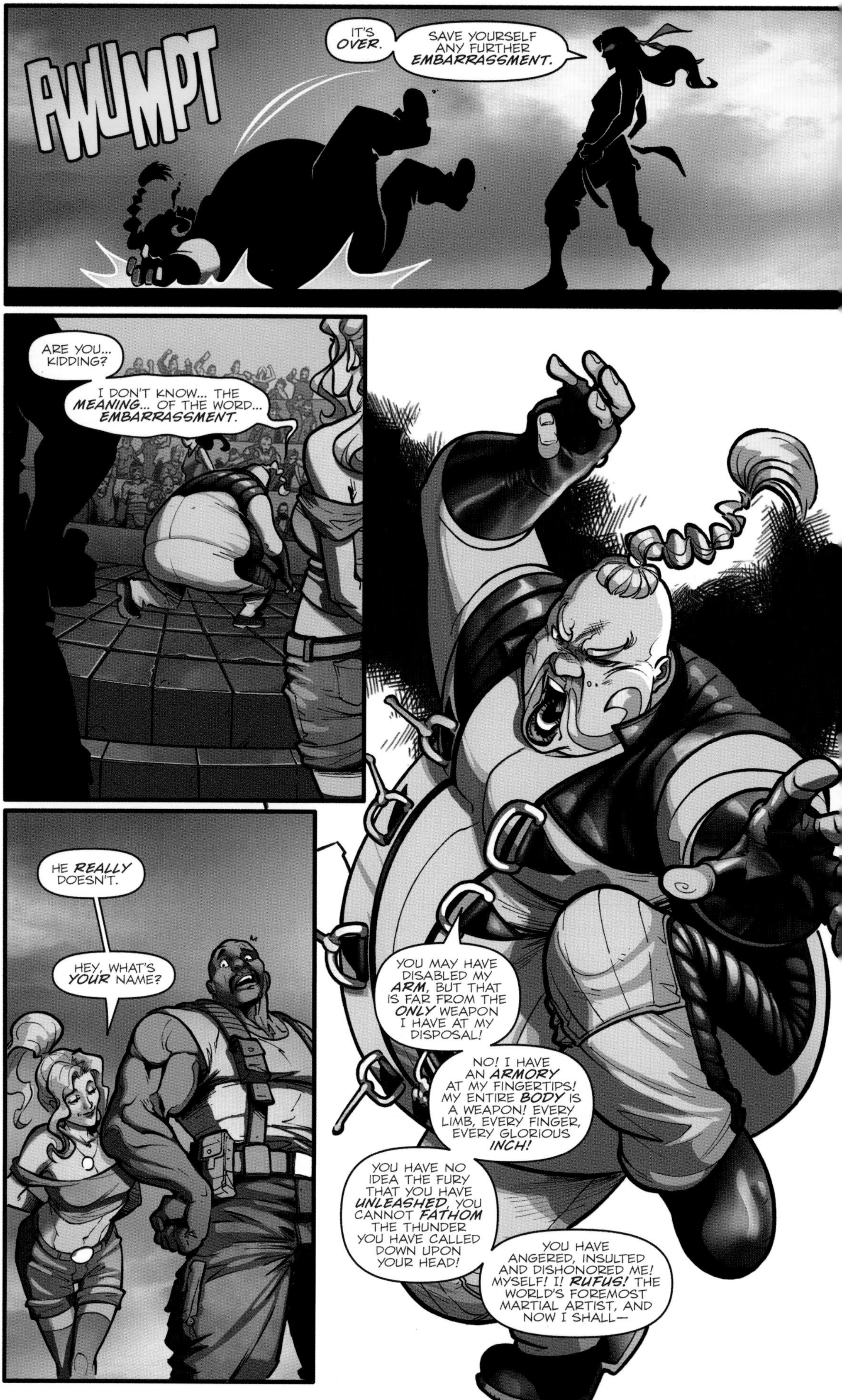
AWUMPT
IT'S OVER.
SAVE YOURSELF ANY FURTHER EMBARRASSMENT.
ARE YOU... KIDDING?
I DON'T KNOW... THE MEANING... OF THE WORD... EMBARRASSMENT.
HE REALLY DOESN'T.
HEY, WHAT'S YOUR NAME?
YOU MAY HAVE DISABLED MY ARM, BUT THAT IS FAR FROM THE ONLY WEAPON I HAVE AT MY DISPOSAL!
NO! I HAVE AN ARMORY AT MY FINGERTIPS! MY ENTIRE BODY IS A WEAPON! EVERY LIMB, EVERY FINGER, EVERY GLORIOUS INCH!
YOU HAVE NO IDEA THE FURY THAT YOU HAVE UNLEASHED, YOU CANNOT FATHOM THE THUNDER YOU HAVE CALLED DOWN UPON YOUR HEAD!
YOU HAVE ANGERED, INSULTED AND DISHONORED ME! MYSELF! I! RUFUS! THE WORLD'S FOREMOST MARTIAL ARTIST, AND NOW I SHALL—

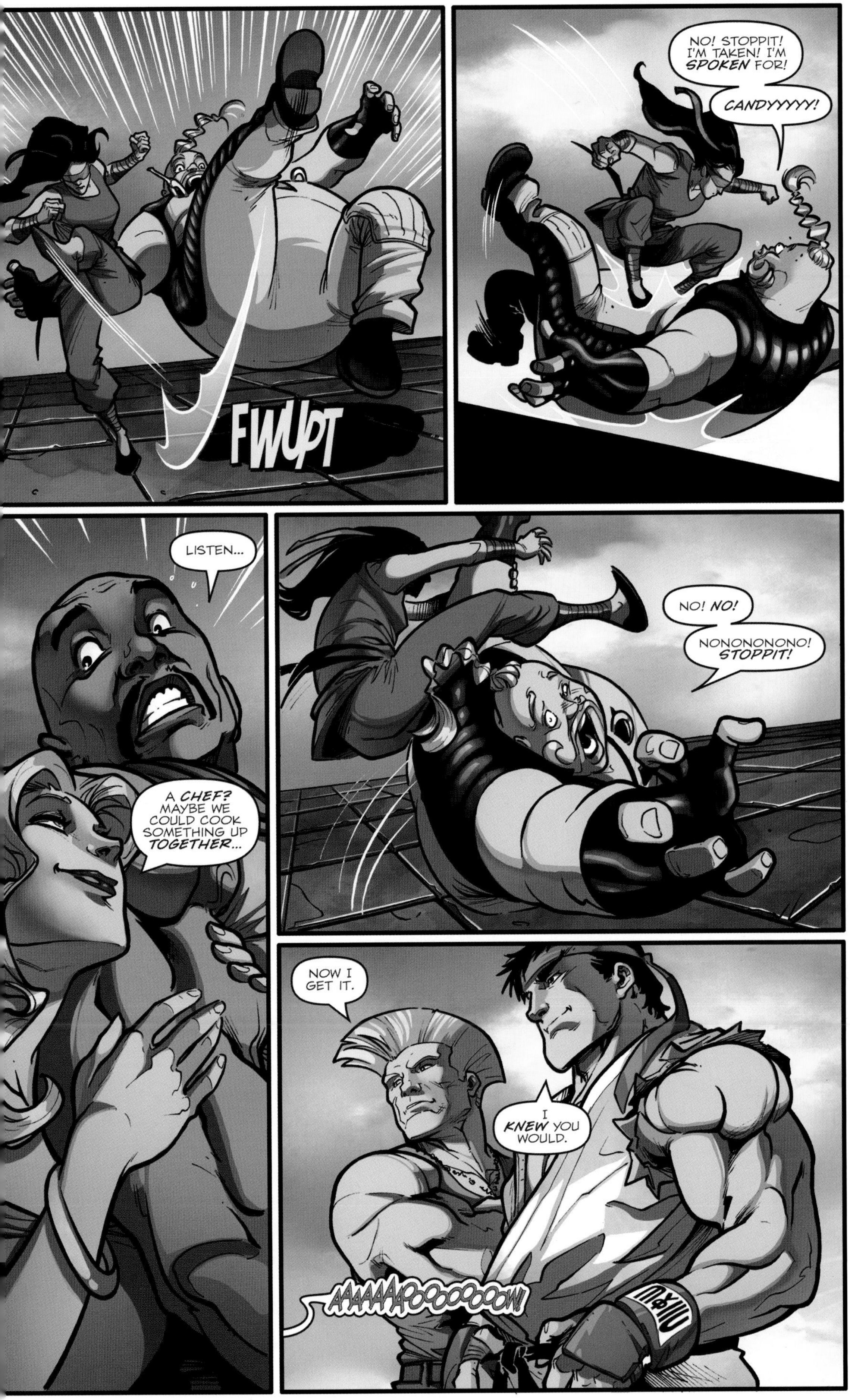
FWUPT
NO! STOPPIT! I'M TAKEN! I'M SPOKEN FOR!
CANDYYYYY!
LISTEN...
A CHEF? MAYBE WE COULD COOK SOMETHING UP TOGETHER...
NO! NO!
NONONONONO! STOPPIT!
NOW I GET IT.
I KNEW YOU WOULD.
AAAAAAPOOOOOOOOW!

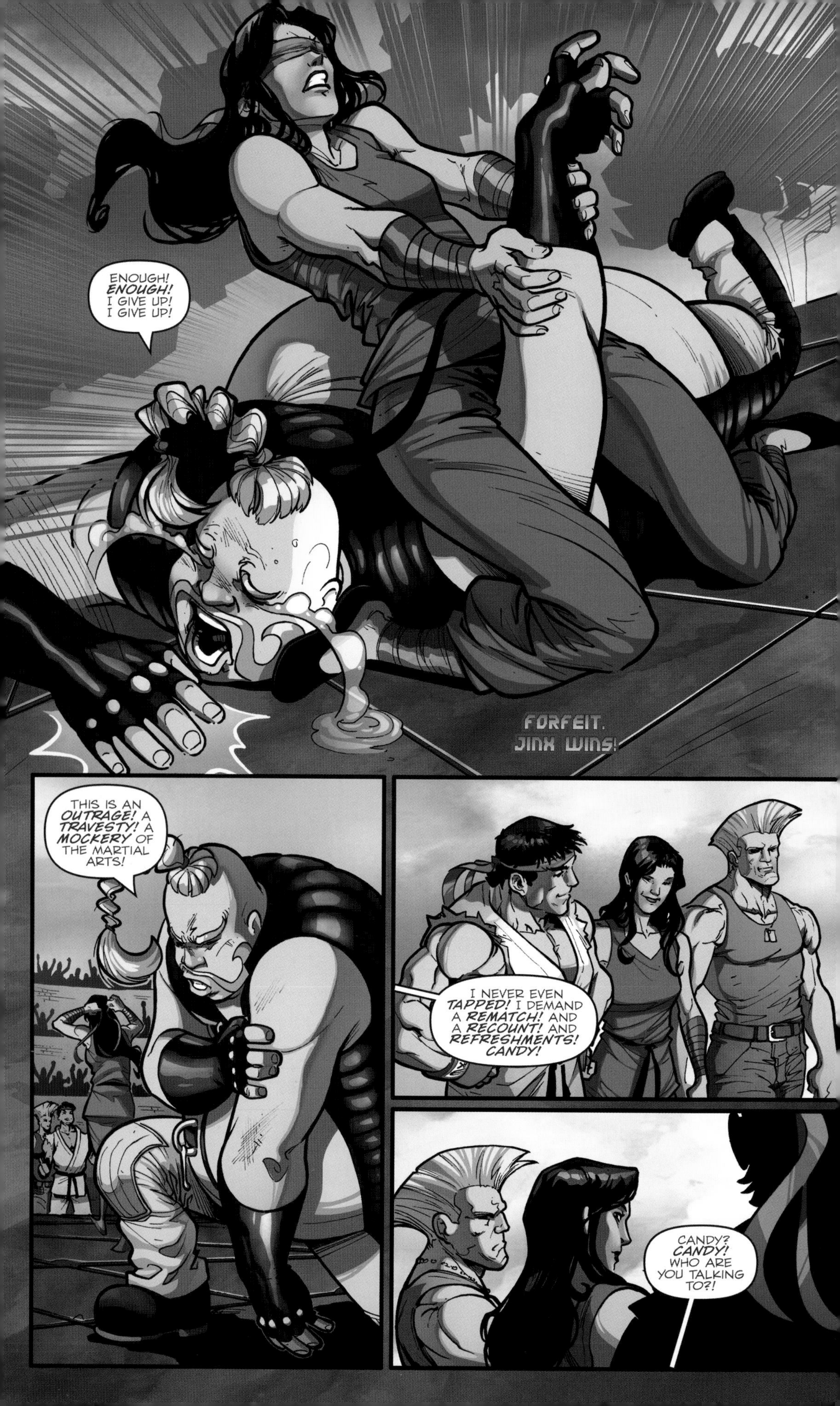
ENOUGH! ENOUGH! I GIVE UP! I GIVE UP!
FORFEIT. JINX WINS!
THIS IS AN OUTRAGE! A TRAVESTY! A MOCKERY OF THE MARTIAL ARTS!
I NEVER EVEN TAPPED! I DEMAND A REMATCH! AND A RECOUNT! AND REFRESHMENTS! CANDY!
CANDY? CANDY! WHO ARE YOU TALKING TO?!

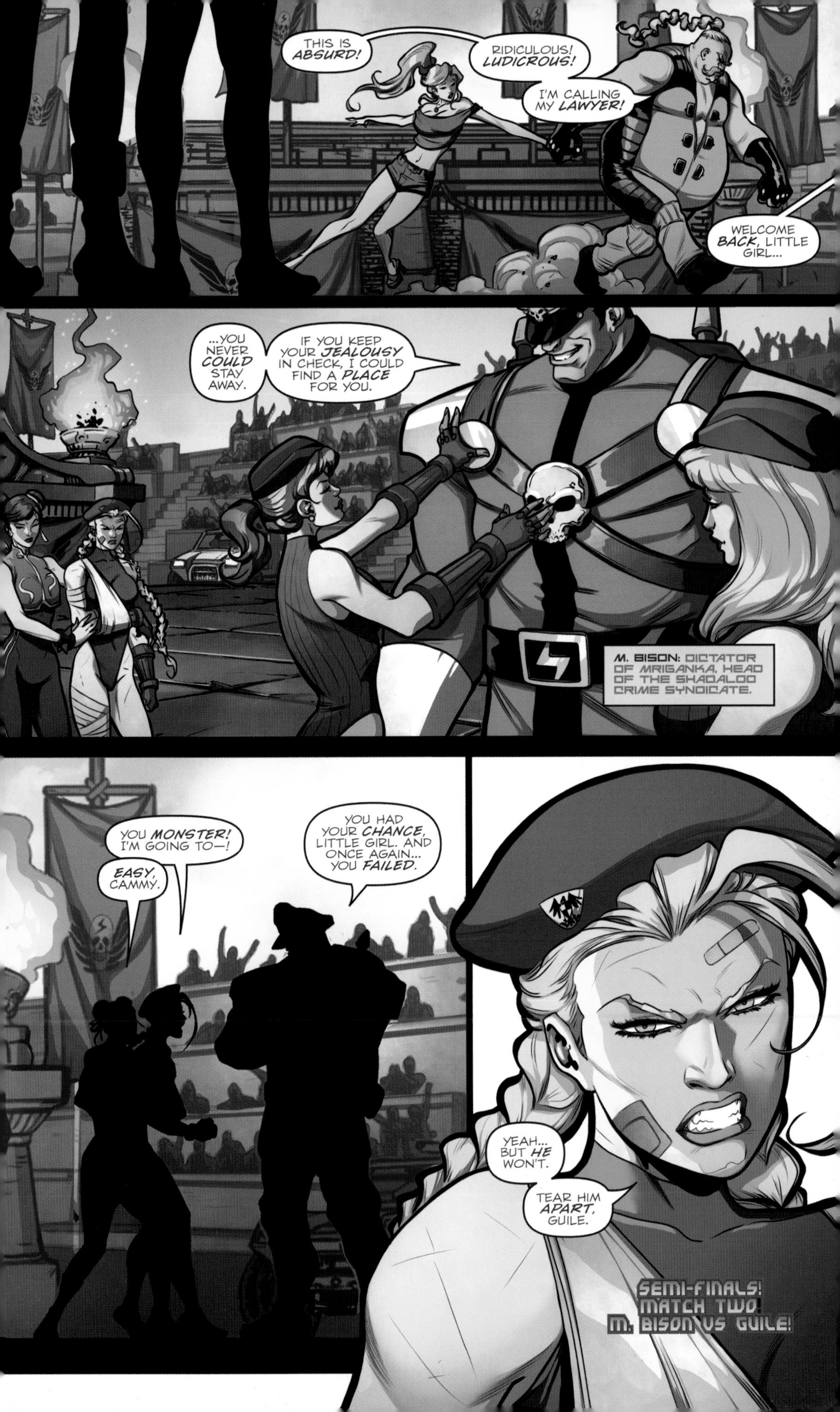
THIS IS ABSURD!
RIDICULOUS! LUDICROUS!
I'M CALLING MY LAWYER!
WELCOME BACK, LITTLE GIRL...
...YOU NEVER COULD STAY AWAY.
IF YOU KEEP YOUR JEALOUSY IN CHECK, I COULD FIND A PLACE FOR YOU.
M. BISON: DICTATOR OF MRIGANKA, HEAD OF THE SHADALOO CRIME SYNDICATE.
YOU MONSTER! I'M GOING TO—!
EASY, CAMMY.
YOU HAD YOUR CHANCE, LITTLE GIRL. AND ONCE AGAIN... YOU FAILED.
YEAH... BUT HE WON'T.
TEAR HIM APART, GUILE.
SEMI-FINALS! MATCH TWO M. BISON VS GUILE!

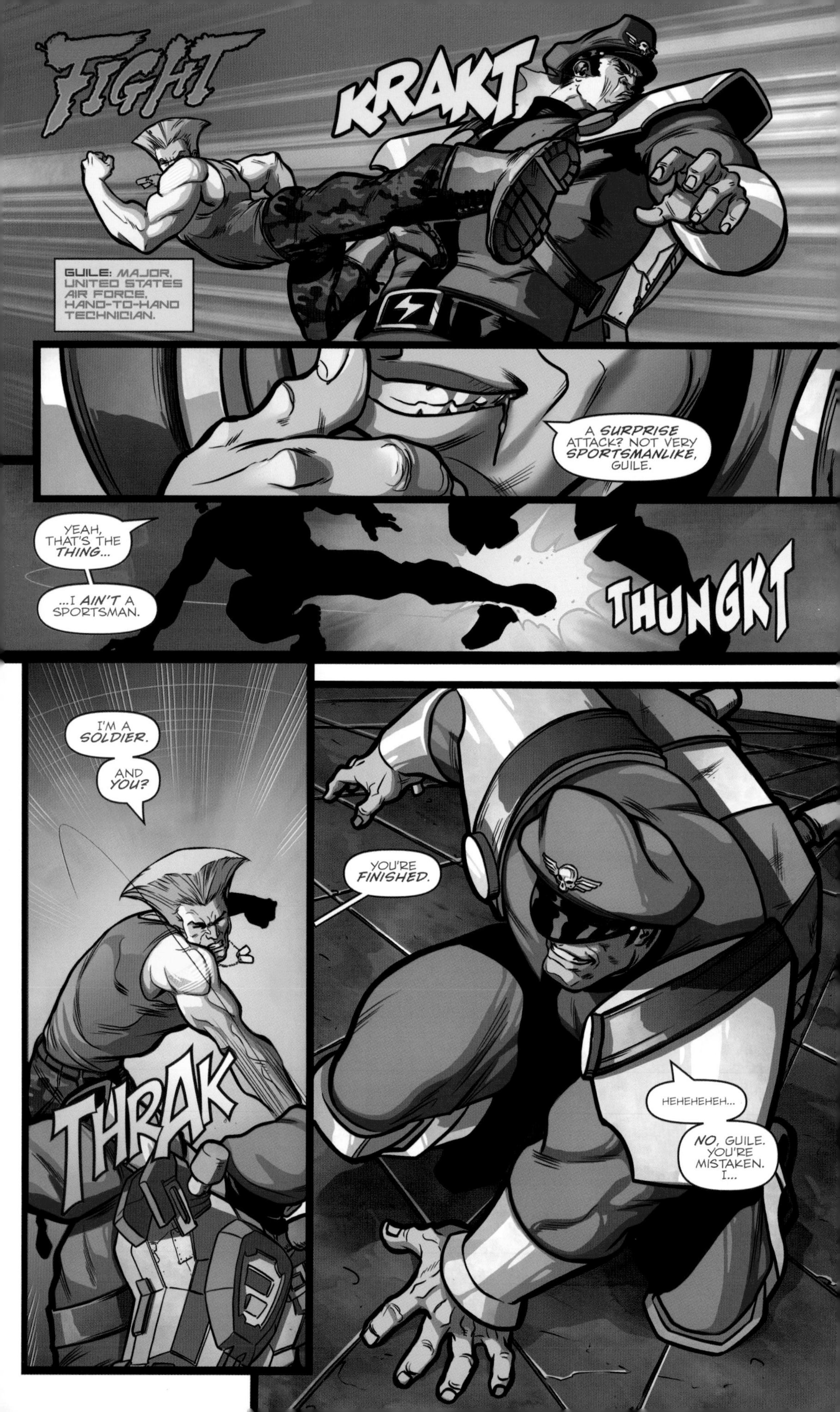
FIGHT
KRAKT
GUILE: MAJOR, UNITED STATES AIR FORCE, HAND-TO-HAND TECHNICIAN.
A SURPRISE ATTACK? NOT VERY SPORTSMANLIKE, GUILE.
YEAH, THAT'S THE THING...
...I AIN'T A SPORTSMAN.
THUNGKT
I'M A SOLDIER.
AND YOU?
THRAK
YOU'RE FINISHED.
HEHEHEHEH...
NO, GUILE. YOU'RE MISTAKEN. I...

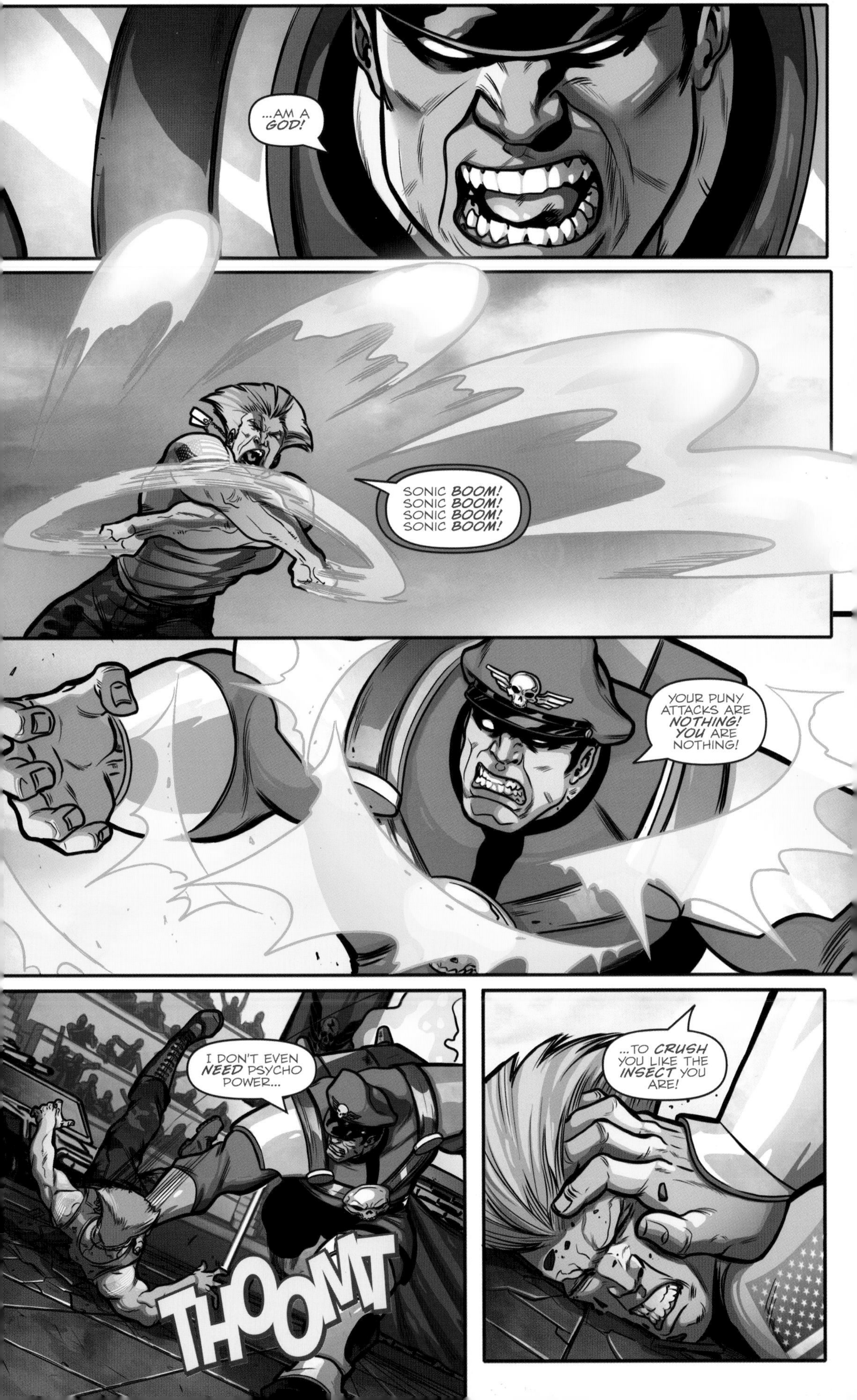
...AM A GOD!
SONIC BOOM! SONIC BOOM! SONIC BOOM! SONIC BOOM!
YOUR PUNY ATTACKS ARE NOTHING! YOU ARE NOTHING!
I DON'T EVEN NEED PSYCHO POWER...
THOOMT
...TO CRUSH YOU LIKE THE INSECT YOU ARE!

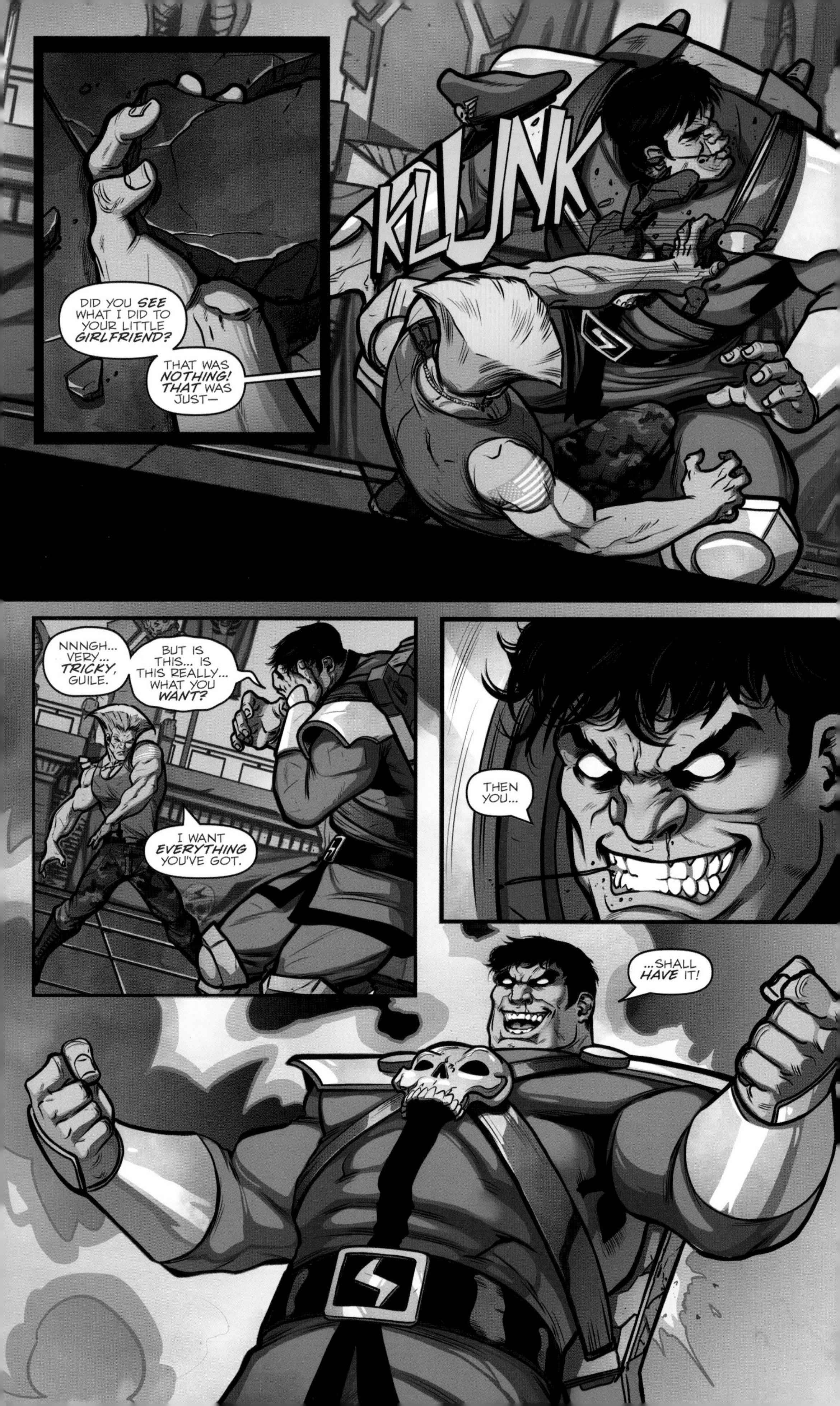
DID YOU SEE WHAT I DID TO YOUR LITTLE GIRLFRIEND?
THAT WAS NOTHING! THAT WAS JUST—
KLUNK
NNNGH... VERY... TRICKY, GUILE.
BUT IS THIS... IS THIS REALLY... WHAT YOU WANT?
I WANT EVERYTHING YOU'VE GOT.
THEN YOU...
...SHALL HAVE IT!

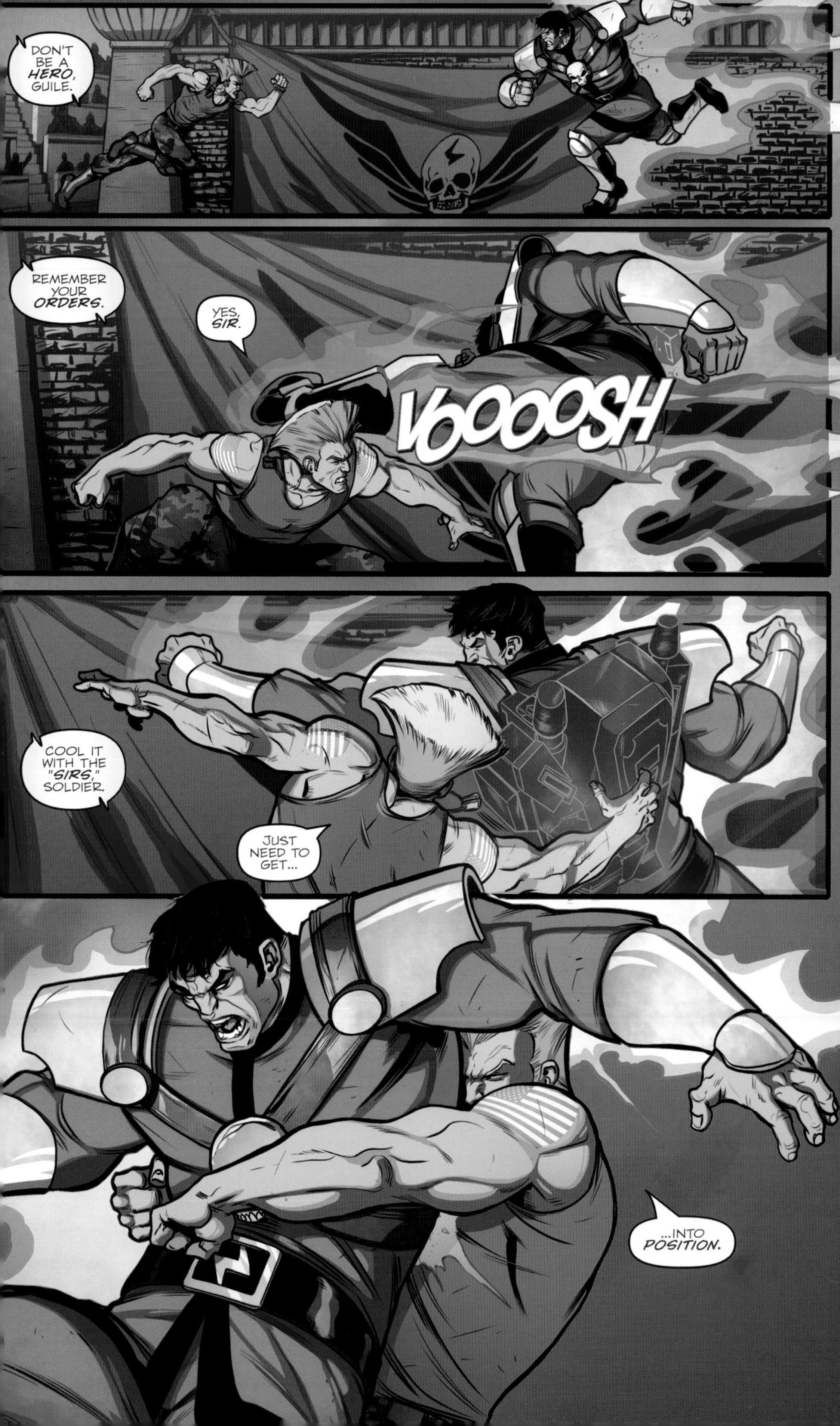
DON'T BE A HERO, GUILE.
REMEMBER YOUR ORDERS.
YES, SIR.
VOOOOSH
COOL IT WITH THE "SIRS," SOLDIER.
JUST NEED TO GET...
...INTO POSITION.

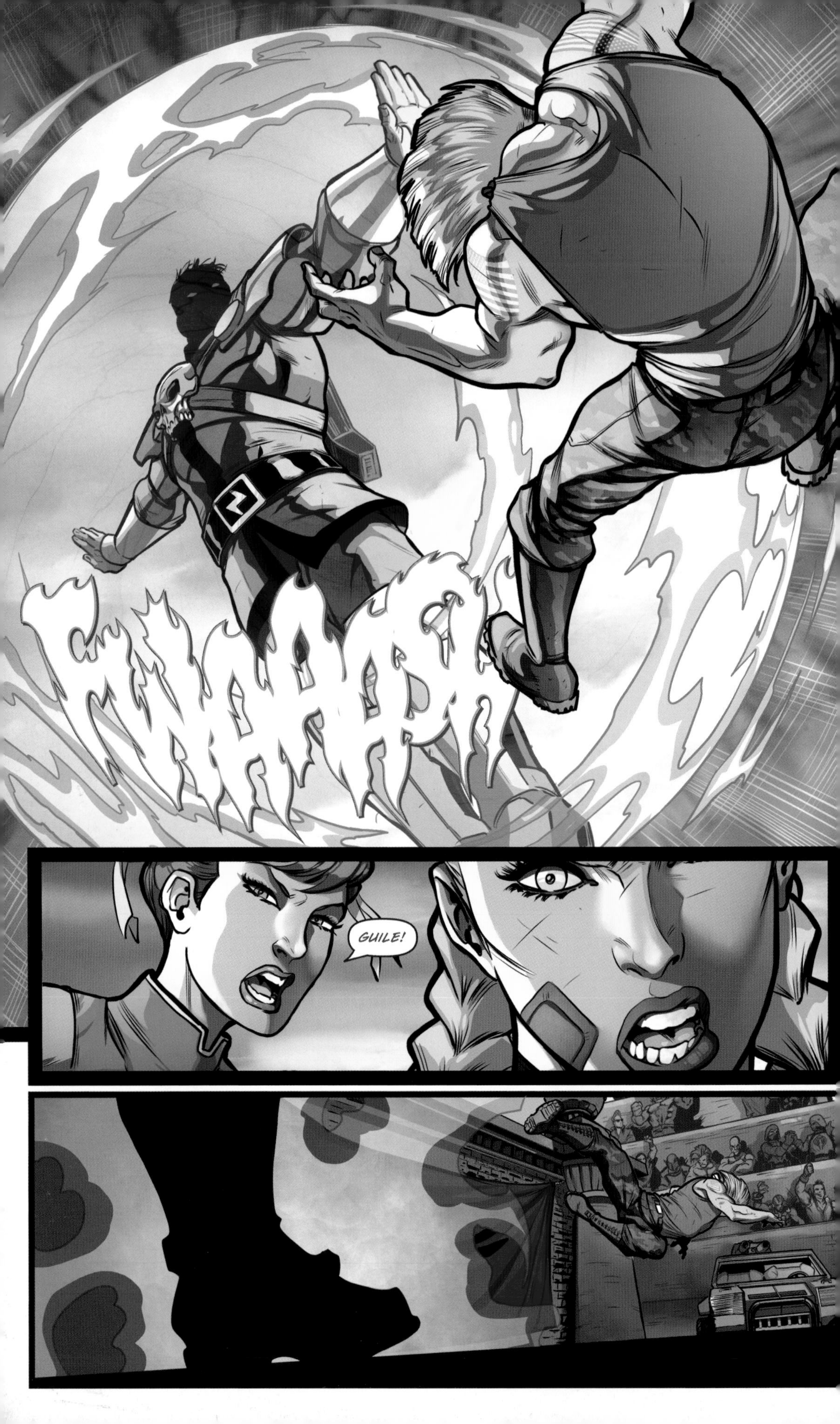
GUILE!

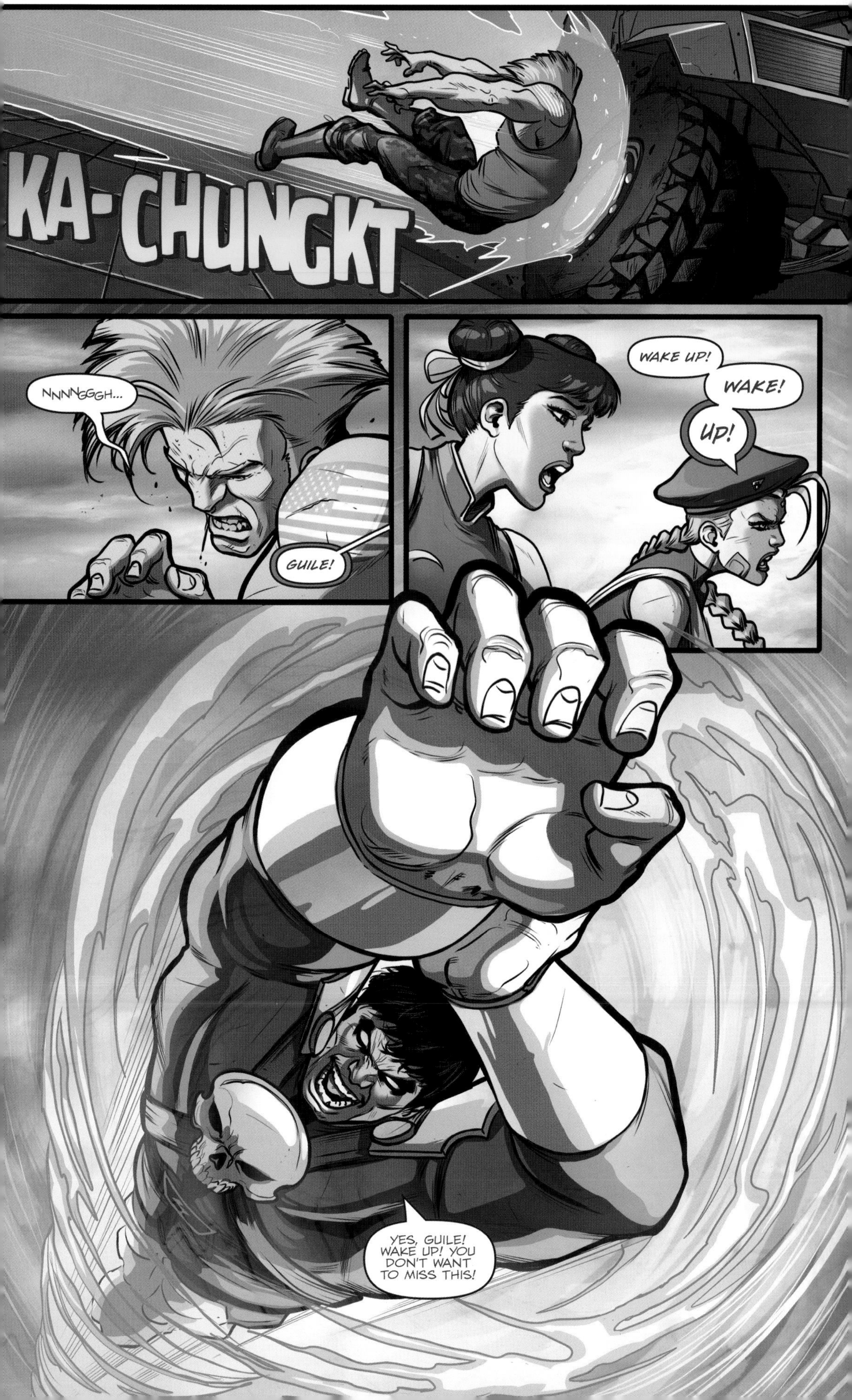
KA-CHUNGKT
NNNNGGGH...
GUILE!
WAKE UP!
WAKE!
UP!
YES, GUILE! WAKE UP! YOU DON'T WANT TO MISS THIS!

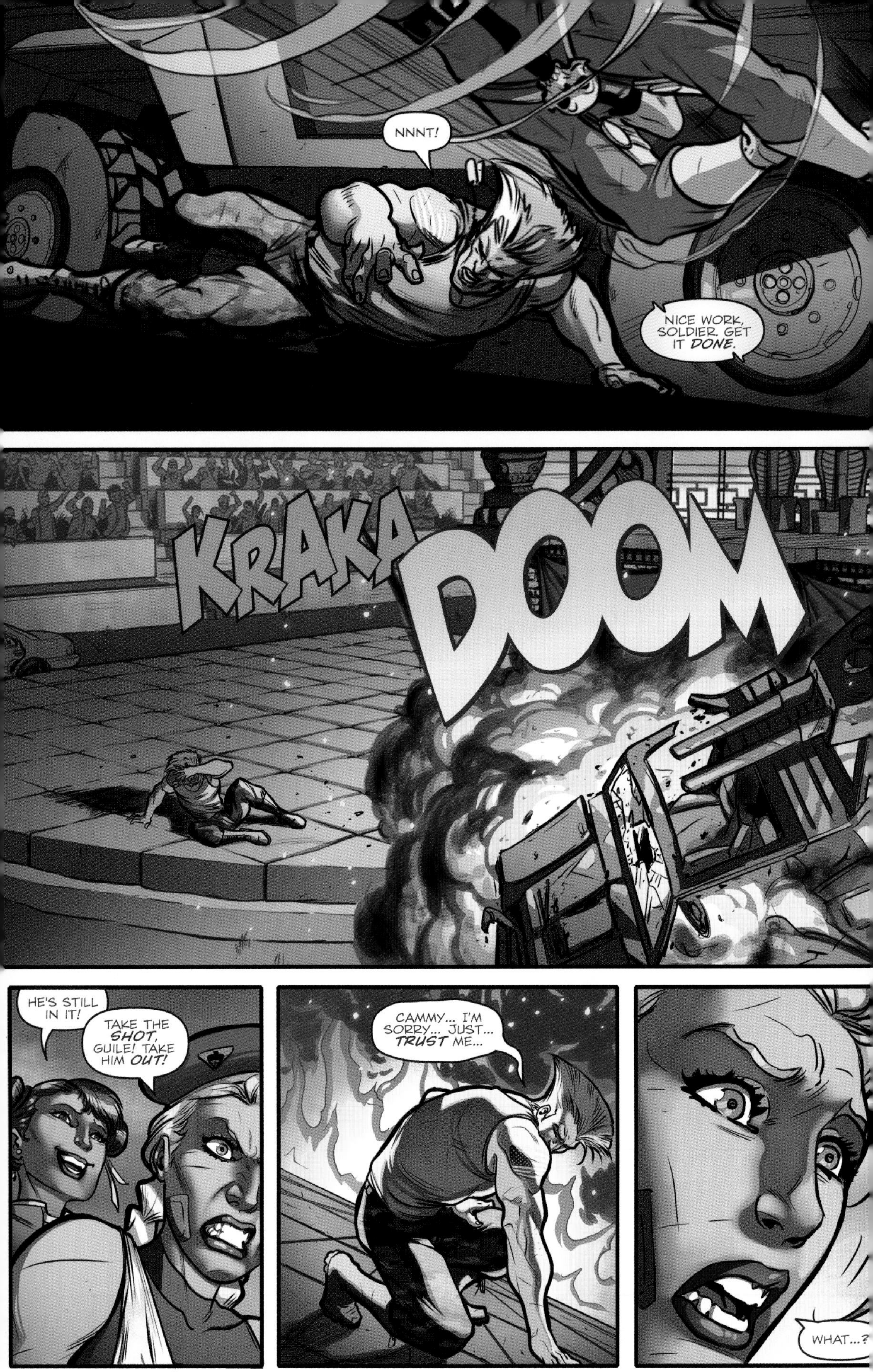
NNNT!
NICE WORK, SOLDIER. GET IT *DONE*.
KRAKA DOOM
HE'S STILL IN IT!
TAKE THE *SHOT*, GUILE! TAKE HIM *OUT*!
CAMMY... I'M SORRY... JUST... *TRUST* ME...
WHAT...?

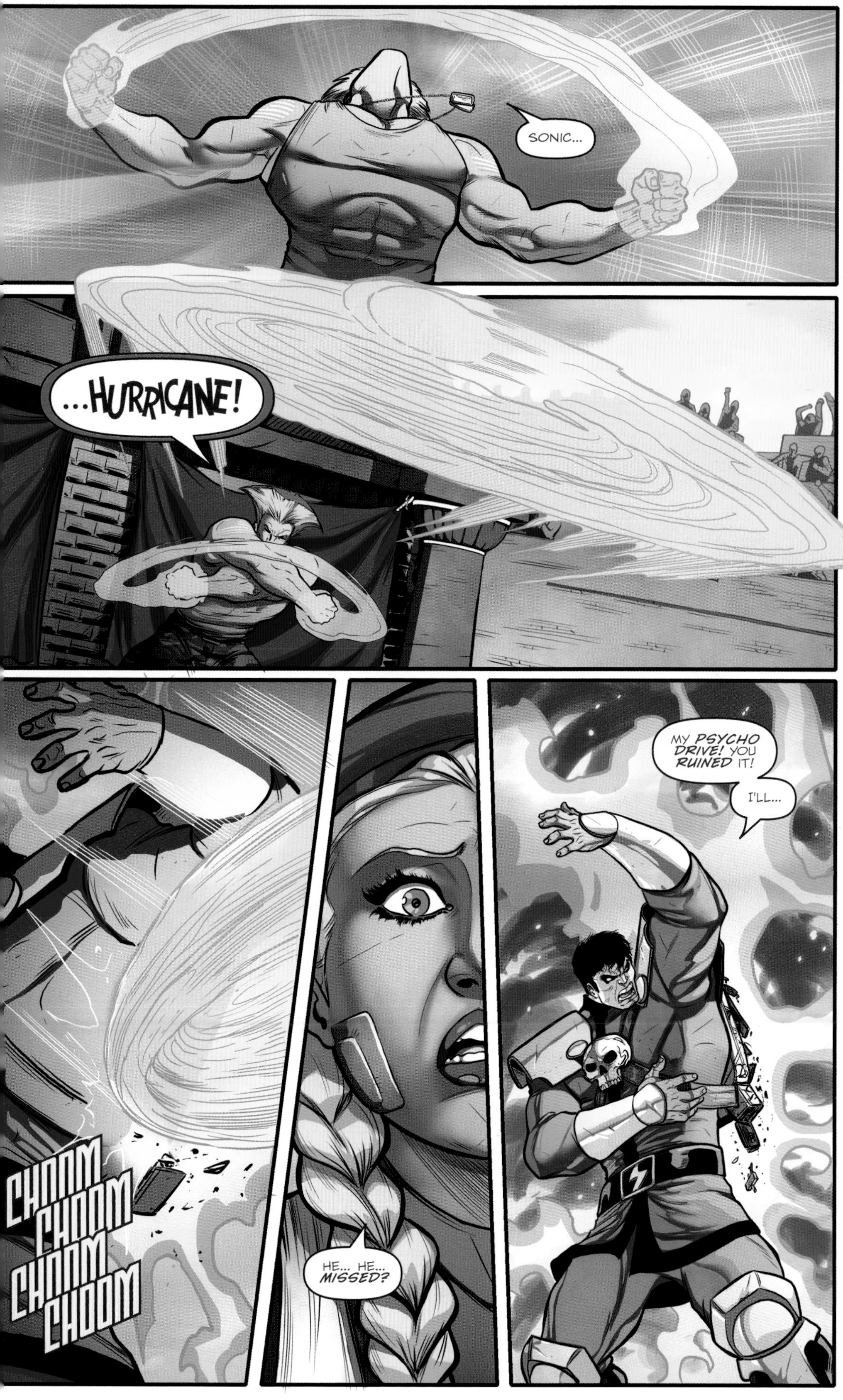
SONIC...
...HURRICANE!
CHOOM CHOOM CHOOM CHOOM
HE... HE... MISSED?
MY PSYCHO DRIVE! YOU RUINED IT!
I'LL...

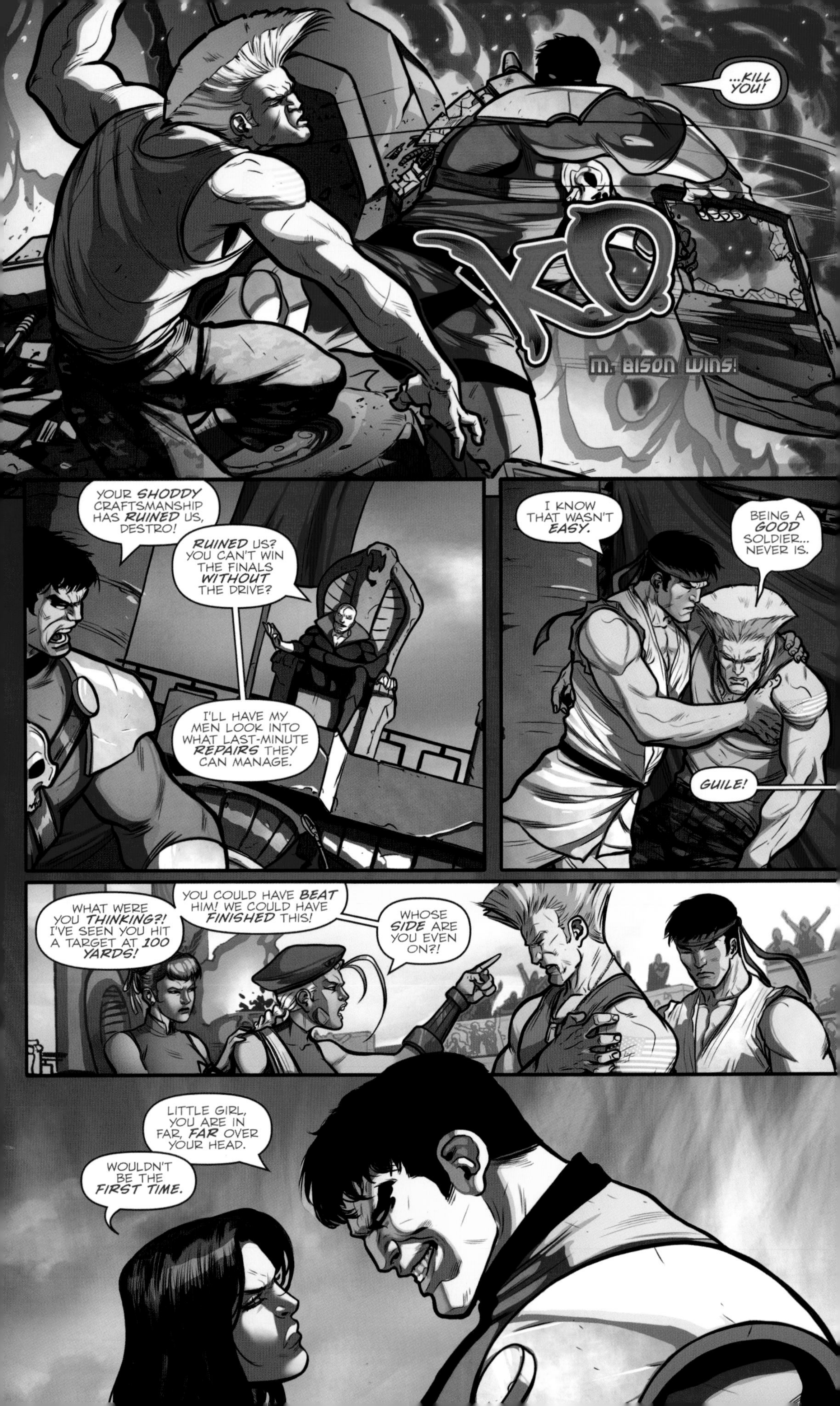

...KILL YOU!
KO
M. BISON WINS!
YOUR SHODDY CRAFTSMANSHIP HAS RUINED US, DESTRO!
RUINED US? YOU CAN'T WIN THE FINALS WITHOUT THE DRIVE?
I'LL HAVE MY MEN LOOK INTO WHAT LAST-MINUTE REPAIRS THEY CAN MANAGE.
I KNOW THAT WASN'T EASY.
BEING A GOOD SOLDIER... NEVER IS.
GUILE!
WHAT WERE YOU THINKING?! I'VE SEEN YOU HIT A TARGET AT 100 YARDS!
YOU COULD HAVE BEAT HIM! WE COULD HAVE FINISHED THIS!
WHOSE SIDE ARE YOU EVEN ON?!
LITTLE GIRL, YOU ARE IN FAR, FAR OVER YOUR HEAD.
WOULDN'T BE THE FIRST TIME.

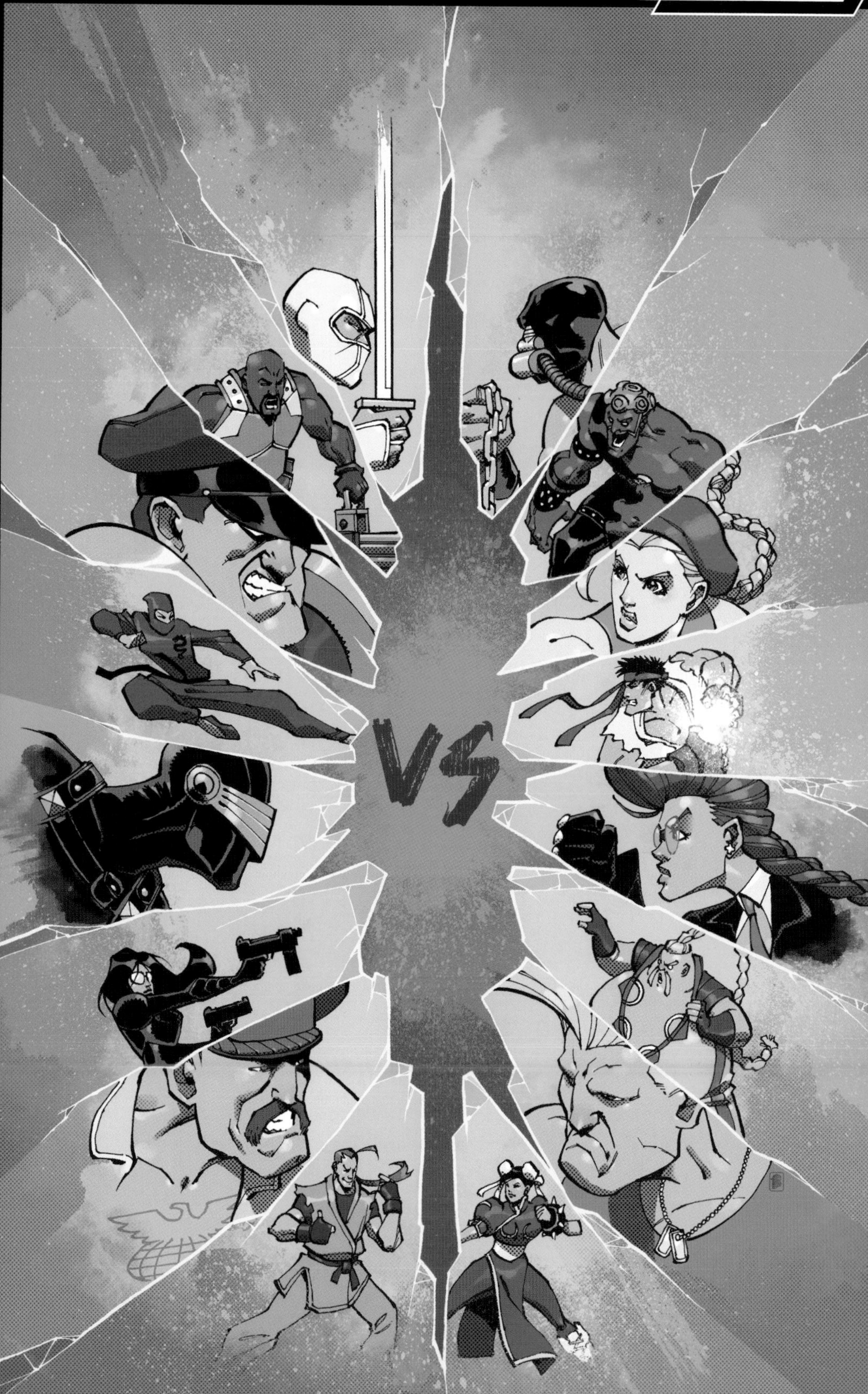
VS

CHAPTER 5

World Warrior
Tournament Bracket

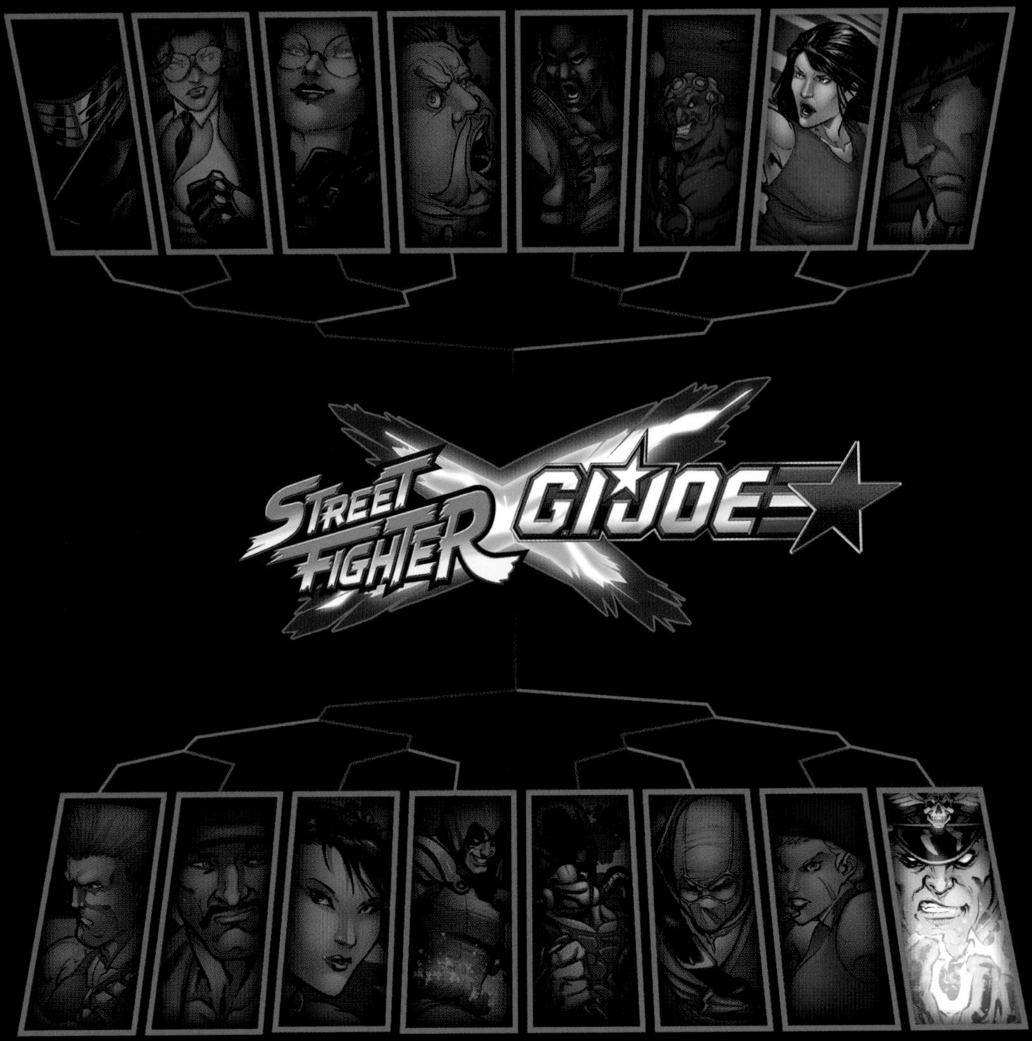
STREET FIGHTER
G.I. JOE

JINX vs. M. BISON

FINALS

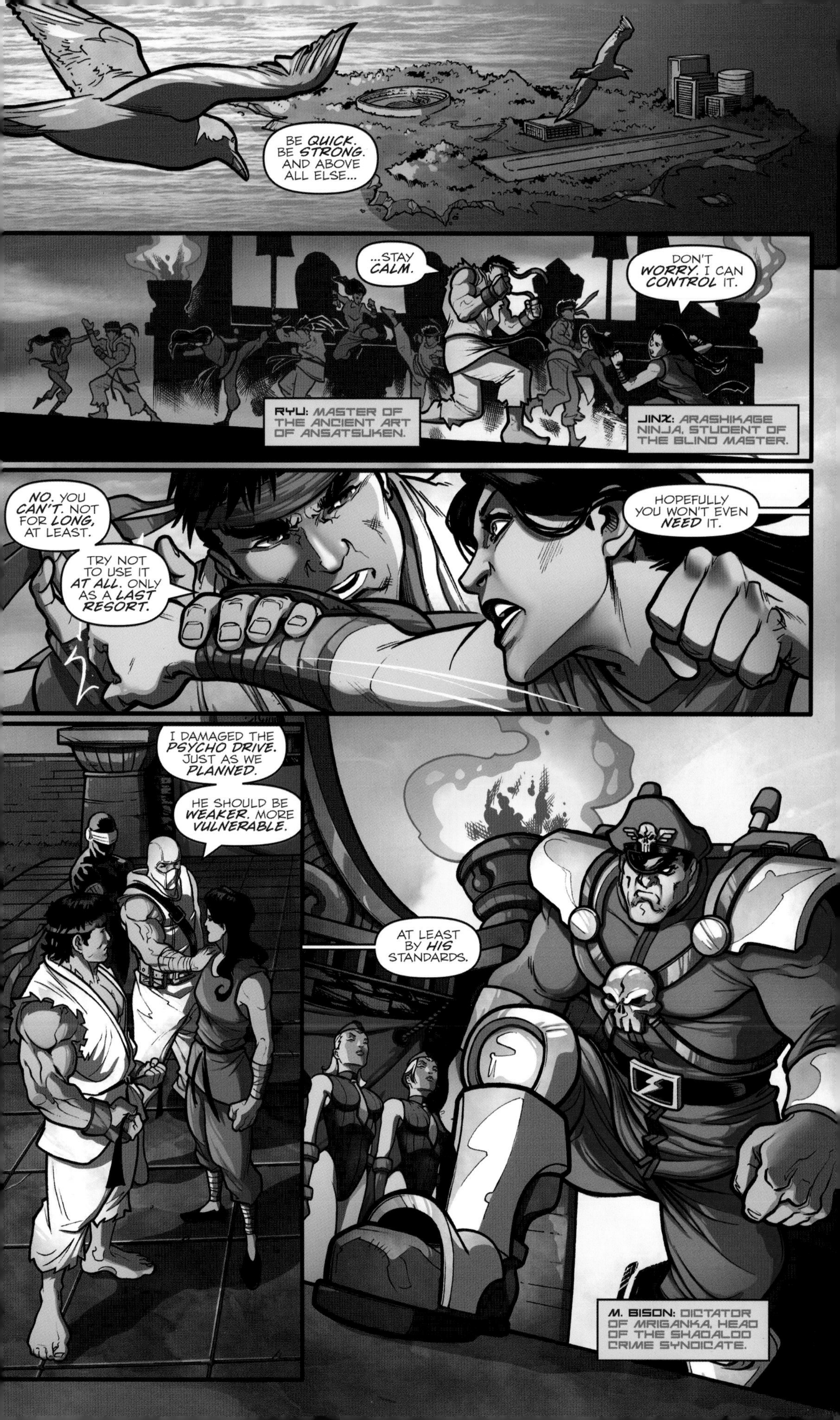
BE QUICK. BE STRONG. AND ABOVE ALL ELSE...
...STAY CALM.
DON'T WORRY. I CAN CONTROL IT.
RYU: MASTER OF THE ANCIENT ART OF ANSATSUKEN.
JINX: ARASHIKAGE NINJA, STUDENT OF THE BLIND MASTER.
NO. YOU CAN'T. NOT FOR LONG, AT LEAST.
TRY NOT TO USE IT AT ALL. ONLY AS A LAST RESORT.
HOPEFULLY YOU WON'T EVEN NEED IT.
I DAMAGED THE PSYCHO DRIVE. JUST AS WE PLANNED.
HE SHOULD BE WEAKER. MORE VULNERABLE.
AT LEAST BY HIS STANDARDS.
M. BISON: DICTATOR OF MRIGANKA, HEAD OF THE SHADALOO CRIME SYNDICATE.

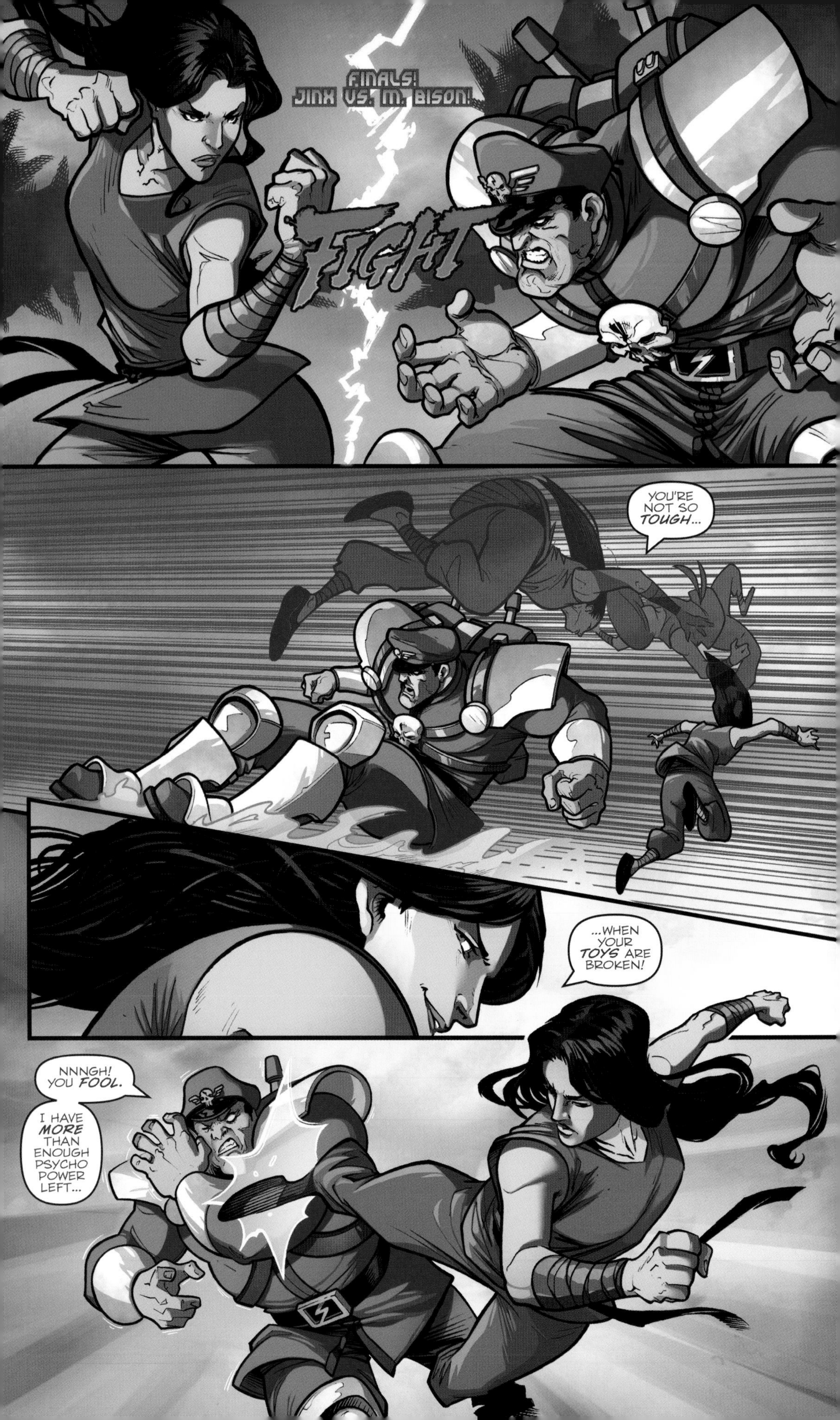
FINALS!
JINX VS. M. BISON!
FIGHT
YOU'RE NOT SO TOUGH...
...WHEN YOUR TOYS ARE BROKEN!
NNNGH! YOU FOOL.
I HAVE MORE THAN ENOUGH PSYCHO POWER LEFT...

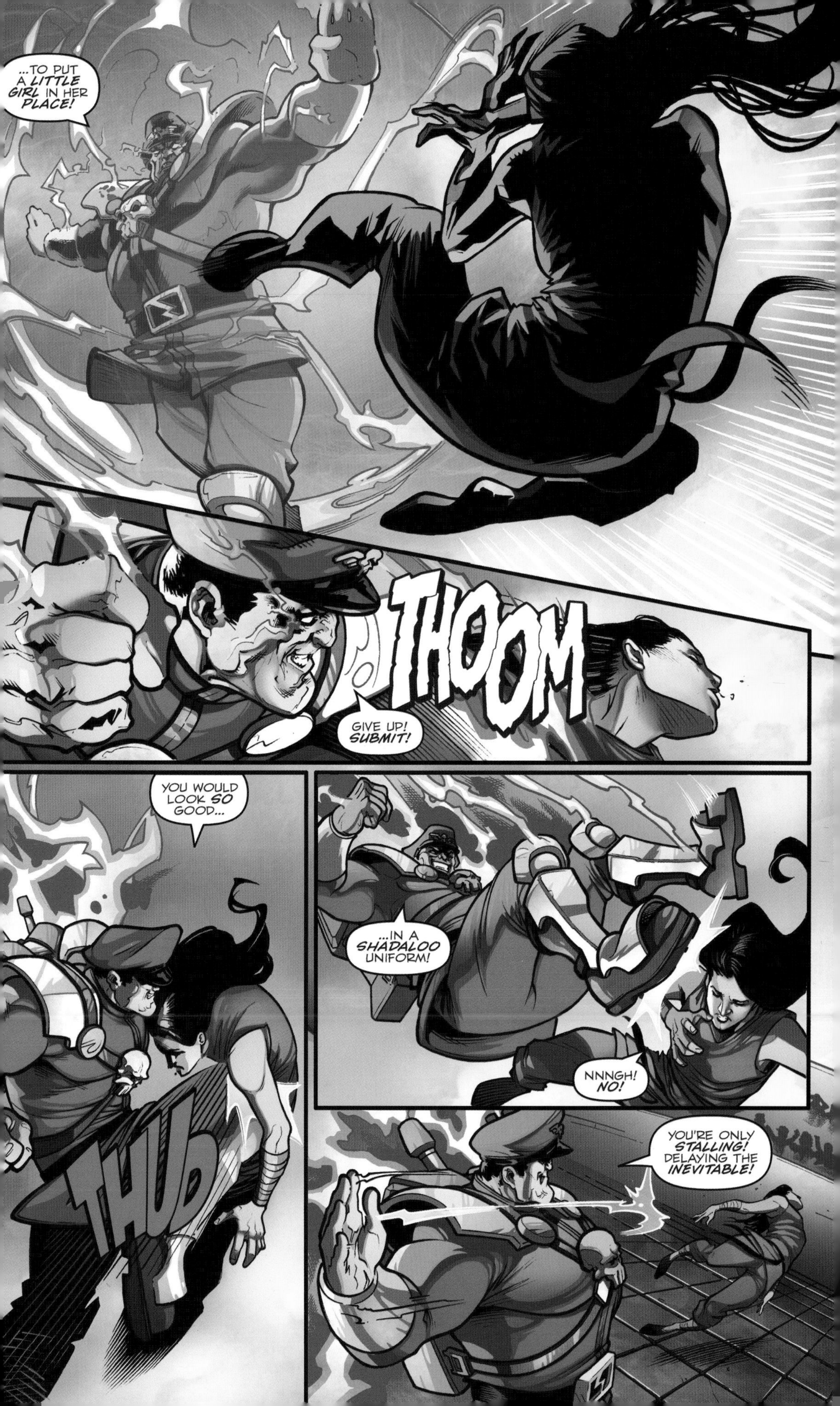

...TO PUT A LITTLE GIRL IN HER PLACE!
THOOM
GIVE UP! SUBMIT!
YOU WOULD LOOK SO GOOD...
THUD
...IN A SHADALOO UNIFORM!
NNNGH! NO!
YOU'RE ONLY STALLING! DELAYING THE INEVITABLE!

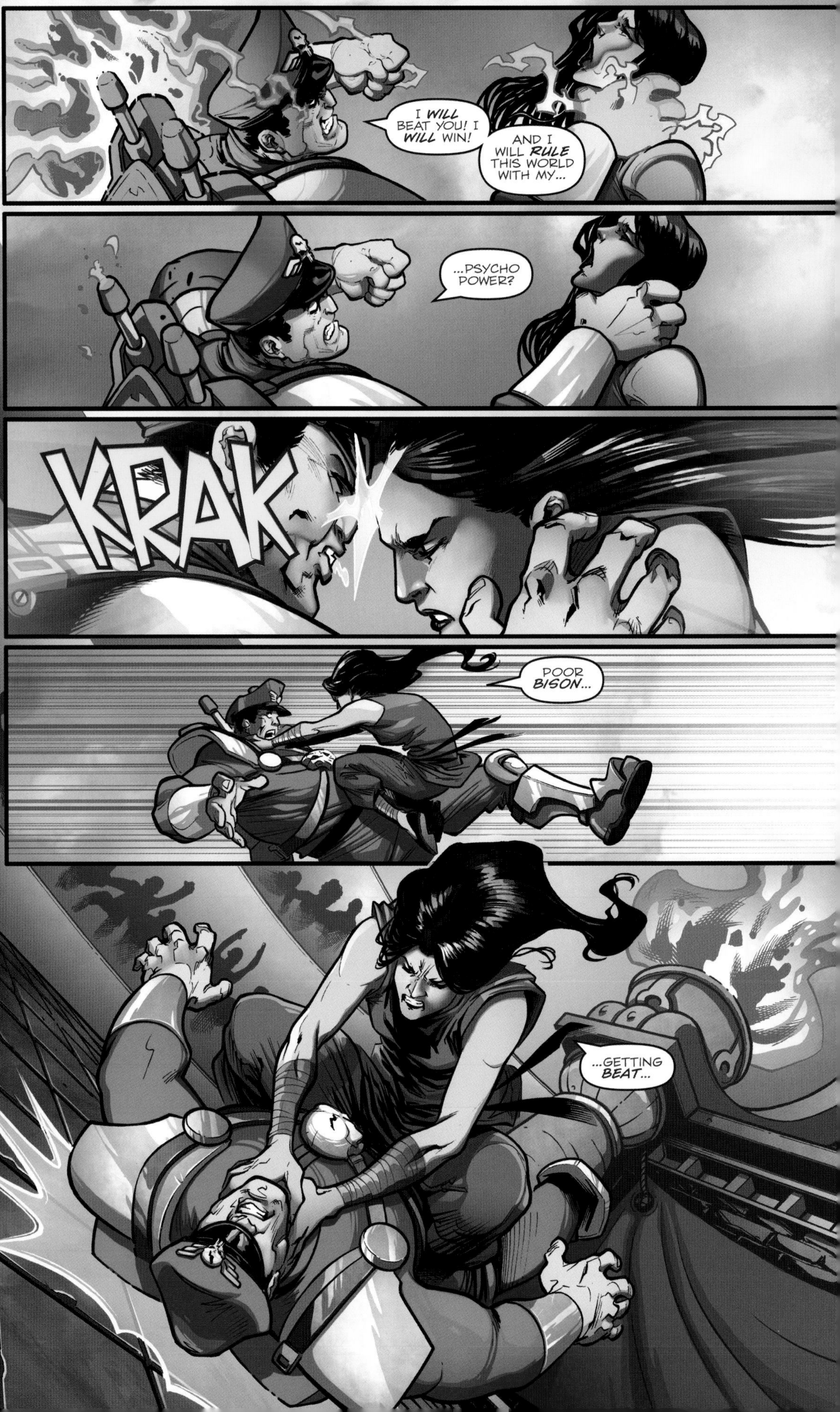
I WILL BEAT YOU! I WILL WIN!
AND I WILL RULE THIS WORLD WITH MY...
...PSYCHO POWER?
KRAK
POOR BISON...
...GETTING BEAT...

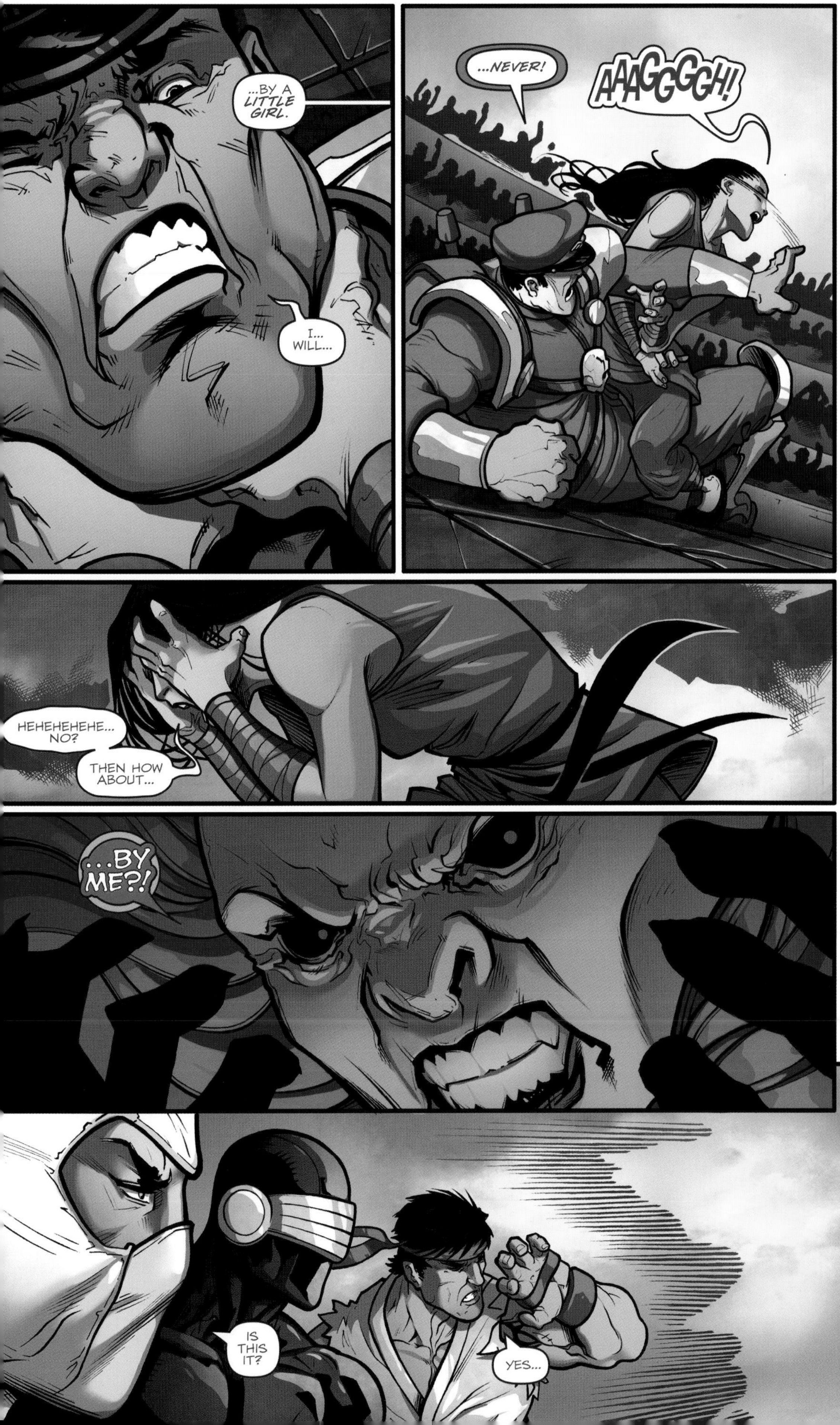
...BY A LITTLE GIRL.
I... WILL...
...NEVER!
AAAGGGGH!
HEHEHEHEHE... NO?
THEN HOW ABOUT...
...BY ME?!
IS THIS IT?
YES...

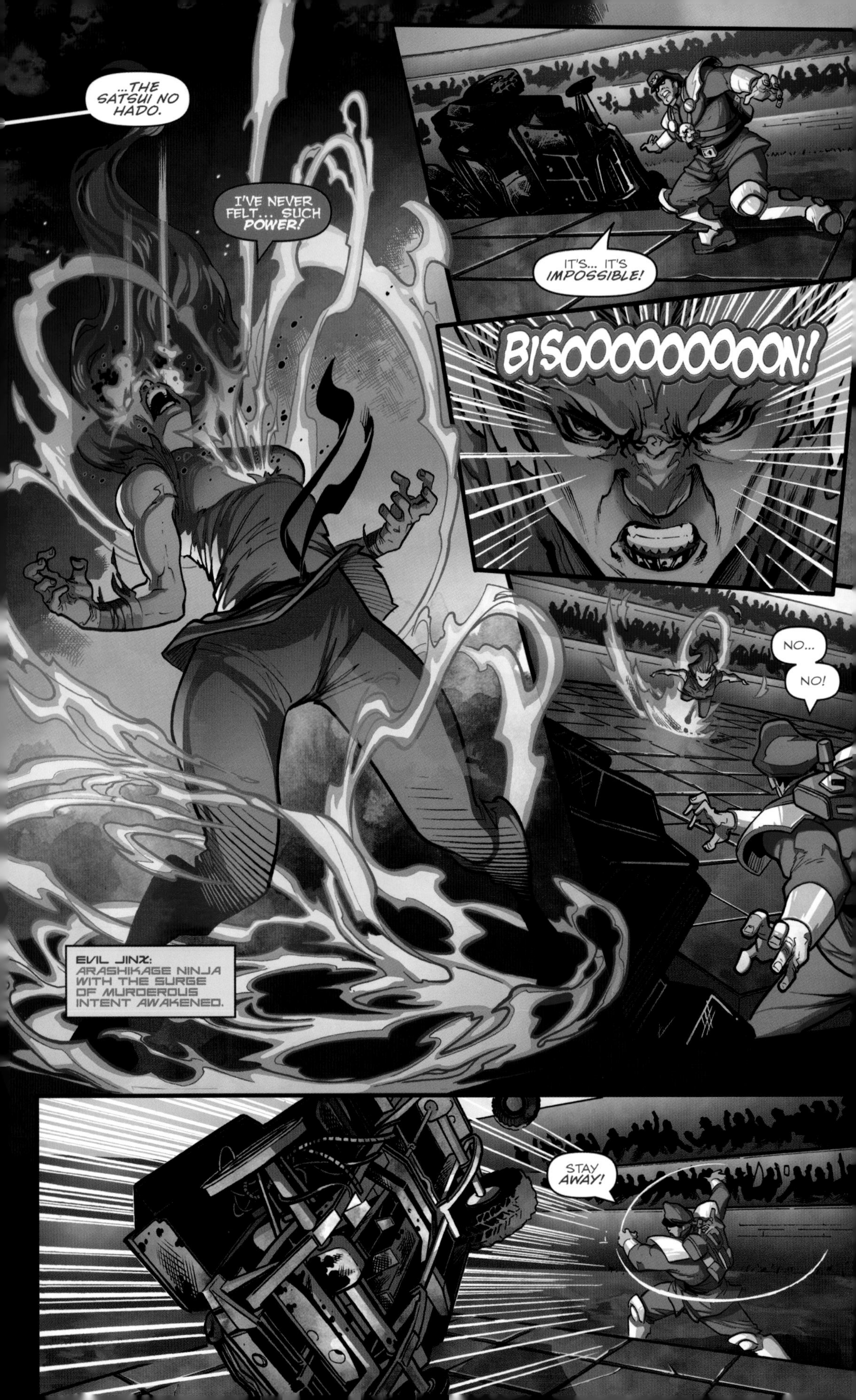

...THE SATSUI NO HADO.
I'VE NEVER FELT... SUCH POWER!
EVIL JINX: ARASHIKAGE NINJA WITH THE SURGE OF MURDEROUS INTENT AWAKENED.
IT'S... IT'S IMPOSSIBLE!
BISOOOOOOOOON!
NO...
NO!
STAY AWAY!

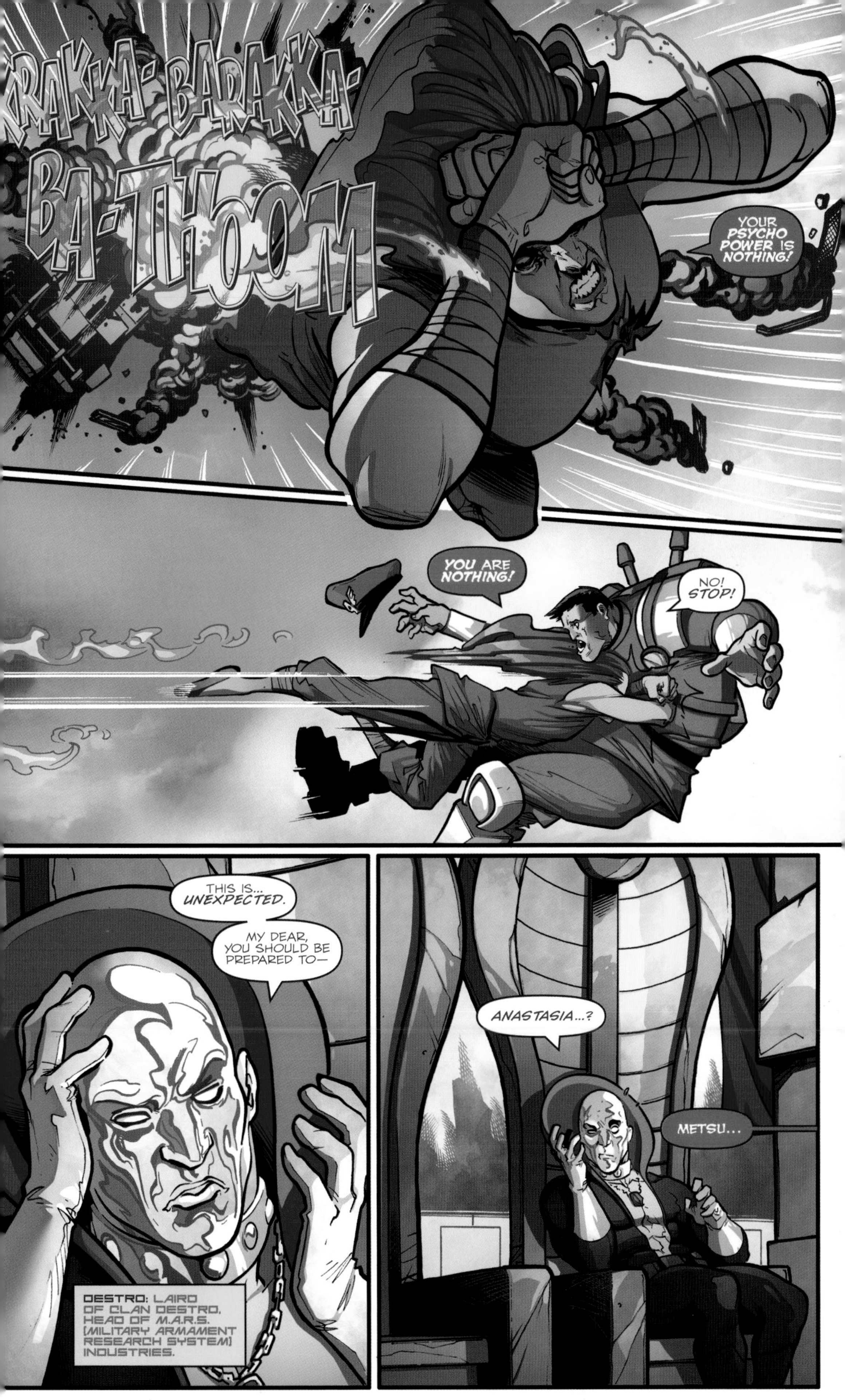
BRAKKA-BADAKKA-
BA-THOOM
YOUR PSYCHO POWER IS NOTHING!
YOU ARE NOTHING!
NO! STOP!
THIS IS... UNEXPECTED.
MY DEAR, YOU SHOULD BE PREPARED TO—
DESTRO: LAIRD OF CLAN DESTRO, HEAD OF M.A.R.S. [MILITARY ARMAMENT RESEARCH SYSTEM] INDUSTRIES.
ANASTASIA...?
METSU...

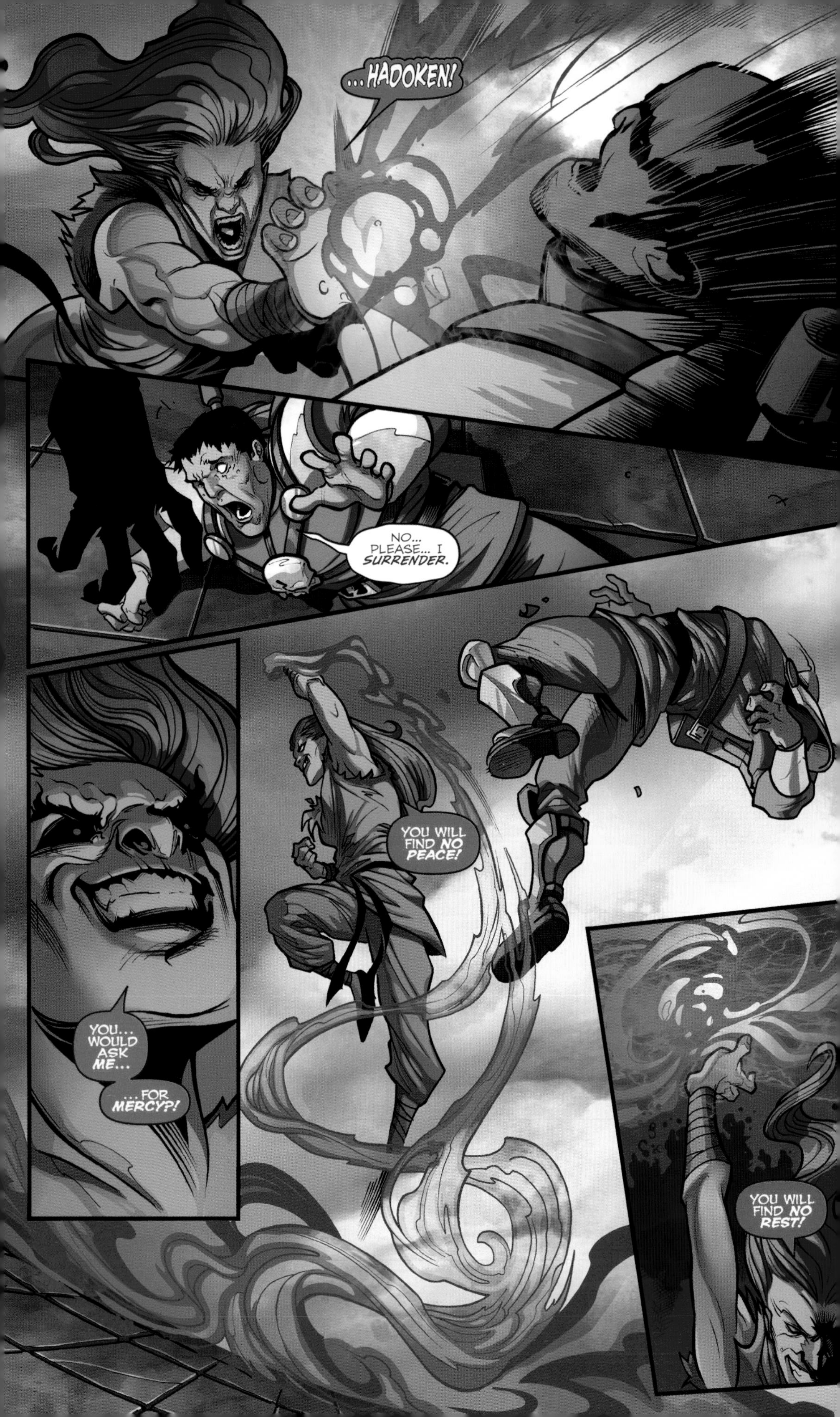
...HADOKEN!
NO... PLEASE... I SURRENDER.
YOU... WOULD ASK ME...
...FOR MERCY?!
YOU WILL FIND NO PEACE!
YOU WILL FIND NO REST!

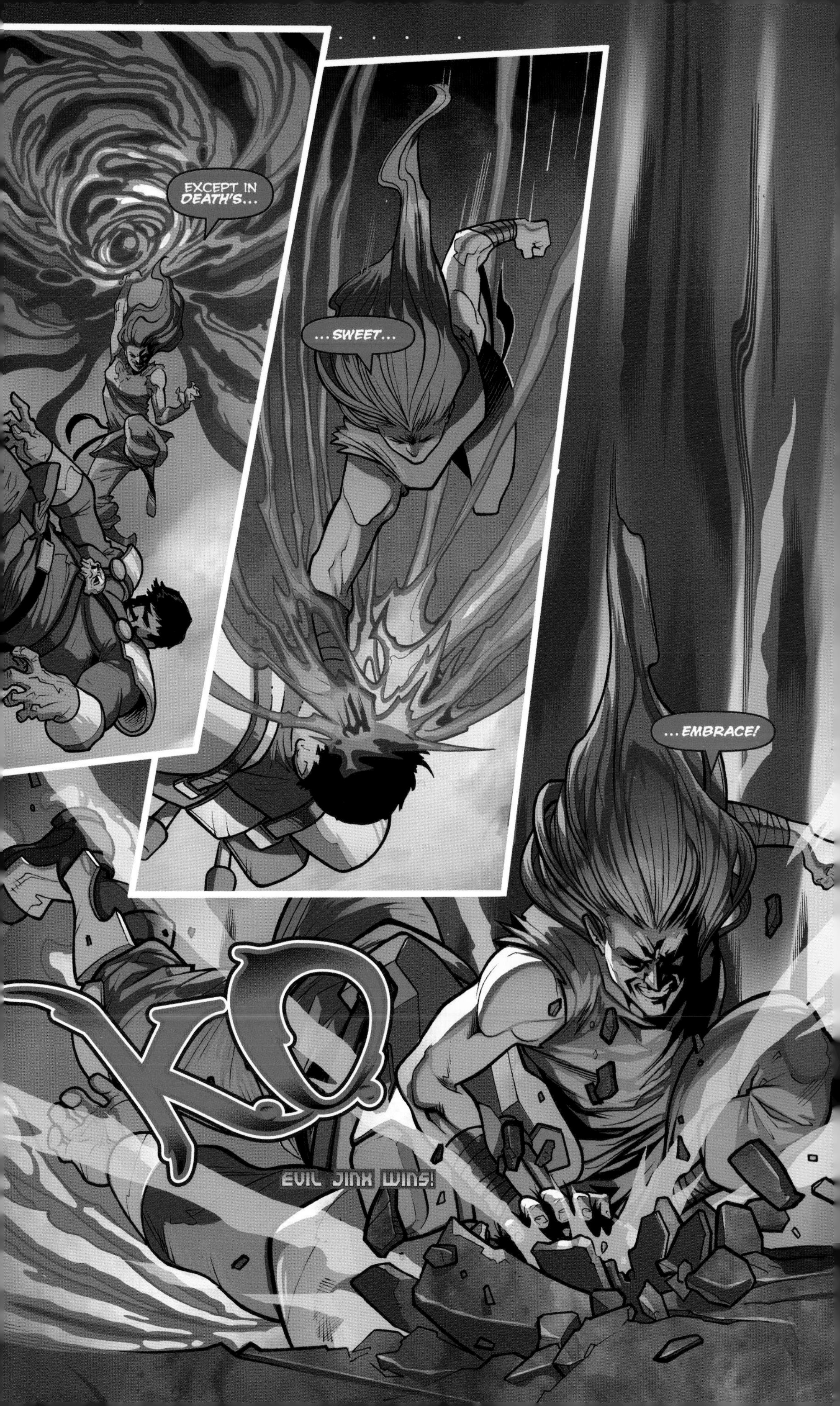
EXCEPT IN DEATH'S...
...SWEET...
...EMBRACE!
KO
EVIL JINX WINS!

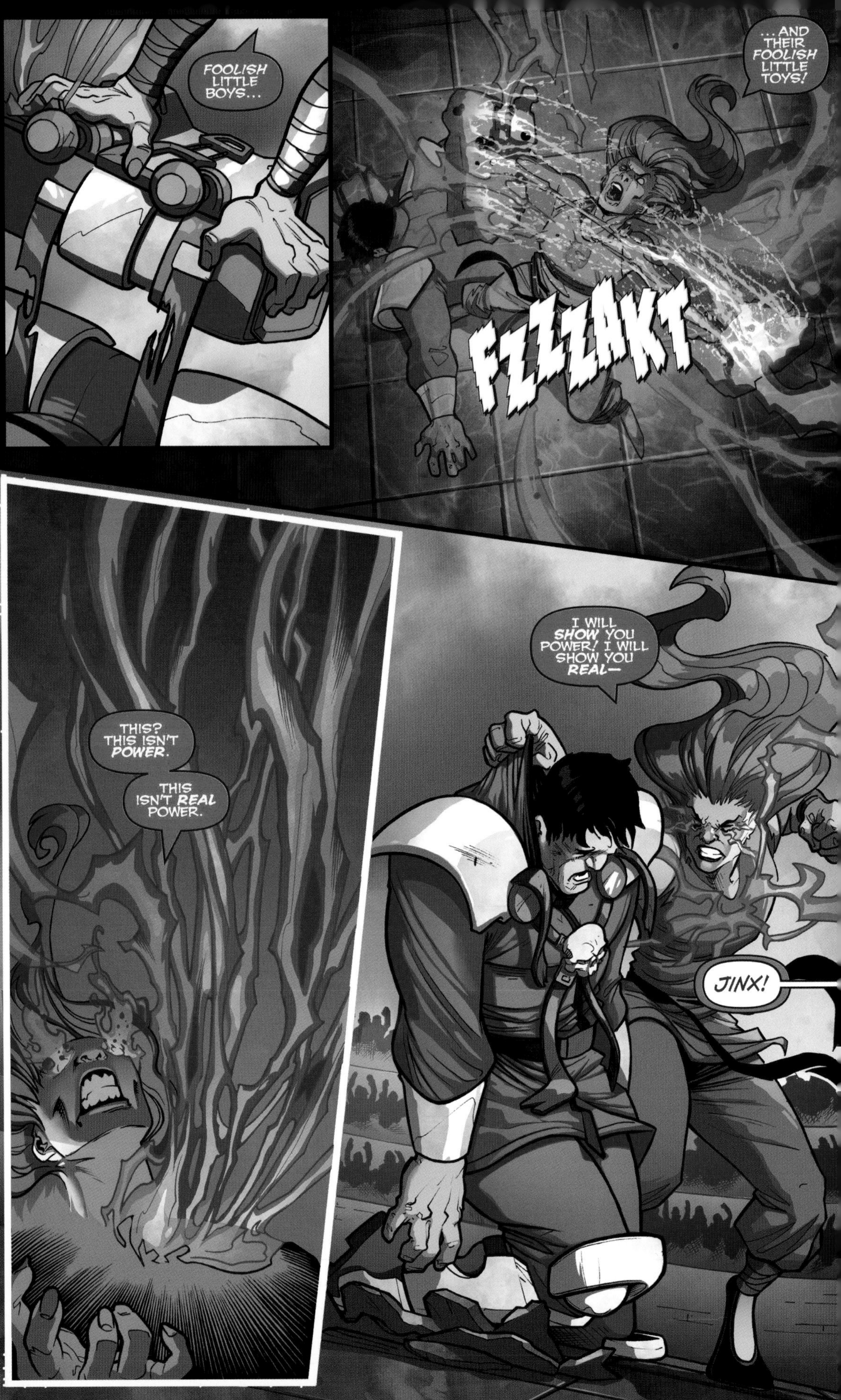
FOOLISH LITTLE BOYS...
...AND THEIR FOOLISH LITTLE TOYS!
FZZZAKT
I WILL SHOW YOU POWER! I WILL SHOW YOU REAL—
THIS? THIS ISN'T POWER.
THIS ISN'T REAL POWER.
JINX!

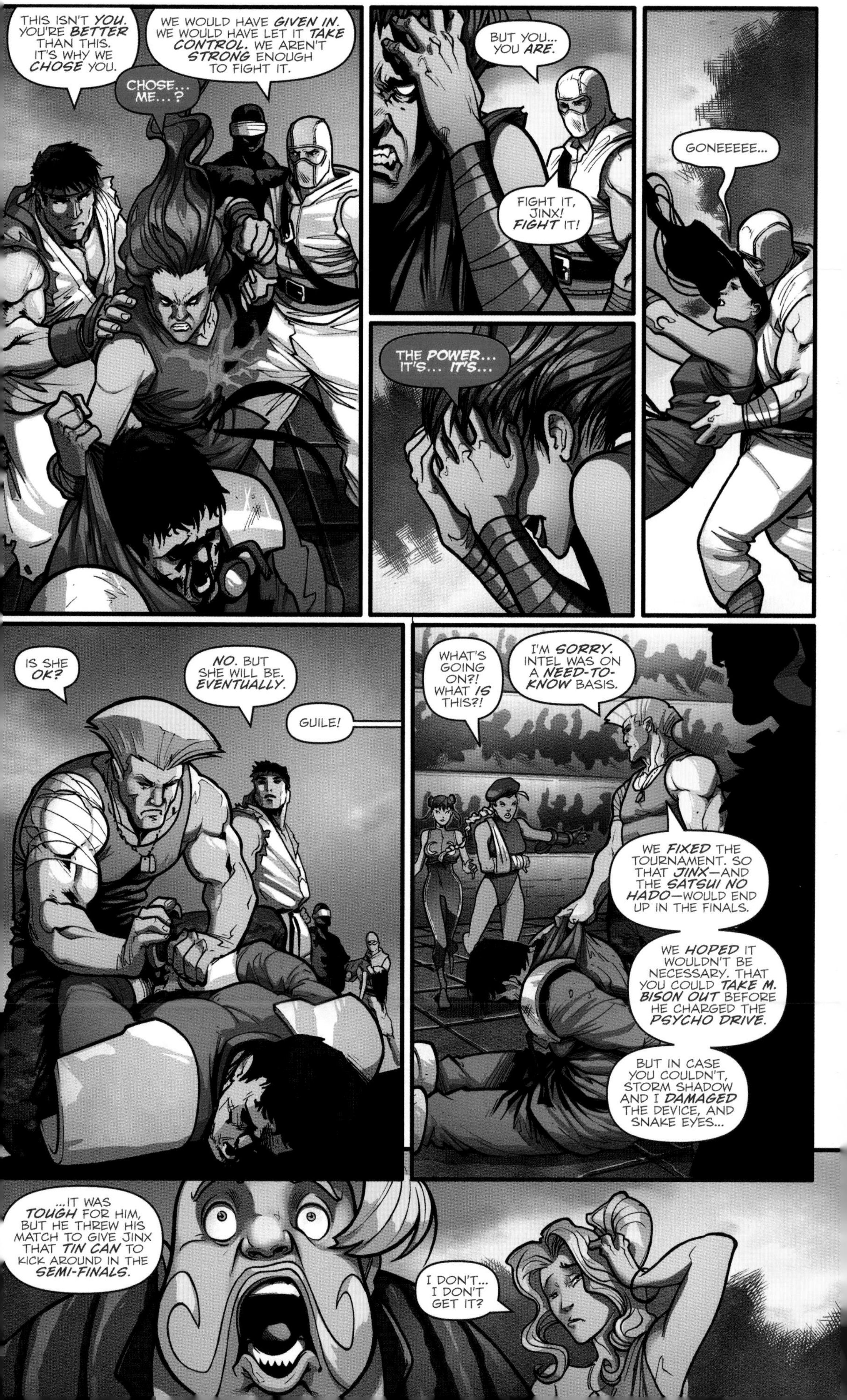
THIS ISN'T YOU. YOU'RE BETTER THAN THIS. IT'S WHY WE CHOSE YOU.
WE WOULD HAVE GIVEN IN. WE WOULD HAVE LET IT TAKE CONTROL. WE AREN'T STRONG ENOUGH TO FIGHT IT.
CHOSE... ME...?
BUT YOU... YOU ARE.
FIGHT IT, JINX! FIGHT IT!
THE POWER... IT'S... IT'S...
GONEEEEE...
IS SHE OK?
NO. BUT SHE WILL BE. EVENTUALLY.
GUILE!
WHAT'S GOING ON?! WHAT IS THIS?!
I'M SORRY. INTEL WAS ON A NEED-TO-KNOW BASIS.
WE FIXED THE TOURNAMENT. SO THAT JINX—AND THE SATSUI NO HADO—WOULD END UP IN THE FINALS.
WE HOPED IT WOULDN'T BE NECESSARY. THAT YOU COULD TAKE M. BISON OUT BEFORE HE CHARGED THE PSYCHO DRIVE.
BUT IN CASE YOU COULDN'T, STORM SHADOW AND I DAMAGED THE DEVICE, AND SNAKE EYES...
...IT WAS TOUGH FOR HIM, BUT HE THREW HIS MATCH TO GIVE JINX THAT TIN CAN TO KICK AROUND IN THE SEMI-FINALS.
I DON'T... I DON'T GET IT?

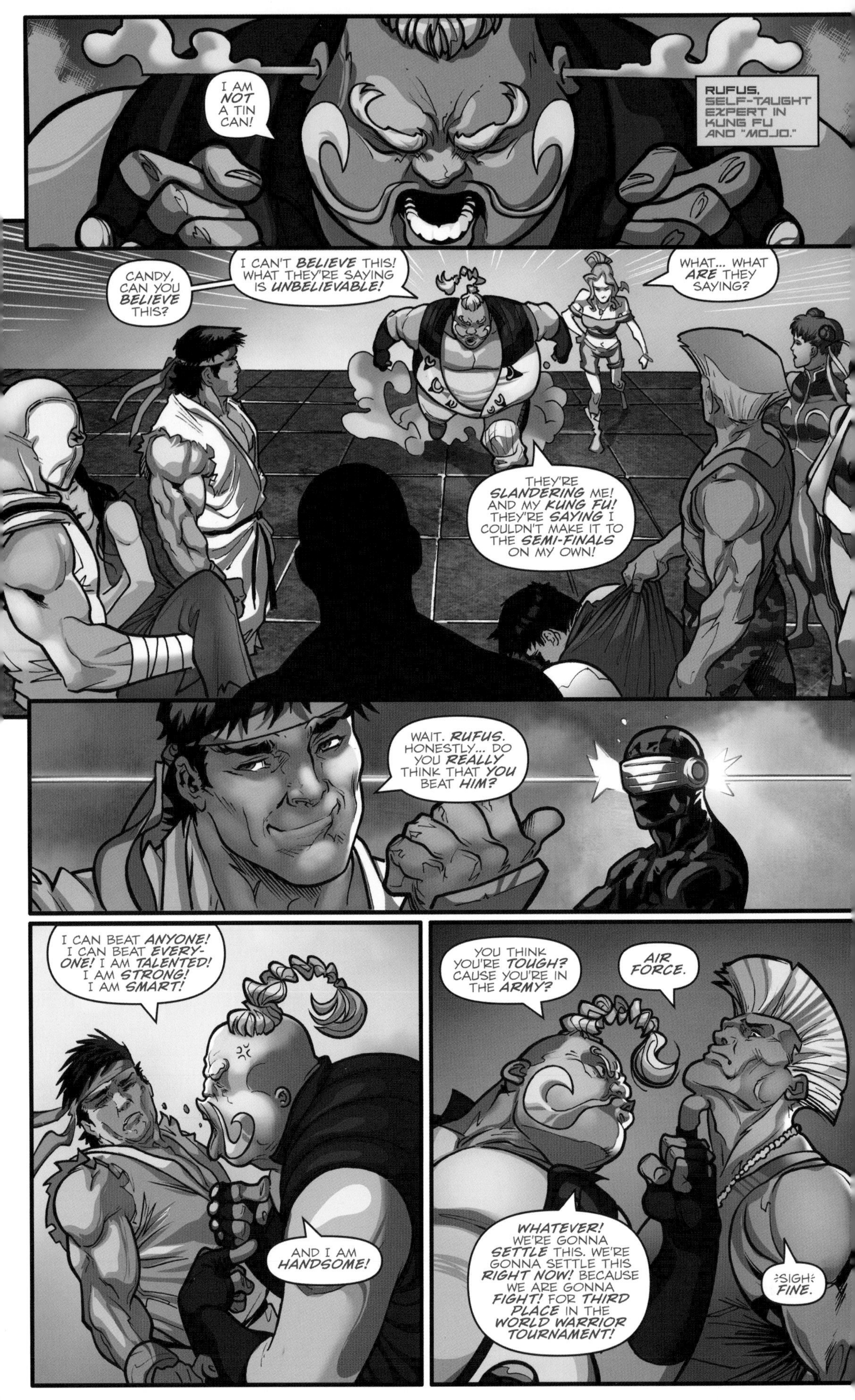
I AM NOT A TIN CAN!
RUFUS, SELF-TAUGHT EXPERT IN KUNG FU AND "MOJO."
CANDY, CAN YOU BELIEVE THIS?
I CAN'T BELIEVE THIS! WHAT THEY'RE SAYING IS UNBELIEVABLE!
WHAT... WHAT ARE THEY SAYING?
THEY'RE SLANDERING ME! AND MY KUNG FU! THEY'RE SAYING I COULDN'T MAKE IT TO THE SEMI-FINALS ON MY OWN!
WAIT. RUFUS. HONESTLY... DO YOU REALLY THINK THAT YOU BEAT HIM?
I CAN BEAT ANYONE! I CAN BEAT EVERY-ONE! I AM TALENTED! I AM STRONG! I AM SMART!
AND I AM HANDSOME!
YOU THINK YOU'RE TOUGH? CAUSE YOU'RE IN THE ARMY?
AIR FORCE.
WHATEVER! WE'RE GONNA SETTLE THIS. WE'RE GONNA SETTLE THIS RIGHT NOW! BECAUSE WE ARE GONNA FIGHT! FOR THIRD PLACE IN THE WORLD WARRIOR TOURNAMENT!
SIGH FINE.

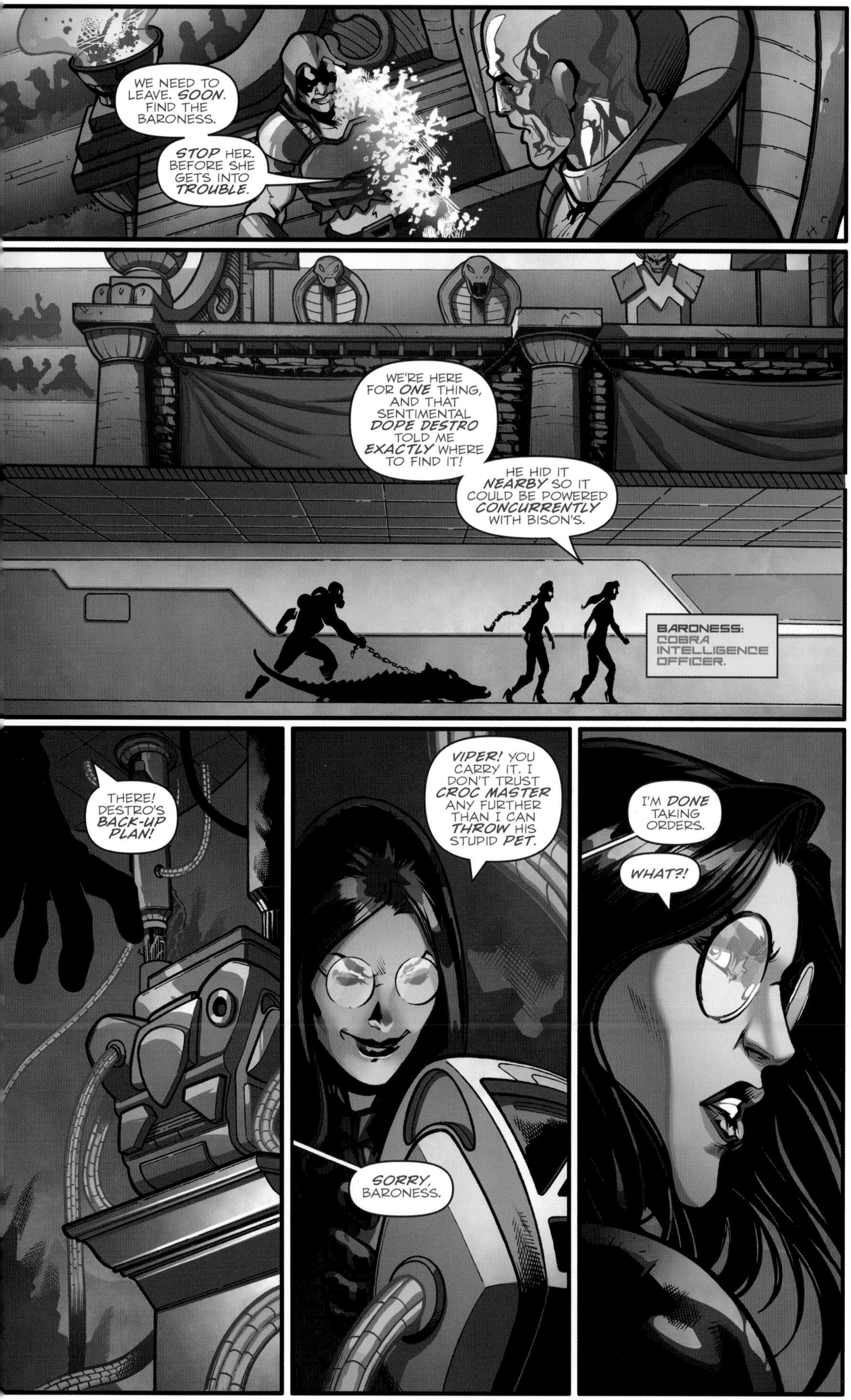
WE NEED TO LEAVE. SOON. FIND THE BARONESS.
STOP HER. BEFORE SHE GETS INTO TROUBLE.
WE'RE HERE FOR ONE THING, AND THAT SENTIMENTAL DOPE DESTRO TOLD ME EXACTLY WHERE TO FIND IT!
HE HID IT NEARBY SO IT COULD BE POWERED CONCURRENTLY WITH BISON'S.
BARONESS: COBRA INTELLIGENCE OFFICER.
THERE! DESTRO'S BACK-UP PLAN!
VIPER! YOU CARRY IT. I DON'T TRUST CROC MASTER ANY FURTHER THAN I CAN THROW HIS STUPID PET.
SORRY, BARONESS.
I'M DONE TAKING ORDERS.
WHAT?!

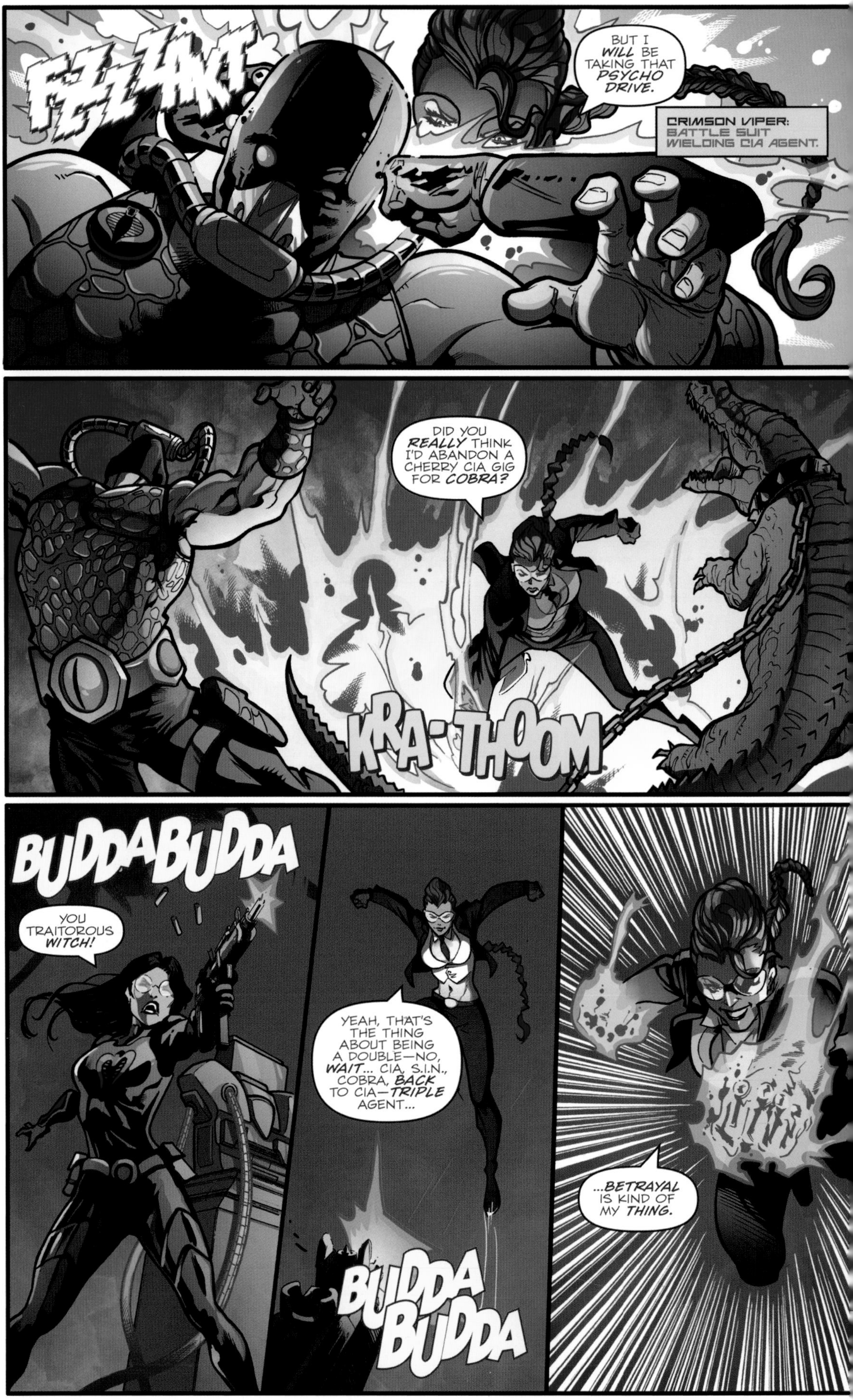
FZZZAKT
BUT I WILL BE TAKING THAT PSYCHO DRIVE.
CRIMSON VIPER: BATTLE SUIT WIELDING CIA AGENT.
DID YOU REALLY THINK I'D ABANDON A CHERRY CIA GIG FOR COBRA?
KRA-THOOM
BUDDABUDDA
YOU TRAITOROUS WITCH!
YEAH, THAT'S THE THING ABOUT BEING A DOUBLE—NO, WAIT... CIA, S.I.N., COBRA, BACK TO CIA—TRIPLE AGENT...
BUDDA BUDDA
...BETRAYAL IS KIND OF MY THING.

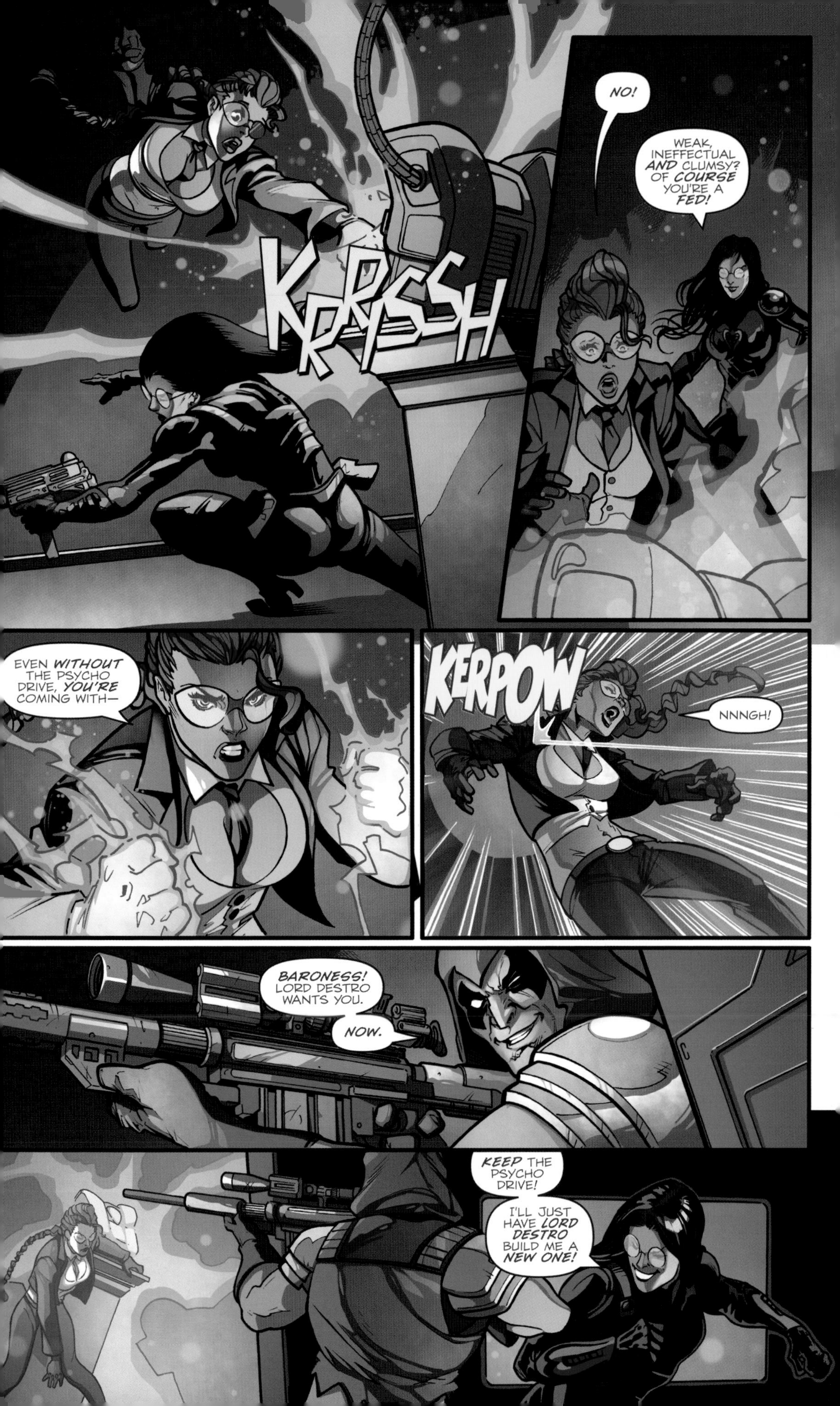
KRRISSH
NO!
WEAK, INEFFECTUAL AND CLUMSY? OF COURSE YOU'RE A FED!
EVEN WITHOUT THE PSYCHO DRIVE, YOU'RE COMING WITH—
KERPOW
NNNGH!
BARONESS! LORD DESTRO WANTS YOU.
NOW.
KEEP THE PSYCHO DRIVE!
I'LL JUST HAVE LORD DESTRO BUILD ME A NEW ONE!

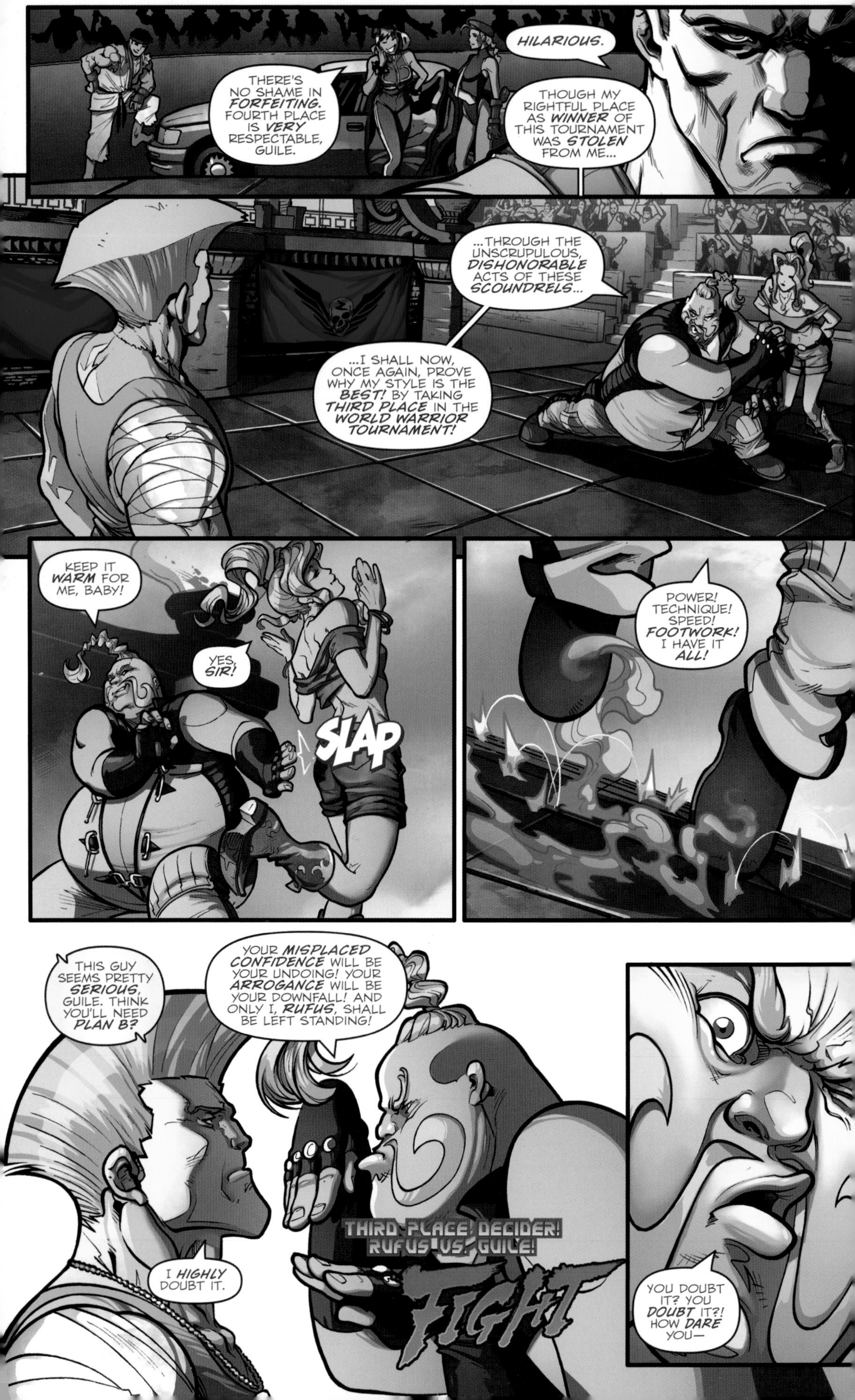

THERE'S NO SHAME IN FORFEITING. FOURTH PLACE IS VERY RESPECTABLE, GUILE.
HILARIOUS.
THOUGH MY RIGHTFUL PLACE AS WINNER OF THIS TOURNAMENT WAS STOLEN FROM ME...
...THROUGH THE UNSCRUPULOUS, DISHONORABLE ACTS OF THESE SCOUNDRELS...
...I SHALL NOW, ONCE AGAIN, PROVE WHY MY STYLE IS THE BEST! BY TAKING THIRD PLACE IN THE WORLD WARRIOR TOURNAMENT!
KEEP IT WARM FOR ME, BABY!
YES, SIR!
SLAP
POWER! TECHNIQUE! SPEED! FOOTWORK! I HAVE IT ALL!
THIS GUY SEEMS PRETTY SERIOUS, GUILE. THINK YOU'LL NEED PLAN B?
YOUR MISPLACED CONFIDENCE WILL BE YOUR UNDOING! YOUR ARROGANCE WILL BE YOUR DOWNFALL! AND ONLY I, RUFUS, SHALL BE LEFT STANDING!
I HIGHLY DOUBT IT.
THIRD PLACE DECIDER! RUFUS VS. GUILE!
FIGHT
YOU DOUBT IT? YOU DOUBT IT?! HOW DARE YOU—

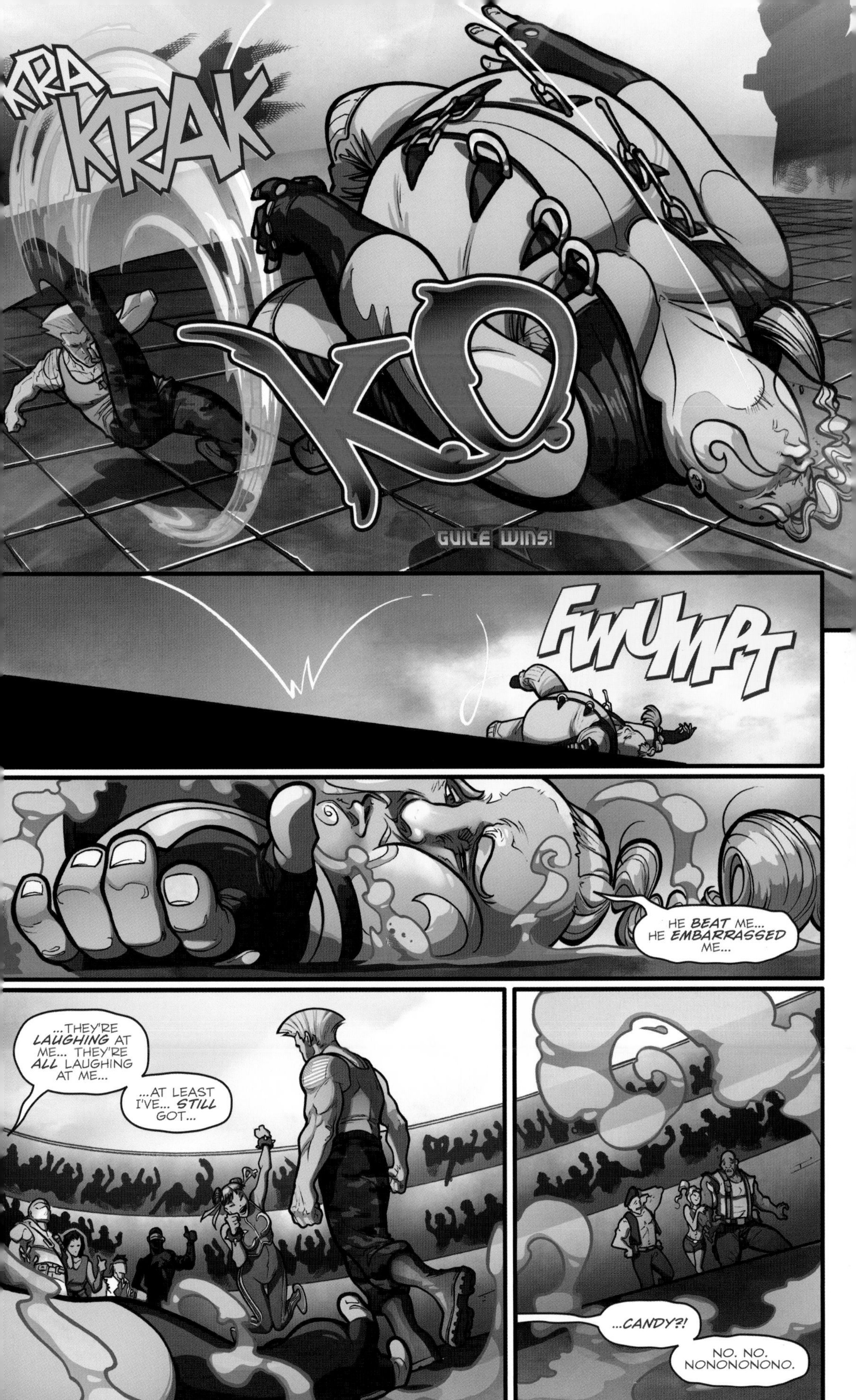
KRA KRAK
K.O.
GUILE WINS!
FWUMPT
HE BEAT ME... HE EMBARRASSED ME...
...THEY'RE LAUGHING AT ME... THEY'RE ALL LAUGHING AT ME...
...AT LEAST I'VE... STILL GOT...
...CANDY?!
NO. NO. NONONONONO.

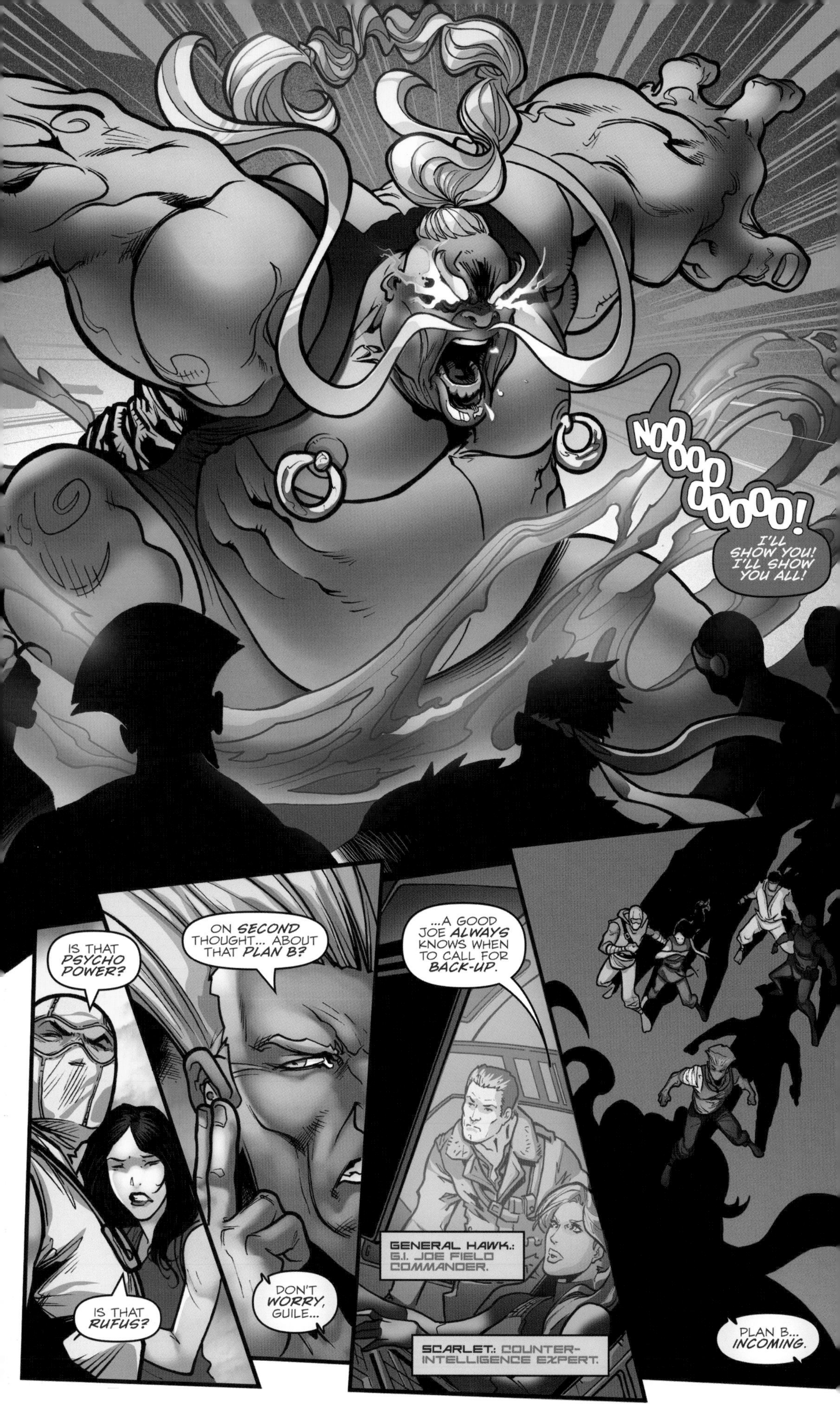
NOOOOOOOOOO!
I'LL SHOW YOU! I'LL SHOW YOU ALL!
IS THAT PSYCHO POWER?
IS THAT RUFUS?
ON SECOND THOUGHT... ABOUT THAT PLAN B?
DON'T WORRY, GUILE...
...A GOOD JOE ALWAYS KNOWS WHEN TO CALL FOR BACK-UP.
GENERAL HAWK.: G.I. JOE FIELD COMMANDER.
SCARLET.: COUNTER-INTELLIGENCE EXPERT.
PLAN B... INCOMING.

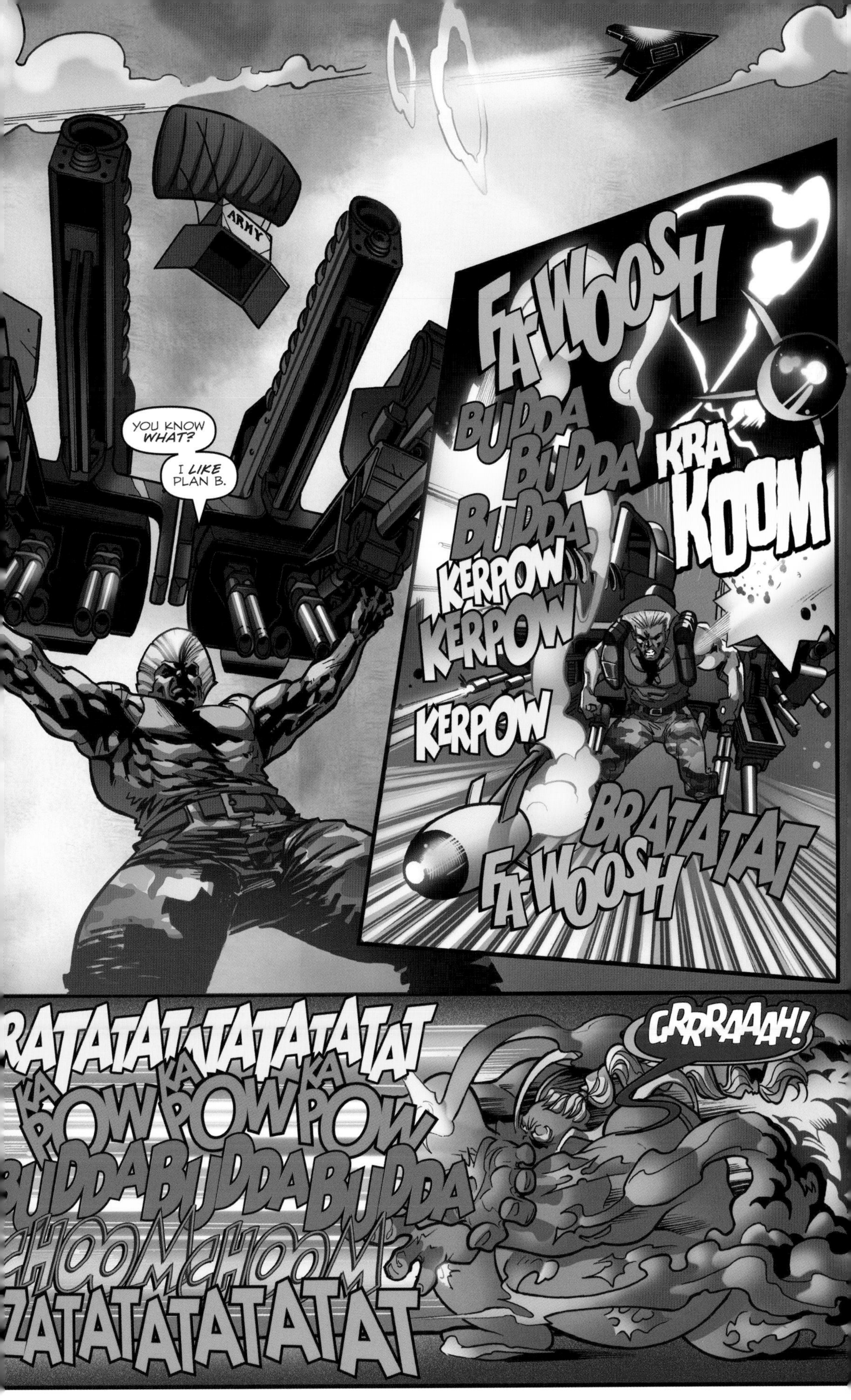
YOU KNOW WHAT?
I LIKE PLAN B.
FA-WOOSH
BUDDA BUDDA BUDDA
KRA KOOM
KERPOW KERPOW
KERPOW
BRATATAT
FA-WOOSH
RATATATATATATATATAT
KA POW KA POW KA POW
BUDDA BUDDA BUDDA
CHOOM CHOOM
ZATATATATATATAT
GRRRAAAH!

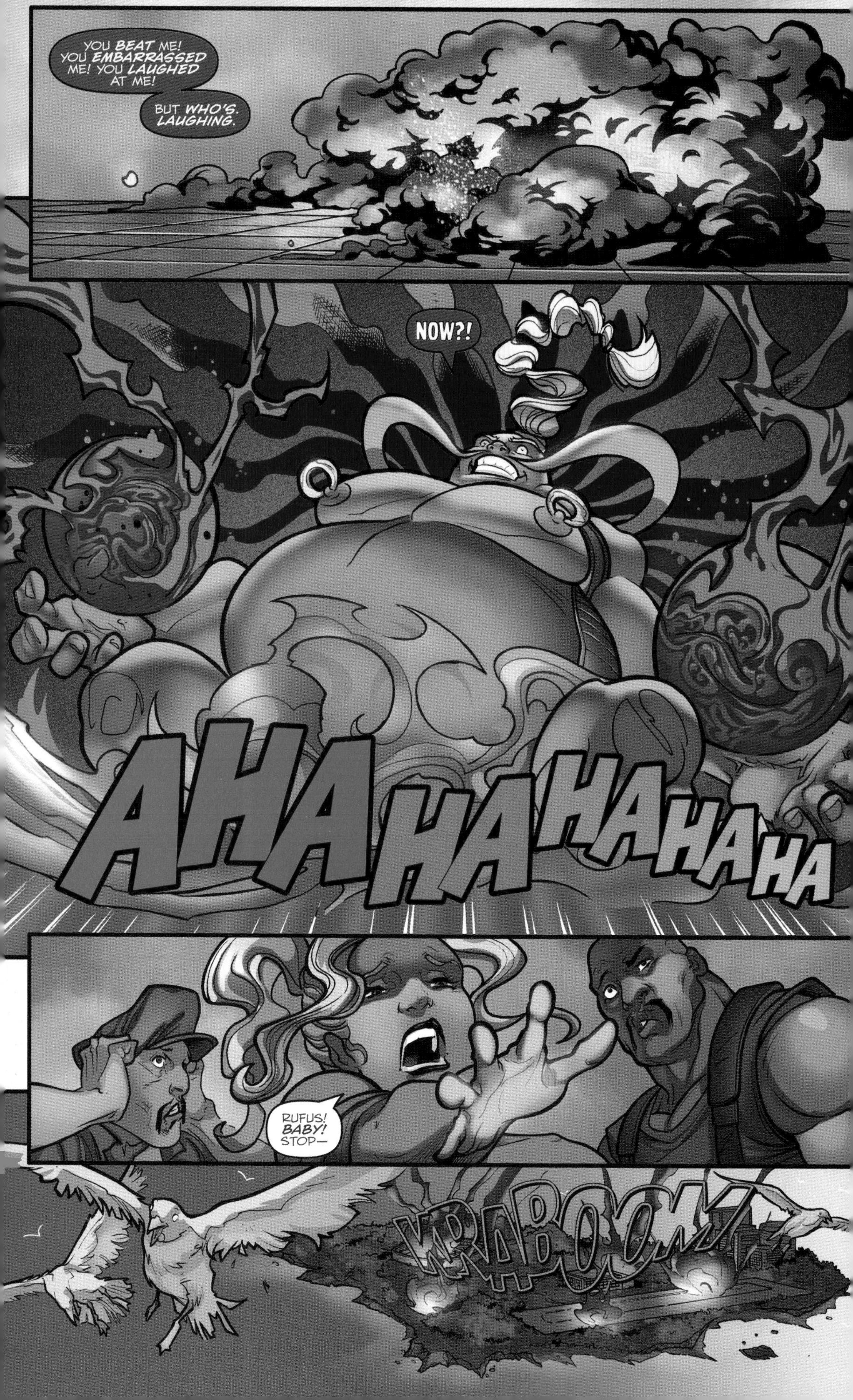
YOU BEAT ME! YOU EMBARRASSED ME! YOU LAUGHED AT ME!
BUT WHO'S. LAUGHING.
NOW?!
AHAHAHAHAHAHA
RUFUS! BABY! STOP—
KRABOOM!

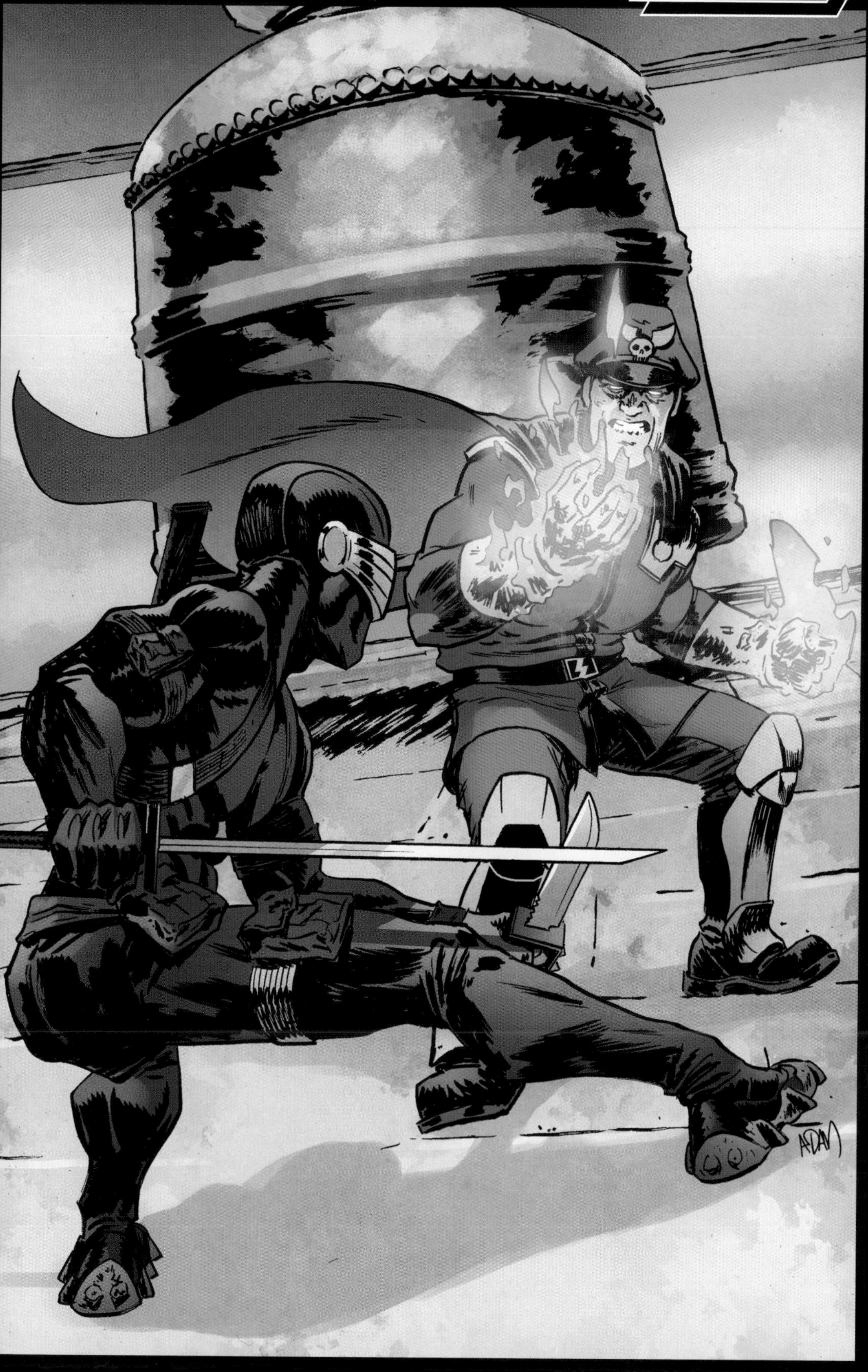
ADAM

CHAPTER 6

WORLD WARRIOR TOURNAMENT BRACKET

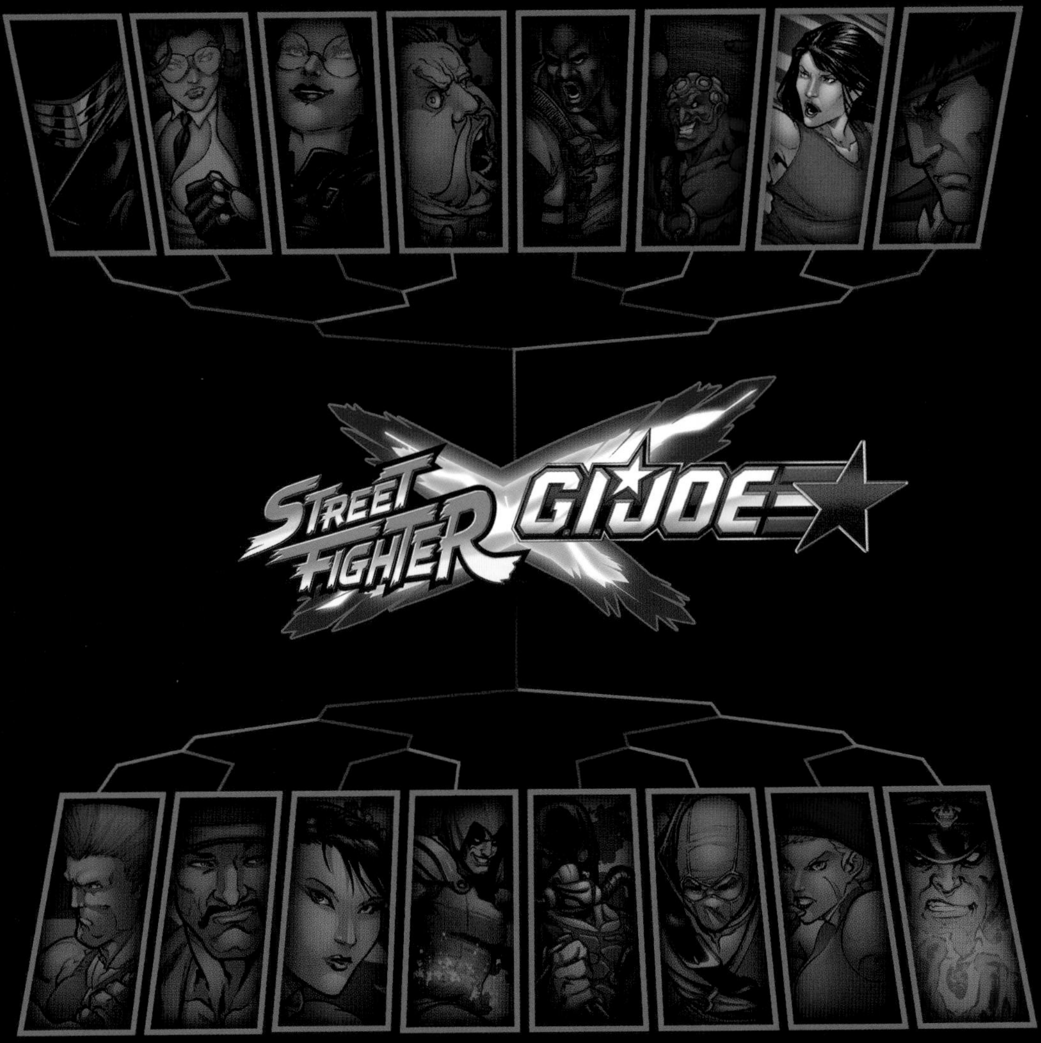
STREET FIGHTER
G.I. JOE

JINX

WINNER!

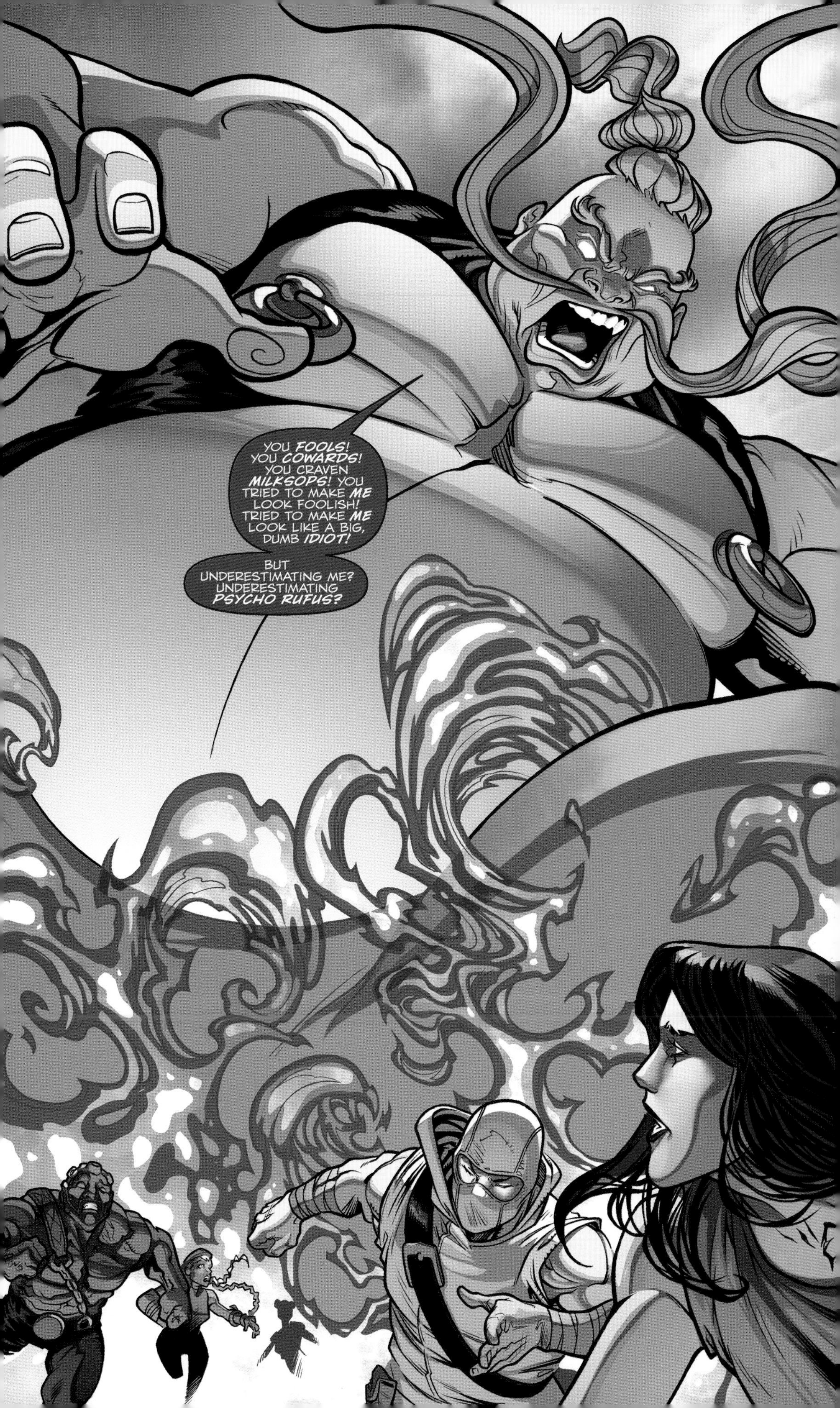
YOU FOOLS! YOU COWARDS! YOU CRAVEN MILKSOPS! YOU TRIED TO MAKE ME LOOK FOOLISH! TRIED TO MAKE ME LOOK LIKE A BIG, DUMB IDIOT!
BUT UNDERESTIMATING ME? UNDERESTIMATING PSYCHO RUFUS?

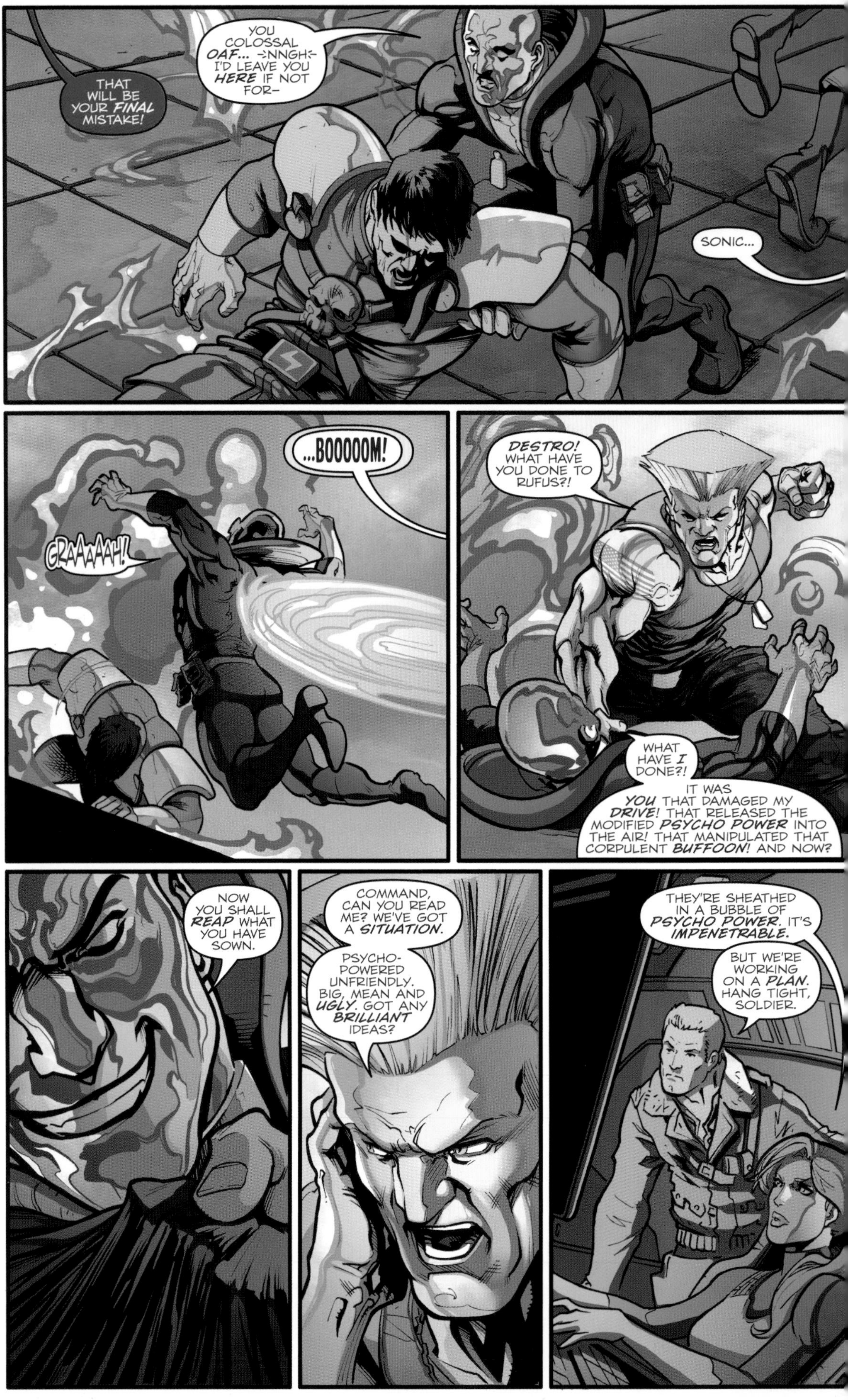
THAT WILL BE YOUR FINAL MISTAKE!
YOU COLOSSAL OAF... -NNGH- I'D LEAVE YOU HERE IF NOT FOR-
SONIC...
...BOOOOOM!
GRAAAAAH!
DESTRO! WHAT HAVE YOU DONE TO RUFUS?!
WHAT HAVE I DONE?!
IT WAS YOU THAT DAMAGED MY DRIVE! THAT RELEASED THE MODIFIED PSYCHO POWER INTO THE AIR! THAT MANIPULATED THAT CORPULENT BUFFOON! AND NOW?
NOW YOU SHALL REAP WHAT YOU HAVE SOWN.
COMMAND, CAN YOU READ ME? WE'VE GOT A SITUATION.
PSYCHO-POWERED UNFRIENDLY. BIG, MEAN AND UGLY. GOT ANY BRILLIANT IDEAS?
THEY'RE SHEATHED IN A BUBBLE OF PSYCHO POWER. IT'S IMPENETRABLE.
BUT WE'RE WORKING ON A PLAN. HANG TIGHT, SOLDIER.

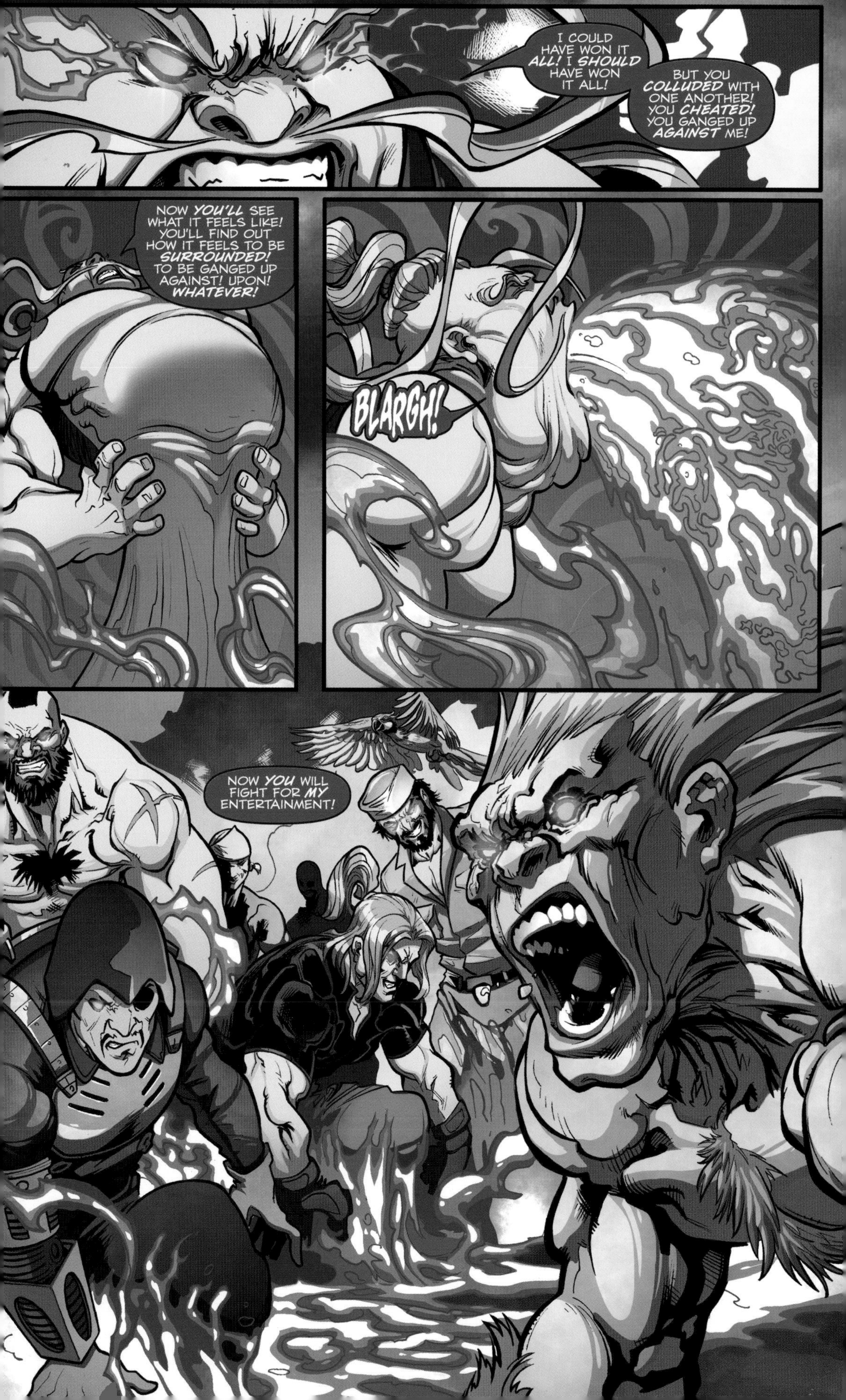
I COULD HAVE WON IT ALL! I SHOULD HAVE WON IT ALL!
BUT YOU COLLUDED WITH ONE ANOTHER! YOU CHEATED! YOU GANGED UP AGAINST ME!
NOW YOU'LL SEE WHAT IT FEELS LIKE! YOU'LL FIND OUT HOW IT FEELS TO BE SURROUNDED! TO BE GANGED UP AGAINST! UPON! WHATEVER!
BLARGH!
NOW YOU WILL FIGHT FOR MY ENTERTAINMENT!

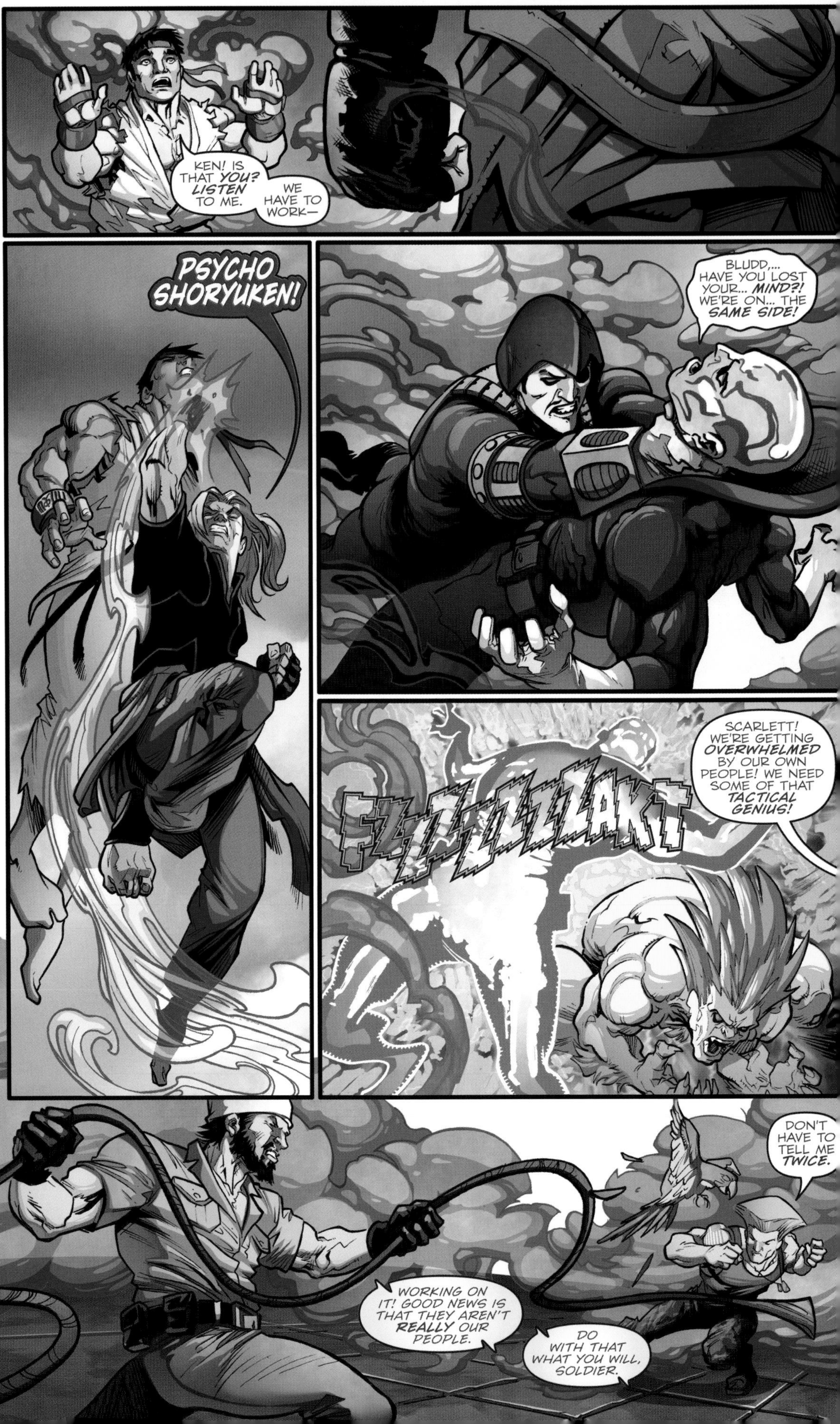
KEN! IS THAT YOU? LISTEN TO ME.
WE HAVE TO WORK—
PSYCHO SHORYUKEN!
BLUDD,... HAVE YOU LOST YOUR... MIND?! WE'RE ON... THE SAME SIDE!
SCARLETT! WE'RE GETTING OVERWHELMED BY OUR OWN PEOPLE! WE NEED SOME OF THAT TACTICAL GENIUS!
DON'T HAVE TO TELL ME TWICE.
WORKING ON IT! GOOD NEWS IS THAT THEY AREN'T REALLY OUR PEOPLE.
DO WITH THAT WHAT YOU WILL, SOLDIER.

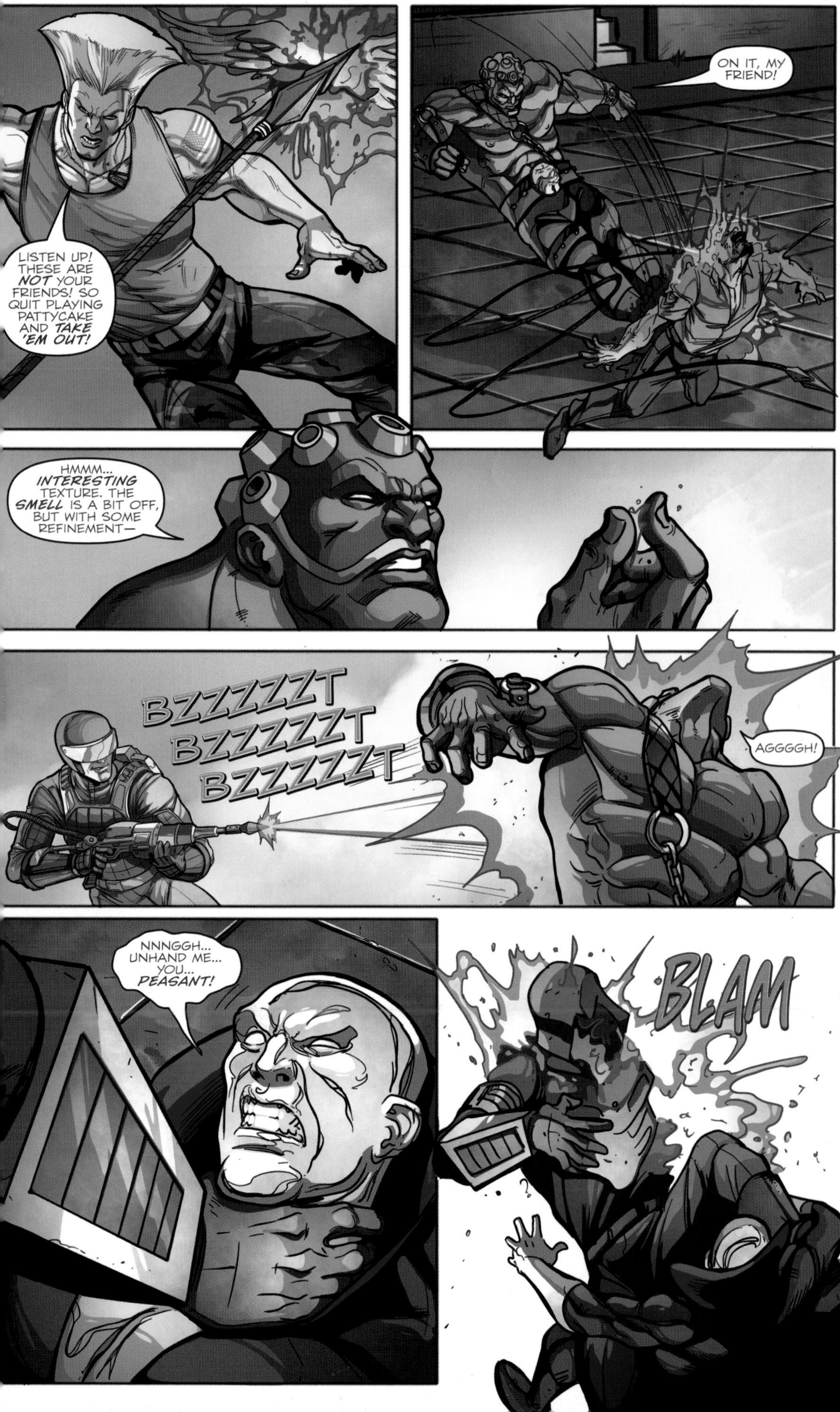
LISTEN UP! THESE ARE NOT YOUR FRIENDS! SO QUIT PLAYING PATTYCAKE AND TAKE 'EM OUT!
ON IT, MY FRIEND!
HMMM... INTERESTING TEXTURE. THE SMELL IS A BIT OFF, BUT WITH SOME REFINEMENT—
BZZZZZZT BZZZZZZT BZZZZZZT
AGGGGH!
NNNGGH... UNHAND ME... YOU... PEASANT!
BLAM

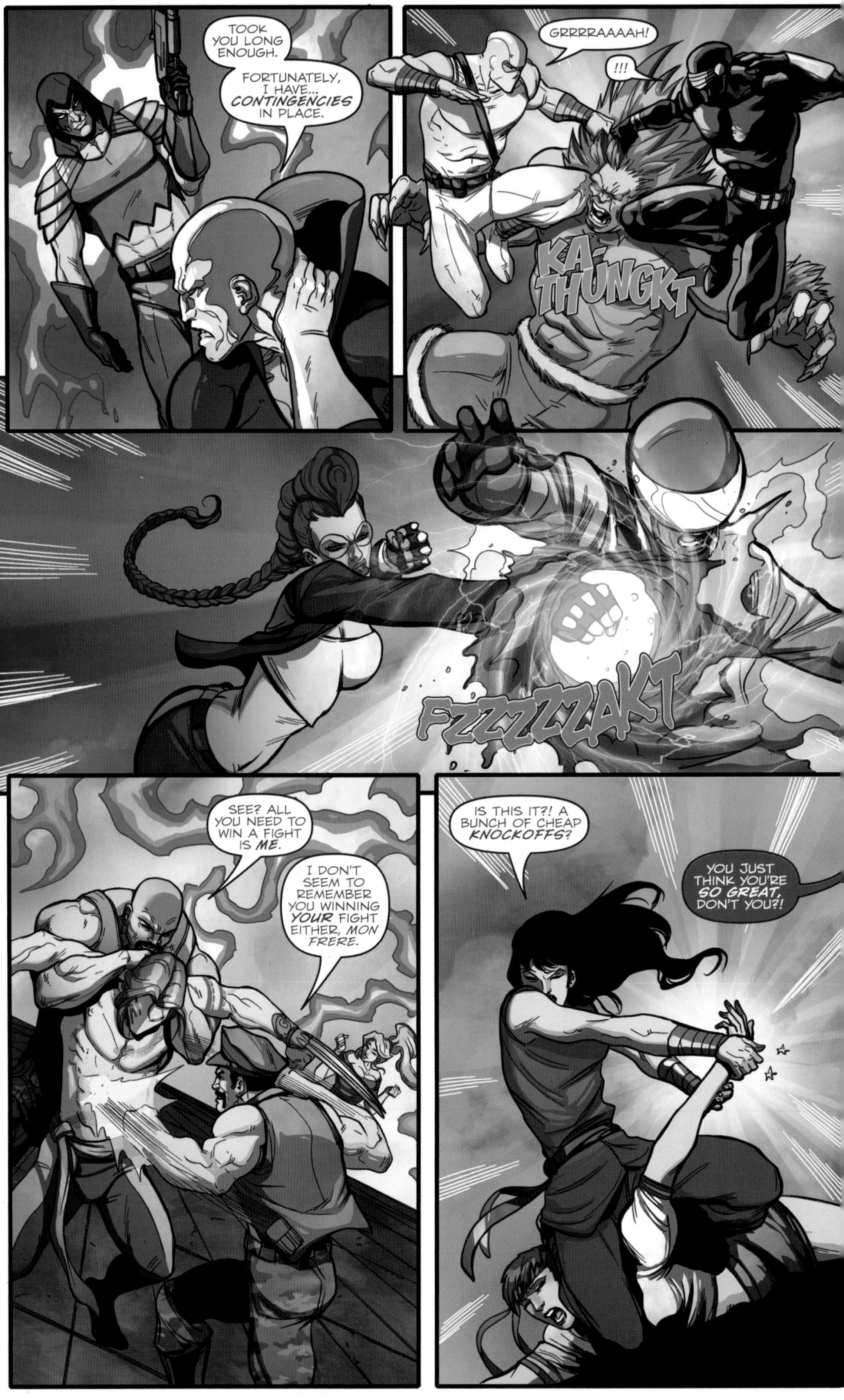
TOOK YOU LONG ENOUGH.
FORTUNATELY, I HAVE... CONTINGENCIES IN PLACE.
GRRRRAAAAH!
!!!
KA-THUNGKT
FZZZZZZAKT
SEE? ALL YOU NEED TO WIN A FIGHT IS ME.
I DON'T SEEM TO REMEMBER YOU WINNING YOUR FIGHT EITHER, MON FRERE.
IS THIS IT?! A BUNCH OF CHEAP KNOCKOFFS?
YOU JUST THINK YOU'RE SO GREAT, DON'T YOU?!

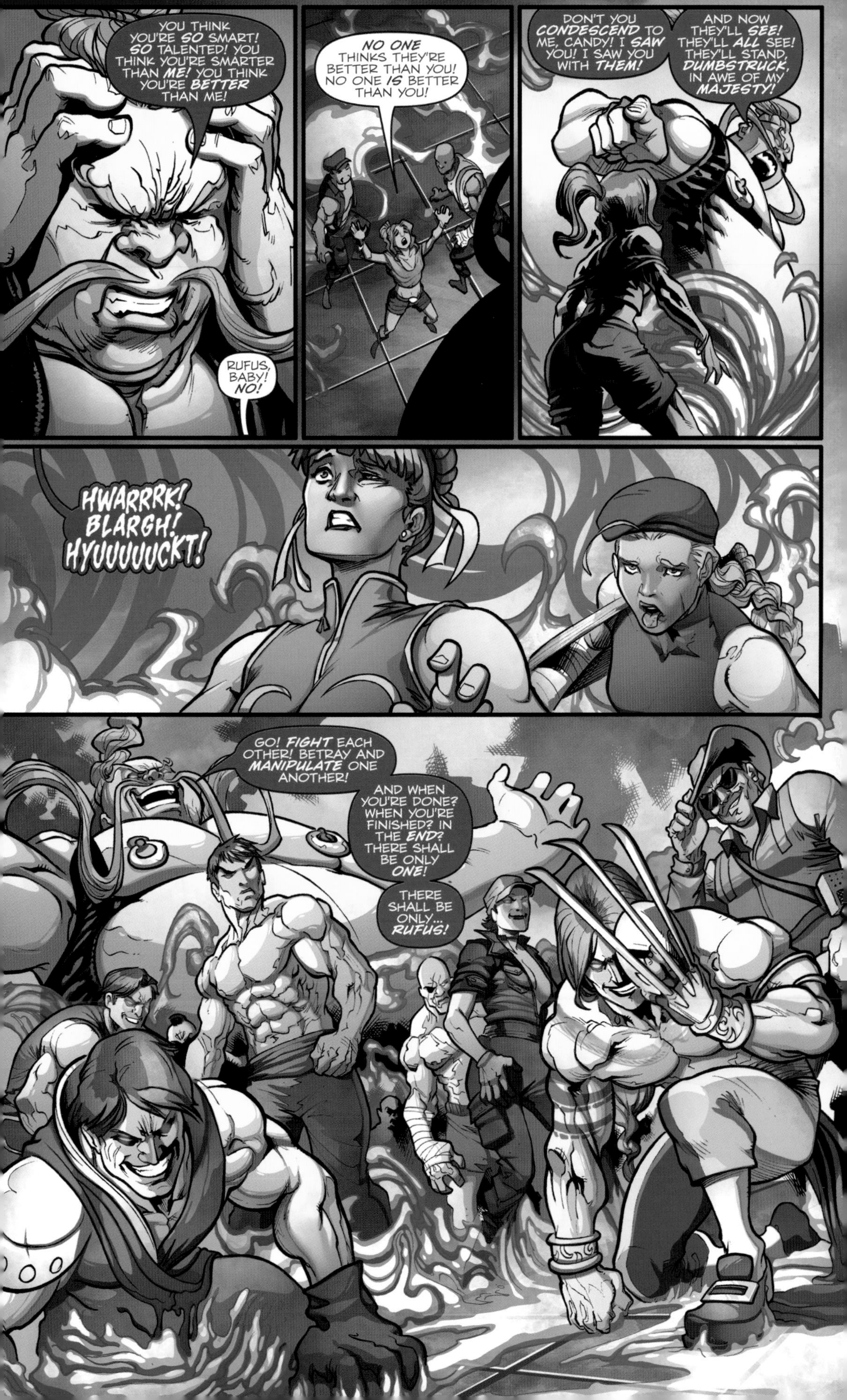
YOU THINK YOU'RE SO SMART! SO TALENTED! YOU THINK YOU'RE SMARTER THAN ME! YOU THINK YOU'RE BETTER THAN ME!
RUFUS, BABY! NO!
NO ONE THINKS THEY'RE BETTER THAN YOU! NO ONE IS BETTER THAN YOU!
DON'T YOU CONDESCEND TO ME, CANDY! I SAW YOU! I SAW YOU WITH THEM!
AND NOW THEY'LL SEE! THEY'LL ALL SEE! THEY'LL STAND, DUMBSTRUCK, IN AWE OF MY MAJESTY!
HWARRRK! BLARGH! HYUUUUUCKT!
GO! FIGHT EACH OTHER! BETRAY AND MANIPULATE ONE ANOTHER!
AND WHEN YOU'RE DONE? WHEN YOU'RE FINISHED? IN THE END? THERE SHALL BE ONLY ONE!
THERE SHALL BE ONLY... RUFUS!

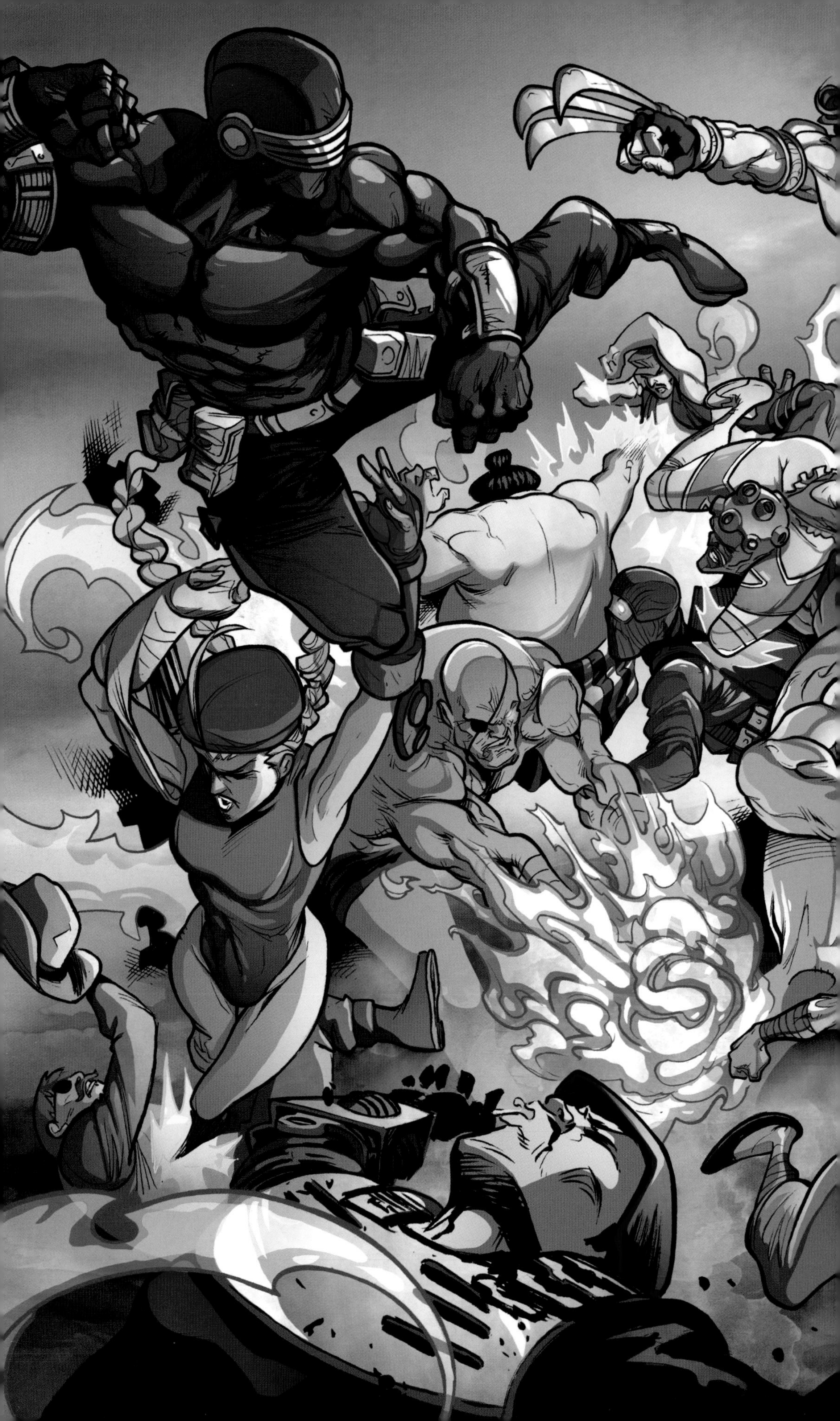

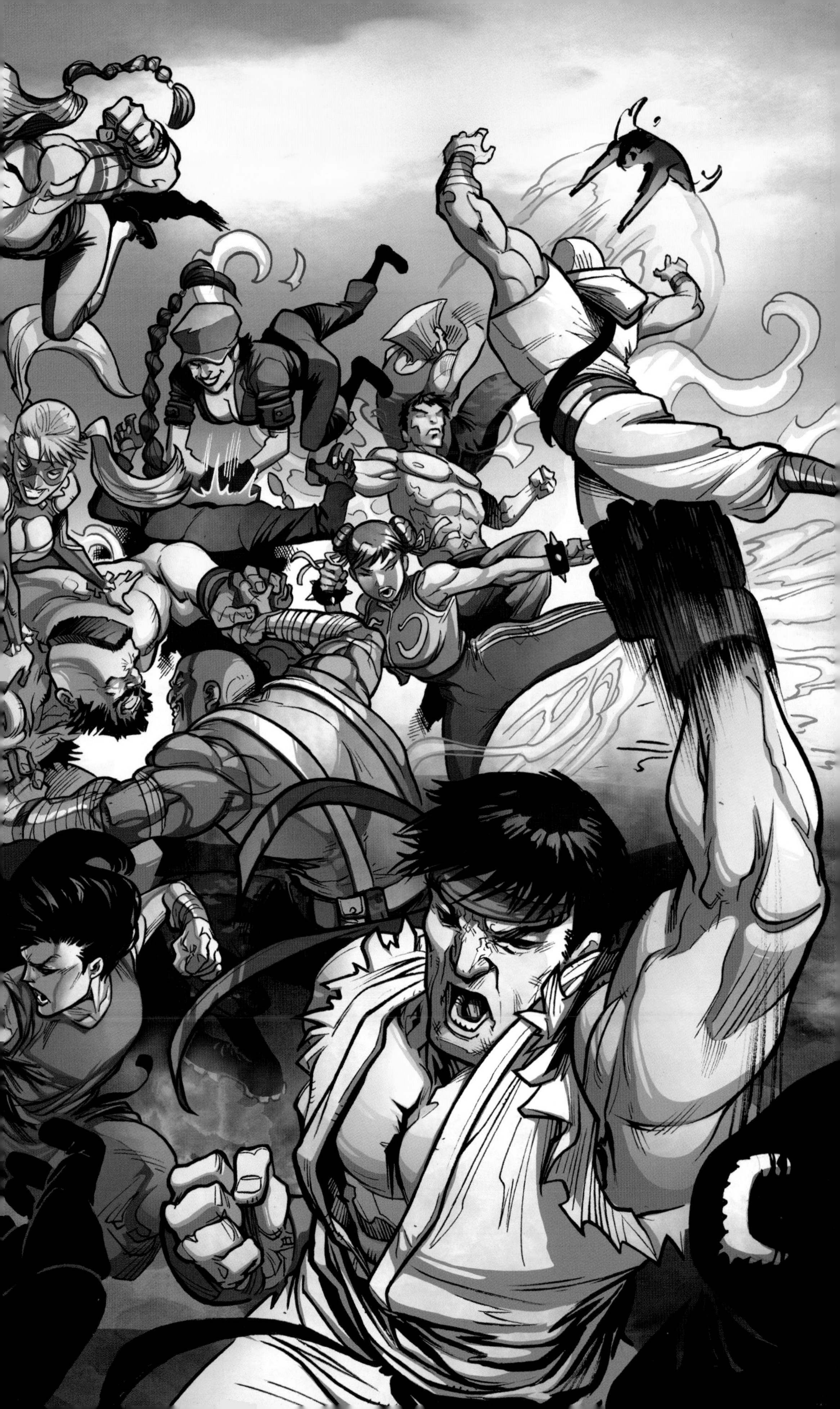

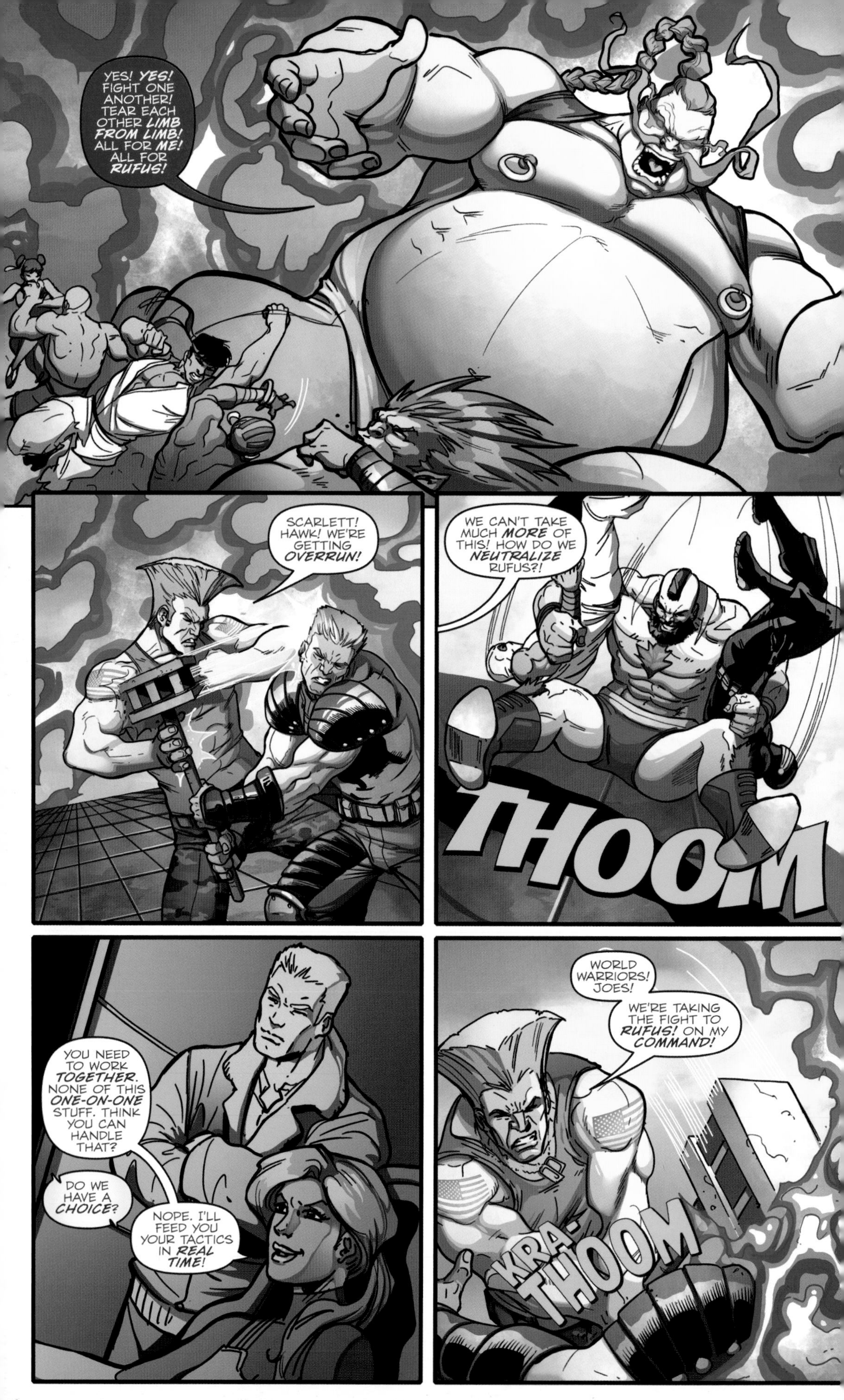

YES! YES! FIGHT ONE ANOTHER! TEAR EACH OTHER LIMB FROM LIMB! ALL FOR ME! ALL FOR RUFUS!
SCARLETT! HAWK! WE'RE GETTING OVERRUN!
WE CAN'T TAKE MUCH MORE OF THIS! HOW DO WE NEUTRALIZE RUFUS?!
THOOM
YOU NEED TO WORK TOGETHER. NONE OF THIS ONE-ON-ONE STUFF. THINK YOU CAN HANDLE THAT?
DO WE HAVE A CHOICE?
NOPE. I'LL FEED YOU YOUR TACTICS IN REAL TIME!
WORLD WARRIORS! JOES!
WE'RE TAKING THE FIGHT TO RUFUS! ON MY COMMAND!
KRA-THOOM

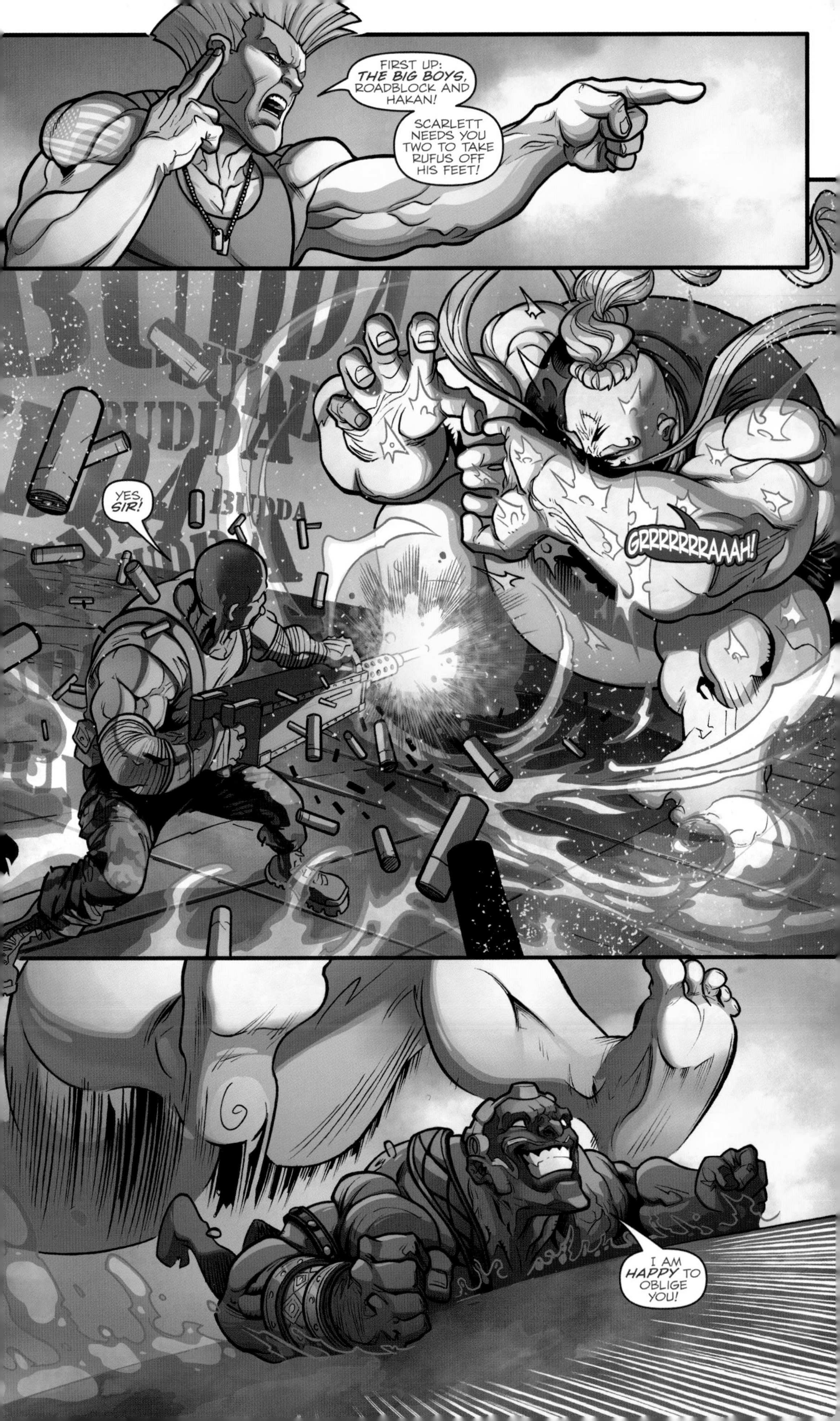
FIRST UP: THE BIG BOYS, ROADBLOCK AND HAKAN!
SCARLETT NEEDS YOU TWO TO TAKE RUFUS OFF HIS FEET!
BUDDA BUDDA BUDDA BUDDA
YES, SIR!
GRRRRRRRAAAH!
I AM HAPPY TO OBLIGE YOU!

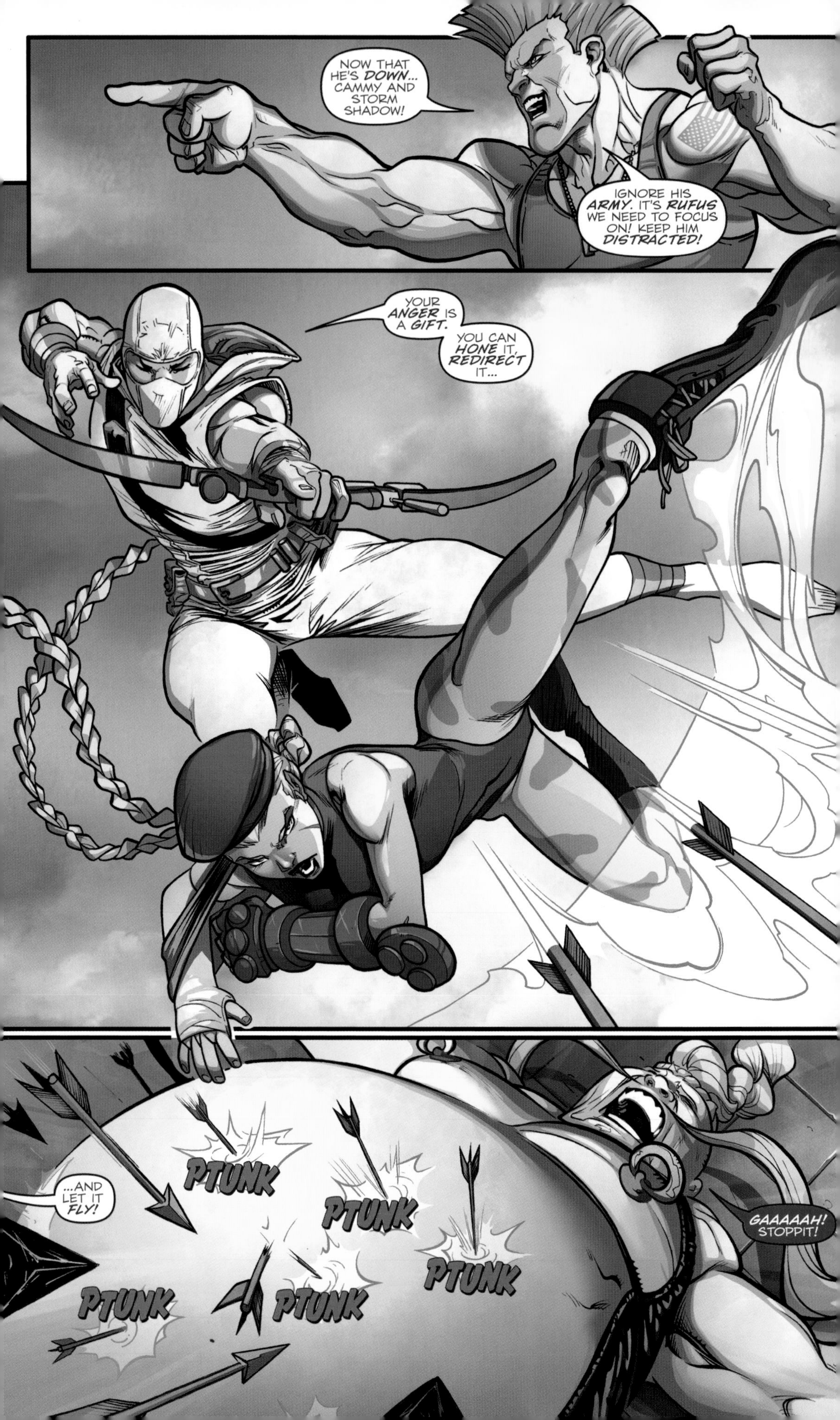
NOW THAT HE'S DOWN... CAMMY AND STORM SHADOW!
IGNORE HIS ARMY. IT'S RUFUS WE NEED TO FOCUS ON! KEEP HIM DISTRACTED!
YOUR ANGER IS A GIFT.
YOU CAN HONE IT, REDIRECT IT...
...AND LET IT FLY!
PTUNK
PTUNK
PTUNK
PTUNK
PTUNK
GAAAAAH! STOPPIT!

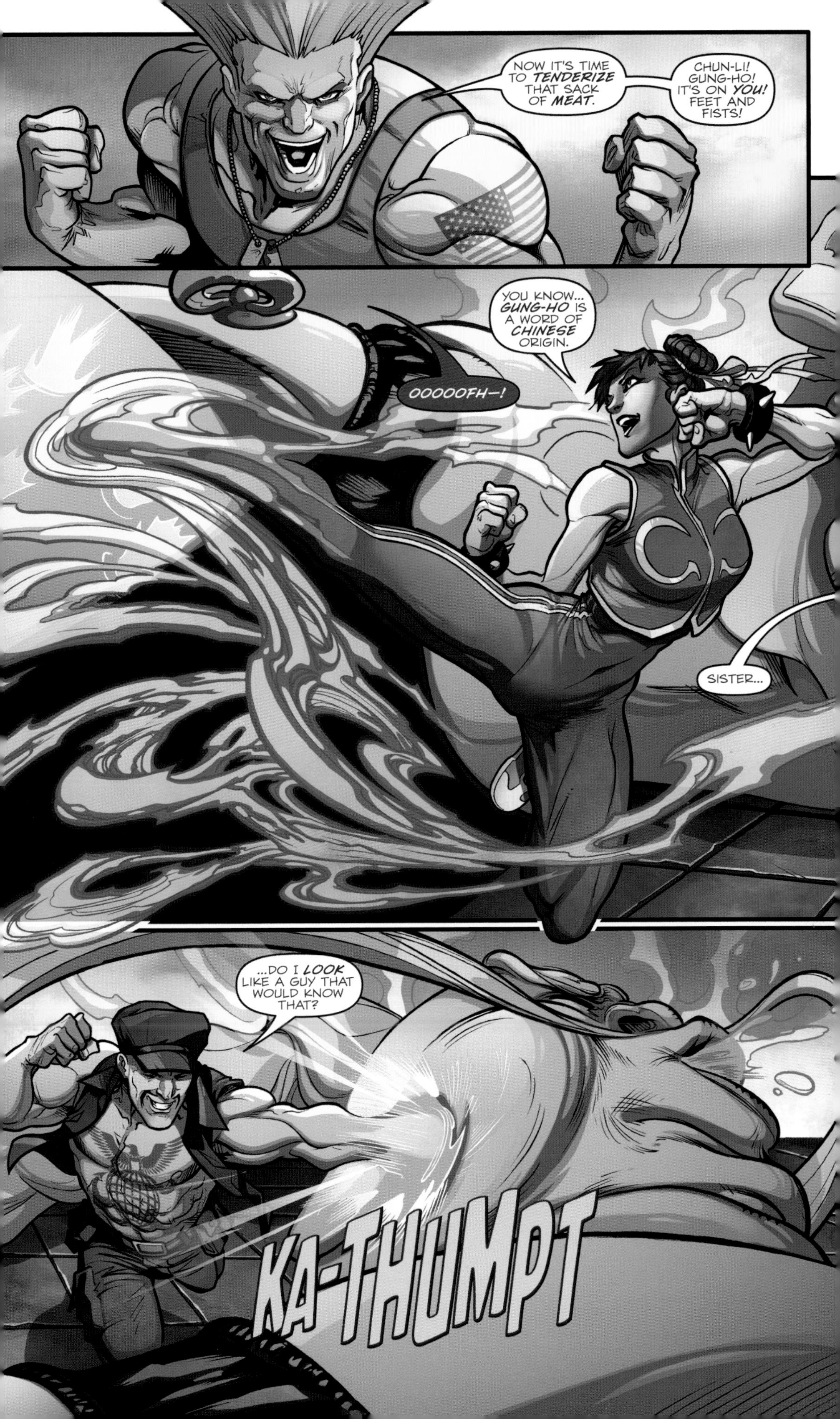
NOW IT'S TIME TO TENDERIZE THAT SACK OF MEAT.
CHUN-LI! GUNG-HO! IT'S ON YOU! FEET AND FISTS!
YOU KNOW... GUNG-HO IS A WORD OF CHINESE ORIGIN.
OOOOOFH—!
SISTER...
...DO I LOOK LIKE A GUY THAT WOULD KNOW THAT?
KA-THUMPT

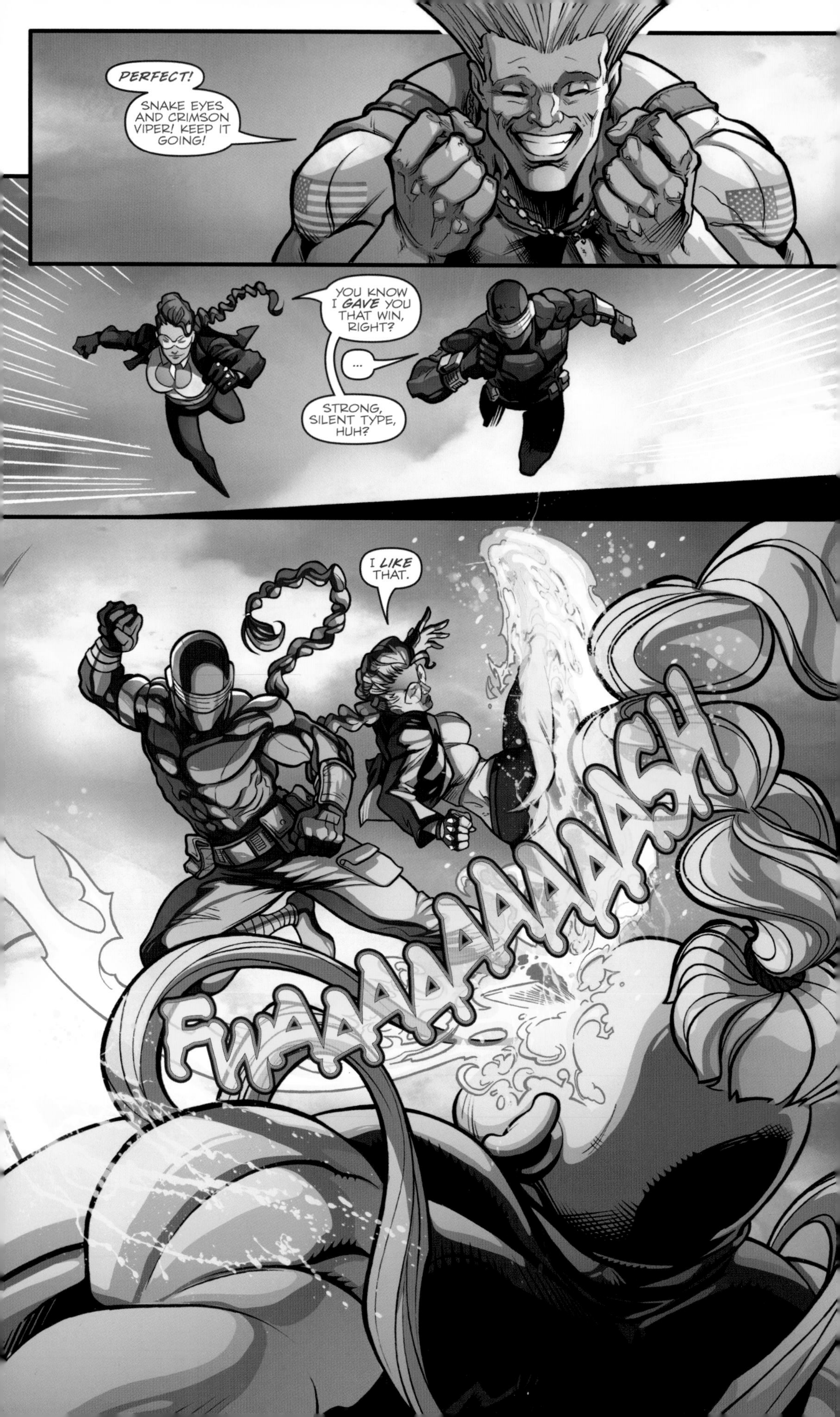
PERFECT!
SNAKE EYES AND CRIMSON VIPER! KEEP IT GOING!
YOU KNOW I GAVE YOU THAT WIN, RIGHT?
...
STRONG, SILENT TYPE, HUH?
I LIKE THAT.
FWAAAAAAAASH

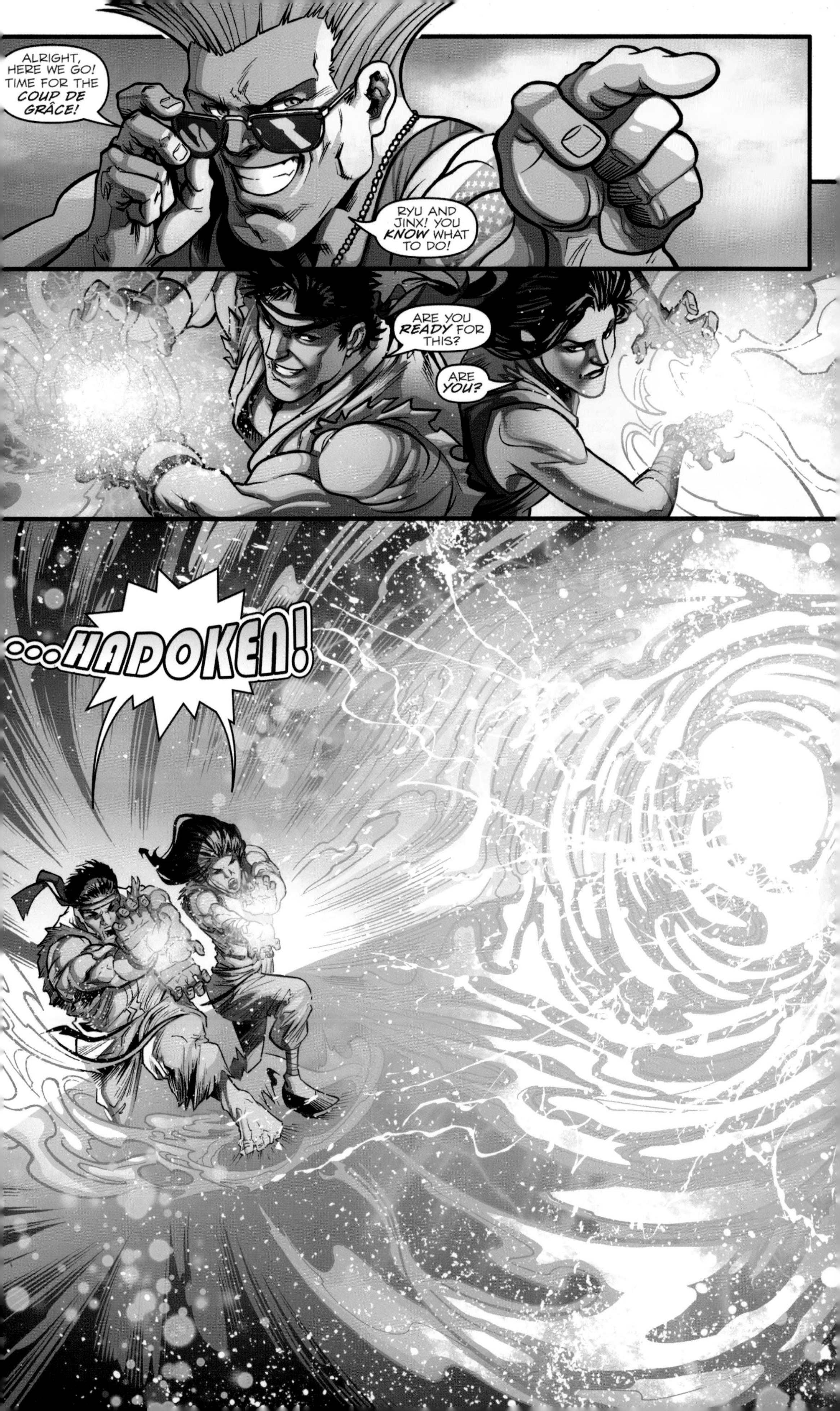
ALRIGHT, HERE WE GO! TIME FOR THE *COUP DE GRÂCE!*
RYU AND JINX! YOU *KNOW* WHAT TO DO!
ARE YOU *READY* FOR THIS?
ARE *YOU?*
...HADOKEN!

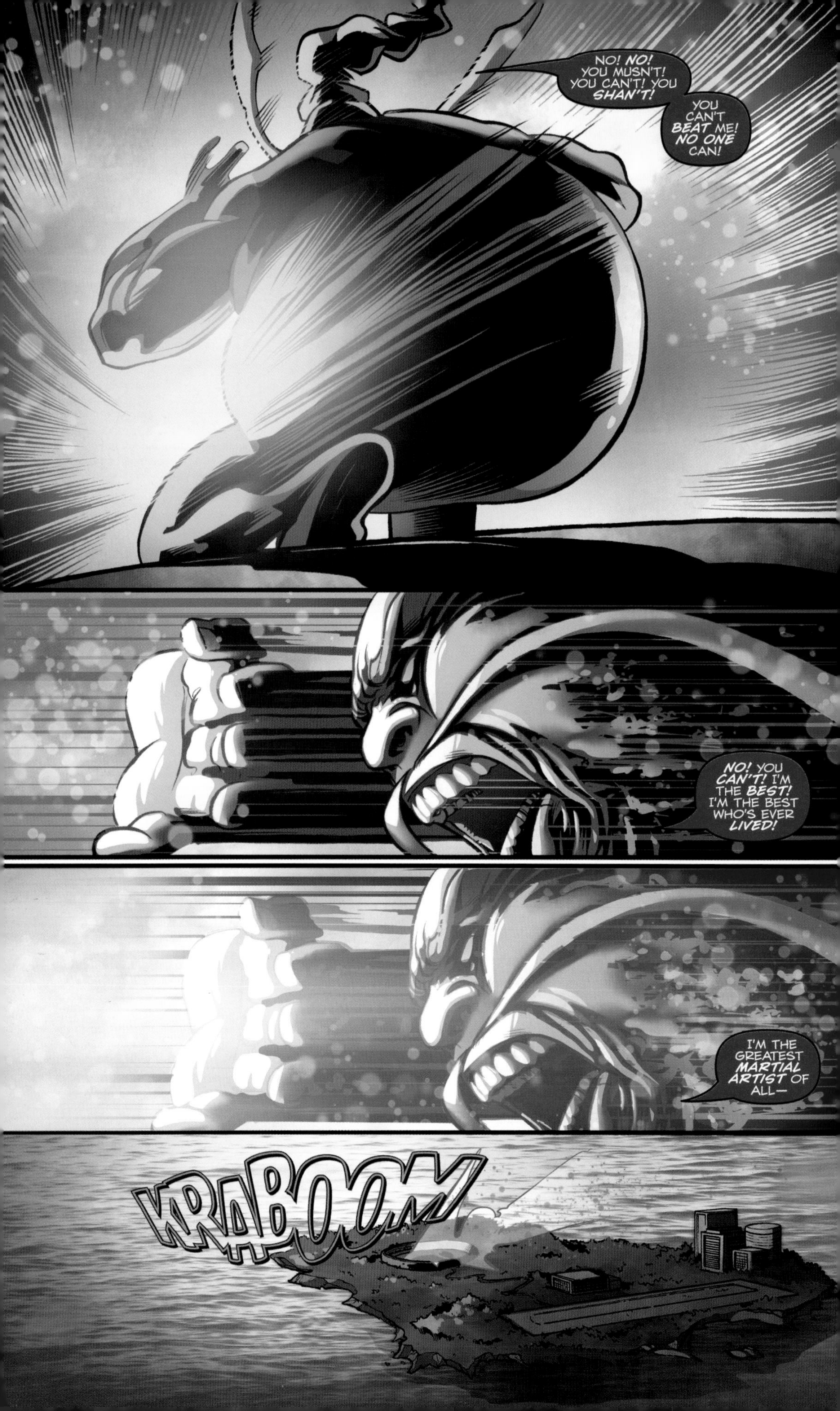

NO! NO! YOU MUSN'T! YOU CAN'T! YOU SHAN'T!
YOU CAN'T BEAT ME! NO ONE CAN!
NO! YOU CAN'T! I'M THE BEST! I'M THE BEST WHO'S EVER LIVED!
I'M THE GREATEST MARTIAL ARTIST OF ALL—
KRABOOM

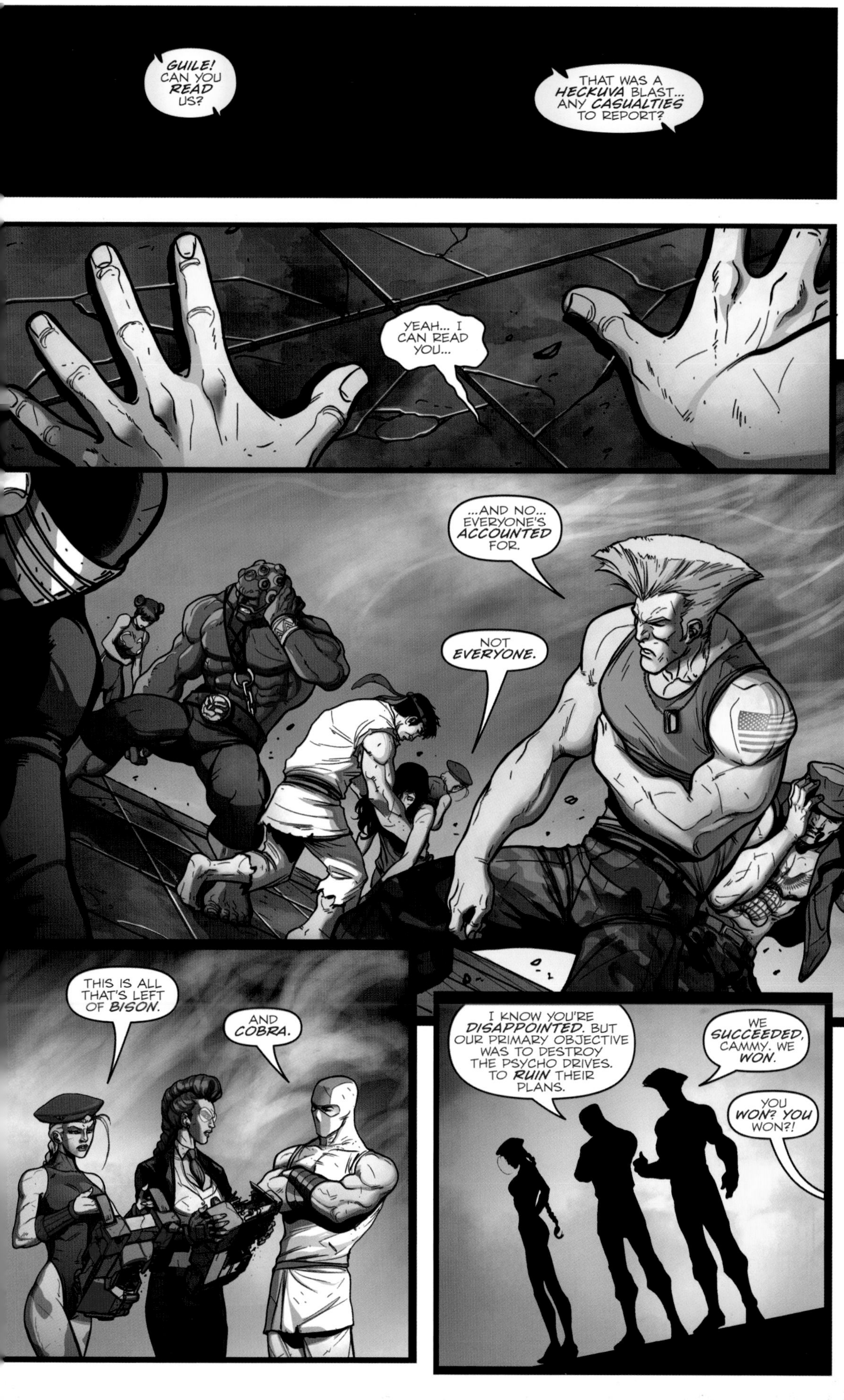
GUILE! CAN YOU READ US?
THAT WAS A HECKUVA BLAST... ANY CASUALTIES TO REPORT?
YEAH... I CAN READ YOU...
...AND NO... EVERYONE'S ACCOUNTED FOR.
NOT EVERYONE.
THIS IS ALL THAT'S LEFT OF BISON.
AND COBRA.
I KNOW YOU'RE DISAPPOINTED. BUT OUR PRIMARY OBJECTIVE WAS TO DESTROY THE PSYCHO DRIVES. TO RUIN THEIR PLANS.
WE SUCCEEDED, CAMMY. WE WON.
YOU WON? YOU WON?!

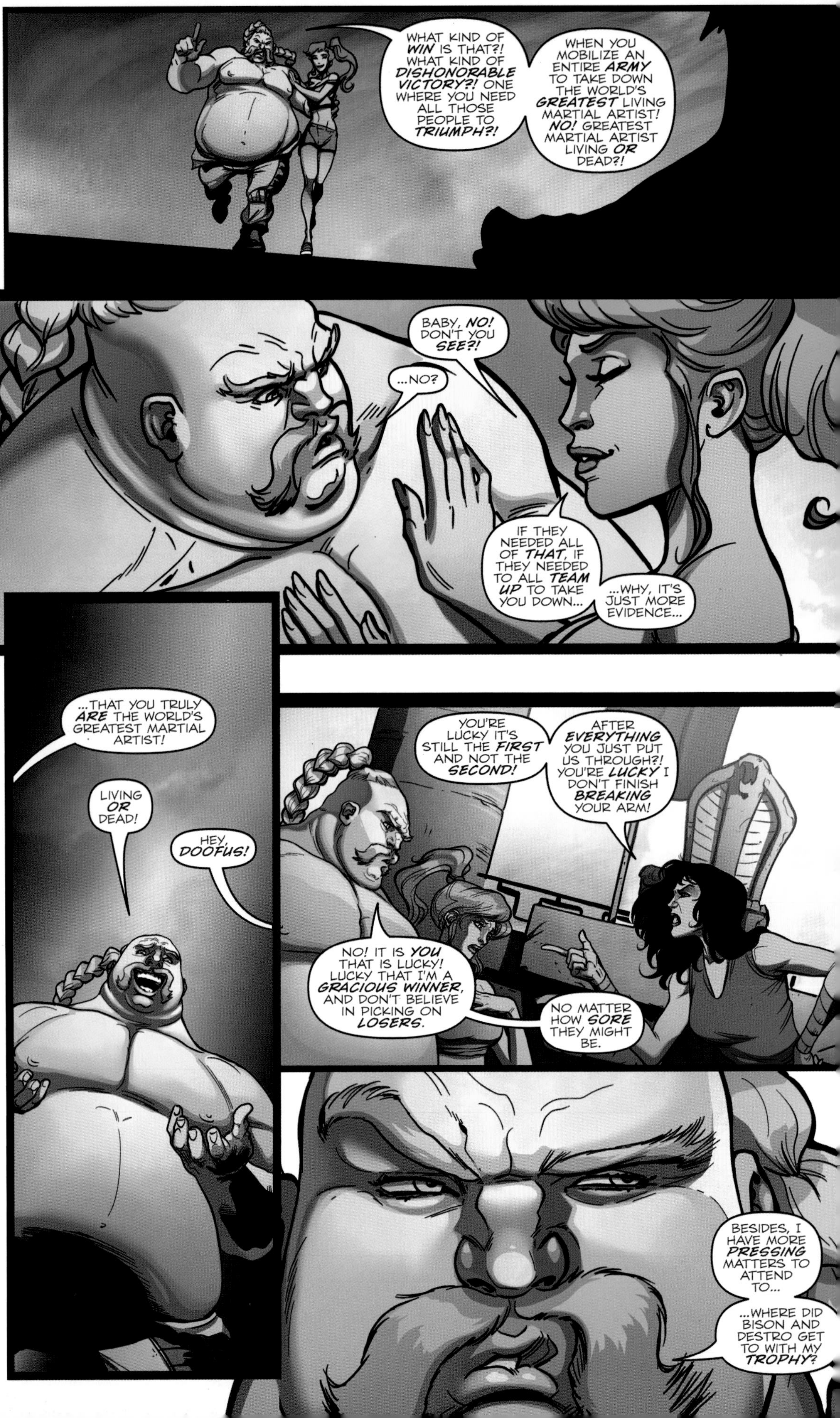
WHAT KIND OF WIN IS THAT?! WHAT KIND OF DISHONORABLE VICTORY?! ONE WHERE YOU NEED ALL THOSE PEOPLE TO TRIUMPH?!
WHEN YOU MOBILIZE AN ENTIRE ARMY TO TAKE DOWN THE WORLD'S GREATEST LIVING MARTIAL ARTIST! NO! GREATEST MARTIAL ARTIST LIVING OR DEAD?!
BABY, NO! DON'T YOU SEE?!
...NO?
IF THEY NEEDED ALL OF THAT, IF THEY NEEDED TO ALL TEAM UP TO TAKE YOU DOWN...
...WHY, IT'S JUST MORE EVIDENCE...
...THAT YOU TRULY ARE THE WORLD'S GREATEST MARTIAL ARTIST!
LIVING OR DEAD!
HEY, DOOFUS!
YOU'RE LUCKY IT'S STILL THE FIRST AND NOT THE SECOND!
AFTER EVERYTHING YOU JUST PUT US THROUGH?! YOU'RE LUCKY I DON'T FINISH BREAKING YOUR ARM!
NO! IT IS YOU THAT IS LUCKY! LUCKY THAT I'M A GRACIOUS WINNER, AND DON'T BELIEVE IN PICKING ON LOSERS.
NO MATTER HOW SORE THEY MIGHT BE.
BESIDES, I HAVE MORE PRESSING MATTERS TO ATTEND TO...
...WHERE DID BISON AND DESTRO GET TO WITH MY TROPHY?

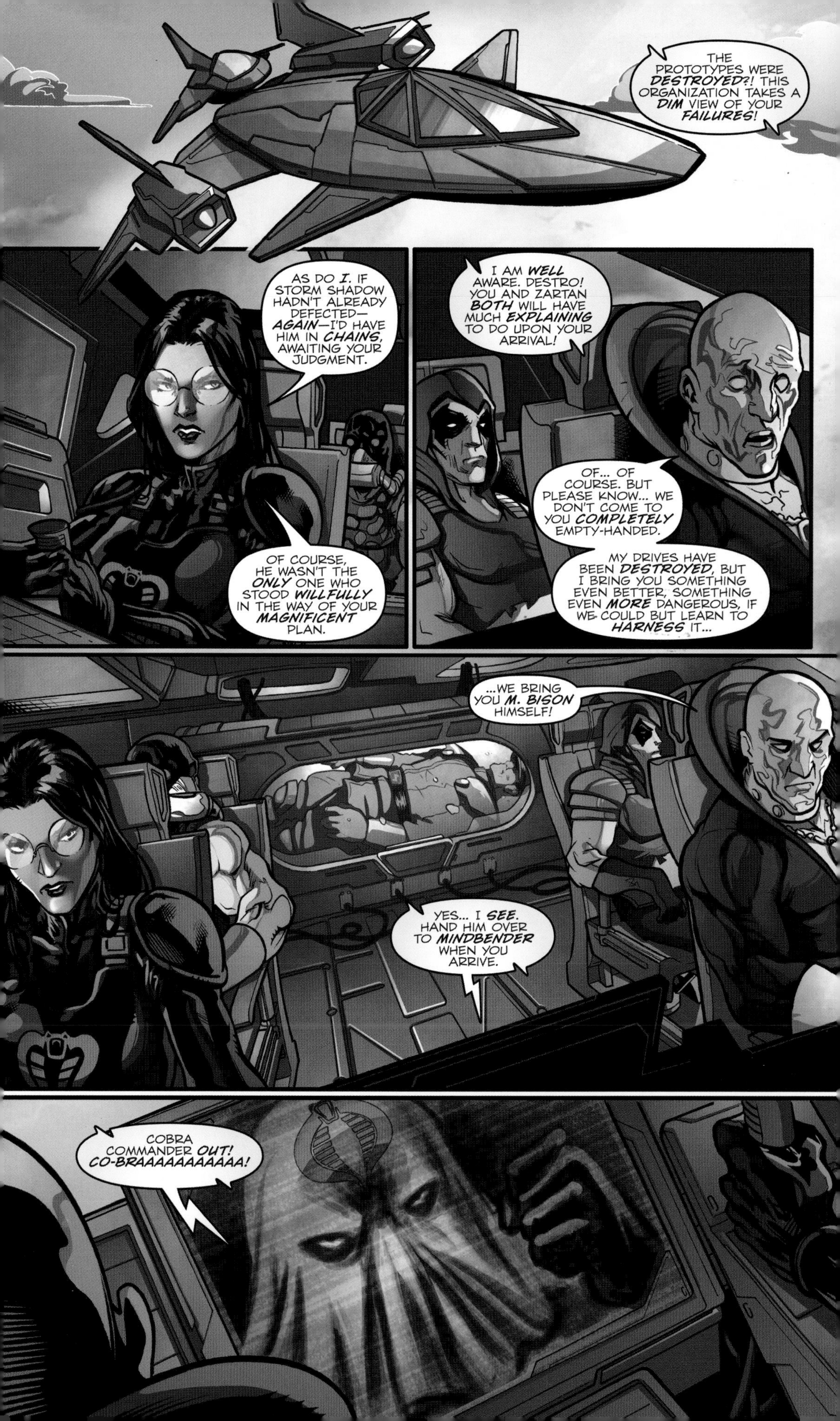
THE PROTOTYPES WERE DESTROYED?! THIS ORGANIZATION TAKES A DIM VIEW OF YOUR FAILURES!
AS DO I. IF STORM SHADOW HADN'T ALREADY DEFECTED—AGAIN—I'D HAVE HIM IN CHAINS, AWAITING YOUR JUDGMENT.
OF COURSE, HE WASN'T THE ONLY ONE WHO STOOD WILLFULLY IN THE WAY OF YOUR MAGNIFICENT PLAN.
I AM WELL AWARE. DESTRO! YOU AND ZARTAN BOTH WILL HAVE MUCH EXPLAINING TO DO UPON YOUR ARRIVAL!
OF... OF COURSE. BUT PLEASE KNOW... WE DON'T COME TO YOU COMPLETELY EMPTY-HANDED.
MY DRIVES HAVE BEEN DESTROYED, BUT I BRING YOU SOMETHING EVEN BETTER, SOMETHING EVEN MORE DANGEROUS, IF WE COULD BUT LEARN TO HARNESS IT...
...WE BRING YOU M. BISON HIMSELF!
YES... I SEE. HAND HIM OVER TO MINDBENDER WHEN YOU ARRIVE.
COBRA COMMANDER OUT! CO-BRAAAAAAAAAAA!

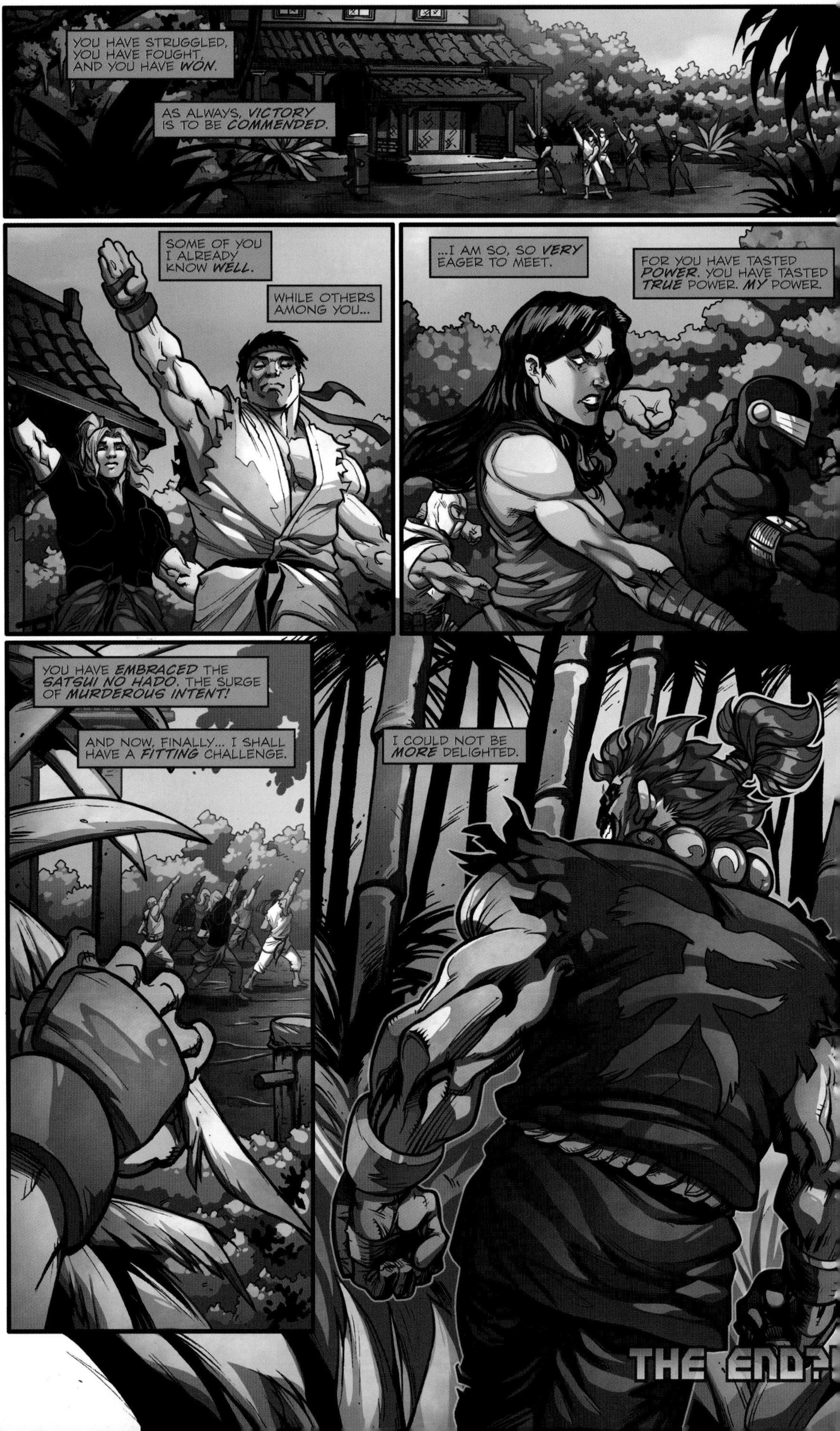
YOU HAVE STRUGGLED, YOU HAVE FOUGHT, AND YOU HAVE WON.
AS ALWAYS, VICTORY IS TO BE COMMENDED.
SOME OF YOU I ALREADY KNOW WELL.
WHILE OTHERS AMONG YOU...
...I AM SO, SO VERY EAGER TO MEET.
FOR YOU HAVE TASTED POWER. YOU HAVE TASTED TRUE POWER. MY POWER.
YOU HAVE EMBRACED THE SATSUI NO HADO. THE SURGE OF MURDEROUS INTENT!
AND NOW, FINALLY... I SHALL HAVE A FITTING CHALLENGE.
I COULD NOT BE MORE DELIGHTED.
THE END?!

ART BY ADAM RICHES

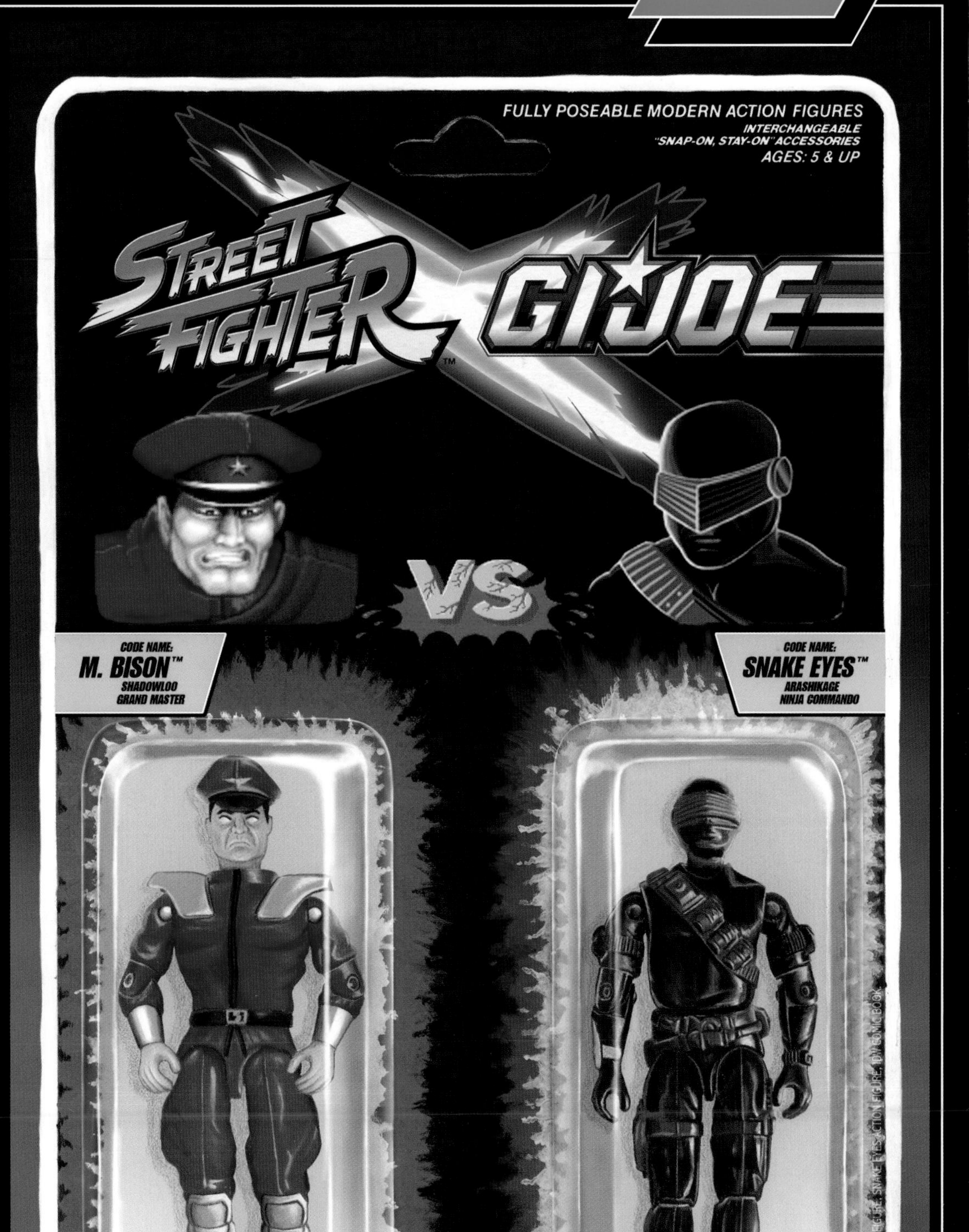
FULLY POSEABLE MODERN ACTION FIGURES
INTERCHANGEABLE
"SNAP-ON, STAY-ON" ACCESSORIES
AGES: 5 & UP
STREET FIGHTER™
G.I. JOE
VS
CODE NAME:
M. BISON™
SHADOWLOO
GRAND MASTER
CODE NAME:
SNAKE EYES™
ARASHIKAGE
NINJA COMMANDO
INCLUDES: M. BISON ACTION FIGURE, SNAKE EYES ACTION FIGURE, IDW COMIC BOOK.
CAPCOM
HASBRO

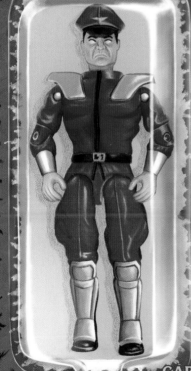

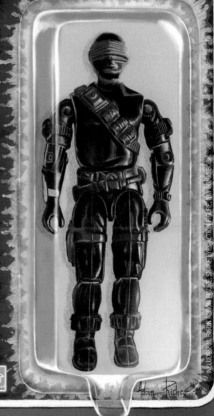

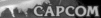

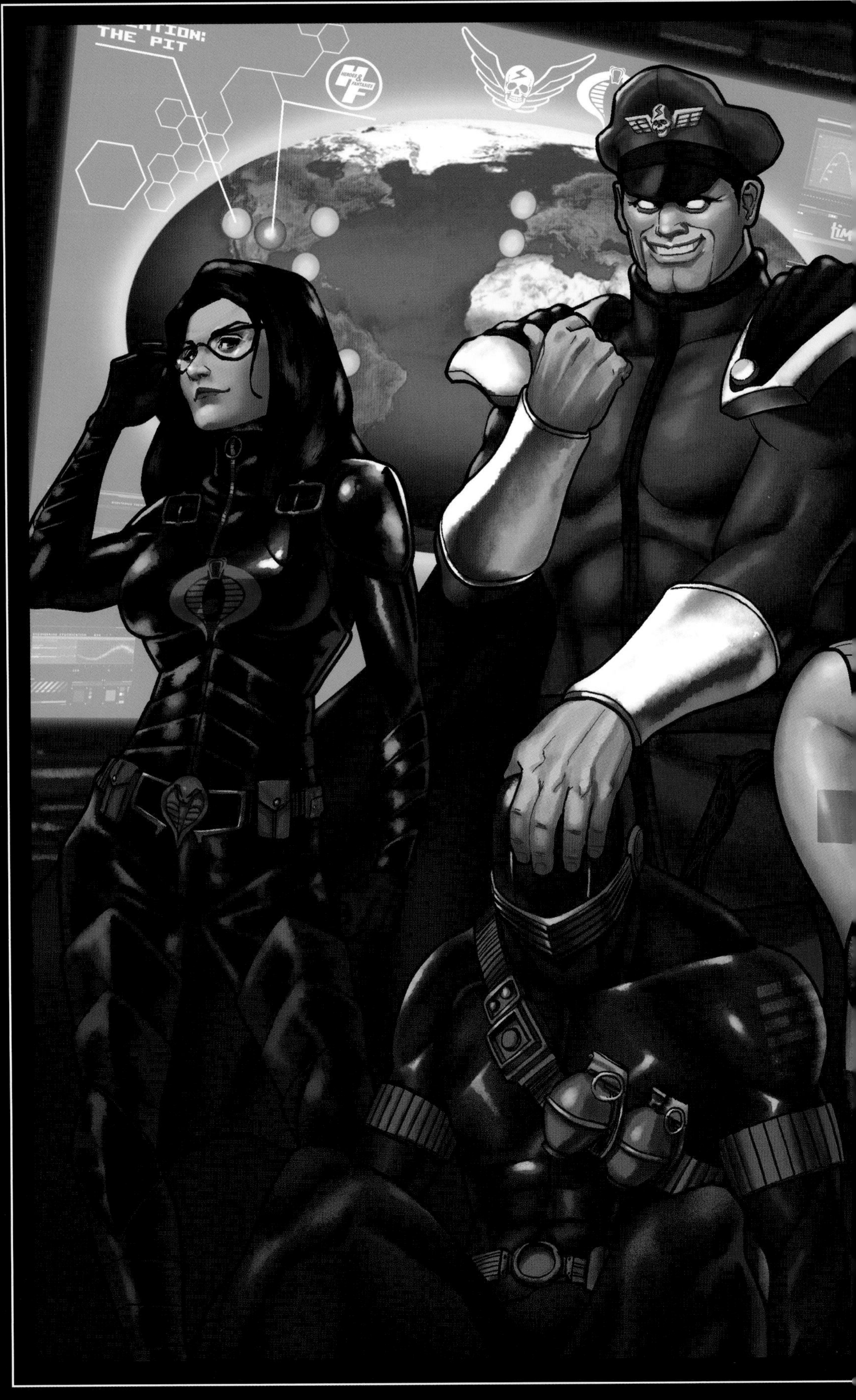
THE PIT

ART BY TIM "NINJAINK" LIM

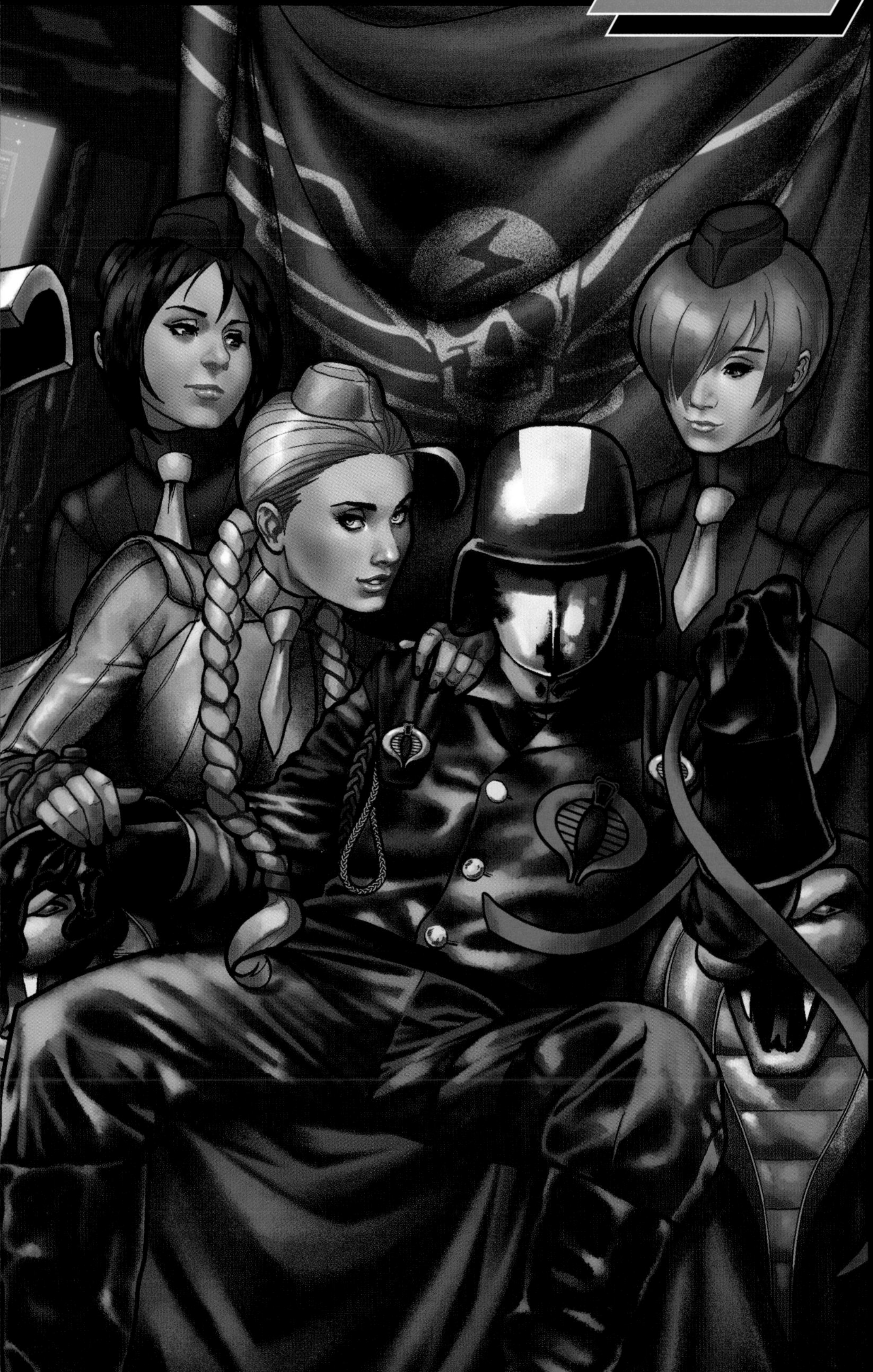

ART BY MIKE CHOI

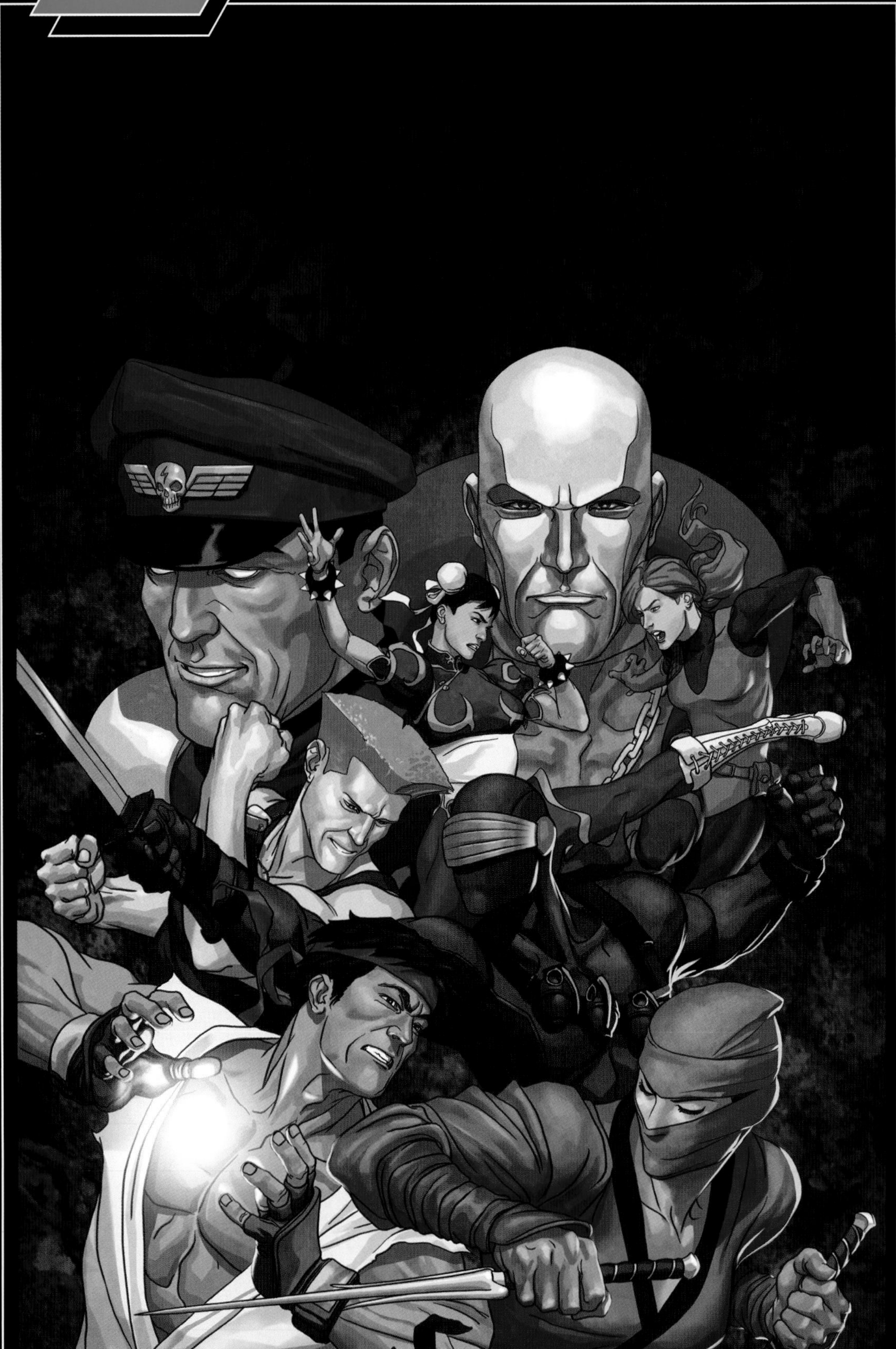

ART BY COREY LEWIS

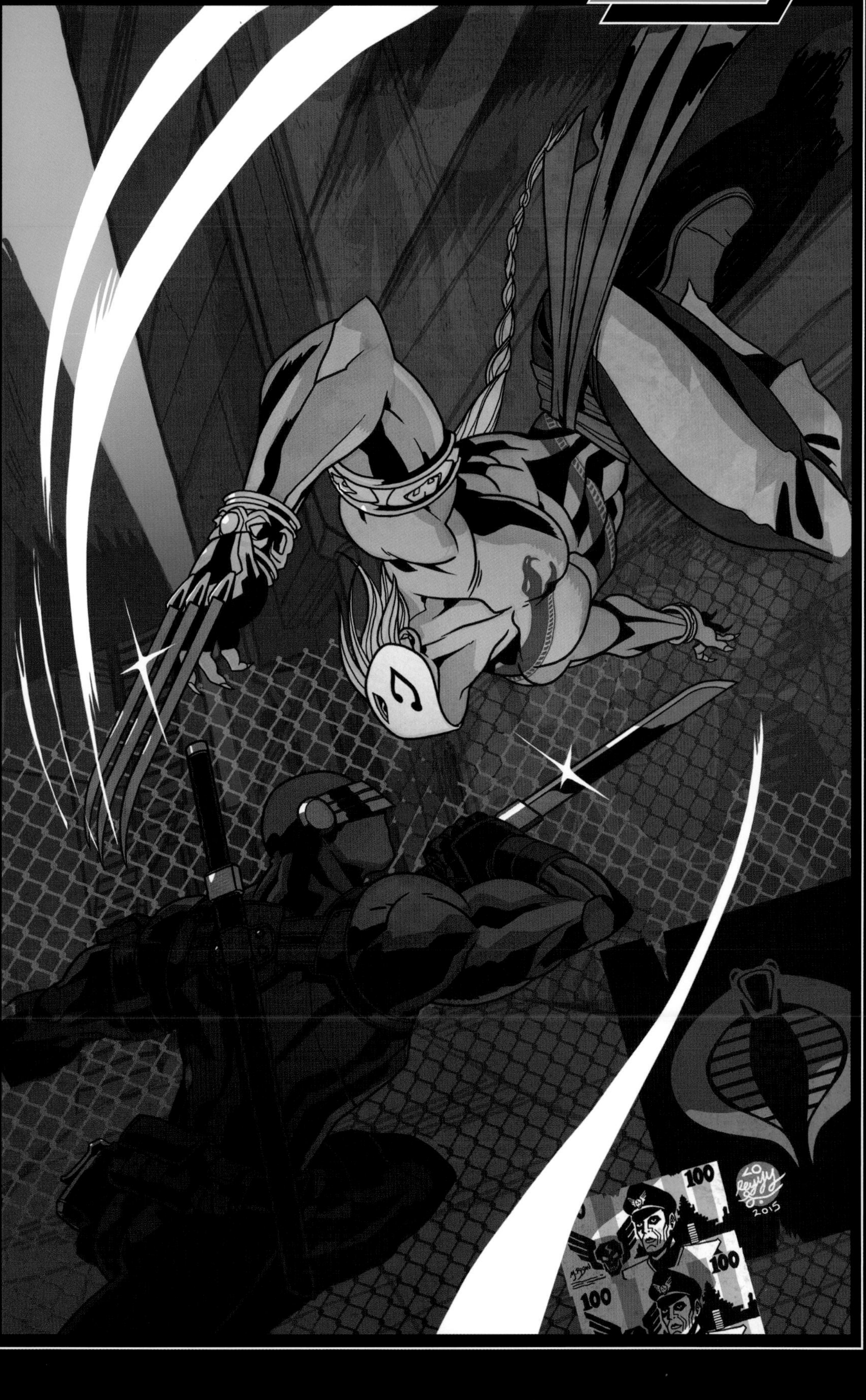

ART BY DEREK CHARM

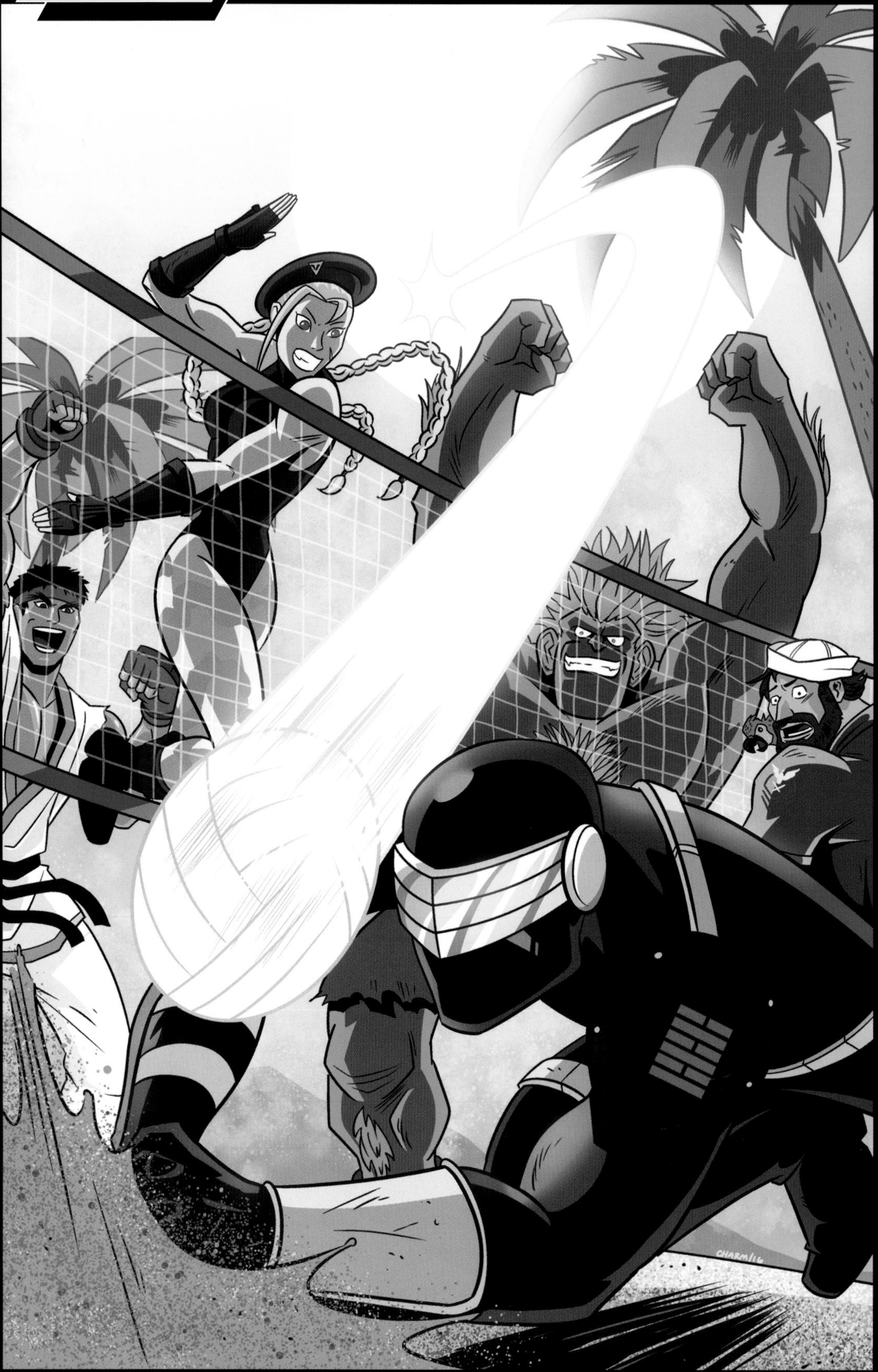
CHARM/16

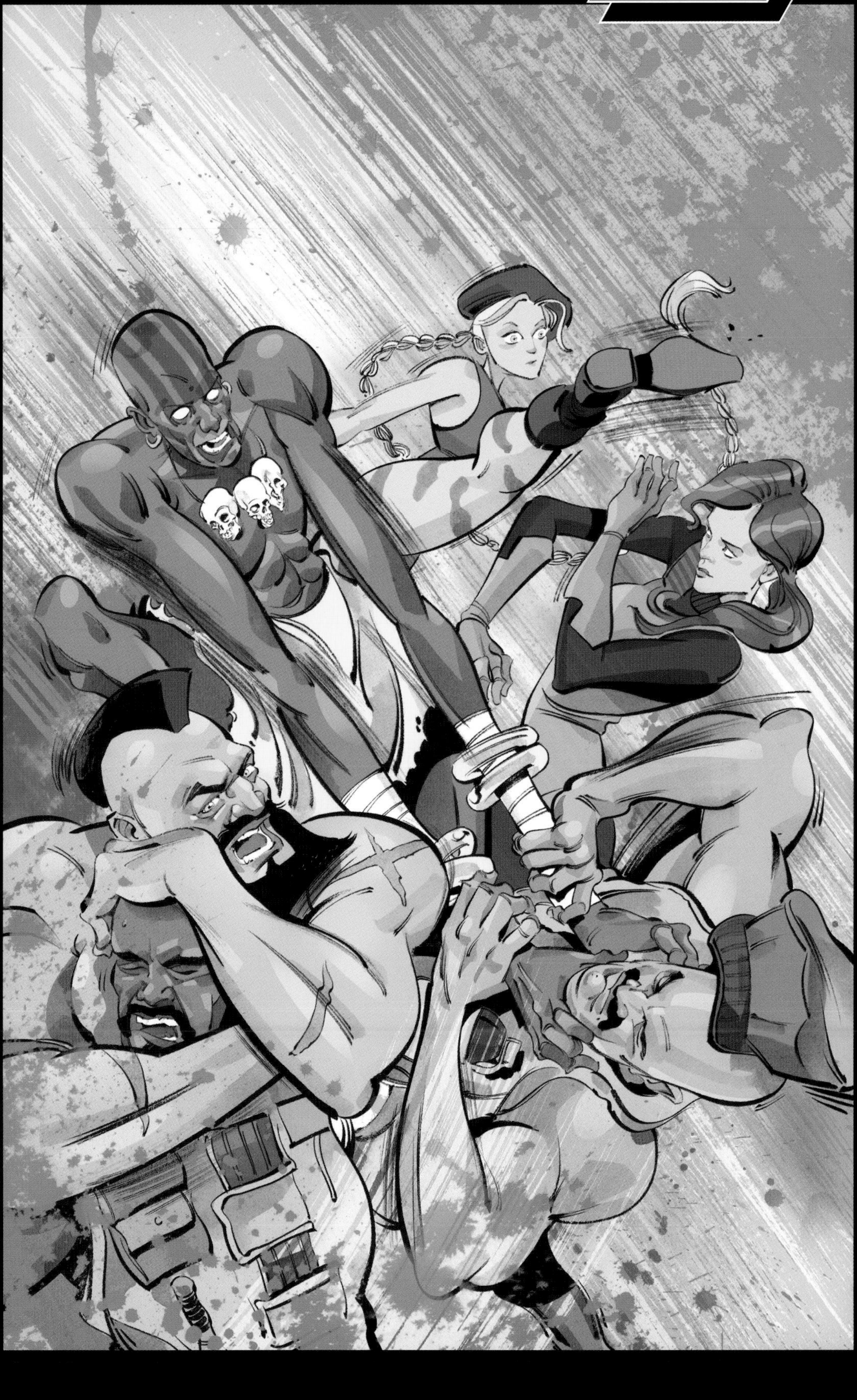

ART BY ZACH HOWARD
COLORS BY NELSON DÁNIEL

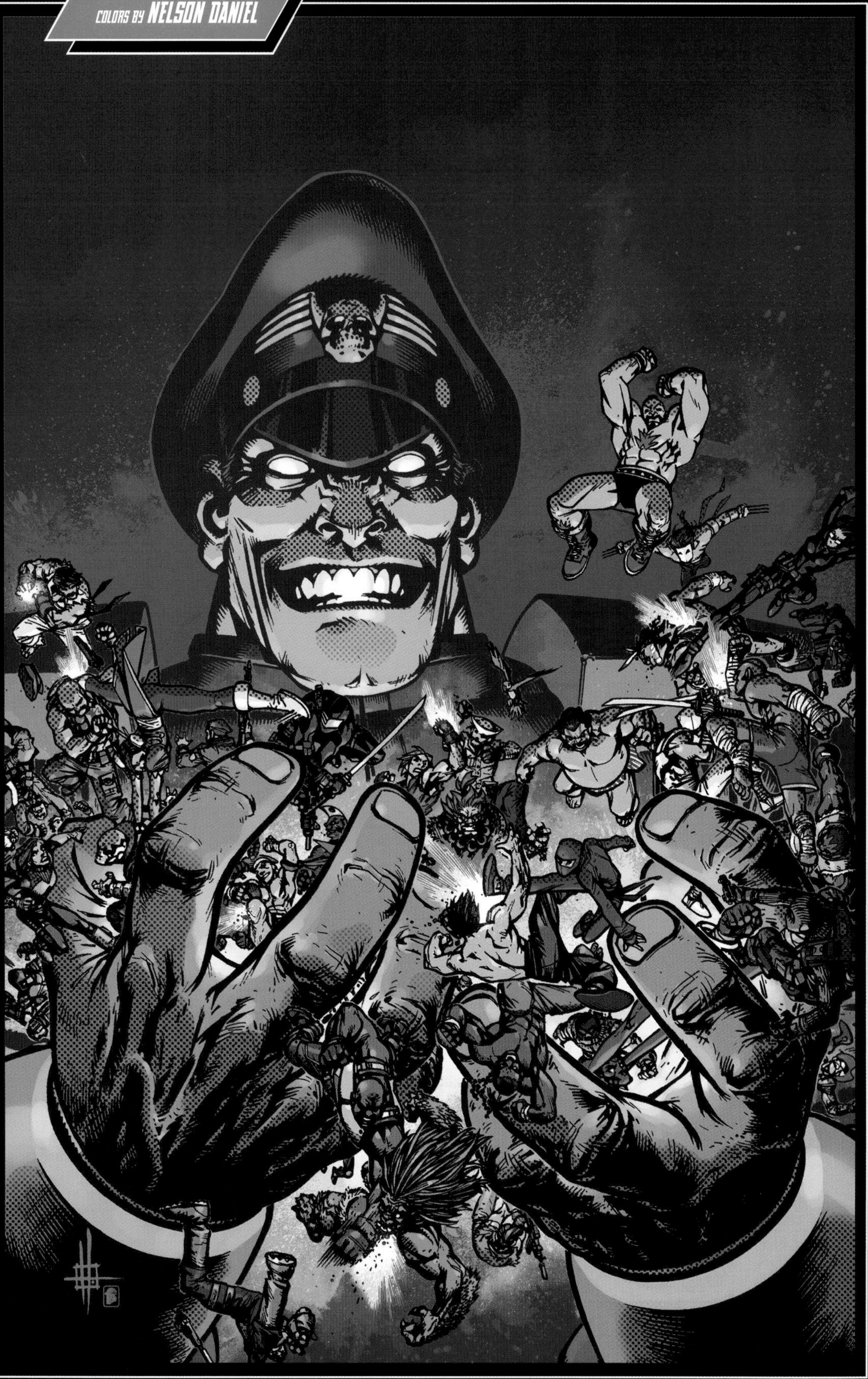

COLORS BY DAVID GARCIA CRUZ

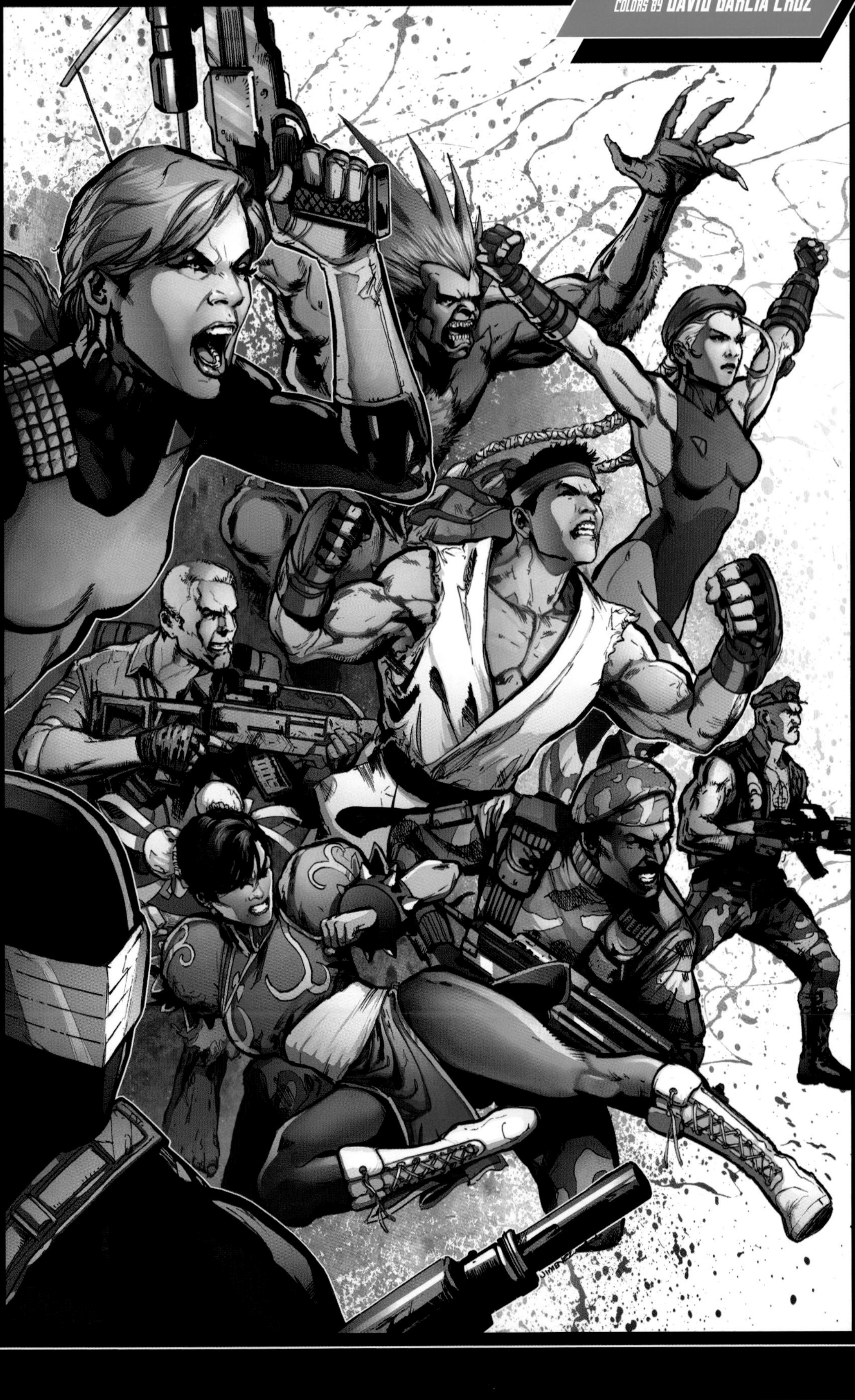

ART BY RAMON VILLALOBOS
COLORS BY ALLEN PASSALAQUA

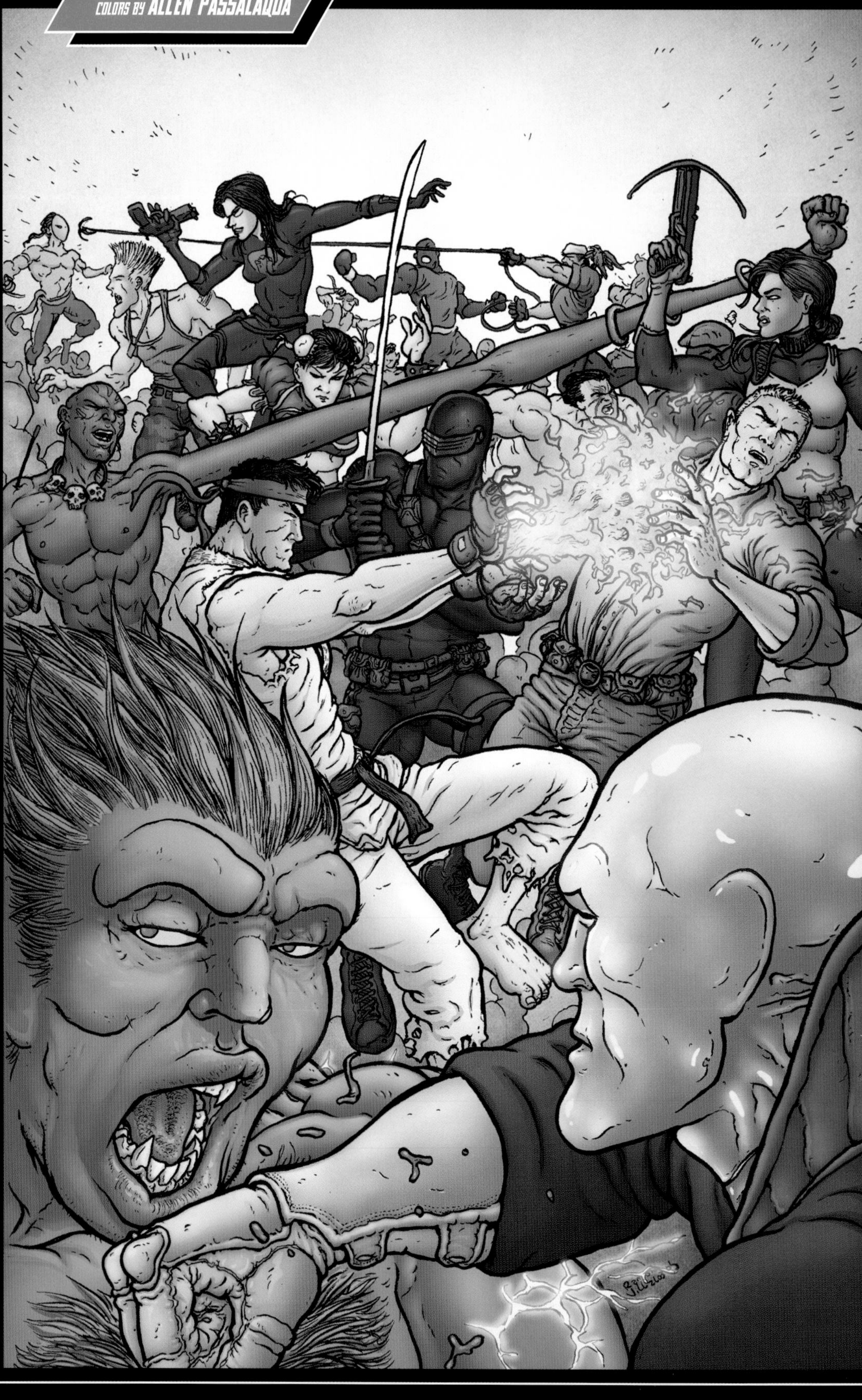

ART BY KHARY RANDOLPH
COLORS BY JOHN RAUCH

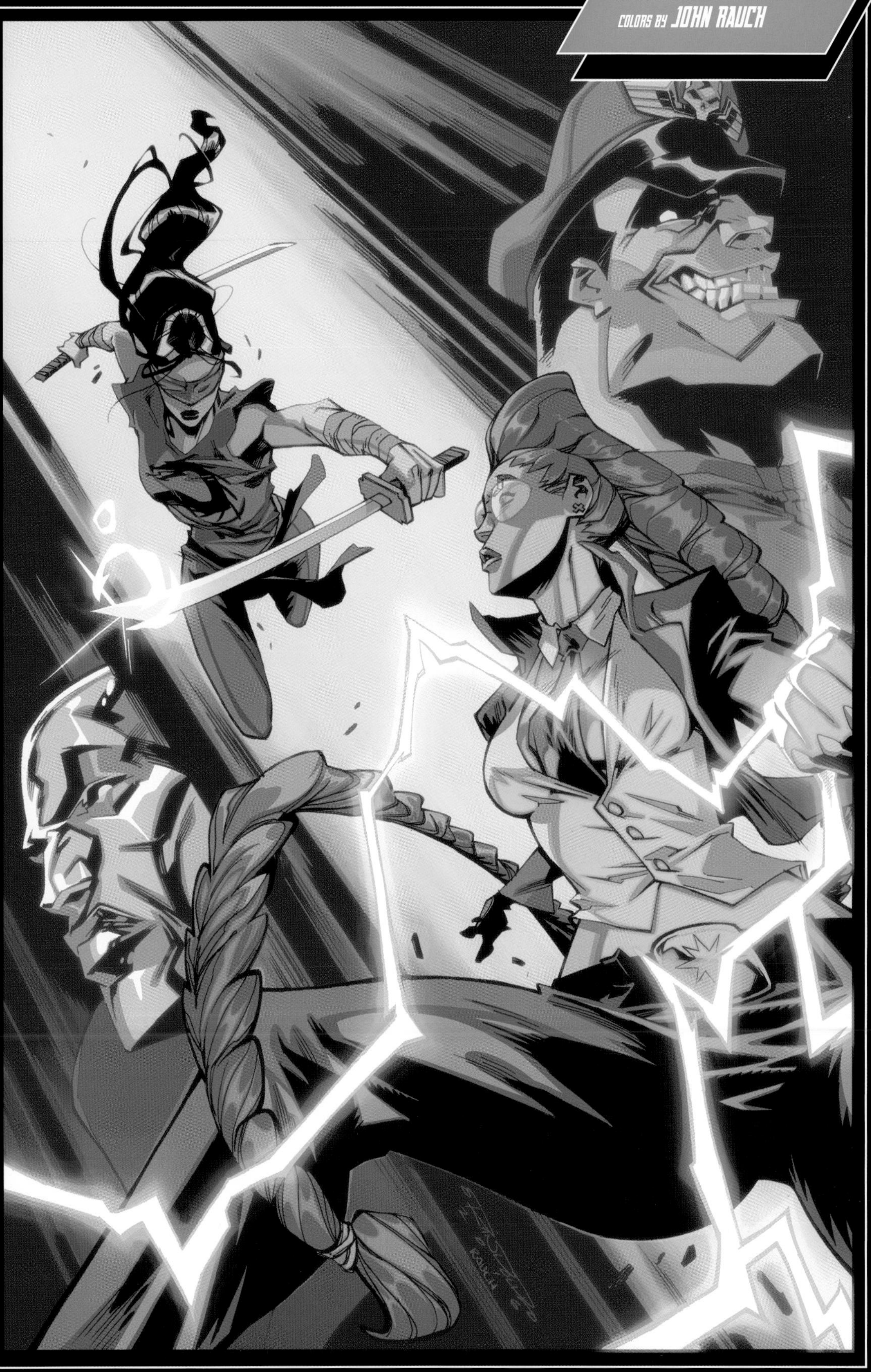

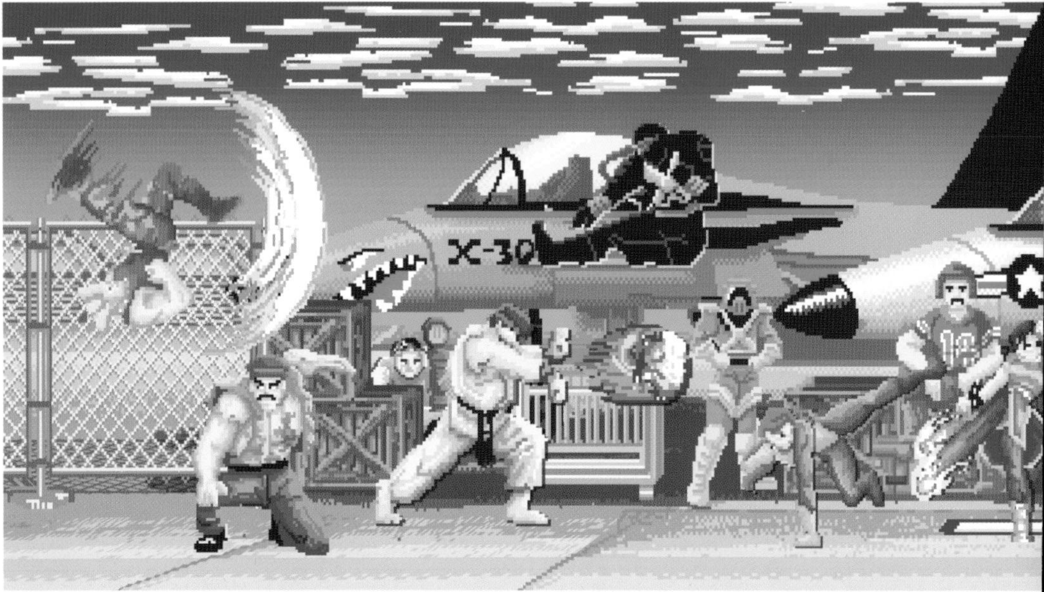
X-30

ART BY MATT WAITE

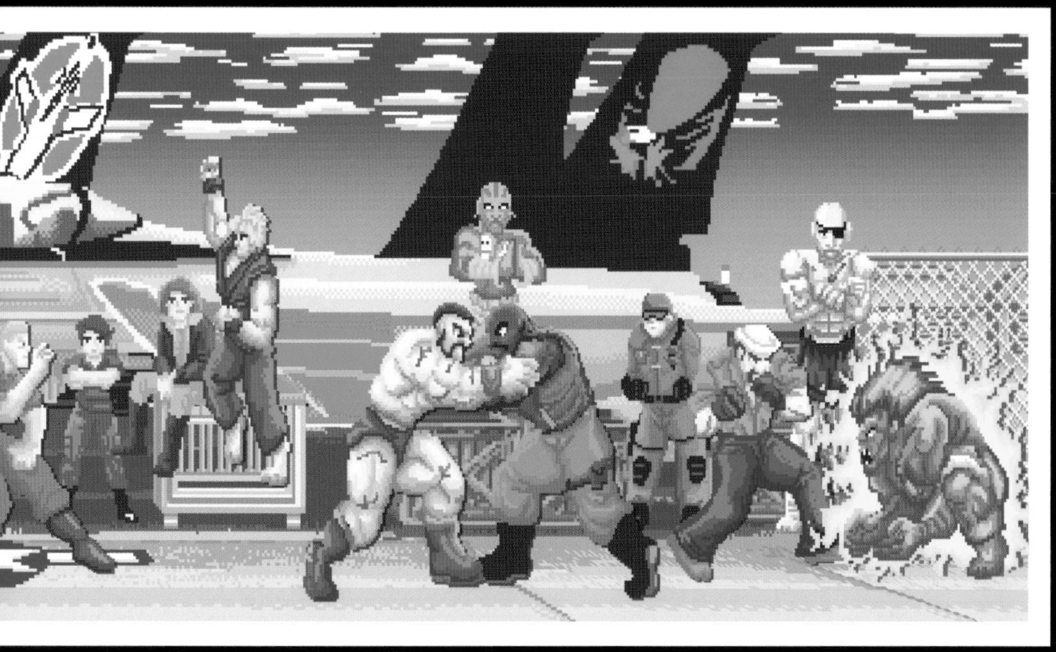

ART BY EMILIO LAISO

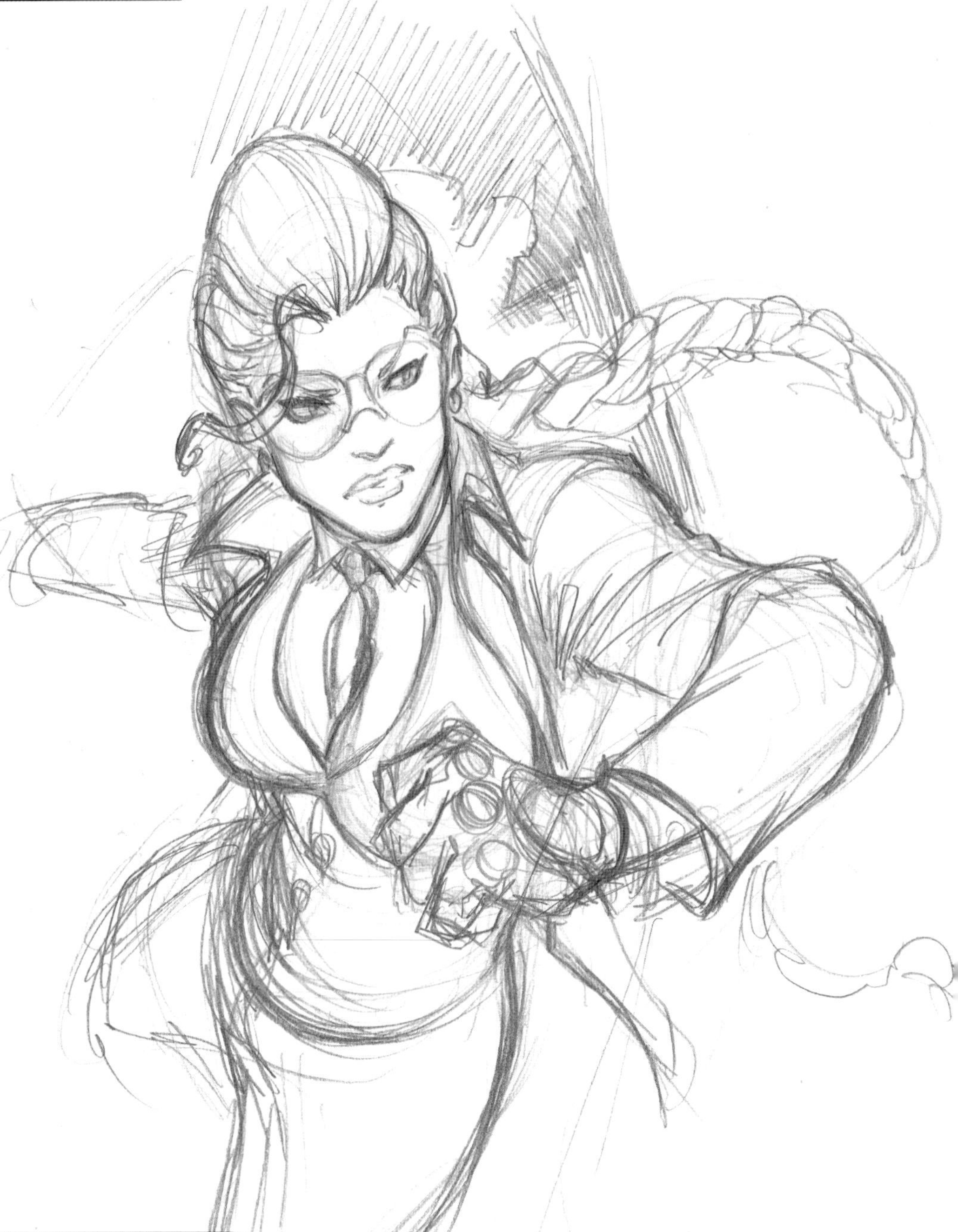

STREET FIGHTER

CRIMSON VIPER

"Miss Perfect"

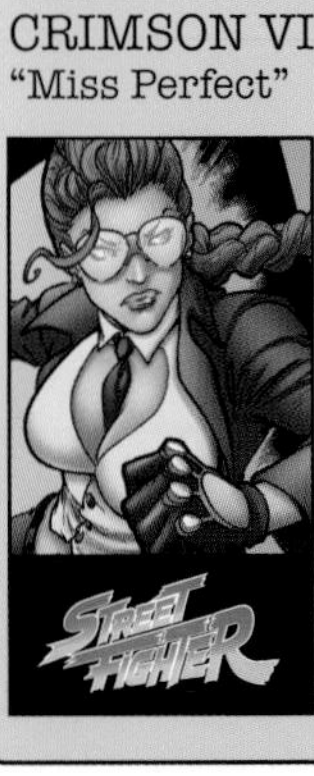
STREET FIGHTER

HEIGHT: 175 cm WEIGHT: 56 kg BLOOD TYPE: AB
FIGHTING STYLE: Using secret spy gadgets
SIGNATURE MOVES: Burning kick, Seismic Hammer, Thunder Knuckle
COUNTRY OF ORIGIN: U.S.A.

Crimson Viper is an enigma. Though she has been known to work with organizations as varied as the C.I.A. and the nefarious S.I.N., her true allegiances are, as of now, unclear. What is abundantly clear, however, is the threat that she poses to anyone standing in her way. Viper's most dangerous asset is her high-tech battlesuit, which protects her while also allowing her to deal out heinous amounts of damage.

"Whether you're talking about her looks or the 1,000,000 volts she packs in her left glove, Crimson Viper is a knockout. But even when you get past her ability to electrocute you, set you ablaze or crumble the earth beneath your feet, you're still dealing with an incredibly capable martial artist."

ART BY EMILIO LAISO

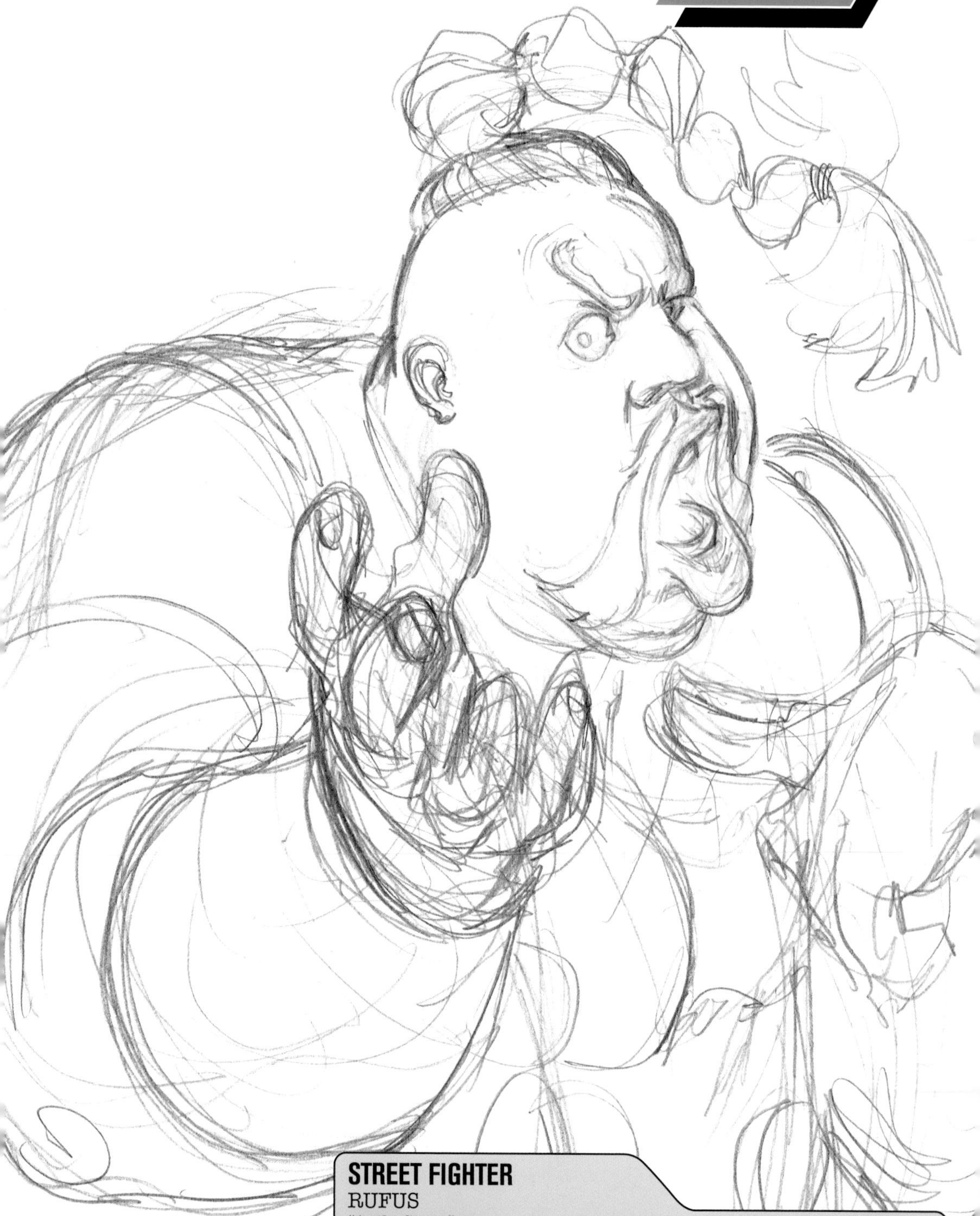

STREET FIGHTER

RUFUS

"Agile Giant"

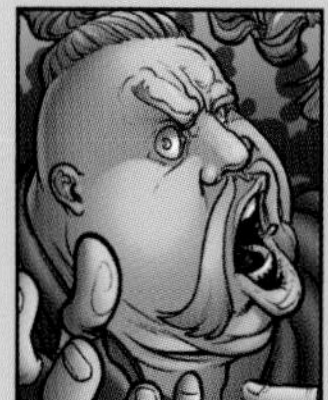

HEIGHT: 195 cm WEIGHT: 185 kg BLOOD TYPE: O
FIGHTING STYLE: (What he thinks is) kung fu
SIGNATURE MOVES: Galactic Tornado, Messiah Kick, Snake Strike
COUNTRY OF ORIGIN: U.S.A.

Unlike most World Warrior Tournament competitors, Rufus is almost completely self-taught. He developed his skills through mail order correspondence courses and kung fu movies before spending time traveling China and further honing his abilities. While his style is unorthodox to say the least, his massive bulk and painful arrogance belie a shockingly quick, agile and effective martial artist.

"Underestimate this competitor at your own peril. You would be left aghast at the list of martial artists who went confidently into a match against Rufus only to find themselves laid out by his deceptively fast strikes, absurd spinning attacks and relentless rambling."

ART BY EMILIO LAISO

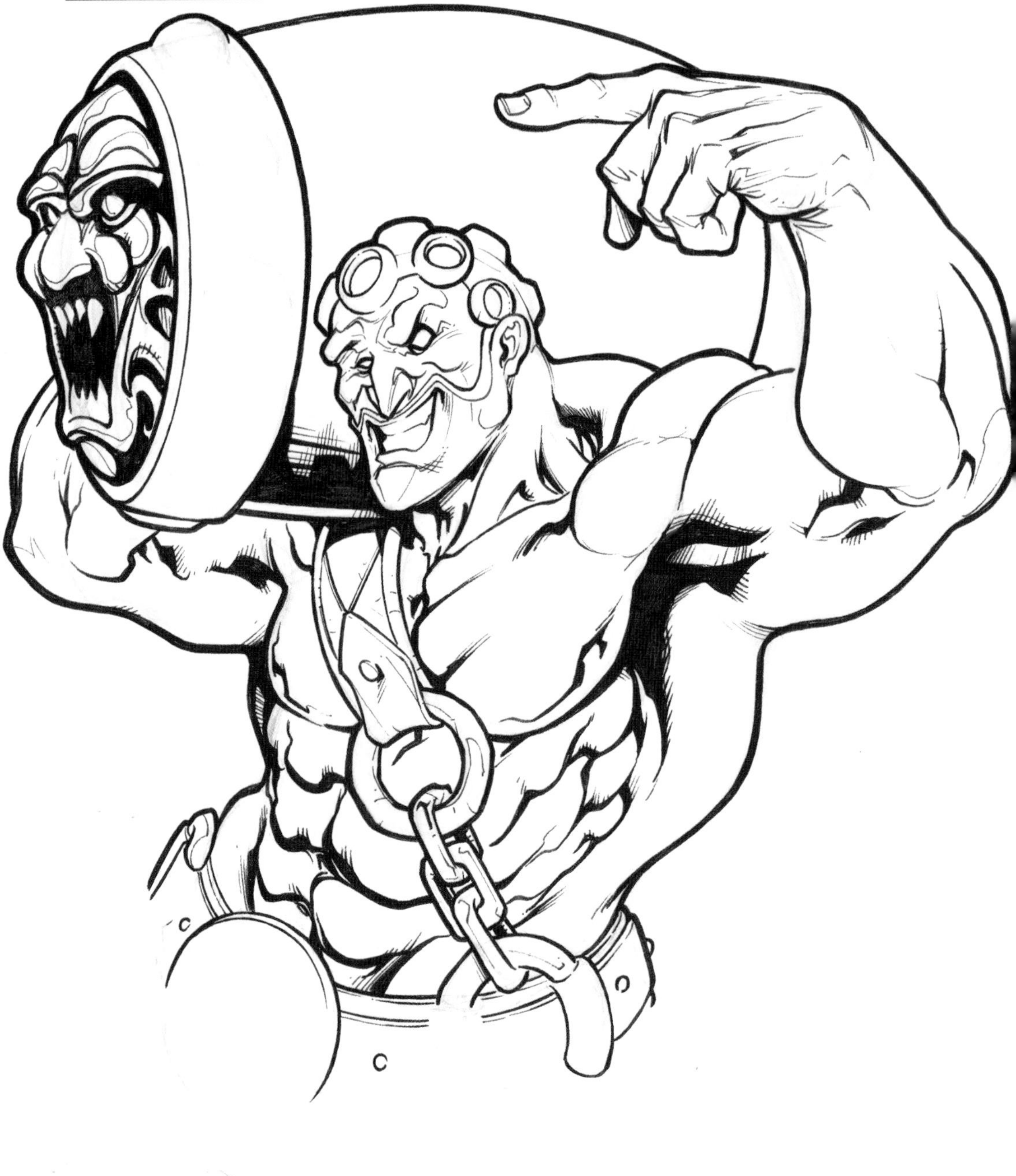

STREET FIGHTER

HAKAN

"The Invincible Czar"

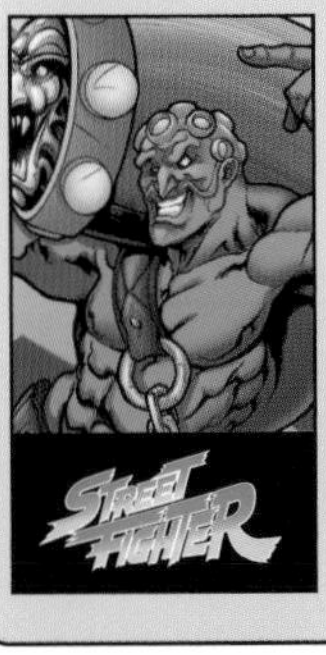
STREET FIGHTER

HEIGHTS: 190 cm WEIGHT: 110 kg BLOOD TYPE: O
FIGHTING STYLE: Yağlı güreş
SIGNATURE MOVES: Oil Shower, Oil Coaster, Oil Combination Hold
COUNTRY OF ORIGIN: Turkey

Hakan fights for fame. Not for himself, but for the popularization of his company, the world's leading edible oil manufacturer, and Turkey's national sport, a peculiar type of oil wrestling known as yağlı güreş. To that end, the good-natured Hakan uses not only his massive size but his viscous (and delicious) oils to his advantage during his matches.

"Hakan is the president of a multinational corporation, the father of more daughters than we can keep track of and, frankly, an all-around great guy. But don't let his outgoing nature or outrageous appearance fool you: Hakan is a formidable and, ahem, slippery opponent."

ART BY EMILIO LAISO

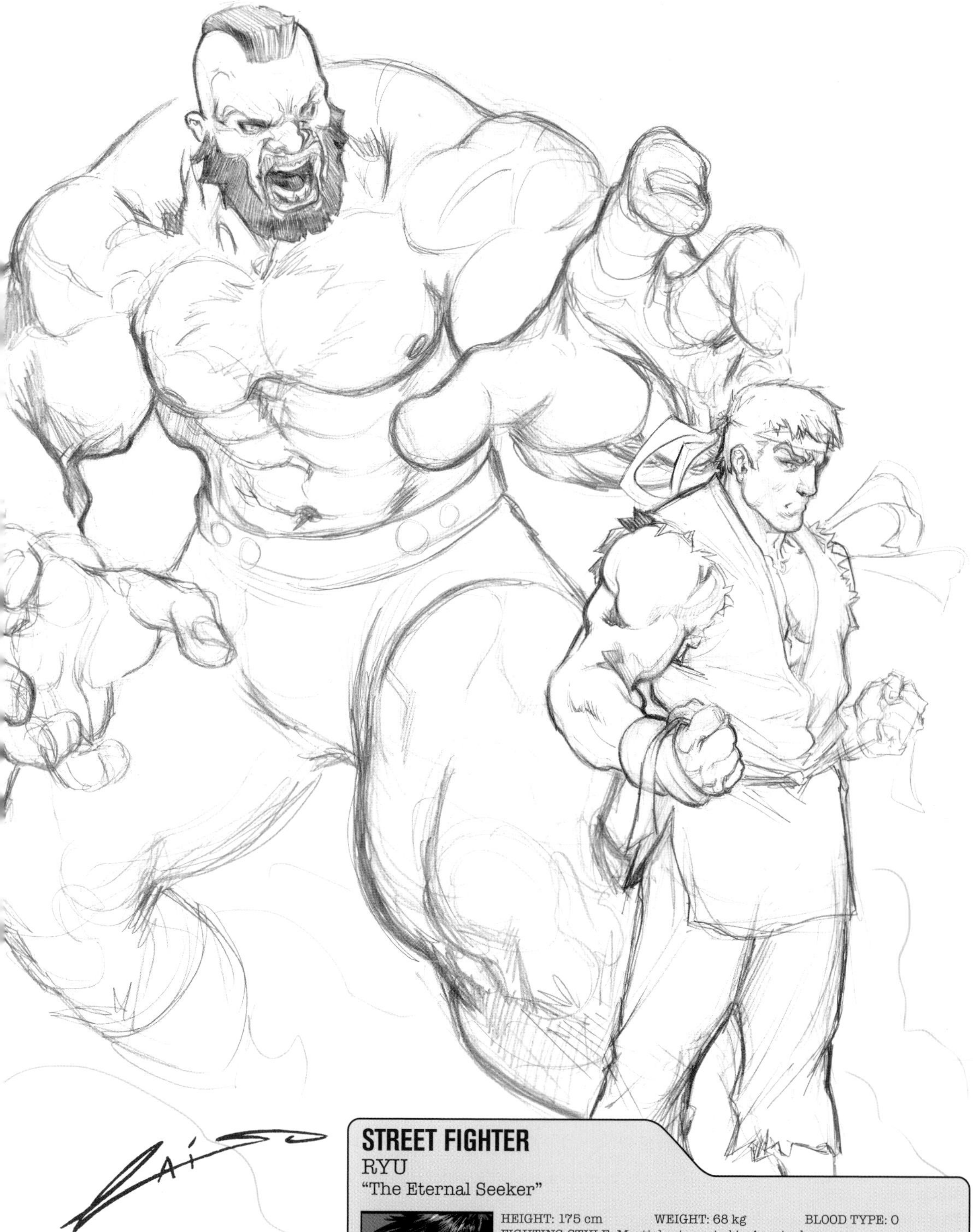

STREET FIGHTER

RYU

"The Eternal Seeker"

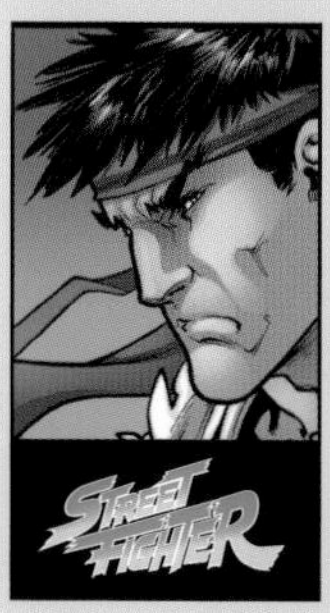
STREET FIGHTER

HEIGHT: 175 cm WEIGHT: 68 kg BLOOD TYPE: O
FIGHTING STYLE: Martial arts rooted in Ansatsuken
SIGNATURE MOVES: Hadoken, Tatsumaki Senpukyaki, Shoryuken
COUNTRY OF ORIGIN: Japan

Ryu – along with his best friend Ken – was trained in the art of Ansatsuken by Gouken, who taught both warriors how to harness their ki to perform devastating attacks. But that power came with a significant risk: The temptation to give in to the Satsui no Hado, "The Killing Intent." Though Ryu possesses incredible fighting abilities, they must be closely monitored in order to keep the Satsui no Hado in check.

"Even without the Satsui no Hado, Ryu is one of the most formidable fighters to ever compete in the World Warrior Tournament. But when he gives in, when he succumbs to the Satsui no Hado, Ryu becomes something else entirely... something dark, hateful and unbelievably powerful."

ART BY EMILIO LAISO

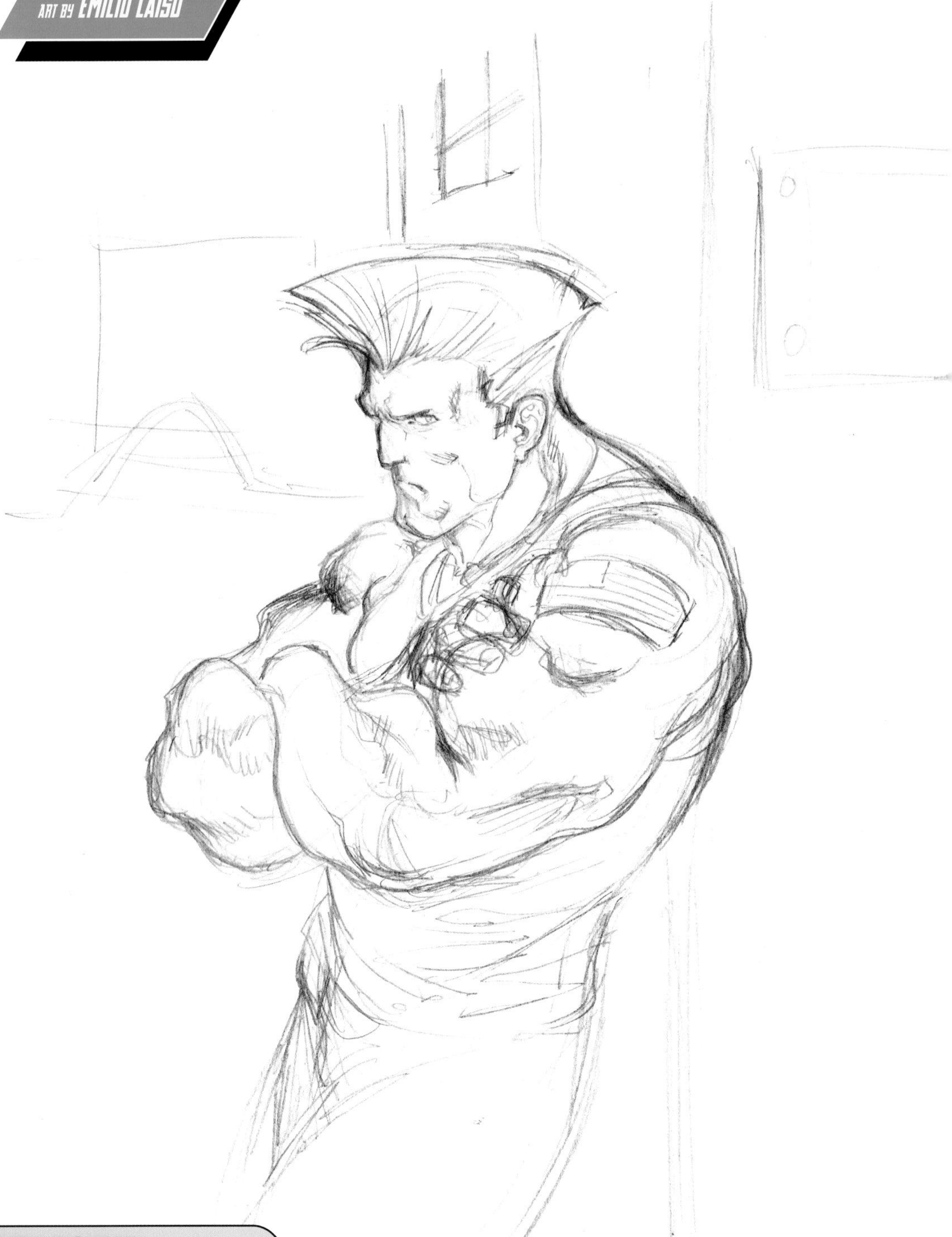

STREET FIGHTER

GUILE

"The Sonic Blade"

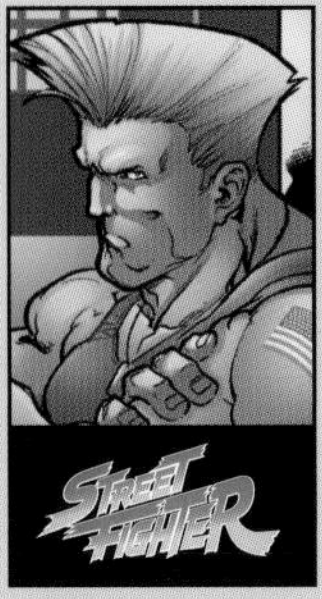

STREET FIGHTER

HEIGHT: 182 cm WEIGHT: 86 kg BLOOD TYPE: O
FIGHTING STYLE: Martial arts and professional wrestling
SIGNATURE MOVES: Flash Kick, Sonic Boom
COUNTRY OF ORIGIN: USA

After his friend and fellow Air Force lieutenant, Charlie Nash, went missing during an investigation of Shadaloo, Guile made it his life's mission to take down the group's leader, M. Bison. But when he exhausted his options in the court of law, Guile set out on his own, using his idiosyncratic blend of combat-approved martial arts and professional wrestling to bring Bison to justice.

"His hulking physique, American flag tattoo, fatigues and... unique hairstyle might make him look like just another meathead, but Guile is much, much more. Underneath that shock of blonde hair hides the brain of a tactical genius, as Guile is an expert at reading and predicting his opponents' movements."

ART BY EMILIO LAISO

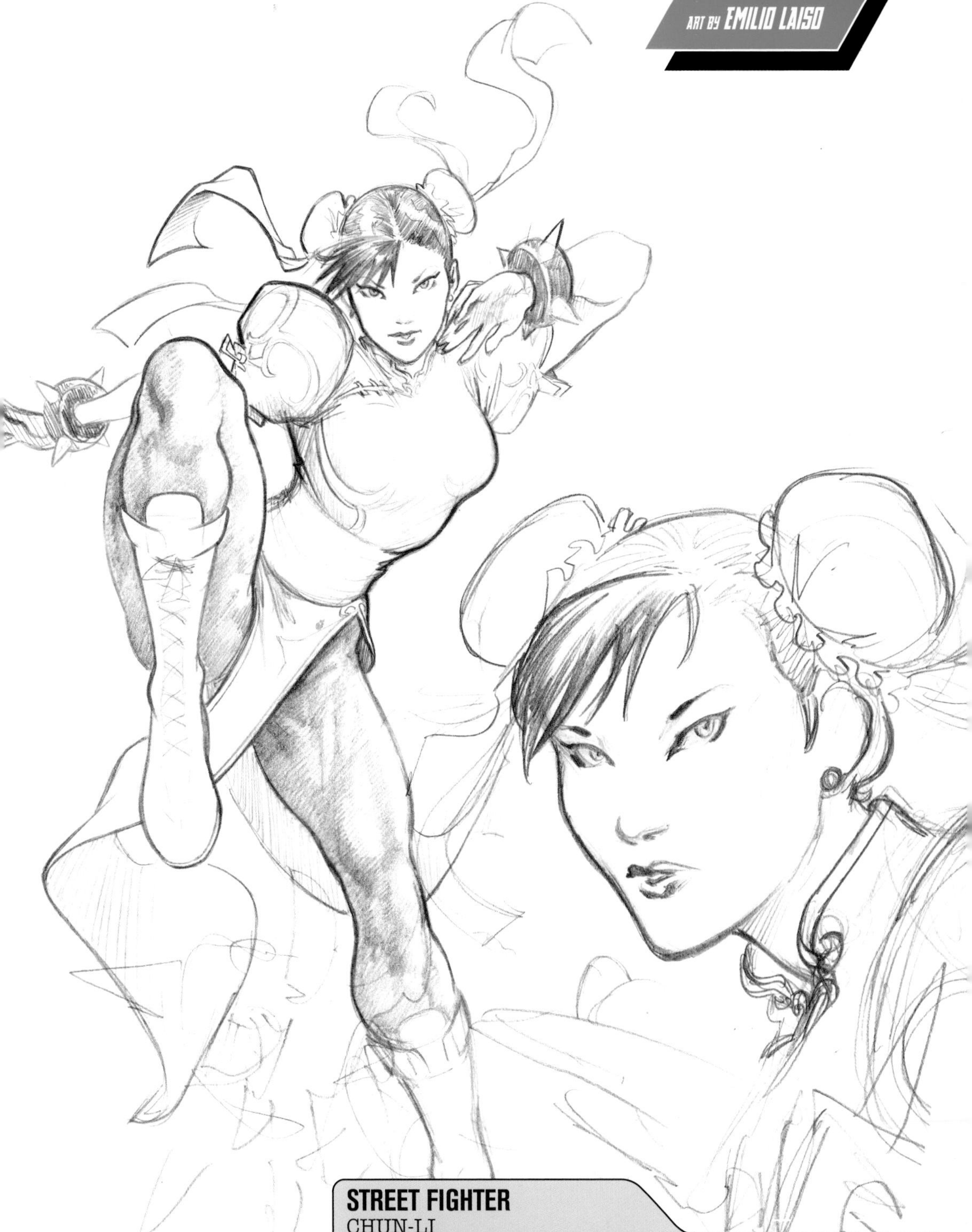

STREET FIGHTER

CHUN-LI

"The Strongest Woman in the World"

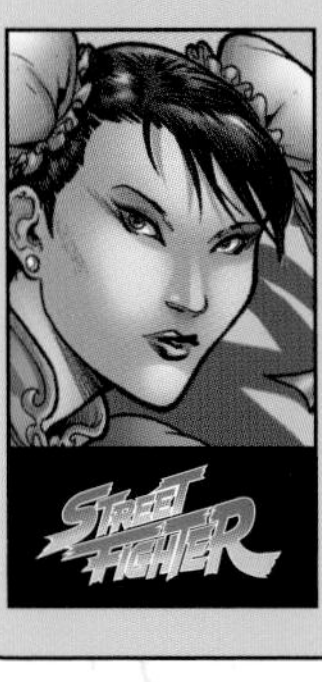
STREET FIGHTER

HEIGHT: 169 cm WEIGHT: She'll Never Tell BLOOD TYPE: A
FIGHTING STYLE: Chinese Martial Arts
SIGNATURE MOVES: Kikoken, Lightning Kick, Spinning Bird Kick
COUNTRY OF ORIGIN: China

Following a youth spent immersed in traditional Chinese martial arts, Chun-Li became an Interpol agent in the hopes of finding her missing father, eventually teaming up with Air Force lieutenant Charlie Nash. Though fighting was initially just a way for Chun-Li to gather information, training and competing has since become an end in and of itself for her.

"'Strongest Woman in the World'? How about just one of the strongest people in the world, period, full-stop. But what makes Chun-Li truly formidable in combat isn't just her legendary leg strength, it's the quick, fluid movements she uses to deliver those bone-crushing kicks."

ART BY **EMILIO LAISO**

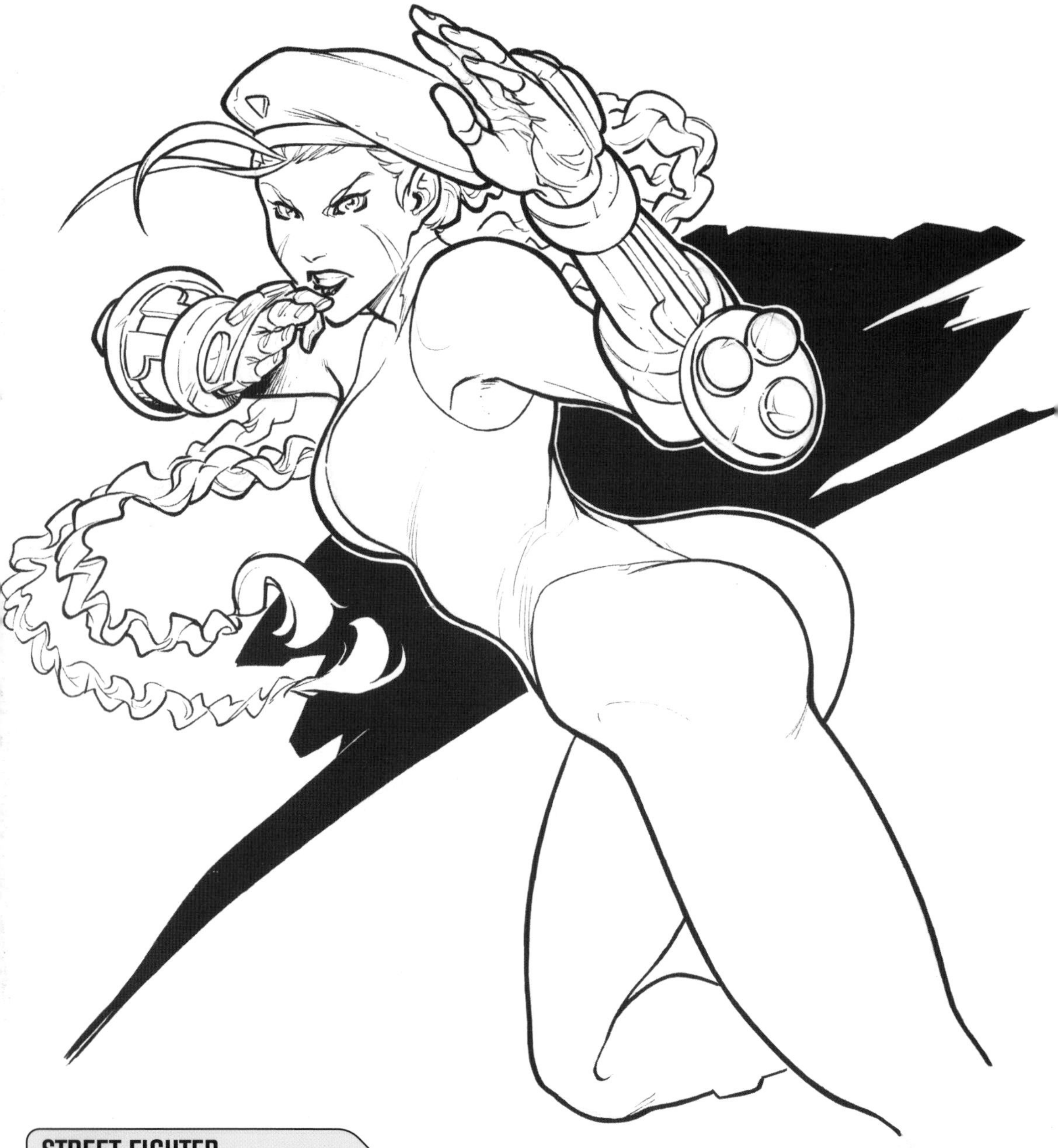

STREET FIGHTER

CAMMY

"The Stinging Bee"

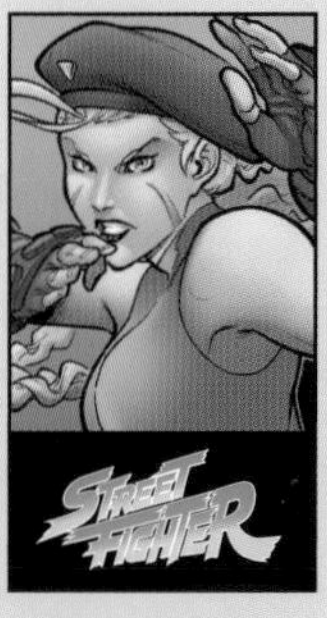
STREET FIGHTER

HEIGHT: 164 cm WEIGHT: 46 kg BLOOD TYPE: B
FIGHTING STYLE: Shadaloo Fighting techniques, Special Forces training
SIGNATURE MOVES: Cannon Spike, Cannon Strike, Spiral Arrow
COUNTRY OF ORIGIN: United Kingdom

Originally created by M. Bison, who called her Killer Bee, Cammy was a part of the dictator's personal guard. Eventually, she began to break down the walls of Shadaloo's brainwashing and developed a mind of her own, making her way into the Special Operations Unit known as Delta Red, where she was tasked with a single mission: Kill M. Bison.

"More than any other World Warrior, Cammy has an axe to grind. Not only was she Bison's slave... she was also his clone. But while the dictator's DNA might make her quick-to-anger and brusque, it also makes her a devastatingly effective hand-to-hand combatant."

ART BY EMILIO LAISO

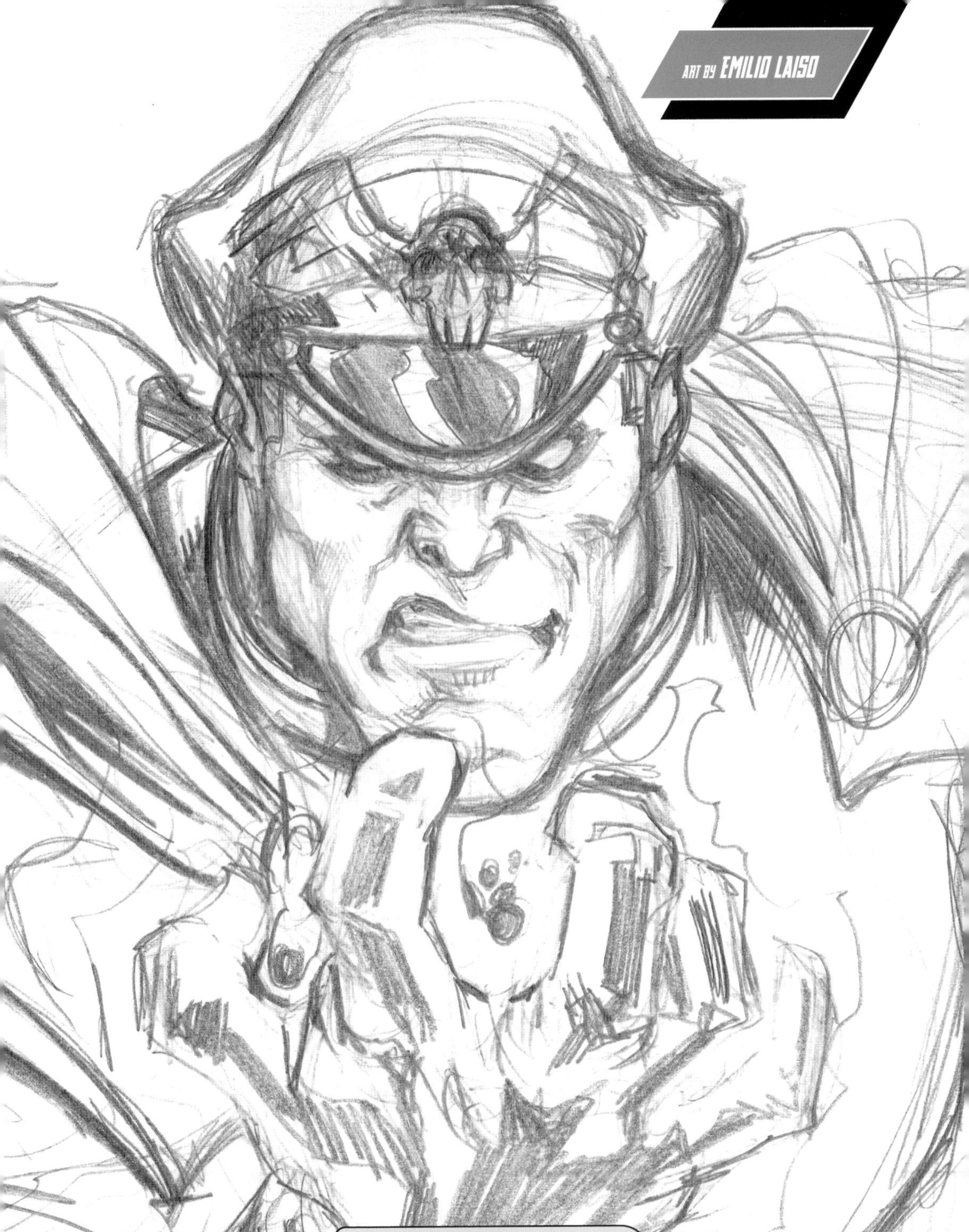

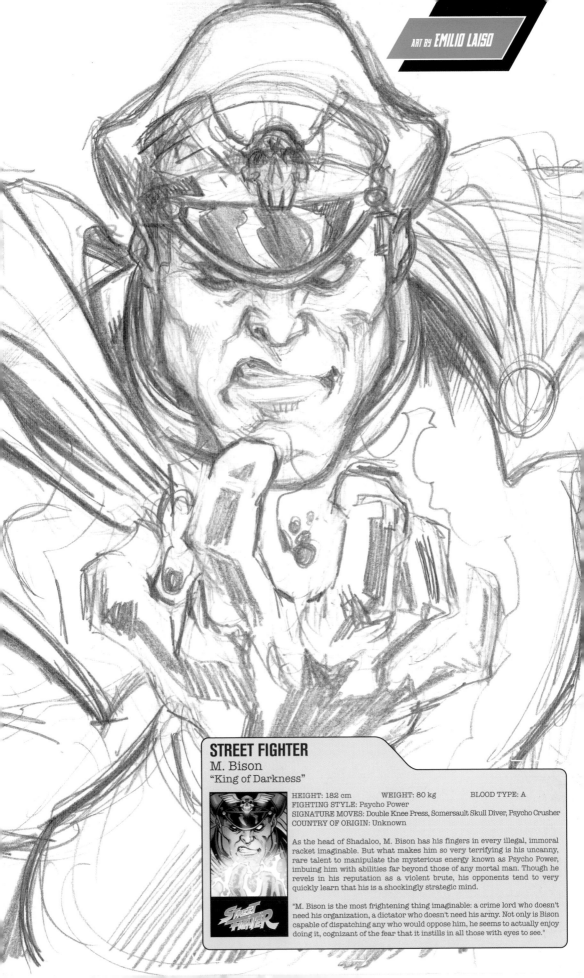

STREET FIGHTER

M. Bison

"King of Darkness"

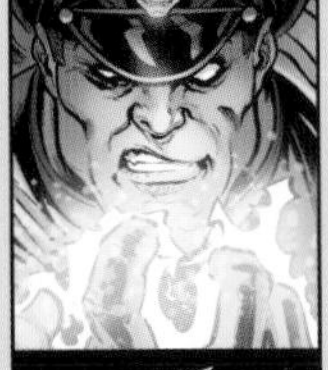

HEIGHT: 182 cm WEIGHT: 80 kg BLOOD TYPE: A
FIGHTING STYLE: Psycho Power
SIGNATURE MOVES: Double Knee Press, Somersault Skull Diver, Psycho Crusher
COUNTRY OF ORIGIN: Unknown

As the head of Shadaloo, M. Bison has his fingers in every illegal, immoral racket imaginable. But what makes him so very terrifying is his uncanny, rare talent to manipulate the mysterious energy known as Psycho Power, imbuing him with abilities far beyond those of any mortal man. Though he revels in his reputation as a violent brute, his opponents tend to very quickly learn that his is a shockingly strategic mind.

"M. Bison is the most frightening thing imaginable: a crime lord who doesn't need his organization, a dictator who doesn't need his army. Not only is Bison capable of dispatching any who would oppose him, he seems to actually enjoy doing it, cognizant of the fear that it instills in all those with eyes to see."

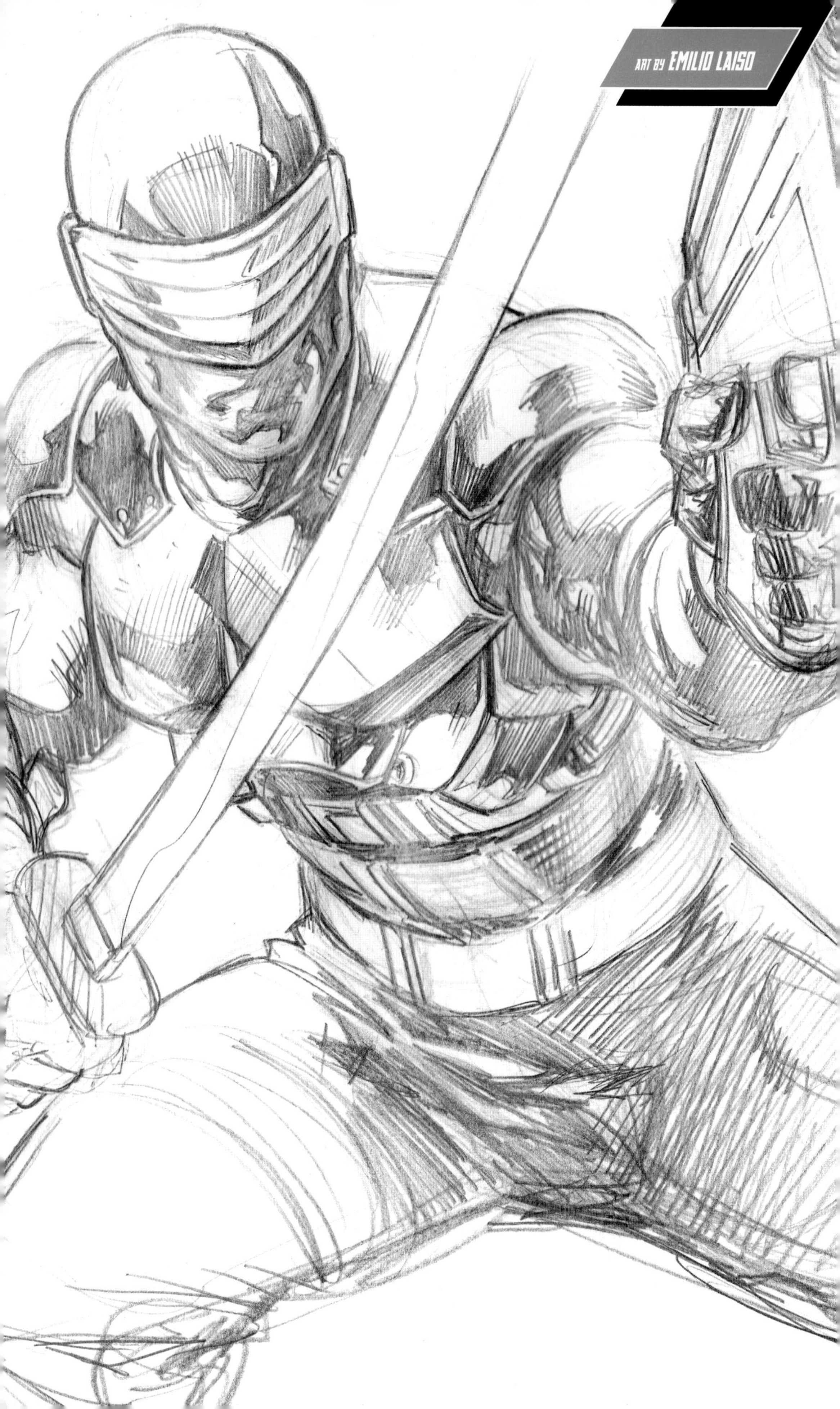

ART BY EMILIO LAISO

2016 STREET FIGHTER x G.I. JOE QUALIFYING ROUND RESULTS

Even with 16 different combatants throwing down within the pages of Street Fighter x G.I. Joe, there's no getting around it: Some of your favorites probably didn't make the cut. So, in an effort to appease you, our dear readers, while also providing a bit of background on how the current brackets came to be, we have provided the results from the 2016 World Warrior Tournament qualifying rounds. Enjoy, and cross your fingers that your favorites learn from their losses on their way to a better showing next year.

—Aubrey

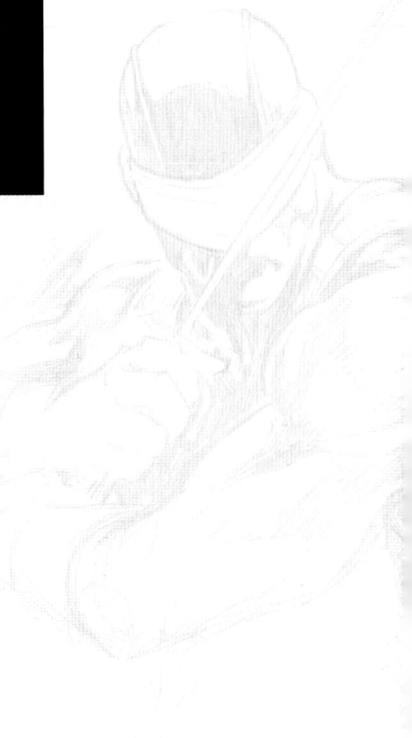

SNAKE EYES DEF. KEN

A perfect example of how important your place in the brackets can be, perennial favorite Ken Masters had a poor draw, and ended up having to face Snake Eyes in his very first contest. Though their martial-arts skills were evenly matched, good scouting and a single, expertly thrown shuriken gave the Arashikage ninja the upper hand.

CRIMSON VIPER DEF. MUNITIA

Though Snake Eyes' use of a shuriken already established a liberal interpretation of the phrase "hand-to-hand combat," this particular fight sealed the deal. This match was a flurry of electricity, flames, gunfire and explosions, but when the smoke cleared, it was Crimson Viper standing tall.

THE BARONESS DEF. ELENA

This qualifying round match featured a Baroness squaring off against a Princess, but there was nothing refined or regal about their brawl. The Baroness utilized what appeared to be kickboxing techniques to great effect, grounding Elena repeatedly. Though she managed to get a second wind, ultimately, the capoeira fighter lost due to a controversial match stoppage.

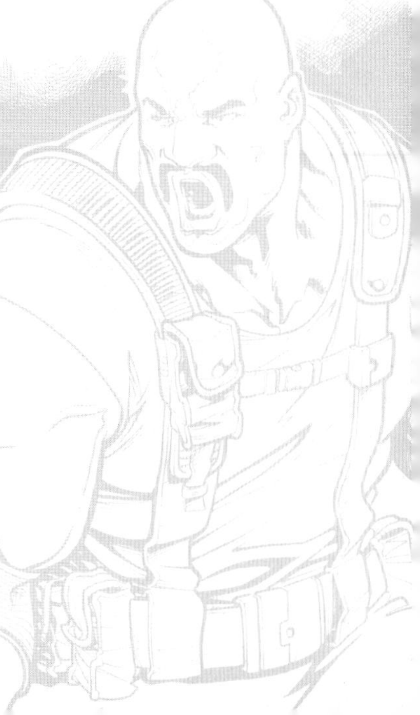

RUFUS DEF. COVER GIRL

Though Rufus appeared at the World Warrior Tournament with his girlfriend Candy in tow, he made no effort to hide his infatuation with Cover Girl. In fact, during their match, Rufus seemed more interested in putting his opponent in rather unique "holds," than actually fighting her, leading the G.I. Joe operative to forfeit the match in an effort to "Just get away from him."

ROADBLOCK DEF. ZANGIEF

If there is one contest from the qualifiers that I wish we could have shown, it would have been this, perhaps the best Hoss Match I have ever had the pleasure to witness. Though neither competitor is a slouch when it comes to the martial arts, this match wasn't about skill or technique, it was about one thing and one thing only: power. To Zangief's shock, however, his Spinning Piledriver only seemed to inconvenience Roadblock, who dusted himself off and dropped the Red Cyclone with nothing more sophisticated than a right hook.

HAKAN DEF. SHIPWRECK

From his time sailing the Mediterranean, Shipwreck was more than familiar with not only Hakan, but his use of yağlı güreş and those world-renowned oils. But even with that foreknowledge and preparation, Shipwreck and his pet, Polly, found themselves lying on the ground, staring at the sky, covered in olive oil. Fortunately for Polly, however, Hakan and his company are committed to protecting the environment, so he quickly cleaned the greased-up parrot.

JINX DEF. BLANKA

Post-match, Jinx admitted that this was the first time she had ever faced someone with the natural ability to shoot electricity out of their body. Blanka, however, never one to fight strategically, showed his hand too early, which gave Jinx the opportunity to utilize her speed to repeatedly move in and out of range, chopping the massive Amazonian down piece by piece.

RYU DEF. OVERKILL

Ansatsuken is one of the finest, most powerful martial-arts schools in existence, but it is a fighting philosophy designed to fight human beings, not half-man, half-machine monstrosities with gun arms. So, when Ryu squared off against Overkill, he quickly found that his normal strategies would be of no use. Fortunately, not even a cyborg can stand up against a fully charged, massive Metsu Hadoken, and Overkill's systems were overloaded from chi feedback.

GUILE DEF. CRUSHER

Crusher, with his professional background, came into this match expecting to be able to wrestle his way to victory. But after Guile successfully countered a single leg takedown with a nasty guillotine, Crusher realized he might have bitten off more than he could chew. Though the two exchanged holds and throws for almost 20 minutes, a triple rolling vertical suplex put Crusher down for the count.

GUNG-HO DEF. DHALSIM

Though Dhalsim claimed to only be competing in order to purchase a new goat for his village, you wouldn't know it once the match started. The yogi used his preternaturally long limbs to strike at his opponent from a distance, but though he hit frequently, the blows had little effect beyond keeping Gung-Ho at arm's length. Eventually, the Joe commando got in close enough to drop Dhalsim with a quick punch combination, emerging victorious and with an only partially singed moustache.

CHUN-LI DEF. QUICK KICK
It was the match-up that martial-arts enthusiasts were dying to see: The Queen of the Lightning Kick vs. The Master of the, well… Quick Kick. As could be expected, the battle was mostly fought with the lower extremities, and to the layperson, could possibly be seen as dull and one-dimensional. But beneath that repetitive surface was a frightful struggle, one which Chun-Li only narrowly won, due to her superior conditioning and stamina.

DAN DEF. SAKURA
Though it likely won't be the last, Dan's victory over Sakura was the first real upset of the tournament. Whether due to Sakura's lack of training, her overconfidence going into the match, the new techniques that her opponent made use of, or perhaps some combination of the three, perennial underdog Dan was able to pick up a decisive victory, shocking everyone in Mriganka and the Vegas betting parlors.

STORM SHADOW DEF. FEI LONG
In a "clash of styles" contest reminiscent of the early days of the UFC, Storm Shadow put his Arashikage ninja skills up against Fei Long's exquisite Jeet Kune Do. In a show of respect for his opponent, the Cobra operative completely disarmed himself prior to the match, leaving a disconcertingly large pile of weapons behind. Though Storm Shadow was ultimately the victor, there were no hard feelings, as the two shared a silent moment of respect for one another and their respective styles.

CROC MASTER DEF. ALEX
Much like Crusher in his match against Guile, Alex entered this contest expecting to punish his opponent with his wrestling acumen. Unfortunately, there are two things that Alex didn't consider: 1) that Croc Master's alligator-wrestling skills could translate to humans, and 2) that the World Warrior Tournament bylaws permitted the use of trained, man-eating crocodiles.

CAMMY DEF. FIREFLY
Though his skills aren't quite Arashikage level, Firefly's ninja abilities are nothing to scoff at, and as a result, this match was a fast-paced affair, pitting Firefly's arsenal of strikes against Cammy's incendiary combos. Though Firefly tried to take his opponent out with a set of surreptitiously placed explosives, Cammy was too quick for the detonators, dropping Firefly with her Gyro Drive Smasher.

M. BISON DEF. ROCK N' ROLL
Poor Rock N' Roll never stood a chance.

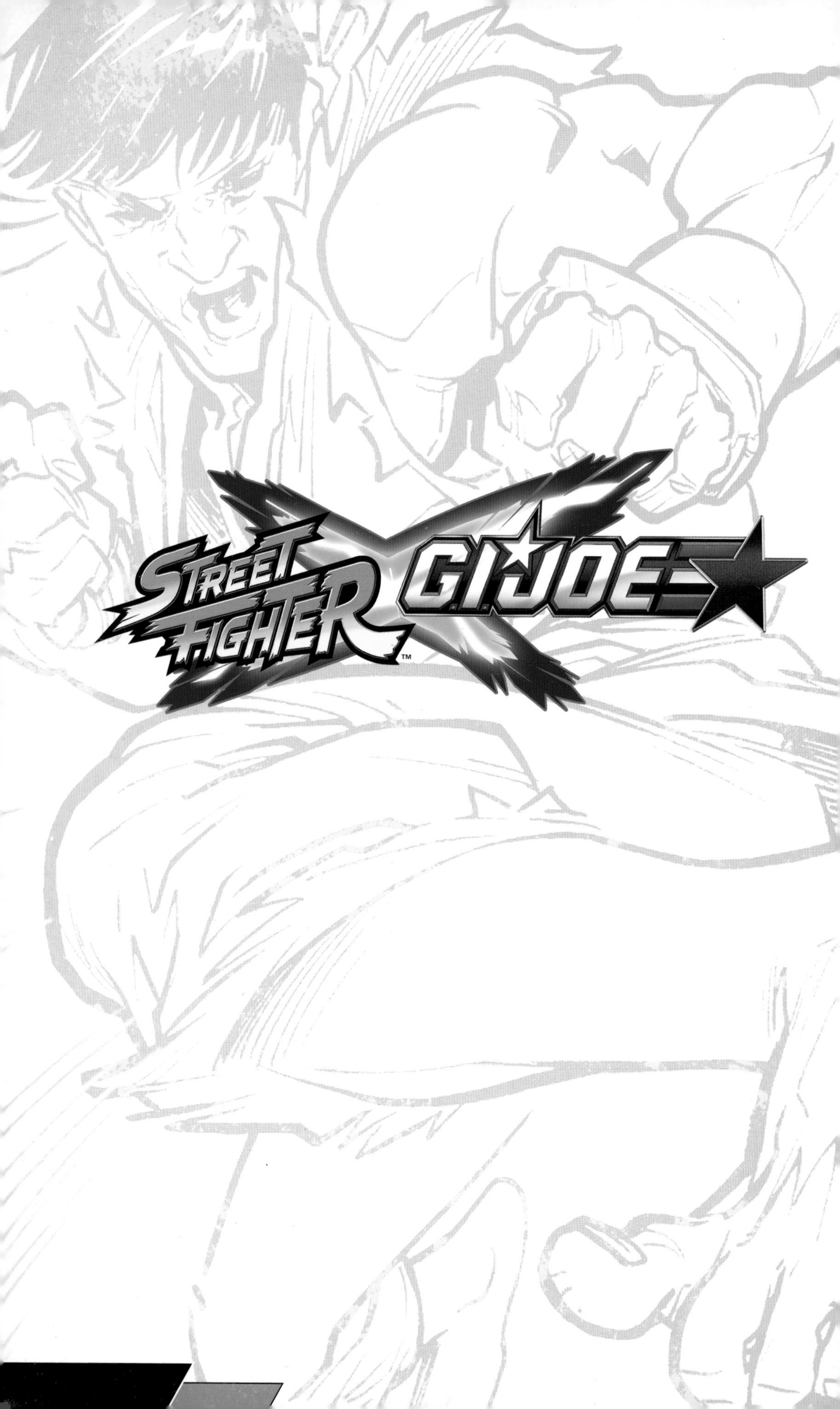
STREET FIGHTER
G.I. JOE